ILLUSTRATED

WORLD

ENCYCLOPEDIA

ILLUSTRATED

WORLD

ENCYCLOPEDIA

10

ILLUSTRATED WORLD ENCYCLOPEDIA, INC.

NEW YORK

Geometry

geometry

Geometry is one of the branches of mathematics. Geometry is used to measure shapes, sizes, and distances. The word comes from Greek words meaning "earth" and "measure." Geometry was used by the Egyptians and other ancient peoples, at least six thousand years ago, to measure land and to build big buildings.

Plane geometry is used to measure a flat surface, such as land or the top of a table. *Solid geometry* is used to measure things that are, or could be, solid, such as a block of stone or a tin can. Geometry is not usually taught before high school, because to learn geometry you should know something about arithmetic and algebra, which are other branches of mathematics. Geometry is used by engineers and architects in planning buildings and other structures such as bridges and tunnels. It is important to astronomers, scientists who study the stars. Surveyors, artists, and many other professional men and scientists use geometry in their work.

Geometry deals with things that have dimensions—length, breadth (width), and thickness. A *point* is simply a place or location; it has no dimensions. A *line* is a row of points; it has length but no other dimension. A *plane* has length and breadth but no thickness. A *solid* has all three dimensions.

When two lines intersect (come together) they form an angle. A *flat* surface with three sides is a *triangle,* which means that it has three angles. Angles are measured in *degrees.* All the angles that can be formed around a point will have a total of 360 degrees. When you know the length of two sides and the number of degrees in one angle of a triangle, or when you know the length of one side and the number of degrees in two angles, by geometry you can figure out all the sides and all the angles. There is a special branch of mathematics called *trigonometry,* that deals with triangles.

Hundreds of other figures are dealt with in geometry. There are curves and circles; plane surfaces with four, five, or any greater number of sides; solids with four or more sides, or with curved sides, such as the sphere, the cone, and the cylinder. Among the most important are the square, a four-sided plane figure in which all the sides and all the angles are equal; and the cube, a solid with six flat surfaces, all equal.

EARLY GEOMETRY

The earliest great student of geometry was a man named Thales, who lived in Greece more than 2,500 years ago. Another, who came soon after him, was Pythagoras. The greatest of the early writers on geometry was Euclid, who lived in Greece about 300 B.C. Euclid wrote thirteen books on geometry. They

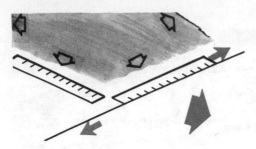

Three basic elements in geometry are the *point*, which has neither size nor shape; the *line*, by which length can be measured, but which has no width; and the *plane*, which is a flat surface, without thickness, extending in any direction.

are called the *Elements*. Except for the Bible and some other religious books, Euclid's *Elements* have probably been read by more people than any other book in history. Most of the geometry taught in high school is taken from six of the thirteen books. In some countries, including England, geometry is called simply *Euclid*. The geometry taught by Euclid is called Euclidean geometry.

EUCLIDEAN GEOMETRY

Euclidean geometry is based on *postulates* and *axioms*. The postulates are statements in geometry that are taken for granted without further explanation or *proof*. They tell us that one, and only one, straight line can be drawn through two points, and that two straight lines cannot

A geometric form can be recognized by its shape. The circle is found in the watch; the triangle in the mountain; and the rectangle in a picture on the wall. A line can be outside the circle, tangent to it, or it can intersect the circle.

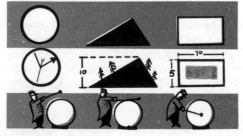

intersect at more than one point. The axioms are other statements that are accepted as self-evident, so obviously true that no proof is needed. For example, "Things equal to the same thing are equal to each other." If $3 + 2 = 5$ and $4 + 1 = 5$, then $3 + 2$ must equal $4 + 1$.

Using these postulates and axioms, Euclid worked out the rules of geometry in a series of *theorems*, or *propositions*. A theorem is something one believes but must prove; a proposition is a statement of what must be proved. Euclid proved his theorems by a kind of reasoning called *logic*. Logical reasoning uses statements that are known to be true and draws conclusions from them.

Many people have studied Euclidean geometry to help them think more clearly.

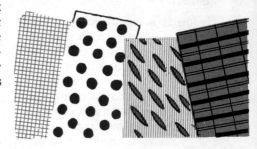

Various geometric forms are used in making attractive patterns for textile designs.

There is a story that Abraham Lincoln, before he became President of the United States, once borrowed a geometry book, so that he could learn how the theorems were proved in the book. This helped him think more clearly when he was arguing law cases in court.

Special types of geometry, called *projective* and *descriptive* geometry, are important in drawing plans and blueprints for buildings and other structures. Architects and draftsmen study them in college.

NON-EUCLIDEAN GEOMETRY

There are other kinds of geometry besides Euclidean geometry. These are called non-Euclidean geometry. They start out with one or more postulates that

The basic geometric forms are also found in advertising and in box designs.

are different from Euclid's. One kind is called *hyperbolic* geometry. It was invented by two European mathematicians more than a hundred years ago. It disagrees with Euclid's postulate that one and only one line can be drawn through a point parallel to a given line.

The triangle and cylinder are important geometric forms used in architecture.

In another kind of non-Euclidean geometry, called *elliptic* or *Riemann* geometry, there is a postulate that says no parallel lines can be drawn. This geometry was used by Albert Einstein when he developed his famous theory of relativity.

Geometric symmetry in this building makes for a feeling of calm and restfulness.

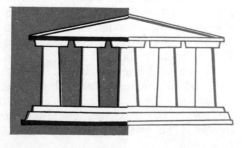

geopolitics

Geopolitics is the study of how geography affects politics. It is also called *political geography.* It teaches that the policy of a nation must be to gain or to hold the territory where its people can grow the food and find the minerals that they need, and where they will be safest from attack. Also valuable are places of strategic importance—that is, important only when fighting a war—such as the Rock of Gibraltar, a British possession that is of value only as a naval base.

Germany, especially during the time when it was governed by the Nazi Party of Adolf Hitler, is the country that is most often thought of in connection with geopolitics.

The word geopolitics was first used in 1917 by a Swede named Rudolf Kjellen. Though Kjellen was not a German he thought that all the Germanic peoples, which include the Swedish and other Scandinavian peoples, should get together.

An Englishman named Halford Mackinder, in 1904, had written that a territory in the center of Europe and Asia, which territory he called the "heartland," was necessary to any nation that wanted to control the world. A German general named Karl Haushofer taught these ideas in Germany and they had a great influence on Hitler's government, which came into power in Germany in 1933. Hitler tried to conquer the "heartland" in World War II, but of course he was beaten. The ideas called geopolitics are totally lacking in justice and morality.

George, Lake

Lake George, in the eastern part of the state of New York, is one of the most beautiful lakes in the United States. It is a narrow body of water, 33 miles long and only two or three miles wide. Most of the lake is deep, and the water is unusually clear. The lake is dotted with tiny islands, and along the shore the foothills of the mighty Adirondack Moun-

The beauty of Lake George with its many islands makes it ideal for summer vacations.

N.Y. State Dept. of Commerce

tains rise to about two thousand feet. Lake George drains into Lake Champlain. There are fishing and swimming at Lake George in the summer, and skiing and other winter sports in the winter. At Lake George Battleground Park there are ruins of great forts that were used during the French and Indian War and also in the American Revolution. The French discovered Lake George about three hundred years ago. It was named for George III, king of England.

George, Saint

St. George is the patron saint of England. A patron saint is a special guardian and protector. Many of the stories you read about St. George are legends, that is, they are not really true but are marvelous tales. The most famous story about St. George is that he killed a dragon in a terrible fight in order to save a king's daughter. St. George was a real person who died in the year 303. Very little is known about him except that he was known to have been a very holy man and a popular hero.

The Cross of St. George, which is an emblem, or sign, was put on the English flag five hundred years ago and you will find it there today.

George, King of England

There were six kings of England named George. The first four of them belonged to the house (family) of Hanover, the royal family that originally ruled the small kingdom of Hanover, in Germany. The last two English kings named George were members of the House of Windsor, which is the name of the royal family in England today.

George I lived about two hundred and fifty years ago. He was born in 1660, and became elector (king) of Hanover in 1698. In 1714 he became king of England because he was a grandson of King James I of England. George I spoke no English, and was not very much interested in English affairs. Under his rule, the cabinet, which acts for the Parliament, became stronger in England than it had ever been before. George I died in 1727.

George II, the son of George I, became king when his father died. He was a wiser king than his father, but he too was more interested in German affairs than in English affairs. During the reign of George II, England fought several wars and became very powerful. George II died in 1760.

George III was the grandson of George II. He was born in 1738 and became king in 1760, and it was against George III that the American colonies fought and won the Revolutionary War. George III was much more interested in English politics than either George I or George II, but he was not a good king, and was unpopular with his people. During the last years of his reign, George III became insane. His son, the Prince of Wales, took his place and became George IV in 1820, when George III died. George IV was born in 1762, so he was 58 years old before he became king. He was also an unpopular king. He reigned for about ten years, and died in 1830.

George V, the grandson of the great Queen Victoria, was born in 1865 and became king in 1910. Although he was a good and popular ruler, England had to face many serious problems during his reign. Chief among these problems were the rising labor problems of the country, the difficulties of English rule in Ireland and India, and then World War I. During the rule of George V, the royal fam-

George I   George II   George III

George IV   George V   George VI

ily of England changed its name to the house of Windsor.

George VI was the younger son of George V. He became king when his brother, Edward VIII, abdicated (gave up the throne) in 1936. George VI was a very popular king and the English people loved him and his family very much. The years of his rule were very difficult years because George VI became king just before World War II, and he died shortly after the war. All through the years of the war, George VI remained with his people, helping them and giving them courage to fight the war to victory. When George VI died, in 1952, his eldest daughter was crowned as Queen Elizabeth II.

George, Henry

Henry George was an American author who became famous by writing one book. It was called *Progress and Poverty,* and in it George told why he thought people were poor and how they could be helped. He felt that a country's land belongs to its people and that all have an equal right to the use of the earth. However, it is not possible or practical for all men to use the land, so George thought that the government should have a single tax, on the land alone, which would be enough to run the country. Henry George was born in Philadelphia in 1839 and later moved to California. After working at many jobs and often suffering from poverty, he moved to New York. Here George became well known as a lecturer and writer. He published *Progress and Poverty* in 1879. In 1886 he ran for mayor of New York and almost won the election even though the major political parties opposed him. When he died in 1897 huge crowds attended his funeral.

George Junior Republic

The George Junior Republic is a village where all the work is done, and the government is run, by teen-age boys and girls. It is called a republic because, as in a country that is called a republic, the government is run by its citizens, the people who live there. The citizens of the George Junior Republic are boys and girls 16 to 21 years old. They all must work on the farms or in the industries of their village. Everyone has a voice in the government. The George Junior Republic is in New York State, in the United States, so it has to obey the laws of the state and the nation, but when special decisions have to be made about affairs in the village, all the citizens meet to discuss their problems and make their laws.

The George Junior Republic was started in 1895 by a man named W. R. George. Mr. George was looking for a way to help boys and girls who were delinquent, that is, who had disobeyed the law. They were unhappy and uncared for, and they might have grown up to be criminals. George thought that if these boys and girls had a chance to work and to take charge of their own government, they might learn to be good and responsible citizens. So he started the George Junior Republic as a place to try out his ideas. The George Junior Republic has proved to be very successful. People have come from all over to study it. Some other villages like the George Junior Republic have been set up in other places, and it has been imitated by schools and institutions and prisons. They are helping boys and girls by giving them a chance to support themselves and to run their own government.

Georgetown

For more than a hundred years, from 1714 to 1830, the kings of England were named George, and during this period many towns and settlements in British colonies were named Georgetown in their honor.

George Town is the capital of Penang, a state of the Federation of Malaysia, which is one of the member nations of the British Commonwealth. It is on an island near the Malay Peninsula. The population of George Town is about 235,-000. It is a very modern city and an important seaport. See the articles on MALAYSIA and MALAY PENINSULA.

Georgetown is also the name of a city that is the capital of British Guiana, in South America. It has a population of about 120,000. It is at the mouth of the Demerara River and is an important seaport. In 1940 the British leased some property in Georgetown to the United States for use as a naval and air base.

Georgetown is also a part of Washington, D.C., the capital of the United States. Until 1878 it was a separate town. It is a residential section, with many old houses, some of them dating back more than two hundred years. Georgetown University, the oldest college in the United States conducted by the Roman Catholic Church, is in Georgetown. It was founded in 1789 and is for men only. In 1961 there were 6,065 students enrolled.

There are several cities in the United States named Georgetown.

George Washington Bridge

The George Washington Bridge is a bridge across the Hudson River, connecting Manhattan, in New York City, and Fort Lee, New Jersey. It is a suspension bridge, which is a bridge held up by cables hung from great towers. The towers of the George Washington Bridge are 600 feet above water, and the cables are each three feet thick. The main span of the bridge is 3,500 feet long.

The George Washington Bridge is one of the longest suspension bridges in the world. It was completed in 1931. Millions of automobiles, trucks, and buses stream across the bridge every year. Because of the growing traffic, a second level was added to the bridge in 1961 and 1962 underneath the original roadway, doubling its capacity.

Georgia

Georgia is a state in the south of the United States, and was one of the original thirteen colonies. Since the Civil War, Georgia has grown so important as an industrial state that it is now called the Empire State of the South. Georgia was named after King George II of England by the first English settlers.

In area, Georgia ranks 21st in size among the states, with 58,876 square miles. In population it ranks 15th, with more than four million people living there. In 1788, it was the fourth colony to become a state. The capital is Atlanta.

THE PEOPLE OF GEORGIA

About a fifth of the people of Georgia

Georgia Dept. of Commerce

The State Capitol building in Atlanta.

are farmers. They grow large quantities of cotton and corn, and produce more watermelons and peanuts than any other state. The peaches they grow are also famous throughout the country. The people who live in the cities work in factories, making many products such as cotton goods, clothing, peanut butter, and paper.

If you visit Georgia, you will notice that there are almost as many colored people as white people. There are more Negroes in Georgia than in any other state—more than a million. Most of them work on farms or are laborers in factories.

The earliest settlers in Georgia were the English, who came there about 220

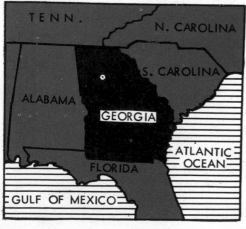

years ago. They were followed by people from Switzerland, Germany, and France, who wanted to escape from these countries because they could not worship God as they pleased. Today, almost all Georgians are American-born. Many are proud that they are southerners and that Georgia was one of the states that formed the Confederate States of America in 1861, and fought against the Union in the Civil War. In Georgia, you will see old Confederate flags in many places, and monuments to soldiers who died in the Confederate armies.

The churches are very important in the social life of the Georgians. Nearly everyone goes to Sunday School and to church, and, especially in the smaller towns, people have their clubs and parties and picnics through their churches.

WHAT GEORGIA IS LIKE

If you travel through Georgia, you will find that the north, central, and southern regions are quite different. In the northern section are part of the Appalachian Mountains, known as the Blue Ridge Mountains. This is a very beautiful part of the state, with deep valleys and steep cliffs covered with valuable timber. It is also rich in minerals, and much gold used to be mined here. The fine marble found in the mountains has been used to build the public buildings in many states and foreign countries.

The central part of Georgia is a plateau. A plateau is a region that is high, like a mountain, but level, like a plain. More people live here than in any other part of Georgia, and some of the most important cities are located in this region. Several rivers flow through the plateau, supplying water power to the manufacturing cities. The farmers grow large quantities of cotton in the fertile areas.

The entire southern part of Georgia is a low plain, where peanuts, watermelons, and other crops are grown. There are also large pine forests from which the people get turpentine and rosin. Along the coast

are marshes, the largest being the Oke-
fenokee Swamp, where many animals and
birds live.

As in other southern states, one can see
many small fur-bearing animals—the
raccoon, the squirrel, and others that people like to hunt. There are some wild
animals such as the wildcat, bear, and al-
ligator.

Although Georgia is in the south, it
is not as uncomfortably hot as one might
think. The climate is varied and healthful.
In the mountains, it is quite cold, with ice
and snow in the winter. In the plateau it
is warm in summer, but not hot. Only in
the southern plain are the summers very
hot. Most of the state has a mild climate,
with an average temperature of 48 degrees in January and 80 degrees in July.

The rivers of Georgia are very useful
for transportation. The most important
are the Chattahoochee, the Altamaha, and
the Savannah. Located on the Savannah
River is the famous Savannah River
Plant, where one of the most important
chemicals for the hydrogen bomb is
made. Railroads and highways reach
nearly all parts of the state.

GOVERNMENT OF GEORGIA

Georgia, like other states, has a governor (elected for a four-year term) and
a legislature, called the General Assembly and composed of a Senate and a House
of Representatives with members elected
for two-year terms. Judges are elected for
six years. The capital is Atlanta. There
are 159 counties.

Like other states of the deep South,
Georgia tried to evade the laws that require Negro and white students to attend
the same schools, using all legal devices
and sometimes illegal violence. By 1966
there was some integration in many of
Georgia's 1,400 elementary schools and
550 high schools, and in most of the 49
colleges and universities, of which the
principal ones (some of them famous) are:

University of Georgia, at Athens. Enrollment, 7,010 in 1961 (co-ed).

Thurston Heckler, Atlanta

**Stone Mountain, near Atlanta, is the largest
piece of granite in the world. A memorial
to the Confederate States of America is
carved on its top.**

Georgia Dept. of Commerce

**The brick arches and walls of Fort Pulaski
took many years to build, but during the
Civil War they could not withstand the
new rifled cannons of the Union army.**

Dept. of State Parks, Atlanta

**The warm Georgia climate makes swim-
ming in this pool at the beautiful Franklin
Delano Roosevelt State Park a very pleasant way to spend a summer day.**

Georgia Institute of Technology, at Atlanta. Enrollment, 5,133 in 1961 (co-ed).

Georgia State College of Business Administration, at Atlanta. Enrollment, 3,126 in 1961 (co-ed).

Woman's College of Georgia, at Milledgeville. Enrollment, 765 in 1961 (women only).

Emory University, at Atlanta. Enrollment, 3,963 in 1961 (co-ed).

Mercer University, at Macon. Enrollment, 1,342 in 1961 (co-ed).

CHIEF CITIES OF GEORGIA

The leading cities of Georgia, with populations from the 1960 census, are:

Atlanta, population 487,455, the state capital and largest city in the state. There is a separate article about ATLANTA.

Savannah, population 149,245, the second-largest city in the state. There is a separate article about SAVANNAH.

Columbus, population 116,779, the third-largest city, manufacturing center, in the western part of the state.

Augusta, population 70,626, fourth-largest city, cotton trading center, in the eastern part of the state. There is a separate article about AUGUSTA.

Macon, population 69,764, fifth-largest city, commercial and industrial center, in the central part of the state.

GEORGIA IN THE PAST

More than four hundred years ago the Spanish, under Hernando De Soto, were the first white people to visit Georgia. They were searching for gold, but did not find any, and moved on to the Mississippi River. Some years later, other Spanish explorers came to Georgia, as did the French and English. But the first permanent settlement was not made until 1733, when King George II of England gave James Oglethorpe the right to start a colony there. Oglethorpe wished to start a settlement for people who were poor and in debt, and who wished to begin a new life. He also saw it as a place where Protestants from Europe could live and worship God as they pleased. People from many countries came to the colony, which was located where Savannah now stands. In 1736, the first Sunday School in America was started there and, a few years later, the first orphanage in the country was built.

1. The Savannah River is important in Georgia and many industries are located along its banks. Barges carry oil and coal up and down the river to the cities.

2. The Coca Cola factory in Atlanta makes enough soft drinks to quench the thirsts of most of the people in Georgia. How many thousands of bottles do you think are stacked here for shipping?

3. People in Georgia mine fuller's earth with this machinery. Fuller's earth is an important product in the state and is used in making soaps and to take the color out of vegetable oils.

Georgia State Chamber of Commerce

Georgia Dept. of Commerce Photos

3

4

Savannah Chamber of Commerce

1. An Atlanta steel plant hums with activity as the sparks fly and the molten steel is ready to be poured into the molds in the lower left-hand corner.

2. Two men, on a lake in one of Georgia's state parks, are exploring the strange and beautiful territory, where the trees grow right out of the water.

3. The map shows the variety of products for which Georgia is famous.

4. The "seatrain" *Savannah* travels between Savannah and New York, carrying loaded railroad cars. It makes the round trip once a week and is a familiar sight in the busy ports of Savannah and New York.

5. Fishing boats with their big nets catch many kinds of fish off the Georgia coast and supply the city markets.

Dept. of State Parks, Atlanta

2

ELIZABELL
ST. MARYS, GA.

5

Savannah Chamber of Commerce

1. Sergeant William Jasper Monument in Savannah was built to honor one of Georgia's Revolutionary War heroes.
2. An air view of the important city of Savannah on the Savannah River.
3. The beautiful fountain in Forsyth Park, Savannah, is modeled after the one in the *Place de la Concorde* in Paris.
4. Ben Hill, a house built in 1855, is now the home of the president of the University of Georgia, in Athens.
5. Savannah's Telfair Academy, built by the famous architect William Jay.
6. Office buildings in Atlanta.

Georgia Dept. of Commerce

Georgia State Chamber of Commerce

Georgia was the last of the thirteen colonies to be settled, and for a time it did not flourish. However, land could be bought on very easy terms, and many wealthy South Carolinians moved in, bringing their slaves. Farming and cattle-raising helped Georgia to prosper.

The Georgians fought in the Revolutionary War, though they were so far south that sometimes they did not know how the war was going in New England. In 1788 Georgia became a state.

It was in Georgia that Eli Whitney invented the cotton gin, which made the growing of cotton more profitable than ever. You can read about the COTTON GIN in a separate article. The people in Georgia planted great fields of cotton, and wanted the Negroes to cultivate them. Slavery became very important as Georgia grew into one of the biggest cotton-producing states. There were large plantations whose rich owners lived in fine mansions and owned hundreds of slaves. When Abraham Lincoln was elected president in 1860, and it appeared that the slaves would be set free, Georgia was one of the southern states that seceded from the Union.

In the Civil War, Georgia suffered more destruction than almost any other Confederate state. The Battle of Chickamauga, in September, 1863, lasted two days, and they were called the two bloodiest days of the war. The following year, the Union troops under General Sherman captured Atlanta and set fire to it. With an army of 60,000 soldiers, Sherman then began his famous march to the sea, destroying villages, towns, and countryside as he went. At the end of the war, three-quarters of Georgia's wealth had been destroyed. The state was in ruins and the people were very poor. Carpetbaggers controlled the state government and robbed it of millions. However, the people gradually rebuilt Georgia, though it was not readmitted to the Union until 1871. The state prospered as the Georgians developed their industries.

Several events of importance occurred in Georgia. In 1819, the first transatlantic steamer sailed from Savannah and crossed the Atlantic Ocean to England in 25 days. The following year the first railroad in America, with horse-drawn cars, was built near Savannah. In this same city, the first American Girl Scout troop was organized in 1912.

Georgia has long since recovered from the hardships that followed the Civil War. Today it is a flourishing farming and industrial state.

Franklin D. Roosevelt is closely associated with Georgia, although he was not born there. He founded the famous Warm Springs Foundation, at Warm Springs, in 1927, to help people who had infantile paralysis.

PLACES TO SEE IN GEORGIA

Chattahoochee National Forest, 1,165,-000 acres, in the northern part of Georgia, on U.S. Route 76. Superb mountain scenery; wild turkeys; streams well-stocked with fish; picnic areas.

Fort Frederica National Monument, 210 acres, off southeast coast, on St. Simon Island, five miles from Brunswick, on U.S. Route 17. Built by Gen. James Oglethrope (1736–1748), during the struggle between Spain and England for control of what is now the southeastern part of the United States.

Fort Pulaski National Monument, 5,364 acres, in the southeast, on Savannah Beach, 12 miles west of Savannah, on U.S. Route 80. Early nineteenth century fort, with moat and drawbridge; fired on by Union soldiers in the Civil War; first proved the total ineffectiveness of old-style masonry fortifications.

Ocmulgee National Monument, 683 acres, in central Georgia, in Macon, on U.S. Route 41. Unique remains of mounds and prehistoric towns of an ancient tribe of Indians; museum with Indian relics.

Bethesda Orphanage, in the southeast, in Savannah, on U.S. Route 17. The oldest orphanage in the United States; opened in 1740. During the Civil War it was used as a military hospital.

Kennesaw Mountain National Battlefield Park, 2,883 acres, in the northwest, west of Marietta, on U.S. Route 41. Historic field on which occurred one of the two heavy attacks made by General Sherman on Confederate troops in his campaign against Atlanta.

Slave Market, in Louisville, on U.S. Route 1. Built in 1758, in the center of town; slaves were sold here.

Tallulah Gorge, in the north, on U.S. Route 17. A steep-sided crevice, 1,000 feet deep; may be reached by trail. Along the descent is a stone profile resembling the head of a witch, 35 feet high.

The Little White House, in western Georgia, at Warm Springs, on U.S. Route 27. Used by President Franklin D. Roosevelt during his lifetime. It was here that he died in 1945.

Bonaventure Cemetery, 4 miles east of Savannah, on U.S. Route 17. One of the most beautiful cemeteries in the country; magnificent oak trees, Spanish moss, and flowers.

GEORGIA. Area, 58,876 square miles. Population (1965 estimate) 4,357,000. Capital, Atlanta. Nickname, Empire State of the South. Motto, Wisdom, Justice, Moderation. Flower, Cherokee rose. Bird, brown thrasher. Song, "Georgia." Joined the Union January 2, 1788; one of 13 original states. Official abbreviation, Ga.

Georgian Bay, an extension of Lake Huron, in the southern part of Ontario, Canada. The bay has many islands to which people go for summer vacations: see the article on Lake HURON.

Georgian S.S.R.

The Georgian Soviet Socialist Republic is a region that is usually called Georgia, which is the same as the name of the state in the United States. It is one of the fifteen republics in the UNION OF SOVIET SOCIALIST REPUBLICS, about which you can read in a separate article.

It is less than half the size of the state of Georgia, having about 27,000 square miles, but about the same number of people, about four million, live there.

The people of Georgia speak a language of their own, called Georgian, but other languages such as Russian, Armenian and Turkish are also spoken. For many hundreds of years the women of Georgia have been considered very beautiful. Some famous men have come from Georgia, among them Joseph Stalin, the former premier of Russia.

For many years the Georgians were almost all farmers and raisers of livestock. In the southern part of Georgia, they raised mulberry trees for silk and also grew grapes. During the past forty years other industries have begun to grow. Factories have been built in Tbilisi (or Tiflis) the capital city, and also in Batum, a large port on the Black Sea. The oil industry is especially important at Batum. Georgia has large coal fields, and its manganese mines are among the largest in the world. There are big forests, which are cut for lumber.

In the south of Georgia the climate is warm and moist, and in the east are high mountains and dry plains called *steppes*. The two largest rivers are the Kura and the Rion.

GEORGIA IN THE PAST

Georgia began as an independent kingdom about 2,300 years ago. During most of the last 1,500 years Georgia has been ruled by other nations, and about 150 years ago most of it was taken by Russia. For a short time after 1917, Georgia was an independent republic. In 1921 it became part of the U.S.S.R.

geranium

The geranium is a colorful flower that is grown in the warmer parts of the United States. The flower has small, four-petaled blossoms at the top of a stem. The leaves are light green with lines of darker green running through them in a pattern.

Geraniums are usually very red, but they can also be white, yellow, rose, or even purple. Potted geraniums (grown in flowerpots or in window boxes) grow from ten inches to a foot and a half high, but in California they may grow to a height of four feet when planted out-of-doors. An oil with a rich, pungent odor is taken from some kinds of geranium. It is used to make perfume and to give a pleasant odor to soap.

geriatrics

Geriatrics is a new branch of medicine that studies diseases of older people. In the past one hundred years medical science has become successful in conquering many diseases that used to kill large numbers of people. As a result many more people are living today in the older age groups. These new large groups of older people have their own medical problems, and the study and treatment of these is called geriatrics. The doctor who specializes in them is a geriatrician.

Of course older people have many of the same diseases as younger people, but they are more likely to get some diseases and less likely to get others; so the geriatrician specializes in the diseases that older people are most likely to have trouble with. These are diseases that have something to do with parts, or organs, of the body which may gradually wear out. Mainly it is the veins and arteries, or blood vessels, that wear out in such places as the heart (causing heart trouble), or the brain (causing cerebral hemorrhage, or bleeding within the brain). Cancer is another disease studied by geriatrics because it is often caused by long wear and irritation in different parts of the body. Also, there is mental disease that can be caused by the wearing out of blood vessels of the brain in older people. It is like mental disease in younger people except that they usually cannot remember things, or think clearly. In all diseases of geriatrics older people need much care and attention.

germ

A germ is the first stage in the life of any living thing. The part of a plant that develops into its seed is called the germ of the plant. The tiny egg that develops into a human being or animal is called a germ cell.

Usually when we say germs we mean disease germs or BACTERIA, about which you can read in a separate article.

German language and literature

The German language is spoken in Germany and Austria, and also Switzerland, where it is one of the three official languages (along with French and Italian). In many other countries to which German-speaking people have emigrated, there are people who speak both German and the language of their new country. This is true of the United States, to which more than five million German-speaking people have moved in a little more than a hundred years. Besides all this, German is taught in most colleges and in many other schools throughout the world. It is a very valuable language to scientists and scholars, because many great scientific books have been written in German.

Altogether, there are about ninety million people in the world who speak German. Only Chinese, English, Spanish and Russian are spoken by more people.

The modern German language grew out of the languages spoken by the Germanic tribes that settled in northern and central Europe more than two thousand years ago. Several other modern languages are closely related to German. English is a Germanic language, because the Angles and Saxons who moved into England about 1,500 years ago were Germanic peoples. Even more closely related to German are the Dutch language and the Scandinavian languages (Norwegian, Swedish, Danish, and Icelandic).

All these languages, like nearly all European languages, belong to the Indo-European family of languages, called Indo-Germanic by German scholars.

HIGH AND LOW GERMAN

The German word for their language is *Deutsch*. It is spoken in many forms, or dialects, but it has two main branches, *platt Deutsch* (meaning "Low German," the oldest form of the language, which is still spoken in the low, flat regions of northern Germany) and *hoch Deutsch* (meaning "High German," the language spoken in the high, mountainous regions of the south). High German is the language taught in the schools and the language in which German literature is written. Low German is more like English.

The German way of arranging words in a sentence is so different from the English way that sometimes it seems funny to English-speaking people. The great humorist Mark Twain was one of those who poked fun at it. Of course, one way is as good as another; it is all a matter of what you are used to. Where we would say, "At three o'clock we saw the man get into his car," the Germans would say, "At three o'clock have we the man into his car get in seen."

In the German language, separate words can be combined to form one long word. It is as though in English we spoke of a person who is slightly insane as a "partlyoutofhismindperson." These long words, too, can seem funny to a person who is not used to them, but they are really quite easy to understand.

German is more of an inflected language than English is. That means that the words have different endings, depending on how they are used in the sentence. In English, an example of inflection can be found in such words as *he, him, his,* where the same word has different spellings depending on how it is used. In many cases a mark called the *umlaut* is used in the spelling of German words to show a change in the pronunciation of an *a, o,* or *u.* For example, *Mann* is the German word for *man,* and *Männer* is the word for *men.* This is one case in which the same sort of change occurs in English.

In German spelling, a noun (name of anything) always begins with a capital letter.

English used to be the same kind of inflected language German is, until less than a thousand years ago. Gradually, the English people stopped using many of the special forms of their words. The German people kept on using them.

GERMAN LITERATURE

Until the present (twentieth) century, German literature was noted chiefly for its great poetry and its scientific literature. One of the great works of German literature is Martin Luther's translation of the Bible. The poet GOETHE (about whom there is a separate article), who was born about two hundred years ago, ranks among the greatest poets of all time, along with Greece's Homer, Rome's Virgil, Italy's Dante, and England's Shakespeare. Friedrich von Schiller, who lived in the same period as Goethe, wrote great poetry and plays, some of which can be read at their best in English because they were translated by one of England's greatest poets, Samuel Taylor Coleridge. Gotthold Lessing was Germany's great playwright of this same period. Strangely enough, Shakespeare is considered by the Germans to be one of their greatest playwrights because his plays were so admirably translated (by August Wilhelm von Schlegel) that they seem as good in German as in English.

Americans have a particular fondness for the poetry of Heinrich Heine and for the novels of Thomas Mann, because they have been so widely read in their translations, but there is equally great German literature that is not so familiar to English readers. Many great philosophers, such as Immanuel Kant, were German and wrote in the German language. The novel was a neglected form of literature in Germany for many years, though Goethe wrote some novels and E. T. H. Hoffman, about 150 years ago, wrote several fine novels. Hoffman is well-known in English-speaking countries because the composer Offenbach wrote a light opera, *Tales of Hoffman,* based on his stories.

German measles

German measles is a disease caused by a virus, which is a tiny form of life—even smaller than a germ—and can cause disease when it enters the human body. German measles is a different disease from measles, although the signs of it are somewhat the same. Usually a person does not have German measles more than once.

German measles starts in much the same way as a cold, with a headache, a runny nose, and perhaps a slight fever. Later the skin breaks out in a light rash that itches a great deal. A person is likely to have German measles in the winter or spring, and children are more likely to catch it than grownups. German measles does not last more than a few days, and the patient is not very sick.. It is not a serious disease, except that it can be very dangerous to a woman who is pregnant, that is, a woman who is going to have a baby. German measles can harm the unborn child in several ways, particularly by damaging its heart.

German shepherd

The German shepherd is one of the largest, strongest, and at times fiercest of all dogs. It was used for many years in Germany to guard flocks of sheep and cattle, and for police work. The present German shepherd has been bred carefully since about 1900, so all dogs of the breed look pretty much alike. Today German shepherds are trained to guide the blind. They are also kept as pets, because they are very loyal to their own people, and when they are properly trained are wonderful protectors for children. Many people persist in calling the German shepherd a German police dog, but this is not correct.

The K-9 corps of dogs in both World War I and World War II had great numbers of German shepherds, trained for war

Abadee Kennels

German shepherd dogs are used in movies because they follow directions easily.

work, and many of these fine dogs were awarded medals for special acts of heroism and bravery. Many German shepherds are used as watchdogs in stores, factories, and government buildings, and they do a fine job at that also.

The German shepherd stands about 23 inches high at the shoulder, and it is about 29 inches from the front of the chest to the base of the tail. It weighs anywhere between 65 and 85 pounds. It has ears that stand up straight, and a curved, bushy tail. Males are both larger and heavier than females. Although you can see German shepherds in colors that vary from dark brown or blackish to a light shade of tan, the most common color is wolf-gray and tan, with black markings.

German silver

German silver is a whitish metal made by combining copper, nickel and zinc. A lot of the silverware which we use on the table is made of German silver that has been coated with real silver. German silver is harder than real silver and it can be polished to shine brightly, but it loses its shine very easily. If vinegar or other strong mixtures are mixed with German silver, they form a solution that is poisonous. German silver should not be used with such liquids or with fruits, if the real silver coating has worn off. German silver was given this name because it was first made in Germany.

Germany

Germany

Germany is the name used by English-speaking people for a large section of Central Europe where the people speak the German language and are descended from early inhabitants of Europe who were called Germans, or Teutons.

When World War II began in 1939, Germany was a single country, the richest and most powerful in Europe. The German people called it *Deutschland*. About eighty million people lived there, more than half as many as then lived in the United States, though the area of

Germany was only about 145,000 square miles, or not quite the size of the state of California.

Germany regained its independence some years after World War II but was divided into two countries. One took the name Federal Republic of Germany, and is usually called West Germany; in this country there is free enterprise. The other part of Germany, the eastern part, came under the control of Russia and has a Communist government; it calls itself the Democratic Republic of Germany, but it is not a democracy as that word is understood in America. This part of Germany is usually called East Germany.

In the past, Germany was made up of many small countries, which often fought among themselves. Nevertheless most of the people felt that they were one nation, because they share the same language and literature and history. They have never stopped feeling that way, and in the period after World War II, the chief ambition of most Germans has been to unite West and East Germany to make a single nation again.

THE GERMAN PEOPLE

Most of the people who live in Germany are descended from several different Germanic tribes that settled in northern and central Europe more than two thousand years ago. Some of these tribes went to other countries such as France,

German Tourist Information Photos

On this page are pictures of Berlin, the former capital of Germany, and Bonn, the present-day capital of West Germany.

1. One of the beautiful lakes in Berlin.
2. The Potsdamer Platz was once the center of Berlin. It now marks the border between the East and West sectors of Berlin.
3. The Kurfürstendam is still the most fashionable shopping center in Berlin.
4. Beethoven's birthplace in Bonn.
5. The city hall in Bonn is small, but it is a beautiful old building.
6. Natural History Museum in Bonn.

German Tourist Information Photos

Left: A German fisherman casts his net into the Main River, near Frankfurt. *Right:* One of the fine churches in Dresden. It was badly damaged in World War II.

Spain, England, and the Scandinavian countries (Norway, Sweden, and Denmark). The others became the German people as we know it today.

The people of Germany speak the language called German, about which you can read in the article on GERMAN LANGUAGE AND LITERATURE. There are many dialects, or slightly different forms of this language.

The Germans who live in the north are mostly Protestants, but among those who live in the south there are many Roman Catholics. The largest group of Protestants are Lutherans. Martin Luther, who began this church more than four hundred years ago, was a German.

No people in the world have been better educated or more advanced in science than the Germans. This has been the chief reason that Germany has been so powerful in manufacturing and also in war. Germany's population has often been so big that there was not enough land for all the people, and Germany has tried to take territory from neighboring countries. This has led to wars in which the Germans have fought against several other powerful countries at the same time, and so have lost.

HOW THE PEOPLE LIVE

The people of Germany live very much as do the people of the United States and Canada. Many of them live in large cities and work in offices or factories near by. The industries of Germany are very well developed and produce many different things. Germany has been one of the leaders in the manufacture of machinery, iron and steel products, chemical goods, and scientific equipment. Germany's factories and cities were greatly damaged and in many cases destroyed during World War II, but the people in West Germany worked very hard to rebuild their country, and by about 1960 they had not only rebuilt but had improved and modernized their industries. Today West Germany is one of the leading industrial nations of the world, and the people live better than ever. East Germany did not match this recovery.

About thirty per cent of the land of West Germany is good for farming. The German farmers are very modern and raise many different crops. In the north they raise potatoes and rye, in the central areas they grow wheat and other grains, and in the south there is chiefly dairy farming and the raising of livestock.

German Tourist Information Photos

Left: People in Cologne enjoying lunch near the magnificent Cologne cathedral. *Right:* Assmannshausen, on the Rhine River, is famous for its fine vintage wine.

Not only are the German people hard workers, but they have always been great scholars. German scientists have always been among the best in the world. Many of the great books of the world have been written by Germans, and much of the world's most beautiful music was composed by German composers such as Wagner, Bach, and Beethoven.

There are also nineteen important universities in Germany, and many American students go to these universities to study.

WHAT THE COUNTRY IS LIKE

The eastern part of Germany, the Communist part, is mostly level plains lying between the Elbe and Oder Rivers. West Germany, which is more than twice as large as East Germany, with a total area of about 95,000 square miles, is divided into several important regions. The southern part is mountainous. It includes the Bavarian plateau, which averages nearly 1,600 feet above sea level. A plateau is high, like a mountain, but level like a plain. The Zugspitze Mountain, in this region, is the highest point in Germany, almost 9,800 feet high. This part of Germany is noted for its dairy industries. Much of the land is covered with large forests, which supply a great deal of West Germany's wood and timber needs.

The central part of Germany is low, hilly country, with many level plains. This is the largest part of West Germany. The northern part of Germany is a low plain that reaches to the North Sea.

There are several important rivers in Germany. In the south, the Danube rises in the Black Forest and flows eastward through Germany, across the Bavarian plateau, and into Austria. The other important rivers of Germany flow northward. The Rhine, perhaps the most important river in Germany, begins in Switzerland, flows all the way through Germany, and then enters Holland. The Elbe and the Oder, both important rivers in East Germany, also flow north. The Elbe empties into the North Sea and the Oder into the Baltic Sea.

On these important rivers many boats go up and down stream, carrying all kinds of freight. Many canals connect the rivers, and the rivers and canals provide Germany with a network of cheap transportation for all sorts of freight. Important industrial centers and cities are linked by modern *Autobahnen* (thruways).

Germany's extensive network of railroads, greatly damaged during World War II, has been rebuilt and changed almost entirely to electric and Diesel traction. Its fleet of merchant ships, also destroyed during the war, is now larger than it was in 1939. Germany is taking part in civil aviation again and has its own airline.

The climate of Germany is much like the climate of the northern New England states, but it is not as damp. This is the general climate of Western Europe. The average summer temperature is about 65 degrees, and there are usually snows and freezing temperatures during the winter. The people who live in the mountain valleys in the south have a somewhat warmer climate, but there are heavy snows in the mountains. Many people go there to enjoy winter sports.

HOW THE PEOPLE ARE GOVERNED

After the defeat of Nazi Germany, the country was divided into four zones. In 1949, the three zones that had been controlled by the Western Allies (the United States, Great Britain, and France), became the Federal Republic of Germany. The Russians, who dominate East Germany, have refused to permit free elections that might result in a union of West and East Germany as one nation again.

German Tourist Information Photos

1. The head of a 700-year-old statue in the Cathedral of Aachen, north Rhineland, shows the skill of medieval German artists. The statues of Aachen Cathedral are famous for their beauty.
2. An 800-year-old castle, near Aachen, is used now as a shelter for young hikers.
3. Vineyards and orchards on steep slopes bordering the Rhine produce fine wine, apples, pears, and plums.

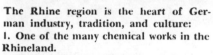

The Rhine region is the heart of German industry, tradition, and culture:
1. One of the many chemical works in the Rhineland.
2. Busy sewing-machine operators make women's coats in a Rhineland factory.
3. Hard-working laborers in a vineyard do not have time to observe the beauty of the Rhine River, far below them.
4. Boats on the Rhine pass the Lorelei Mountain, famous in German folklore.
5. The medieval inn of a Rhineland town.
6. A shrine beside a Rhineland vineyard.

German Tourist Information Photos

German Tourist Information Office

Left: Violin makers, father and son, work at their craft in the Black Forest. **Right:** Pride in their fields shows in the faces of these Westphalian peasants.

The government of West Germany made its capital in the city of Bonn. The government is headed by a president, who is elected every five years. The lawmaking body is the parliament, which has two houses: the Bundestag, whose members are elected every four years by popular vote, and the Bundesrat, whose members are appointed by the legislatures of the German states. The president of Germany selects a chancellor or prime minister representing the strongest political party in the parliament.

The Democratic Republic of Germany, which is made up of the zone of East Germany and a part of the city of Berlin, has a constitution very much like the constitution of Soviet Russia. The leaders of this government are under the orders of Soviet officials stationed there.

THE CITIES OF GERMANY

The largest city of Germany, Berlin, is divided into two sections: West Berlin, and East Berlin. Berlin was the capital of Germany before the war. There is a separate article about BERLIN.

In West Germany there are several important cities. The largest is Hamburg, which has a population of about 1,800,-000. Munich, the capital of the state of Bavaria, is a city of more than a million. It is an important industrial as well as cultural center. It has an old, famous university and many good theatres. A large number of artists and writers live there. Cologne, famous for its old cathedral, is the third-largest city in West Germany with a population of about 800,000. Other big cities are Essen, which is a steel and machine building center, Frankfurt-am (on the)-Main, and Düsseldorf, both centers of banking, business, and insurance. Bonn, the capital of West Germany, is quite small in comparison with these other cities.

German Tourist Information Photos

1. Two German girls in country dress gather spring-time blossoms before an old village church in the Black Forest region in south Germany.
2. A shepherd tends his flock in a meadow near an old ruined castle in Baden, in south Germany.
3. A leader directing a German country dance whistles to signal a change of step. He will crack his whip to show what step comes next. The style of his three-cornered hat is 200 years old.
4. Many statues still remain in place on a wall of the famous Heidelberg Castle, partly ruined when it was struck by lightning 200 years ago.
5. A peaceful village nestles against a wooded slope in a hilly region of West Germany.

In East Germany, the important cities are Leipzig, which is an important center for publishing and printing as well as commercial trade; Dresden, which is an important railroad center and port on the Elbe River; and Chemnitz, which is an important textile manufacturing city. Chemnitz is now called Karl Marxstadt, in honor of the founder of Communism.

GERMANY IN THE PAST

During the early days of the Roman Empire, about two thousand years ago, the lands that now make up most of Germany were inhabited by many Germanic tribes, some of which came from central Asia. About 1,100 years ago, the Germanic tribes were united into one powerful country under the great king Charlemagne.

After the death of Charlemagne, the eastern part of his kingdom became the kingdom of Germany. This kingdom broke up into small countries, which became part of the HOLY ROMAN EMPIRE, about which there is a separate article. One of these small kingdoms, which was called Prussia, soon became much stronger than the others. In 1871, William I, King of Prussia, was made German Emperor (in German, the Kaiser), uniting all the German countries north of Austria. This was the beginning of the modern German state. Germany's trade and industries were built up, and the country became very strong.

The Prussian leaders of Germany were not satisfied with the development of foreign trade and home industries. They wanted to make a great world empire out of Germany. Their ambition had much to do with starting World War I.

Germany and its allies lost this war, and had to give up most of their land and all their outside colonies. A new constitution was adopted, and Germany became a republic. This new German government was known as the Weimar Republic, because its constitution was adopted at the German city of Weimar.

THE THIRD REICH

In German, the word *Reich* means "realm," or "nation." The First Reich was the old empire, called the Holy Roman Empire, which lasted until the year 1806. The Second Reich was the German empire under the kings of Prussia. The Weimar Republic replaced the Second Reich. It was not a bad government, but in the 1920s and 1930s people in all countries became very poor. Even in the United States, the richest of all countries, there was a great depression. Germany, made poor by its loss of World War I, was in the worst possible condition to stand a depression. The German people were suffering from very bad living and working conditions. The different political parties of Germany were all blaming one another for these problems.

One of these political parties was the National Socialist Party, which is usually called the Nazi Party. In 1933 this party managed to seize control of the government. Adolf Hitler, the Nazi leader, was first made chancellor (prime minister), and then when he had become powerful enough, he made himself dictator. He called the country the Third Reich and called himself *der Führer,* which means "the leader." Under Adolf Hitler and his Nazi Party, the German people lost all their freedoms, freedom of worship, freedom of speech, the freedom of the press, and the other rights of people who live in a free and democratic country. Hitler persecuted and eventually murdered millions of Jews, and he also fought against the Roman Catholic and other Christian Churches.

Adolf Hitler had no honesty in dealing with foreign countries and, by threatening war, he seized Austria and part of Czechoslovakia. He wanted still more territory, so he made a treaty with the Communist government of Russia, which was just as dishonest as he was, to conquer and divide several small countries. In 1939, Hitler started World War II by invading Poland. Most of the German people idolized Hitler, approved of the things he did, and willingly let him lead them into war.

Germany was successful at first. Soon nearly all of Europe was under German domination. Hitler betrayed his Russian friends and invaded Russia too. His fatal mistake was in declaring war on the United States in 1941. Germany was the strongest European power, but American power proved to be far greater. In 1945 the Allies forced Germany to surrender and the four chief victor nations, the United States, Great Britain, France and Russia, took control of Germany. In 1955 West Germany regained independence and in 1959 East Germany officially became independent, though still under Soviet domination.

GERMANY. Area, 137,558 square miles. Population (1964 estimate) 75,358,000. Language, German. Religion, mainly Lutheran and Roman Catholic. Government divided as follows (excluding Berlin):

DEMOCRATIC REPUBLIC OF GERMANY (East Germany). Area, 41,479 square miles. Population (1964 estimate) 17,068,000. Government, republic. Monetary unit, the Deutsche mark, also called Ostmark, worth about 6 cents (U.S.).

FEDERAL REPUBLIC OF GERMANY (West Germany). Area, 95,738 square miles. Population (1964 estimate) 58,290,000. Government, republic. Monetary unit, the Deutsche mark, worth about 25 cents (U.S.). Flag, three wide horizontal bars of black, red and gold.

germicide

Germicides are chemicals that kill germs. Chlorine, which is a chemical put in drinking water in a big city, is a germicide. Chlorine is also used to kill germs in the water of many swimming pools. Iodine is a germicide. We usually speak of germicides as "antiseptics" or "disinfectants." Antiseptic and disinfectant have much the same meaning, but chemicals used for living things are usually called antiseptics and chemicals used on non-living things, such as dishes, are called disinfectants.

germination

Germination is the process by which seeds grow into plants. We usually speak of it as *sprouting*. Every living thing begins with a germ or embryo. In the case of plants the embryo is in the seed; the outer parts of the seed are food that enables the embryo to grow until it is large enough to burst the outer coat of the seed. The same thing happens in the case of an egg, which contains the embryo of a chicken and food to feed it. When the chicken is large enough, it bursts the eggshell.

The seed of every plant in the world has the same living parts, or organs, that are necessary for germination. In every seed there is a part that will eventually grow into a root. There is a part called the *hypocotyl* that will grow into the plant's stem. There is a third part that will grow into the leaf or leaves.

Seeds need the right amounts of water and air, and the right temperature, in order to sprout. Too little or too much water or air, or the wrong temperature, may stop the process of germination. For example, many seeds die when too much water stops air from getting to them. This happens when soil in gardens and fields is too wet and does not have good drainage (places to soak up the excess water). The time needed for germination differs in various types of seed. The seed of a grass or vegetable usually takes less time to sprout than the seed of an oak tree. Some seeds have been known to germinate overnight, and the seeds of some mountain plants may take ten years to germinate.

A proper knowledge of germination is necessary for farmers and plant growers.

Geronimo

Geronimo was a famous chief of the warlike Apache Indians. He became famous in the 1870s for his attacks on the villages and settlements of the white men in Arizona. He was captured and put on

an Indian reservation, and with the rest of the tribe he was forced to become a farmer. Farming was something entirely new to the Apaches, since they had always lived by hunting and by raiding other tribes. In 1881, Geronimo and a small band of Apaches broke away from the reservation and began again to live by raiding the white settlers. The government sent General Crook, a famous Indian fighter, to capture Geronimo and his followers, and in 1886 Crook finally caught them. As Crook and his men were taking the Indians back to their reservation, they escaped but were captured soon again. Even though the Indians were far outnumbered by the Army, Geronimo refused to surrender unless the government would allow him and his men to return to their families. After serving two years in prison, Geronimo lived peacefully until he died in 1909 at the age of about eighty-four.

Gerry, Elbridge

Elbridge Gerry was an American patriot who took part in the organization of the first government of the United States. Gerry was born in 1744, in Massachusetts. At that time the American colonies in North America still belonged to England, but Gerry agreed with the people who thought that the colonies should be independent from England. Gerry was elected to the Continental Congress, and when the Congress wrote the Declaration of Independence, which said that the colonies would set up their own government, Gerry was one of the signers. From that time on, Gerry held many posts in the government of the new country.

During the Revolutionary War, he worked hard at getting supplies needed for the army of the colonies. After the war, he was one of the members of the con-vention that wrote the Constitution of the United States. He was elected to the first Congress. Later he was sent to France as a representative of the United States government. For a while, he was governor of Massachusetts. While he was governor, some changes were made in the organization of the voting districts of Massachusetts. These changes did not seem very fair, and the people made up a new word, "gerrymander," to describe the unfair changes that were made by Gerry's government. This word is still used today, and people who talk about *gerrymandering* mean changing voting districts unfairly. The last post that Gerry held was the office of vice-president of the United States. He was elected vice-president in 1812, and was still in office when he died in 1814.

Gerry had a grandson, Elbridge Thomas Gerry, who lived from 1837 to 1927. Elbridge Thomas Gerry is remembered as a reformer. He was especially interested in children, and he was a leader in organizing the Society for the Prevention of Cruelty to Children, which tries to see that children are taken care of, and not mistreated.

gerrymander

Gerrymander is a word made up in the United States more than a hundred years ago to describe a special kind of political trickery. Each state in the United States is divided into districts from which members of the House of Representatives are elected. Sometimes politicians change the districts so that their party will get its votes in the districts where the votes will do them the most good. Elbridge Gerry was Governor of Massachusetts in 1812 when the districts in Massachusetts were changed to give his party more power. One of the new districts in Massachusetts was of such a strange shape that a newspaper editor, who was politically opposed to Gerry, called it a "gerrymander" because it was authorized by Gerry and looked like a huge salamander, a lizardlike animal with a long tail. Since that time any changing of the districts of a state for unfair political purposes has been called *gerrymandering*.

Gershwin, George

George Gershwin was a famous American composer. He started as a writer of popular songs but he also wrote some more serious music that is performed by symphony orchestras. He is best remembered now for *An American in Paris* and *Rhapsody in Blue*. He also wrote  many musical shows, including *Of Thee I Sing,* for which he received a Pulitzer Prize,. and *Porgy and Bess,* one of his most ambitious works. His popular songs include "Swanee" and "The Man I Love." George Gershwin was born in Brooklyn, New York, in 1898 and died in 1937, when he was only 39 years old.

His brother, Ira Gershwin, became a very successful writer of lyrics for popular songs, including the lyrics for *Of Thee I Sing.* He was born in New York City in 1896.

Gestapo

The Gestapo was the secret state police in Germany when it was ruled by the Nazi party. The word comes from the first syllables of the German words *Geheime-Staats-Polizei,* which means "secret state police."

The Gestapo was formed in 1933, when Adolf Hitler and the Nazis took control of Germany. Members of the Gestapo were not controlled by a "Bill of Rights" as American police are. They arrested anyone who criticized the government or who was against the Nazis, and their spies were everywhere. The Gestapo came to be feared by everyone, even by important officials of the government.

Hermann Goering was the first chief of the Gestapo, but in 1935 Heinrich Himmler got control of it. This gave Himmler more actual power than anyone in Germany except Hitler.

The Gestapo was responsible for the upkeep and guarding of large concentration camps and secret prisons in Germany. Not only did it torture and starve hundreds of people, but it also killed great numbers of prisoners, especially those who were Jewish, in poison-gas chambers.

A branch of the Gestapo was set up in every nation defeated or occupied by the Nazi armies during World War II.

gestation

Gestation is the growth of the young inside its mother. The length of time that this growth takes is called the *gestation period.*

The period of gestation in human beings, the time between the fertilization of the egg inside the mother and the birth of the fully formed baby, is about forty weeks, or about nine months. There is a separate article on CHILDBIRTH.

The animals that have one baby at a time require longer periods of gestation than those that have litters of several young at a time. The animals that are born singly are completely developed and formed when they are born. Animals born in litters may be incomplete in some respect. Baby rats, for example, are born without hair and with their eyes closed. Kittens and puppies are also born with their eyes closed and cannot walk around right away. Baby colts, however, can walk and stand immediately, and so can calves.

An elephant has twenty to twenty-one months of gestation, a horse eleven months, and a cow nine months. Dogs have a gestation period of only 62 or 63 days, cats 55 to 60 days, and squirrels and rats three weeks.

The animals that carry their newborn young in pouches, such as the kangaroo and opossum, have comparatively short gestation periods. This is because the marsupials, as these animals are called, give birth to young when the babies are still not entirely ready to live in the world by themselves. They must remain in the mother's pouch until they grow a little more, and gain strength. The kangaroo's gestation period is thirty-nine days, the opossum's thirteen days.

Gethsemane

Gethsemane was a garden near the city of Jerusalem. The Gospels of Mark and Matthew in the New Testament tell how Jesus prayed there after he had eaten the Last Supper with his disciples. At that time Roman soldiers were looking for him to arrest him. Because one of his disciples, Judas, betrayed him, the Roman soldiers found Jesus and arrested him, and he was crucified.

Gettysburg

Gettysburg is a small city in southern Pennsylvania. It has become one of the most famous places in American history. Here, from July 1 to July 3, 1863, the Northern army stopped the Confederates, and forced them to give up their plans of invading the North. The Battle of Gettysburg has been called the turning point of the Civil War. For three days the Southerners, who were under the command of General Robert E. Lee, tried to drive back General George G. Meade's Union army, which had taken up a posi-

tion on a long stretch of high ground just south of the town, called Cemetery Ridge. On the final day, the Confederate division of General George Pickett launched a desperate attack on the center of the line. A few men reached the ridge, but they were soon killed. The rest of the Southern soldiers in this heroic charge were either driven back or were killed or wounded. The Northerners lost 23,000 men out of 97,000 who were in the battle. The Southern losses were 28,000 out of 75,000. The battlefield of Gettysburg is now a National Military Park, and every year it is visited by thousands of people. Nearby is a National Cemetery, where many of the soldiers who died in the battle are buried. Abraham Lincoln made his famous Gettysburg Address here when the cemetery was dedicated four months after the battle. Though the speech consists of only 267 words and lasted only four minutes, it is one of the two most famous examples of great writing in American history (the other being the Declaration of Independence).

GETTYSBURG, PENNSYLVANIA. Population (1960 census) 7,960. County seat of Adams County.

geyser

A geyser is a spring of hot water that spouts out of the ground from time to time. A person watching a geyser first hears a rumbling in the earth below his feet, and then a great roar as the spout of water shoots up into the air. Geysers shoot up at regular intervals. Some geysers erupt every few minutes or hours, but there is one geyser that erupts only once every eight years.

Geysers are found only in parts of the earth where there has been recent volcanic activity, that is, where hot lava from deep inside the earth has burst out close to the surface. Mostly geysers are found only in Yellowstone National Park in the United States, in New Zealand, and in Iceland. Geysers are formed by a deep crack in the earth, into which runs rain

Pa. Dept. of Commerce
Part of the Gettysburg battleground.

water and water from inside the earth. The hot lava heats this water until it turns to steam. When the steam reaches a certain pressure it bursts out of the passage, sending tons of water up with it. The time between the eruptions of a geyser depends on how long it takes for the water to drain into the crack and then become hot.

One of the most famous geysers is Old Faithful in Yellowstone Park. It erupts regularly every 65 minutes in a beautiful fountain as high as 125 feet. The Giant is another favorite of sightseers there. It throws up a column of water five feet across and two hundred feet high, and erupts for an hour and a half. Yellowstone Park has seventy geysers.

Geysers build strange and beautiful deposits around the mouth of the crack. These deposits consist of white silica, a mineral the spouting water brings up with it from the earth below.

Ghana

Ghana is a republic in West Africa. It is one of the youngest independent countries in the world, having been a British colony, called the Gold Coast, until March 6, 1957. Then it became independent, as a member of the British Commonwealth of Nations, and joined the United Nations.

More than seven million people live in Ghana and almost all of them belong to the Negro race. The name Ghana was taken from a great Negro empire that existed in central Africa about a thousand years ago. The area of Ghana is 91,843 square miles—about the size of the state of Oregon. This is made up of 79,000 square miles of the original Gold Coast colony (including the Northern territories and Ashanti), plus British Togoland and some smaller regions that were added to Ghana when it became independent. The capital and largest city of Ghana is ACCRA, about which there is a separate article.

Ghana has a seacoast on the Atlantic Ocean. Its principal river is the Volta.

Since Ghana is only a few degrees north of the Equator, the climate is tropical—very hot all year, with a long "rainy season."

Most of the people are farmers. Their principal crop, especially in Ashanti, is cacao, from which cocoa and chocolate come. Ghana has rich deposits of gold and manganese, which are mined, and aluminum, which is not yet mined but can be if the Volta is dammed for hydroelectric power. Most of the people live in villages that are ruled by local kings or chiefs. There are several languages or dialects spoken, but the principal one is Odji, a Sudanese African language. Many of the people follow native religions, but there have been many Christian missionaries in Ghana and especially in the larger cities the children go to Christian schools.

In Ghana, unlike many parts of Africa, all the land belongs to the native people; there are few white residents (about 10,-000 in the whole country) and they own none of the great farms and forests.

In 1960 Ghana became a republic. Its first president was Kwame Nkrumah, who had led Ghana's struggle for independence. Nkrumah's rule became more and more that of a dictator; he stamped out all opposition and put many in prison. In 1962 he was made president for life. Nkrumah was also very ambitious; he wanted to be a leader of all the new nations of Africa. But he did not do very much for the people of his own country. By 1966, Ghana, once one of the most prosperous countries in Africa, was heavily in debt. In February 1966, when Nkrumah was out of the country, the Army seized power and exiled Nkrumah.

GHANA. Area, 91,843 square miles. Population (1964 estimate), 7,537,000. Language, Sudanese (Odji). Religions, Roman Catholic, other Christian, and native. Capital, Accra. Government, republic within the (British) Commonwealth of Nations. Monetary unit, the pound, worth $2.80 (U.S.). Flag, red, gold, green, with black star in center.

Belgian Tourist Office

Some of the churches in Ghent, Belgium, are many hundreds of years old.

Ghent

Ghent is an important city in Belgium. It is the capital of the province of East Flanders. About 455,000 people live there. A canal connects it with the North Sea, making it a seaport. Ghent has been an important trade and manufacturing center for hundreds of years. It is still important in manufacturing, especially cloth and lace, and as a seaport. The people of Ghent are Flemish but speak the Dutch language.

The War of 1812 between the United States and Great Britain was ended by a treaty signed at Ghent in 1814. Henry Clay, John Quincy Adams and Albert Gallatin were among the Americans who helped make the treaty. It was agreed that each country would return to the other whatever lands it had captured during the war. The greatest battle of the War of 1812, the Battle of New Orleans, was fought after the Treaty of Ghent had been signed, because in those days it took so long to get the news of the peace to North America that no one knew the war already had come to an end.

A famous English poet, Robert Browning, wrote a poem called "How They Brought the Good News from Ghent to Aix." It tells about bringing the news of a great victory from Ghent to the city of Aix, in France. The story is imaginary, and was wholly made up by Browning.

ghetto

Hundreds of years ago, before civilized countries generally adopted the principle of religious freedom, many European cities required that all Jews live in a certain section of the city. This section was called the ghetto. It was usually a poor and overcrowded section.

Some of the ghettos were surrounded by walls, and had gates that were locked at night, so that the Jews living in the ghettos had to be home by sundown and could not leave until the next morning. In some European cities there were ghettos that were not required by law. Nearly all the Jews of the city lived in them so that they could more easily follow their ancient customs together. But in most cities the Jews had no choice.

One of the most famous ghettos was the one in Rome, established about 1550. It was located on a few dark streets near the Tiber River, which flooded it yearly. Some Roman rulers were more liberal than others in granting privileges to the Jews, but these ghetto conditions existed in Rome until 1885, when King Victor Emmanuel abolished the ghetto of Rome. Ghettos in other places were gradually abolished after the early 1800s. While the Nazi party ruled Germany and occupied other countries in Europe, the Jews were forced into small sections of the city in Warsaw, the capital of Poland, and Prague, the capital of Czechoslovakia, and these were called ghettos. Also, any section of a big city where nearly all the people are Jews may sometimes be called a ghetto. A famous one was the "Lower East Side" of New York City, from the 1890s to the 1920s.

Ghiberti, Lorenzo

Lorenzo Ghiberti was an Italian sculptor and architect who lived more than five hundred years ago. He is most famous for designing "The Gates of Heaven," two sets of bronze doors for a building called the Baptistry, at Florence, in Italy. He was born in 1378 and died in 1455.

Ghirlandaio, Domenico

Domenico Ghirlandaio was an Italian painter who lived about five hundred years ago. He is famous as the teacher of the great artist Michelangelo. Ghirlandaio painted many scenes from the Bible that were unusual because the people in them are shown wearing the style of clothes worn in Italy five hundred years ago. He did some of the work on the Sistine Chapel in Rome, together with another great painter, Botticelli, and he painted some beautiful frescoes (wall paintings on wet plaster) in the Cathedral of Florence. Ghirlandaio was born in 1449 and died in 1494. His two brothers and his son were also painters.

ghost

A ghost is supposed to be the spirit of a person who has died. Unlike most imaginary spirits, ghosts are not supposed to have any great powers. They can only come back and appear to people in houses, which is called *haunting*. A ghost is supposed to look like steam, so that you can partly see through it. Ghosts are usually pictured in long white robes, and on Hallowe'en people dress up as ghosts in white sheets. Ghosts are supposed to scream, groan, rattle chains, and make other strange noises. This is said to be because they are unhappy to come back to earth, where they are punished for sins they committed when they were alive.

Often the ghosts of murdered people are believed to haunt the place where they were killed. Whole families may be visited by the ghost of a person that an early ancestor killed or injured, or even by the ghost of an ancestor. The Norwegian writer Henrik Ibsen wrote a play called *Ghosts,* which tells about an imaginary family ghost. In Shakespeare's play *Hamlet,* the father of Hamlet appears as a ghost.

There is an organization called the Society for Psychical Research that investigates reports that ghosts have been seen. The Society does this for scientific purposes.

giant

A giant is a creature of human shape but enormously big and strong. There are many stories of giants in the Bible. The giant Goliath was slain by David, and there were whole tribes of giants like the sons of Anak, who were so tall that ordinary people looked like midgets beside them. The ancient Greeks believed in a race of giants called Titans, who fought the gods. The Titans hurled forests and mountains against Olympus, the home of the gods, and laughed at the lightning that Zeus flung back at them. The northern countries have many tales of giants. The Norwegians tell of the giant who had no heart in his body. In India, Cambodia and Ceylon, there were giants who hid their hearts in bird nests to keep them safe. Jack the Giant-killer of the fairy tale was supposed to have lived in Wales. A Cyclops, told about by the great Greek poet Homer, was a one-eyed giant who sometimes helped the gods.

There have been many real giants, too, but they are different from the legendary ones. They are seldom very strong, and they usually do not live long. Many people have grown to be seven feet tall, and some have even reached nine feet. Most circuses have a "tall man," who looks even taller when he stands beside the midget. In the days of ancient Rome an Arabian giant named Gabbaras was captured and exhibited to the people. He was 9 feet, 4 inches tall.

Groups of the stone columns of the Giant's Causeway in Ireland have interesting names such as the Giant's Chimney, the Giant's Wishing-Chair, and Lady Giant's Fan.

Real giantism usually begins in childhood when a gland called the *pituitary* works too hard and produces too much of the substance that enables the body to grow.

Giant's Causeway

The Giant's Causeway is a strange formation of tall rock columns on the northeastern coast of Ireland. There are about 40,000 of these columns, most of them having five or six sides. All of them stand close together. They were actually formed by a great outpouring of lava, or liquid rock, from the earth many millions of years ago, but there is a legend in Ireland that says the Giant's Causeway was made by a man. According to this legend, there was a great Irish hero named Fingal or Finn MacCool who built the Giant's Causeway nearly two thousand years ago as a road for giants to use in crossing from Ireland to Scotland.

gibbon

A gibbon is a tailless ape that lives in the East Indies. When a gibbon stands erect its arms are so long that they nearly touch the ground. As gibbons live in forests and travel about in the trees a great deal, their long arms are very useful for swinging from branch to branch. In the air these animals move with great ease and grace, but on the ground they move awkwardly. Gibbons are the least intelligent of the apes, and are also smaller and thinner than other apes. They have naked, calloused patches on their backs. They are closely related to orangutans and chimpanzees, other members of the ape family. They are also related to the Old World monkeys.

Gibbon, Edward

Edward Gibbon was an English writer of history who lived about two hundred years ago. He is most famous for a work called *Decline and Fall of the Roman Empire.* In this work he tells the story of Rome, from the time of its greatest glory to its downfall almost 1,300 years later. Gibbon was born in 1737 and died in 1794. You can read more about him in the article HISTORY.

Gibbons, James Cardinal

James Gibbons was a famous American Roman Catholic priest who became a cardinal, or prince of the church. He was born in Baltimore, Maryland, in 1834, and he studied for the priesthood at St. Charles College and St. Mary's Seminary in Maryland. He became Archbishop of Baltimore and was made a cardinal in 1886. He is best known for the help he gave the Knights of Labor. The Knights of Labor was a labor union that was banned in Canada because the Canadian government thought that it was a secret society. Cardinal Gibbons persuaded the Pope to praise the Knights because they were helping laborers. The Knights of Labor were accepted in Canada mostly because of Cardinal Gibbons' efforts. He died in 1921.

G.I. Bill of Rights

The G.I. Bill of Rights is a name by which Public Law 346 is known. The law was passed by the Congress of the United States to aid veterans who served in the armed forces in World War II and Korea.

Under this law, the government paid a veteran's necessary school costs and helped him support himself while he was in school or training for a better job. Even veterans who work on farms received special training under the G.I. Bill. Almost eight million veterans received benefits from this law.

Another law, which is not part of the G.I. Bill, provides for even greater help to disabled veterans. These veterans, who were hurt during the war, obtain special training to help them overcome their injuries, such as the loss of an arm or leg. This law is called Public Law 16.

Gibbs, Josiah Willard

Josiah Willard Gibbs was an American scientist who made important discoveries about matter. (Matter is anything that has weight and takes up space.) Gibbs lived about 75 years ago, but people did not recognize the importance of his work until after his death. He died in 1903, and was elected to the Hall of Fame in 1950.

Gibbs was born in New Haven, Connecticut in 1839. He studied at Yale University and also in Paris, France and in Heidelberg, Germany. In 1871 he became professor of mathematical physics at Yale. Six years later, in 1877, he developed a rule called the "Gibbs Phase Rule," which described certain chemical changes in matter that had never been explained before. Most of Gibbs' studies were in the field of thermodynamics, the branch of physics that studies heat. He also wrote several books on mathematical physics.

Gibraltar

Gibraltar is a British colony located at the southern tip of Spain. The colony is actually a huge rock formation just over two miles long and about a mile and a half wide, and it is about 1,400 feet high. It is often called the Rock of Gibraltar. Gibraltar is very important because it guards the Strait of Gibraltar, which is the name of the narrow strip of water connecting the Atlantic Ocean with the Mediterranean Sea. The Strait of Gibraltar separates the southern end of Spain from the northern coast of Africa, and is about seven miles wide at its narrowest point and twenty-five miles wide at its widest point. There is a large naval base at Gibraltar, as well as an important coaling station for ships. Many tunnels have been driven through the rocky ground to connect one part of the colony with another, and large fortifications and gun emplacements have been built there in case of war. Including the soldiers stationed there, more than 25,000 people live at Gibraltar.

Gibraltar has had a very long history. It was captured by the Arabs who crossed into Spain over 1,200 years ago. Later it became a Spanish possession and was finally turned over to the English in

1713. Most of the people who live on the peninsula today, aside from English military personnel, are of Spanish or Italian descent. Most of the people work at the naval base or have jobs in the other military installations.

Many of the animals called BARBARY APES are found at Gibraltar. There is a separate article about them.

Gibson, Charles Dana

Charles Dana Gibson was a famous American artist and illustrator. He is best known as the creator of the "Gibson Girl." She was the central figure in a series of drawings. The Gibson girl was very beautiful and was supposed to be the ideal American girl. (Actually these were drawings of Gibson's wife, who was a great beauty.) These pictures showed the Gibson girl at parties, playing tennis, and playing cards. She wore her hair piled high on her head, and wore a blouse with huge sleeves and a long skirt. The drawings really poked fun at the people of the time by showing how silly some of their fashions were.

Gibson was born in Roxbury, Massachusetts, in 1867. He made drawings to illustrate many stories in leading magazines. He later gave up drawing and became the editor of a magazine. Before he died in 1944 he wrote many books about his travels around the world.

Gideon

Gideon was a hero in the Bible. He lived in Israel more than a thousand years

British Inform. Service

Above: Gibraltar seen from the air. *Below:* A British officer with the famous apes of Gibraltar. A legend says that Gibraltar will remain a British possession as long as the apes remain. *Right:* A naval officer holds the keys of Gibraltar.

before the birth of Jesus. The Jews were troubled then by another desert people, the Midianites, who came into their lands and often killed or stole from them. Once while Gideon was threshing wheat in secret, to hide it from the Midianites, he was visited by an angel who said he could save Israel. Gideon called three hundred friends and relatives to help him fight the Midianites and this little army chased the raiders out beyond Jordan and killed their leaders. The grateful Jews invited Gideon to be king of Israel but he refused.

THE GIDEONS

There is a society called Gideons International that distributes Bibles free of charge to hotel rooms and other places. The society took Gideon's name because of Gideon's obedience to God, as told in the Book of Judges. Gideons International was founded in 1899 in the United States, and has since spread to about thirty countries. It has given away more than two million Bibles to hotels, schools, prisons, ships, and military camps. During World War II the Gideons distributed Bibles among the men in the armed services.

Gila monster

A Gila monster is a poisonous lizard that is found in the sandy deserts of the southwestern United States and Mexico. It is a reptile with a long, narrow, heavy body and thick tail and head. It is called the Gila monster because it was first noticed in the valley of the Gila River in Arizona. A large Gila monster may be nearly two feet long, which is very large for a lizard. It has a rough, warty skin, usually black and yellow. The Gila monster has large teeth. Some of the teeth have a groove down the side that allows the poisonous saliva to flow into wounds made by the teeth. Human beings have died from its bite. Gila monsters eat worms, centipedes, and bird and lizard eggs.

Am. Museum of Natural History
A Gila monster crawling in the desert.

Gila River

The Gila River, more than five hundred miles long, rises in the mountains of New Mexico and flows westward across Arizona. It flows into the Colorado River. On its way it forms canyons in the mountains and fertile valleys in the flat plains. Southern Arizona would be much drier than it is if the Gila River and its tributaries did not irrigate its dry land.

Gilbert Islands

The Gilbert Islands are in the western part of the Pacific Ocean. There are 16 coral islands in the Gilberts. These islands are called atolls, and about 33,000 people live on them. The islands belong to England, but they were captured by Japan in World War II. Almost two years later, on November 21, 1943, a strong American fleet sailed to the two largest islands, Tarawa and Makin, and landed troops who defeated the Japanese there. You can read about TARAWA in a separate article. The Gilberts were then used as bases for American bombers.

Gilbert, Sir Humphrey

Sir Humphrey Gilbert was the first Englishman to establish a British colony in the New World. He was born in England in 1539, and he went to school at Oxford, one of England's best universities. Later he became an army officer and fought for England in many foreign coun-

N.Y. Public Library
Left: W. S. Gilbert. **Right:** A. S. Sullivan.

tries. From his half-brother, Sir Walter Raleigh, he learned to love the sea. He became interested in finding a Northwest Passage across the seas from Europe to China, and he persuaded Queen Elizabeth I of England to outfit him for a voyage.

Gilbert's first trip in search of the Northwest Passage was a complete failure. His second trip was a success, but not the kind he expected. He did not find a Northwest Passage. Instead he landed in Newfoundland, where he founded a small fishing village and claimed the land for England. In 1583, while he was returning to England in his small ship, he was lost in a storm.

Gilbert and Sullivan

Sir William Gilbert and Sir Arthur Sullivan were two Englishmen who wrote comic operas together. These are plays with some of the words set to music and much of the story told in songs. In them certain customs and habits, some of them English and others worldwide, were satirized (made fun of). Gilbert wrote the words and Sullivan wrote the music. Their comic operas were by far the most popular written during their time, which was about sixty years ago. Many of them are still so popular that they are constantly being performed.

Among the most popular comic operas that Gilbert and Sullivan wrote together are *The Mikado, The Pirates of Penzance, Trial by Jury, H.M.S. Pinafore, Iolanthe,* and *The Yeomen of the Guard.*

A special theater, the Savoy Theater, was built in London in 1881 by the producer Richard D'Oyly Carte to put on the Gilbert and Sullivan operas. The companies that put them on were often called Savoyards. There is still an English company called the D'Oyly Carte Company that performs these operas.

Sir William Schwenck Gilbert was born in 1836. He was first a military officer and later worked in a government office. He also studied and practiced law. In 1861 he began to publish humorous poetry, which was very well liked. One collection of his poems is called *Bab Ballads.* Then he and Sullivan began writing comic operas together. Even though Gilbert and Sullivan worked together they often quarreled, and sometimes did not speak to each other for weeks at a time. They would send their work back and forth by messengers. In 1890 they had a very serious quarrel and did not speak or work together for six years.

Prominent Englishmen are often rewarded by being knighted and allowed to use "Sir" before their names. Sullivan was knighted in 1883. Gilbert had hurt Queen Victoria's feelings by insulting the British Navy in *H.M.S. Pinafore,* and he was not knighted until 1907, six years after the Queen's death. He died in 1911.

Read also the article about Sir Arthur SULLIVAN.

Gilead

Gilead was the name of a land told about in the Bible. It was also the name of a mountain and a city in that land. Gilead was a region east of the Jordan River. It was an upland region of pastures and woods. It was especially known for the spices and the balm, a sweet-smelling oil or ointment, that came from there. Gilead is mentioned often in the Bible. It was given as a home to the tribes of Reuben and Gad, and to part of the tribe of Manasseh. The great Hebrew prophet and preacher Elijah came from the land of Gilead.

Gilgamesh

Gilgamesh is the greatest hero of Babylonian and Assyrian mythology, the stories the Babylonians and Assyrians told about their gods and goddesses. Gilgamesh was daring in battle, the most handsome man of his time, and the wisest. Other men called him "the Powerful, the Perfect, and the Wise."

All the women fell in love with him and the men became jealous. They asked the goddess Ishtar to create a rival to Gilgamesh, and Ishtar told Aruru, another goddess, to make Engidu his rival. Engidu was as handsome and as wise as Gilgamesh. He was big and unbelievably strong, and knew everything about the past and future. But he did not like people and spent his time in the forest, living with the animals. Engidu was supposed to have had the body of a bull and the chest and head of a man.

When Gilgamesh and Engidu met and fought, the earth shook for miles around. At last Gilgamesh won. Engidu and Gilgamesh became friends after this and fought many battles and had many adventures side by side. When Engidu got sick and died, Gilgamesh learned to fear death. He left the country in search of a magic tree called the Tree of Life, which could make him live forever. He asked a wise man for directions to the Tree and as the wise man gave him directions, he also told him the story of a great flood that covered the earth. Gilgamesh wandered in the wilderness for a long time and had many battles and adventures while searching for the Tree.

gills

Gills are the organs by which fish breathe, just as human beings breathe with their lungs. Gills are tiny blood vessels behind the head of the fish. They take oxygen out of the water that the fish takes in through its mouth. If you look at the throats of most fish, you will see four or five small slits. These openings are called gill slits. The fish opens his mouth at regular intervals and takes in water. When he closes his mouth, the water is forced through the slits over the tiny gills. The blood in the gills takes the oxygen from the water. The oxygen is then carried to other parts of the body by the blood stream. The water is let out of the body through the gill slits, and this is the way fish breathe. The gills of the fish must be wet in order for them to breathe, because dry gills do not work. This is why fish die if they are kept out of water.

ginger

Ginger is a spice used in cooking. It gives food a special flavor and a sharp taste. You can taste this spice in ginger tea, ginger beer, ginger candy, ginger ale, and gingersnap cookies. There are other forms of ginger, the dried ginger root, which lasts for a long time, and the green or young root, which looks like an onion.

All these forms of ginger come from the root of the ginger plant, which grows in the tropics, in England, in India, in Australia, and other parts of the world.

Left: The flowers of the ginger plant. *Center:* The leaves. *Right:* The root, from which ginger used for flavoring is made.

The part of the plant that grows above the ground consists of reeds, with leaves and flowers growing on separate stalks. When the leaves and flowers wither, the native workers take the roots out of the ground. They wash and dry and scrape the roots and then prepare ginger for its many uses. Ginger is ground for use as ginger powder. Ginger root can be dried and bleached in the sun, making white ginger. The green roots can also be preserved in heavy syrup and eaten as a sweet relish.

Ginger has been used as a food and medicine for thousands of years. The Bible mentions ginger, and the ancient Chinese ate it to make them feel warm inside in cold weather.

gingham

Gingham is a cotton cloth woven in Lancashire, England, in Glasgow, Scotland, and in the United States. The manufacturer weaves the colors into gingham. He does not merely print them on the cloth, as he does with calico. Women use gingham for aprons, dresses, curtains, and upholstery. Men use gingham for sport shirts, and children wear gingham clothes. The different types of gingham are: *chambray,* a plain gingham; *nurse gingham,* which has blue and white stripes; *Scotch gingham,* made in Scotland; *tissue gingham,* which has the feel of cord; *zephyr* or *French gingham,* which is thin and soft; and *madras gingham,* which is woven in many brilliant colors.

ginkgo

The ginkgo is a very ancient tree that grows in China and Japan. It is the only tree left of a large family of trees that grew thousands of years ago. It is sometimes called the maidenhair tree. The ginkgo looks just the same today as it did thousands of years ago when it grew in the forests of ancient times.

The ginkgo can live in cities where harmful gases kill many other kinds of tree, so it is being planted more and more in parks and along streets in the eastern United States. The female trees, which bear foul-smelling fleshy fruits, are not desirable as street trees, however. The ginkgo grows to a height of 60 to 80 feet. Its leaves are fan-shaped. They are on flexible stems and wave in the slightest breeze.

ginseng

Ginseng is a plant from which a valuable drug is made. The ginseng is a low plant. It has three leaves divided into five leaflets each and small, greenish-white flowers. Ginseng has a forked root, and a drug made from the root of the ginseng that is grown in China was used for many years as a medicine. It was so expensive that scientists wanted a cheaper substitute for it. They found one in a member of the same family that grows wild in the United States and Canada. It was then grown commercially for the drug, which is used as a soothing, or quieting, medicine. The ginseng has to be grown in a protected spot because the direct rays of the sun will kill it.

Am. Museum of Natural History

The leaves and fruit of the ginseng.

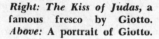

Right: The Kiss of Judas, a famous fresco by Giotto. *Above:* A portrait of Giotto.

Giorgione

Giorgione was a great Italian painter. He worked with a group of painters in Venice, and so we say he belonged to the Venetian school. Very little is known about Giorgione, and there is only one painting that can safely be called his. There are four or five more that were probably painted by him, but experts are not positive.

The one picture known to have been painted by Giorgione is called "The Tempest." It is a landscape, or outdoor scene, with dark clouds in the background. In the picture are a young shepherd boy and a mother with her child. This was one of the first pictures in which the landscape was important. Giorgione, which means "Big George" in Italian, was born about 1477. He died when he was only 33 years old.

Giotto

Giotto was an Italian artist and one of the greatest painters who ever lived. He lived during the Middle Ages, about seven hundred years ago.

At the time Giotto began to paint all pictures were flat-looking. There was little feeling of depth or distance in painting. The ancient Romans had known how to make painted people look real, but during the Middle Ages painters had forgotten how to do it. Painters made their figures tall and wide, and squeezed as many into a picture as possible. Giotto studied very hard and learned how the Romans had made scenes and people look so natural. His paintings look like scenes taken from a play and tell you a story as you look at them.

Giotto's full name was Giotto di Bondone. He was born in Florence, Italy. He drew the first sketches for the lovely bell tower called the Campanile, in the main square in Florence. Most of Giotto's paintings are frescoes, or pictures painted on a plaster wall while the plaster is still wet. All of Giotto's frescoes are scenes from the Bible. They are in churches and cathedrals in Florence and Padua. By the time Giotto died in 1327 his name was known all over Italy, and his fame had spread through most of Europe.

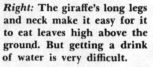

Right: The giraffe's long legs and neck make it easy for it to eat leaves high above the ground. But getting a drink of water is very difficult.

S. Africa Govt. Inform. Office

giraffe

The giraffe is an animal with a very long neck and long legs. It lives in Africa south of the Sahara desert, and it can be seen in many zoos. The giraffe is the tallest of the mammals. (Mammals are animals that nurse their young.) A giraffe may reach a height of eighteen feet, and most of its height comes from its extremely long neck. The giraffe's neck, however, has only seven vertebrae, or neckbones, the same as most other four-legged animals. Giraffes have two bones that stick up from the tops of their heads. These are covered with tufts of hair and look like horns. Giraffes have short, smooth hair, reddish-brown with dark spots. They have short manes and tufts of hair on the ends of their tails. The giraffe has a very long tongue that can stretch so far that the tip becomes small enough to go through a small keyring. Its mouth is shaped somewhat like a cow's, and its lips are muscular. It is a ruminant and chews a cud. A ruminant has three or four stomachs and swallows some of its food whole. This food is stored in the first stomach and brought up again in the form of a cud, which the animal then chews. The giraffe feeds on grass and leaves. It eats a great deal of mimosa, a flowering shrub that grows on the plains where the giraffe lives.

Giraffes are peaceful animals that would rather run away from danger than face it, but they are good fighters if they have to be. They can beat off a lion by kicking their hind legs so fast that it is almost like an explosion in the lion's face. A giraffe can keep up with the fastest horse and outdistance it on uneven ground. It runs by moving both of its legs on the same side at the same time. All four of its legs are the same length, although the front ones look longer. Giraffes were known to the Romans, who exhibited them in spectacles or shows. Thousands of years ago the Egyptians pictured giraffes in their art.

Girard, Stephen

Stephen Girard was an American banker who lived about two hundred years ago. He was born in France in 1750, but when he was 26 he settled in Philadelphia. He made a great deal of money, which he gave generously to the poor.

In his will, Girard left his fortune to build schools. One of these schools is Girard College in Philadelphia, which was intended for orphan boys who wanted to learn a trade. Stephen Girard also lent money several times to the United States government, and in 1814 he paid almost all its war loans himself. He gave his service as well as money. During the yellow fever epidemic in Philadelphia he volunteered to manage a hospital for the sick people, as well as paying for their care. Girard died in 1831.

Giraud, Henri

Henri Giraud was a French general. He was born in 1879. In both World Wars he was captured by the Germans, and both times he escaped. When he escaped in 1941 France had been beaten and occupied by the Germans. Giraud got to North Africa, a French possession that was liberated by British and American forces early in 1942. At that time General Charles de Gaulle commanded the French forces that were not under the control of Germany. Giraud and de Gaulle did not agree on many things, but they were persuaded to work together for the benefit of France. Giraud died in 1949, a few years after the war ended.

Girl Scouts

The Girl Scouts is an organization of girls who meet in small groups to work and play together. These girls learn to be good and helpful citizens. At the same time they have a good time with their friends. The Girl Scout organization was started in England, in 1909, by an English general named Sir Robert Baden-Powell, the same person who started the Boy Scouts organization. This English organization of girls was called the Girl Guides. An American woman named Juliette Gordon Low, who was living in Scotland at that time, became interested in the Girl Guides. When she returned home to America she founded the first Girl Scout group in the United States, in 1912.

The Girl Guide and Girl Scout movement has spread all over the world, and today groups from more than thirty countries belong to the World Association of Girl Guides and Girl Scouts.

WHAT GIRL SCOUTS DO

Any girl ten years old or more can become a Girl Scout. Girls from 7 to 9 years old can join the Brownies, an organization that is connected with the Girl Scouts. Brownie Scouts could be called Junior Scouts. Girls from 10 to 13 are called Intermediate Scouts. When a girl is 14, she may become a Senior Scout if she has been an Intermediate Scout long enough to pass certain requirements.

The Brownies learn songs, dances and handcrafts, and get an idea of what the Girl Scouts do. They are then ready to become good Girl Scouts when they are old enough.

To become a scout, a girl applies for membership in a neighborhood group of scouts called a troop. At the head of each troop is a captain, or leader, a woman especially trained in scouting. A girl who wants to become a scout must first learn something about scouting. She goes to scout meetings. She learns the scout oath, the ten points of the scout law, the scout motto and slogan, and the scout sign, salute, and handclasp.

Within a troop, a Girl Scout becomes a member of a patrol. A patrol is a small group of scouts who work together. There are about eight girls in a patrol, and two or more patrols in a troop. Each patrol has its own name, usually the name of an animal or plant, and its own flag. The scout troop is run in a democratic way, and girl scouts learn about democratic government by practicing it in their troop. Each patrol elects its own leader. The leader has an assistant. All the patrol leaders, together with the troop captain, the troop scribe who keeps records of meetings, and the troop treasurer who collects dues, form the Court of Honor. This court meets to make its own plans and decisions, and everyone helps by making suggestions and giving her own ideas.

Girl Scouts wear uniforms that include a dark green dress, belt, and beret, and a brightly colored neckerchief. They wear the special Girl Scout pin. They wear emblems and badges which show their rank, their troop, and any office they hold and honors they have won. Girl Scouts are divided into three ranks or grades. The lowest is the tenderfoot. Next is second-class scout, and the highest is first-class scout. A girl must pass a test to show that she knows and can do certain things before she can become a tenderfoot. Then she must pass more tests to go into a higher grade.

Girl Scouts learn to be good citizens and helpful friends. A Girl Scout is expected to be loyal, courteous, obedient, thrifty, and clean. She learns to do a good deed every day, and to be useful and helpful to others.

Scouts hold meetings every week, to learn about scouting, to play games, and to work at their many activities. They make plans for hikes and camping trips. They study to pass tests and earn badges.

Senior Scouts help out with younger scouts and experiment in various fields of work that they may choose as careers. In this group many girls go in for Wing Scouting, in which they learn about flying and aviation, or Mariner Scouting, in which they learn about sailing and navigation.

CAMPING AND OUTDOOR LIFE

Girl Scouts have many outdoor activities, through which they learn a great deal about nature, and about how to take care of themselves outdoors. Often scouts take hikes and trips. They cook their meals out-of-doors, and sometimes they camp out.

Scouts must learn many things that are useful to them in their trips. They must know how to follow trails, and how to make road maps. They learn how to plan their trips, and how to get ready the things they need. A camping trip is a success only if the campers know how to take care of themselves, and how to provide the things they need. So a Girl Scout must know how to light a fire. This may seem like a simple thing, but a scout must learn to do it when she has only two matches and no paper to make the fire burn easily. The scout learns that there are many different ways of building a fire for cooking. The scout knows how to broil, bake, or boil her food over the right kind of fire using only a small amount of wood. She knows how different foods can be cooked out-of-doors and what foods to take along on an outdoor trip.

Overnight camping is not much fun without a good shelter, so scouts learn how to put up a tent that will stay up, even if the wind blows. They know how to prevent water from seeping under it. And they learn how to build a shelter from branches that they gather in the woods in case they do not have a tent.

When accidents happen, a Girl Scout must be prepared. Scouts are taught first aid so they can take care of any accidents that happen when there is no doctor nearby.

First aid may mean the difference between life and death. A first-class scout must know how to give artificial respiration so that she can revive a person who has stopped breathing. She also must know what to do about broken bones, serious bleeding, dogbite, snakebite, sunstroke, frostbite, heat exhaustion, fainting, and poisoning.

Many scouts also learn to signal in Morse code, using blinker lights at night and wigwag flags in the daytime. In Morse code each letter of the alphabet is made up of dots and dashes. A dot is a short flash, and a dash a long flash of the blinker light. In wigwag signaling, a two-foot white flag with a red square in the center is waved to the left and right. A wave to the right is a dot, a wave to the

Girl Scouts Photos

Girl Scouts earn merit badges and have fun too by learning skills that will help them to lead healthy, happy, and useful lives:

1. A Girl Scout earns points for a "Child Care" badge by reading a bedtime story to a little boy. Many Girl Scouts earn points by baby-sitting for their neighbors.
2. Girl Scouts learn to darn in company.
3. Two Girl Scouts and their troop leader inspect equipment for a camping trip.
4. A Girl Scout learns to help voters.
5. Girl Scouts learn to tie campers' knots.

left is a dash. In these ways scouts are able to signal emergency messages over long distances.

A scout who knows all these things can have a good time on a camping trip. She knows how to take care of herself. She learns how to do things safely, and how to care for her camping site so that it will be a pleasant place for other campers who follow her. She learns to work together with the other girls. She comes to know the woods and the fields, and to enjoy being close to nature. She also has a great deal of fun.

LEARNING THROUGH SCOUTING

Girl Scouts also learn many useful and interesting things that they use in their everyday lives. Homemaking is one of the many things that Girl Scouts learn about. A family can enjoy its home only if it is taken care of so that everything runs smoothly. So scouts know how to take care of a house and how to plan the work. They learn how to plan and cook good meals that everyone will enjoy. They know how to sew, and how to make useful things.

Two senior Scouts interested in flying learn how Air Force pilots are trained.

Girl Scouts learn how to take care of their health. They know what things are needed for a healthy body, and they develop good health habits. When someone in the family is sick, a scout knows how to be helpful. She studies home nursing, and learns many ways to help a sick person feel comfortable, and get well quickly. Someone who is sick in bed needs special foods and special care, and a scout knows what foods are right. She can help a sick person take a bath in bed. It is not much fun to be sick in bed, but a Girl Scout knows ways to keep a patient comfortable and to entertain a sick person.

A Girl Scout is a good citizen, and she tries to practice good citizenship all the time. She tries to be considerate of other people and to respect their rights. She learns to practice democratic government in her own scout troop. She works on projects that will help her community, and make it a better place to live in. A Scout learns about health and sanitation and safety laws, and she does everything she can to see that the laws are carried out.

Scouts are encouraged to learn useful hobbies, and to do them well. There are more than a hundred hobbies, or skills, that a scout can choose to study. After passing a test in one hobby or skill, she is awarded a merit badge which she wears on her uniform. Merit badges are given in such fields as handicrafts, music, art, dramatics, child care, and nature study.

Girty, Simon

Simon Girty was an American backwoodsman who lived during the time of the Revolutionary War. He was born in Pennsylvania in 1741. When he was a young man he was captured by the Indians and he lived several years with them. He learned their language and ways of living. Then he turned against his own race and became known as "the white renegade." During the Revolution he was in the pay of the English, and led many Indian raids against the American settlers. He was hated and feared by the American frontiersmen for his cruelty, cunning, and savageness. After the war he moved to Canada, where he died in 1818.

Gish, Lillian and Dorothy

Lillian and Dorothy Gish became famous for their acting in some of the first silent movies. In 1915 Lillian Gish acted in the first long movie made by D. W. Griffith, who was one of the earliest movie makers. It was called *Birth of a Nation* and was about the Civil War. Lillian Gish was in other films made by Griffith, including *Way Down East* and *Orphans of the Storm*. She was very pretty and made a great hit with the public and was popular for many years. She was born in 1896 and was only 19 years old when she appeared in *Birth of a Nation*. She later became a popular star in television.

Mus. of Mod. Art

Lillian and Dorothy Gish, shown here in the silent movie, *Orphans of the Storm*, were popular stars during the 1920s.

Dorothy Gish, Lillian's sister, was born in 1898. She also acted in many movies and was the star of *Nell Gwyn* and *Madame Pompadour*. She appeared with her sister in the silent movies *Hearts of the World* and *Romola*. She, too, has become a television actress.

gizzard

The gizzard is the second stomach of birds. It has very thick, muscular sides, or walls, and a tough, horny lining. Birds use their gizzards to grind their food. First, the food is softened in the first stomach by juices that help digestion. Then it is ground up by the second stomach. The gizzard is located in the back of the bird's stomach. Birds that eat hard food have stronger and usually larger gizzards than birds that eat soft foods. Birds that eat grain usually have the strongest gizzards, while birds that eat insects have less strong gizzards. Birds of prey, such as eagles, that eat very little grain, have weak gizzards. Sometimes small stones are found in the gizzards of birds. The birds swallow them to help them grind up their food.

glacier

A glacier is a stream of ice that slides down from the high fields of snow on the tops of mountains. It is a mass of ice blocks broken by huge holes, and as it moves downward it tears bits of the land and mountain with it, changing the shape of the mountain walls and scooping out great valleys. The snowfields where glaciers begin are piles of snow heaped up on mountains so high and cold that the snow keeps falling faster than it can ever melt. The weight of this snow and the slope of the mountains make the snow pull and slide downward and this moving field of snow becomes the glacier. Glaciers are formed when the snow lies about a hundred feet deep from year to year without melting. The speed of the snowfall and the steepness of the slope control the speed of the glacier. Some glaciers move only part of an inch each day. Some push forward several feet. In the Alps, glaciers move ten or twenty inches daily in summer but only half that fast in winter. The fastest glaciers in Greenland travel twenty to ninety feet in a single day. Glaciers may be very wide. Malaspina Glacier in Alaska lies from Mount St. Elias to the ocean and covers about 1,500 square miles.

There are four recognized kinds of glacier. The valley, or mountain, glacier is a glacier that falls from the snowfield like a long river into the valley. When it reaches a level warm enough, it melts. It may reach the sea before it melts. The bits that break off the edge of a mountain glacier and floats in the sea are called icebergs. A hanging glacier is a special kind of valley glacier. It does not become a river of ice. As soon as it falls away from the snowfield it breaks up into ice-falls, which look like waterfalls. These ice-falls are called avalanches, and they in turn may start new glaciers.

A glacier that is formed at the foot of a mountain is called a Piedmont glacier. The Malaspina Glacier is a Piedmont glacier. The small ice sheets, which cover mountains and valleys, and the continental ice sheets, such as are found in Antarctica and Greenland, are the two other kinds of glacier.

The holes in the glacier are caused by the pull and pressure in the ice sheet that help to break up the ice. Also, the curves or rough outlines of the valley in which it travels will shatter the ice. As the glacier goes down its path, part of the ice is melted by the heat of the earth and the sunshine. This melted snow water tunnels its way under the glacier until it comes out at the foot where it may become a real river. The glacier grinds stones to such a fine floury powder that the melted ice water looks milky. Rivers from the foot of glaciers run white with this powdery water.

HOW THE GLACIER CARVES

A glacier can change the whole look of the country it touches. Its action, which tears and scrapes away at mountains and valleys, is called erosion. The ice clings to the rocks and earth around it and tears them away with it, digging huge basins. These basins may fill with rain or melting snow and become lakes. If a mountain is surrounded by glaciers tugging at its sides it may be cut into such jagged peaks as the Matterhorn in Switzerland or the Teton Range in Wyoming. The glacier can also change the land by rubbing and polishing it. Ice files away at the walls surrounding it, smoothing out V-shaped valleys into rounded, smooth-walled, U-shaped ones. Great rocks sometimes tumble into glaciers and become part of them. The rocks file the landscape over which they slide, and the glacier may drop them far away when the ice that carries them dissolves.

All the rocks and earth that the glacier has plowed up and carried on its way downward are left at the foot of its path. These mounds of rock and earth are called *moraines*. Sometimes a moraine will build into a dam that holds back the water and makes a lake after the glacier has melted. Some glaciers are nearly pure ice, but some are so mixed with dirt and rocks they have gathered that they will become almost entirely frozen earth stuck together with a little ice. New Zealand has several glaciers like that. One kind of moraine left by a melted glacier is called a *drumlin*. This is a small hill rounded like the back of a spoon. Many hills in Wisconsin and Michigan are drumlins; so is Bunker Hill, near Boston, left from the end of a glacier.

THE BIGGEST GLACIER

Millions of years ago the ice began to move down from the North Pole in the biggest glacier of all. This huge river of ice poured down for hundreds of years until it covered most of the places where we live now. The ice that lay on America and Europe was thousands of feet thick and millions of square miles wide. The people who lived in those days moved away from this glacier and went farther and farther south to keep warm. Some animals, such as the dinosaurs, were too stupid or clumsy to find warm places to live in, and so they died as the cold grew deeper. The hills of New York and New England were buried under such a heavy sheet of ice that their tops were crushed

The sure-footed bighorn makes its way with confidence through tricky Rocky Mountain terrain carved ages ago by the movement of glaciers.

U.S. Air Force

The glaciers of Mount McKinley National Park form spectacular patterns and make rough going for daring climbers.

Nat'l Travel Office

Huge Ice-Age boulders may be seen in the Glacier Garden in Lucerne, Switzerland.

A highway from Juneau, Alaska, leads visitors to dramatic Mendenhall Glacier.

Alaska Development Board

Swiss Nat'l Travel Service

A glacier stream begins its journey to the lowlands from the jumbled ice mass of a great glacier high in the Bernese Alps of southwest Switzerland.

and rounded down. Out in the west the big continental glacier carved the Yosemite Valley out of the mountains. When the ice did begin to melt, the holes it had cut filled with water and made thousands of lakes and rivers. By now this sheet of ice is melted except around the North Pole and the South Pole.

gladiator

Back in the days of the Roman Empire, nearly two thousand years ago, the people went to arenas as people today go to circuses and theaters, and their favorite entertainment was bloody fights that we would consider too cruel to look at. The men who fought in the arena were called gladiators. They were sometimes captives taken in warfare and sometimes citizens who had been convicted of a crime. Unless they fought in the arena they would be put to death, but as gladiators they had a chance to stay alive for a while. Many gladiators were slaves, and if they became very successful fighters they might be freed. Sometimes the gladiators fought wild animals such as tigers or lions, but often one gladiator would fight another. They fought with swords or knives or other weapons until one fell to the ground. Then the victor would look to the crowd to ask whether to kill the wounded man or let him live. There is a tradition that if the people put out their hands with the thumbs turned down, the victorious gladiator would kill his wounded enemy. But if the people turned thumbs up, the wounded man would be allowed to live.

gladiolus

The gladiolus is one of the flowers you see most often in gardens, in flower shops, in bouquets, and in flower arrangements in the house. It is named from the Latin word for "little sword," because the leaf is long and slender and comes to a sharp point. The flowers blossom in a row at the top of a long stem two or three feet high. The buds at the top of the row come out as the blosssoms at the bottom die. The gladiolus grows in more colors than almost any other flower. It can be seen in almost every color, from white to almost black. Gladiolus grows from a bulblike base, and most of the gladioli that are cultivated here come from a kind that grows wild in South Africa.

Gladstone, William Ewart

William Ewart Gladstone was a great English statesman who lived from 1809 to 1898. He was only 33 years old when he was first elected to the House of Commons, which is part of the Parliament, or lawmaking body, of the English government. For the rest of his life, Gladstone devoted himself to politics and government.

Gladstone was an outstanding speaker and always impressed the people who listened to his speeches. He quickly became a leader in the Liberal Party. Gladstone held many important posts in the government of England, and four times he was prime minister. The prime minister is the head of the English government. Many reforms were introduced into England when Gladstone was head of the government. The right to vote was given to many more people, so that the government of England became more democratic. Under Gladstone, the first complete educational system was set up, so that all English children had to go to school and there were free schools for everyone. Gladstone always worked especially hard to try to help the Irish people. At that time England ruled over all of Ireland. The Irish people were very poor, and they thought that the English government was very unfair to them. Gladstone led the English government to make important changes and reforms in these laws governing Ireland. Gladstone also had other interests. He was an outstanding scholar, and he found time to write many books on religious and historical subjects.

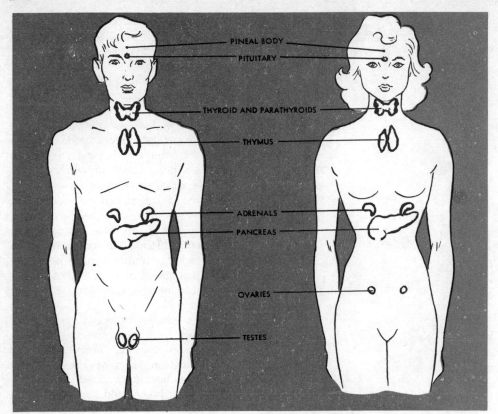

PINEAL BODY
PITUITARY
THYROID AND PARATHYROIDS
THYMUS
ADRENALS
PANCREAS
OVARIES
TESTES

The diagram shows the location of the most important glands in the human body.

gland

A gland is a part of your body that either makes a fluid, or liquid, to be used by the body, or a fluid to be given off from the body; both kinds are very important to help your body grow and live in a healthy way.

ENDOCRINE GLANDS

There are eight different kinds of endocrine glands, or glands that make useful fluids. These glands make different hormones, or chemical fluids, that, when given off into the blood, help the different parts of your body to work all during your life; some of them work at certain ages, and some of them work only when you need their services. But they all work together in a wonderful and delicate machine-like system, so it should be easy for you also to understand that if one of these glands does not work properly, the other glands may all be upset by it. Then unusual things may happen throughout the body. Whether they work right or not is one of the most important things that makes you the kind of person you are, such as tall or short, fat or thin, nervous or easygoing. Each gland is very interesting by itself, and study of it helps you to understand yourself.

1. The *thyroid* is a small gland found on the larynx, or Adam's apple, in your neck. It produces a hormone called *thyroxin* that makes you grow properly. If your gland did not give you enough thyroxin as a child you would become a dwarf, and the lack of growth of your brain would leave you stupid; you would be called a *cretin*. If this happened only when you had grown up, you might de-

Hubert's Museum, Inc.

The circus fat woman may overeat, but she probably weighs about 500 pounds because of faulty thyroid and pituitary glands.

velop a goiter, which is a growth on the neck. If your thyroid produced too much hormone you would be overactive, very nervous, and thin; some people even develop bulging eyes. Doctors can cure most thyroid troubles, especially if they find out soon enough, by adding iodine, which is needed to make thyroxin, or thyroxin from other animals, to your diet; in more serious cases operations are usually successful.

2. The *parathyroids* are four little glands located within the thyroid glands. These glands work all during your life, and their hormone regulates the amount of calcium in your body. Calcium is important to your bones, teeth, blood and muscles. You would die quickly without parathyroid hormone, but the same hormone from sheep can be used for people whose glands do not make enough.

3. The two *adrenal* glands (adrenal means over-the-kidneys) produce hormones for emergencies: when you need to think and act faster, or when you are suddenly afraid or angry at something or somebody. Your excitement excites the adrenals to give off their hormone, *adrenalin,* which spreads through your body in the blood. All your actions become quicker. Another adrenal hormone, *cortin,* is required by your body to make proper use of the foods you need for your energy.

4. The *gonads,* or sexual glands, are the ovaries in woman and the testes in man. They give off hormones from around thirteen years of age until old age. These hormones cause the differences in your body build and actions that make each person different from any other person. Scientists can make these hormones chemically, and they are very helpful in many cases.

5. The *thymus* is a gland under your sternum, or breast bone, which is believed to guide your growth during childhood.

6. Another endocrine gland, the function of which is not completely understood as yet, is the tiny *pineal* gland near the middle part of the brain. It has been suggested that it helps to slow down growth after a certain time of your life.

7. The *pancreas,* under your stomach, makes *insulin* that controls the use and storing of sugar within your body. Since scientists learned the use of insulin they have been able to control the serious disease diabetes, which is caused by lack of insulin, by obtaining the hormone from animals.

8. The *pituitary* gland, near the middle of the brain, is called the "master

gland" because it gives off hormones that cause all the other endocrine glands to work the way they should in order to keep the body healthy. The thyroid gland, the pancreas and the rest must receive hormones from the pituitary before they can do their work. Too much or too little pituitary hormones can make a giant or a dwarf, a thin or a fat person; it can make you weak or strong, intelligent or stupid, nervous or relaxed. Chemists have also learned to make some of the pituitary hormones, which have become important as medicines.

OTHER KINDS OF GLAND

The second kind of gland is one that gives something off from the body. Examples are the kidneys, bean-shaped organs within your lower back, which all during your life clean out the extra water and waste called urine from your body. The urine is passed from the kidneys through tubes to your bladder and then out through your urinary body opening. The kidneys, when healthy, also act to

The bearded woman has overactive adrenal glands. Older women with this disorder often have extra face and body hair.

Hubert's Museum, Inc.

Ewing Galloway

An overactive pituitary gland helped this giant reach a height of 8 feet 7 inches. The midget with an underactive pituitary stopped growing at only 23 inches.

keep the right amount of salt and water in your body. Other glands that give off waste are the tiny sweat glands in your skin.

There are other glands that give off fluids important to life. With the *mammary,* or breast, glands a mother feeds her child milk. There is the *prostate* gland, next to the bladder of man, which gives off a fluid that carries the man's seeds into the body of the woman where they join with her egg to grow into a new human being. In the eyes there are *tear* glands for washing and cleansing the eyeball.

In many parts of the body there are *lymph* glands to keep clean the watery, clear lymph fluid that, in turn, carries off waste and poisons from the millions of tiny cells that make up your body. The digestive glands in your mouth, stomach, liver, and intestines are something like the endocrines because they give off fluids that are used in the body, though not within the blood. These digestive glands give off *enzymes,* or digestive chemicals, that prepare food so your body may use it. There are many other important glands always working to help the wonderful machines that your body is.

glanders

Glanders is a very dangerous disease that attacks horses. When a horse catches glanders it acts much as a human being does when he has a cold. The horse has a runny nose and a fever. It cannot breathe and it may die of suffocation, or smothering. This disease is known all over the world, and both farmers and owners of horses always fear it. Horses can be tested to see if they carry the disease germs, and some countries, such as the United States, import only horses that do not have any glanders germs. This method has worked, and glanders is rarely found in the United States. Sometimes human beings get glanders, too, but not often. Glanders is also known as *farcy.*

Glasgow

Glasgow is the largest city in Scotland and the third-largest city in Great Britain. For hundreds of years it has been one of the most important shipbuilding centers in the world. The city lies on the banks of the river Clyde, on the west coast of Scotland, and there are several miles of good docks on the river for shipbuilding and trading activities of the city. More than a million people live in Glasgow, and besides working on the construction of ships they work in many large factories that produce iron goods, textiles, and other products. Glasgow, with its good harbor, is in the richest coal and iron district of Great Britain, and has become an important city for manufactured goods as well as a trading center. Prestwick International Airport is a major transatlantic stop for several airlines.

Today much of Glasgow is quite modern, and visitors to Glasgow can see the parks, the large public buildings, and the art museums as well as many of the interesting old buildings that were built many years ago. The famous Cathedral of Glasgow, which is an important landmark of the city, was built more than seven hundred years ago. The University of Glasgow was started in 1451. It was aided by the famous Queen Mary of Scots, and later by her son. Today, many plans are being made by the people and civic leaders of the town to build more new buildings, and also to do something about the smoke that comes from the factories and the iron and steel mills, which is always a problem in an industrial city.

GLASGOW. Population (1959 estimate) 1,076,614. Seaport on the Clyde River.

Glasgow, Ellen

Ellen Glasgow was an American writer. She was born in Richmond, Virginia, in 1874, and she lived all her life in the South. She was too delicate to go to school and educated herself by reading the many books in her father's library. Her novels give us a picture of life in the South from the Civil War to modern times.

She was a realist, which means that she wrote about life as it really was, even when this meant writing about unpleasant things. Because of this, her books were never as popular as they should have been, although in 1942 she won the Pulitzer prize, for her novel *In This Our Life.* The Pulitzer Prize is an award given for good writing. Ellen Glasgow died in 1945.

Glass

glass

Glass is a hard material whose greatest value is the fact that it is transparent, that is, it can be seen through. Glass has hundreds of other uses that do not depend upon its being transparent. It is used especially for dishes you drink out of, so much so that you say you drink a "glass of water." Glass is also used for building blocks, and colored glass is used for ornaments and jewelry.

In modern times people have discovered wonderful new ways to make glass. Now, we have very strong glass that will bend and not break. Glass can be made into thread from which cloth can be woven, and it can be used for insulation against heat or cold.

EARLY GLASSMAKING

Glass is made out of sand that has been melted and then allowed to harden. Men learned to make glass thousands of years ago. They must have learned how accidentally when some sand melted in a very hot fire and then hardened into glass. The best glass is made out of white sand that is composed mostly of grains of quartz, a hard rock that glitters when the sun shines on it. This quartz is called silica, and it is the silica that forms glass. Men found that they could make much better glass from sand that was almost pure silica than from sand that contained dirt and other impurities. It was difficult to find sand without some impurities, so men had to find ways to get rid of them. They learned that if they mixed soda with the sand, and boiled the mixture until it became very hot, the soda made some of the impurities boil away. The mixture of soda and sand is called the *batch.* Then someone added crushed limestone to the batch, and he found that this made it boil more quickly, so all glassmakers began to use limestone. Glass made in this way is called *lime glass.*

Men discovered that when they used lead instead of limestone they could make a glass that was clearer and brighter than any glass ever made before. Lead glass is very clear and it sparkles when it is polished. Men began to make glass ornaments out of lead glass. They found that when they added certain materials to the batch, they could make glass of many colors. Most inexpensive jewelry with glass ornaments that you see in stores now is made from lead glass.

One of the wonderful things about glass is that when it is very hot, it is runny,

During World War II, electronic tubes of seamless glass had to be blown by hand.

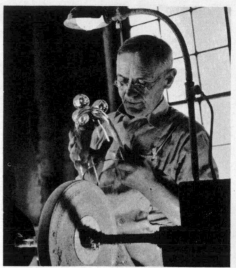

A skilled grinder smooths the rough edge around a hand-blown glass vase.

The molten glass in the clay pot is ready for casting. It will be made into plate glass.

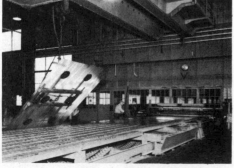

A suction crane lifts a 1,200-pound "blank" of glass, now ready for storage and cutting.

like syrup. Then when it hardens it will keep whatever shape it had when it was a liquid. Men made molds of clay or metal, and they poured the liquid glass into these molds to cool. As the hot glass cooled, it gradually turned from a liquid into a soft mass that could be rolled. Then it could be shaped into plates and cups and bowls and many other objects.

BLOWING GLASS BUBBLES

Next men discovered that much finer (thinner) glass could be made by blowing glass bubbles. Glass bubbles are blown very much as we blow soap bubbles. Instead of blowing just ordinary round bubbles, a good glass blower learned to blow bubbles into almost any shape he wished. We do not know just when glass blowing began, but ancient Egyptians carved pictures on rocks almost four thousand years ago that show some of the early glass blowers. In these pictures, each glass blower holds a slender pipe to his lips. For thousands of years people blew glass in pretty much this same way. The blower used a pipe about six feet long, and this pipe was shaped like a bell at one end. When the glass blower dipped the bell end of his pipe into the hot batch, a small ball of soft, glowing glass stuck to the pipe.

Then the blower placed the opposite end of the pipe to his lips and began to blow gently. Slowly, the bubble of glass formed, and grew larger. The blower raised the far end of the pipe over his head and began to twirl it. Gradually, the bubble took the shape of a vase or goblet, or whatever he wished to make. For a long time, a glass blower needed great skill to do his own work well, because the shape of the bubble depended on how well he could blow glass. Then, blowers learned how to make their work much simpler. They found that they could blow the glass bubble into a mold, so that the bubble would take the shape of the mold, and all of the objects made from one mold would be shaped exactly alike.

A few people now blow beautiful vases and delicate figures and other objects of glass, and men in factories operate great machines that can blow glass. Blown glass now can be made quite easily and it does not cost very much.

GLASSMAKING TODAY

Glassmaking is one of the biggest industries in the United States, employing about 150,000 persons. The glassmakers first remove all of the loose dirt and other impurities from the sand. This is done by special machines. Then, the materials are measured and mixed to make the batch. The large chamber where the materials are mixed is called the *dog house*. It takes about three weeks to heat the giant furnace that must heat the batch.

Most of the furnaces now are heated by electricity, although some of the older furnaces burn coal or gas.

There are two kinds of furnaces that men who work in glass factories use in their work. One kind of furnace holds the batch in huge pots that are placed on ledges above the fire. Another kind of furnace has one great tank that holds the

Owens-Illinois Glass Co.

Years of practice are needed to twist the stem of what will be a gleaming glass cornucopia.

batch, and the heating system is built around the tank. The floor of the tank slants a little, so that as the glass melts it flows towards an opening at the lower end of the tank. A large tank is about one hundred and forty feet long, and it can hold almost two thousand tons of glass. It takes about two days for the glass to melt in the furnace, and then it is ready to be shaped into windows and many other things.

Once men who made window glass had to pour the melted glass onto a table where they used a tool that looked very much like a rolling pin to roll the glass out into thin sheets. Now machines roll the glass. Some window glass is made by machines that blow huge glass bubbles, and these bubbles are cut open and spread out flat.

Plate glass, which is used for mirrors, automobile windshields, and store windows, is clearer and brighter than window glass. Plate glass is rolled in giant rollers, and then ground and polished until it is very clear.

Machines called *pressing* machines press liquid glass into the desired shapes of dishes, drinking glasses, ashtrays, or

Left: A bird painted by Audubon is perfectly reproduced by engraving on the underside of a thin glass dish. *Below:* Light and shadow play on and below the surface of a crystal horse designed by Sidney Waugh. Because glass is light and clear, figurines made of it are a favorite decoration in many homes.

All the natural grace of a fish as it makes its way through the water is caught in the design on the left The special qualities of glass lend themselves to an illusion of grace and lightness that can be achieved with few other materials. Yet the crystal is very heavy.

Steuben Glass, Inc. Photos

bottles. Some machines can press as many as three hundred glass bottles at once. Other machines blow glass electric-light bulbs; more than a billion glass bulbs are blown each year in the United States. Special machines make fine glass for use in telescopes, lenses, and microscopes.

STRONG GLASS

One trouble with glass is that it breaks very easily. Often it cracks when its temperature is changed very suddenly. Modern science has invented many kinds of glass that are hard to break. One of these is a kind of plate glass called *safety glass.* Safety glass is made like a sandwich. It has a thin layer of tough, transparent plastic material between two layers of glass. Sometimes safety glass has as many as five layers of this plastic material. Safety glass will crack but it will not shatter, and it is used particularly in automobile windshields.

There is another special kind of glass that can be boiled and then put on ice, and it will not crack. This kind of glass is called *borosilicate glass,* and it is used to make baking dishes, coffee pots, and other articles that are used in the kitchen for cooking food. Electricity cannot flow through this kind of glass, and so it is used to protect wires and tubes in radios, telephones, and electric power plants.

SPUN GLASS

Men have discovered a wonderful way to spin glass into fibers or threads that can be woven into cloth or fluffed like cotton or wool. This glass feels very fine and silky and it is difficult to believe that it is glass at all. When men make spun glass, they first melt the batch, just as they do to make any other kind of glass. Then the glass is molded into tiny marbles that you can see through. All of these marbles are rolled down a slide into a furnace and melted again. The liquid is sent into a heated chamber that has many tiny holes in the floor, and the glass runs through these holes, and it hardens into soft fine threads. These threads can be spun together to make fine or heavy yarn, or even thick cord. Glass yarn will not burn or stain. It is light and waterproof, and so strong that it will not wear out for a very long time. Scientists now are finding out many ways to use this marvelous new kind of glass.

glasses

Glasses are worn by people who have poor eyesight. Glasses help them to see things clearly and without straining their eyes. Eye doctors, called *oculists* or *ophthalmologists,* or *optometrists,* who are trained to measure a person's ability to use his eyes, find out what kind of glasses a person needs. There are many kinds of eye trouble, and all but a few of them can be helped by the use of glasses.

Years ago people bought glasses from peddlers or through the mail. What they got were magnifying glasses that simply made things look larger. These glasses did not help people to see more clearly without straining their eyes. In some cases, the glasses only increased the eye trouble.

Modern glasses are especially made for the individual wearer by an *optician* (maker of glasses), who carefully grinds the glass or lens for each eye according to the thickness prescribed by the doctor or optometrist. A frame is fitted to the wearer's face so that it rests comfortably on his nose and ears. The lenses are then mounted in the frame.

Some glasses, called *pince-nez,* are clipped to the bridge of the nose and are not supported by the ears. A *monocle* is a single lens that is held in place in the hollow in front of the eye. A *lorgnette* is a frame with lenses for both eyes. It can be held by hand in front of the eyes for short periods of time.

In *bifocals* most of the lens is ground so that the wearer can see things at a distance. The lower part of the middle of the lens is ground so that the wearer can

Better Vision Inst., Inc.

If you find that you are squinting and frowning when you read a book or do your homework, it probably means that your eyes need help. and you should see a doctor.

look at things close to his eyes. A person is usually looking up when he looks at things far away, and looking down when

Many children whose schoolwork has suffered from faulty eyesight can now work easily and well with the proper glasses.

Better Vision Inst., Inc.

he reads, so he automatically looks through the proper lens. The great American statesman, Benjamin Franklin, invented bifocals about two hundred years ago. Today there are even *trifocals*—three kinds of lens for each eye. They are used by people who must have a lens for very close work in addition to the lenses in bifocals. Jewelers, dentists and others who work with small objects use trifocals.

CONTACT LENS

Contact lenses are worn directly on the eyeball, and because of this they must be specially made for the wearer. If they do not fit exactly they can cause discomfort. They are made of a clear plastic material that is ground into lenses just as glass is.

Contact lenses are better for some

GOATS, SHEEP AND HOGS

SHROPSHIRE SHEEP

POLAND CHINA HOG

RAMBOUILLET SHEEP

ANGORA SHEEP

GOATS, SHEEP AND HOGS

CHESTER WHITE HOG

TOGGENBURG GOAT

SUFFOLK SHEEP

DUROC JERSEY HOG

HAMPSHIRE HOG

If you have normal sight, you can see objects that are near and objects that are far away clearly, as in this picture. The drawing shows how light strikes the eye.

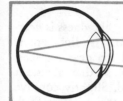

If you are near-sighted, objects that are close up are clear but things far away are blurred, and you need glasses to correct this.

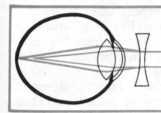

When you are far-sighted, things in the distance are clear, but objects close up are blurred as is shown in this picture of the girl.

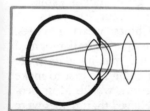

Double vision causes you to see two images of things. In the diagrams, note how the point of light behind the eye falls differently in each instance of faulty eyesight.

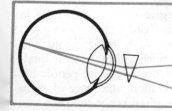

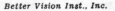

Better Vision Inst., Inc.

Scientists have invented special glasses called contact lenses. Nobody can tell that you have glasses on when you wear them.

kinds of eye trouble than regular glasses. Some actors wear contact lenses for the sake of their appearance, and athletes sometimes wear them because the lenses cannot be broken and therefore are safer. At first, contact lenses were inserted with a special clear fluid in them. The fluid helped magnify and also prevented irritation to the eyeball. The latest contact lenses do not need fluid. They are made to fit only over the iris, the colored part of the eye, and are much more comfortable and can be worn longer than the old kind.

HOW GLASSES HELP

There is a lens in your eye called a *crystalline lens*. It bends the rays of light that enter your eye and brings them to a point or focus on the back of the eyeball called the *retina*. When the focus is right, clear pictures or images of objects are formed by the eye. It is an amazing fact that all images on the retina are upside down. A special part of the brain, called the *occipital lobe,* causes the image to appear right-side up.

Sometimes when the eyeball is too short or the muscles of the eye too weak to control the crystalline lens properly, the light entering the eye is focused too far away from the lens. People who have this trouble are said to be *far-sighted.* They can see distant objects clearly, but not objects that are near by. To correct this defect, slightly convex lenses are used, lenses that are thicker in the middle than at the edges. They help to focus

the light at just the right distance from the crystalline lens so that a distinct image of near objects is formed on the retina. The crystalline lens of the eye is a convex lens.

The opposite of far-sightedness is *near-sightedness,* or *myopia.* The light entering the eye is focused too near the lens, in front of the retina, so that a distant object appears blurred. Slightly concave lenses are used to correct this defect. Such lenses bend the rays of light away from each other so that they are focused on the retina. Concave lenses are thicker at the edges than at the middle.

Some people have what is called *astigmatism.* This happens when the eyeball is curved somewhat like an egg instead of like a round ball. In such cases, lines running up and down may be seen quite distinctly, while lines running from left to right may appear blurred. Specially ground lenses must be used to correct this defect.

WHO FIRST MADE GLASSES

The Chinese are believed to have invented glasses about 2,400 years ago. Marco Polo, the great Italian explorer, journeyed to China about 700 years ago and found many Chinese wearing glasses. At about the same time an Italian named Salvino d'Armati was making glasses. He is given credit for being the first to make glasses in the Western world. Most people at that time believed that glasses were instruments of the devil and should not be used on the eyes, which they thought were a gift from God. That is why when d'Armati died, the inscription on his tombstone read: "Here lies Salvino d'Armati of Florence, the inventor of spectacles. God forgive him his sins. Died in the Year of Our Lord 1317."

The invention of printing, about 450 years ago, did much to improve the quality of glasses. More and more people began to read, and more and more of them found their eyesight was not good enough. Scientists began to study the eye and how to make better glasses for it. As they learned more about eyesight and lenses, they were able to provide people with better glasses.

glass snake

The glass snake is a lizard, but it has no feet as other lizards have. It looks somewhat like a snake, but it has movable eyelids and a stiff armor of scales that prevents it from having the graceful movements of a snake. The glass snake is yellow or greenish-brown, and it is sometimes striped. It get its name because its tail, which is twice the length of its body, can be broken as easily as a piece of glass. If caught by the tail, the glass snake can shed part of its tail. This part will go on wiggling and hold the enemy's attention until the lizard can escape. The tail grows back, but it is slow in becoming as long as it was originally. The glass snake has a lizard's head. It grows to be about two feet long. It is found in southeastern Europe. A smaller kind lives in the Mississippi valley and the southern United States.

glasswort

Glasswort is an herb that grows wild along the seacoasts in many parts of the world. The ash of the glasswort that grows around the Mediterranean Sea contains soda, which was at one time used in glassmaking and soapmaking. Glasswort grows to be about a foot high. It has tiny leaves and flowers that turn red in the fall. The stems of glasswort are very thick and become brittle in cold weather. If you walk across a field of glasswort in winter the flowers crackle and break into bits as if they were glass. Glasswort is not often grown in gardens.

Glauber's salt

Glauber's salt is a chemical compound used as a laxative. It is named for a famous German chemist, Johann Glauber, who lived about three hundred years ago. When he was 21 years old, Glauber was attacked by a fever and he was advised to drink the water from a certain well. After he recovered from his illness, he took from the water of this well some large crystals that looked like rock candy. He called these crystals "the wonderful salt." This salt has been used as a medicine ever since. Glauber's salt is found in many parts of the world.

glaucoma

Glaucoma is a very serious disease of the eye. It often leads to blindness. In glaucoma the eyeball gradually hardens. A person with glaucoma first sees flashes of light and colored rings around objects. He gradually sees less and less. Glaucoma is most common in people over forty. There are medicines that help cure the disease, and sometimes an operation is necessary.

Glendale

Glendale is a city in southern California, near Los Angeles. Its population in 1960 was 119,442. Most of the people work in nearby Los Angeles, but Glendale also has factories, making airplane parts and petroleum products. Forest Lawn Cemetery, one of the world's most elaborate burial places, and Glendale College are there. Glendale was founded in 1887.

Glenn, John H., Jr.

John Herschel Glenn, Jr. was the first American astronaut to orbit the earth. This historic feat took place on Feb. 20, 1962, with millions following the flight by television and radio. Glenn, a Lt.-Colonel in the Marine Corps, circled the earth three times in his Mercury capsule, *Friendship* 7. He travelled 81,000 miles at a top speed of 17,545 miles per hour, reaching a maximum height of 162 miles. Total time of the flight was 4 hours and 56 minutes. Glenn, a former combat and test pilot, was born in Cambridge, Ohio, in 1921.

Schweizer Aircraft Corp. Photos

Gliders are often towed by airplanes. After the cable is released, the glider soars on its own. Note the glider's wide wingspread, which helps it utilize any air currents.

The glider pilot needs great skill to make a belly landing in a small craft. This aluminum glider is very streamlined and gives extra soaring distance.

glider

The glider is an airplane without an engine. It is sent into the air under power from a tow line, or carried by a powered airplane. Once it is in the air the glider is carried along by natural air currents.

The first glider was built in 1810 by an Englishman named Sir George Cayley. His models were too small to carry anyone, but they proved that gliding was possible. Between 1891 and 1896, Otto Lilienthal made man-carrying gliders, and around 1900 the Wright brothers got their first flight training in gliders. Many of these first models were called "hang gliders" because the pilot actually hung in place by his armpits and shifted his body to control the glider.

Except that it has no motor, the glider

is exactly like any other airplane. It has the same type of controls, and is flown the same way. When a glider is ready to be sent aloft, a towing line is attached to the nose, and the other end of the line is hooked to a car or truck, or an airplane. When the glider is towed, it acts just as any airplane would with a propeller, and it rises into the air. When it is as high as necessary, the pilot drops the line. After the glider is in the air, the pilot must look for up-currents to keep him up there, or he would soon glide back to the ground. He knows that the sun shining on flat lands will heat the air over these lands. He also knows that heated air will rise, so he looks for places where these heated air currents are most likely to be found. These hot air currents are called *thermals*. One sign of thermals is flat-bottomed clouds. By staying under these, the pilot keeps his glider in the air.

Official U.S. Air Force Photo

Gliders make no noise, and are valuable for transporting troops that can be landed quietly behind enemy lines.

GLIDERS IN WARTIME

After World War I, Germany was not allowed to have a military air force. When Germany wanted to teach its men how to fly, glider clubs were formed. These clubs were permitted because it was thought that gliders could not be used for war, but this was a mistake. By spending much time in these clubs, German pilots learned how to fly gliders, and when Germany started to build military planes, it had almost 200,000 trained pilots. In this way, Germany had a large air force when it was thought to have none at all.

Other military uses were found for gliders. Since they could be towed by other planes, someone thought of using one powerful airplane as a "locomotive" to pull a "train" of gliders. By using many gliders, large numbers of troops could be flown into combat by only one plane. This was good because gliders are easier and faster to build than airplanes with motors, and cost less. When Germany invaded Crete in 1941, it used glider trains for troops. The United States and England soon caught on to this means of troop transport and used gliders during the invasions of Sicily, France, and Holland. Gliders were also found useful for carrying supplies.

Gliding as a sport has become very popular in the United States, and glider clubs are found all over the country. This is an excellent way to learn to fly, and gliding licenses are issued to people as young as fourteen years of age. For those interested in model-plane aviation, model gliders are among the easiest types to build and fly. People interested in building and flying more complicated types of planes can learn much from gliders.

This big all-metal glider carries soldiers and supplies. One large airplane can tow several of these gliders.

Official U.S. Air Force Photo

Many records have been set in gliders. In 1961, Paul F. Bikle of the United States flew a single-place glider up to 46,267 feet. This is higher than some powered planes can go. In 1952, Charles Atger of France stayed up in the air for 56 hours and 15 minutes, which was more than two days of motorless flying. Another record was set by the United States in 1951, when a glider was flown by Dick Johnson for a distance of 535 miles.

Am. Mus. of Nat. Hist.

The globefish looks like a prickly pear with tiny fins, bulging eyes, stiff mouth and tail. It takes in air, and floats, belly up, on the surface of the water.

globe

A globe is a model of the earth or the heavens. The globe got its name from the earth, which is a sphere and is sometimes referred to as a globe.

A globe of the earth shows all the lands and waters of the earth, drawn to scale. It is called a *terrestrial globe.* Terrestrial means "of the earth." Being the shape of the earth itself, a globe is therefore much more accurate than a flat map. The distance from one place to another is recorded almost exactly while a flat map could very easily be wrong in that distance. Directions, too, are more accurate than on a flat map.

One of the first terrestrial globes was made by a man named Martin Behaim in 1492, the same year Columbus discovered America. Globes are used in the study of geography. The globe is used in schools to show children and students what the world looks like. There are many globes and they are built in many sizes.

A globe of the heavens shows all the stars and planets. It is called a celestial globe. *Celestial* means "of the sky." It is widely used in astronomy, the science that studies the positions, sizes, and motions of all celestial bodies.

globefish

The globefish is an ocean fish that lives in tropical or warm coastal waters. It is sometimes called rabbitfish because it has sharp teeth like a rabbit's. It eats barnacles and small shellfish. Globefish can grow to be a foot long, but those found along the coast of the United States are much smaller. When the globefish is in danger it sucks air into a bladder in its stomach and blows itself up into a big ball. Then it floats on the surface of the water until the danger is past. Globefish are not good to eat and some of them may even be poisonous. They are often kept in a fish bowl or aquarium.

Globe Theatre

The Globe Theatre was built near London, England, more than 350 years ago, in 1598. William Shakespeare, England's greatest playwright, owned part of the theater and his acting company performed there. The first play to be given at the Globe was Shakespeare's *Henry V,* and most of his great plays were first acted there. Later many other famous plays were acted at the Globe.

The Globe was in Southwark, just across the Thames River from the old city of London. You may read about the construction of the Globe and other early English theaters in a separate article on THEATERS.

In 1613, during a performance of *Henry VIII,* a cannon that was shot off in the play set the roof on fire and the Globe burned down. A year later it was rebuilt, but it was destroyed thirty years after that by the Puritans, who felt that it was wrong

J. Crawford and I. Smith

The Globe Theatre was open to the sky; only those in the balconies left and right of the stage were sheltered if it rained. Shakespeare used no scenery. The balcony above the stage might serve as a tower in *Hamlet* or as a real balcony in *Romeo and Juliet*.

for people to go to the theater. Today a small bronze marker on a brick wall shows where the famous Globe Theatre once stood.

glove

A glove is a covering for the hand. The history of the glove reaches back into the earliest days of man's existence. Even the prehistoric caveman used a hand covering that was a kind of glove. The ancient Greeks, Romans and Persians also wore gloves.

The earliest gloves were crude and were more like the mittens that children wear today. They did not have fingers in them. They were worn first to keep the hands warm and to protect them from injury. People in the northern countries of Europe, particularly Sweden, Norway and Germany, used gloves before they were used in England or Spain. Perhaps Caesar's legions, who landed in Britain two thousand years ago—fifty-five years before the birth of Jesus—introduced the glove to England.

At first only men wore gloves. For many years they were worn only by members of the nobility or by high church officials. Today both men and women wear gloves, for warmth and for protection. There are many jobs that require gloves to protect the workers' hands from injury. Many women wear gloves to keep their hands clean, and because without them they are considered poorly dressed for most social occasions.

THE GLOVE AS A SYMBOL

In former days the glove played an important part in the laws and customs of nearly all peoples. It was a symbol of faith, friendship, and authority. Historians think that the glove may have become a symbol because of the habit that men started of shaking hands to express their friendship and good will. It came about that kings and other important people, who could not themselves attend an important meeting, began to send the glove of their right hand as a greeting and as a sign of faith or good intention. A king would send his glove to another king as a guarantee for the safe passage of an ambassador or messenger.

As this custom became more common, gloves were passed between people who were making an agreement of some kind. The glove was a sign that each man intended to live up to his agreement. The glove came to have almost as much legal power as a signature. A young man and a young woman who became engaged to be married exchanged gloves. A soldier riding into battle carried his sweetheart's glove for good luck.

The glove was a sign of truth and honor in the middle ages. A man pledged his allegiance to his king or to his lady by swearing on his glove. A man who felt he had been insulted threw down his glove as a sign that he wished to fight the person who had insulted him. From this custom we get the expression "throwing

Fine gloves are made from leather. Expert craftsmen sort the leather and then carefully prepare it for cutting.

Prepared leather is brought to the cutting tables, where skilled workers quickly cut the leather into individual gloves.

The cut leather is taken to girls operating high-powered sewing machines. They sew the pieces together into gloves.

The best gloves are entirely or partly handsewn. The women doing this work are busy, but often can chat while sewing.

down the gauntlet" (*gauntlet* means "glove") to show that one person is daring another to fight. If a nobleman committed a serious crime, his gloves were often taken away from him.

Women in England first used gloves about four hundred years ago, during the reign of Queen Elizabeth I. Only those who belonged to the court circles were allowed to wear them. The gloves worn by both men and women at this time were perfumed and decorated, often with very costly jewels. Queen Elizabeth herself had three thousand pairs of decorated gloves.

KINDS OF GLOVES

Leather has always been the most popular material for gloves. The leather used for gloves must be flexible as well as soft and long-wearing. We get the expression "fitting like a glove" because gloves have to fit the hand so perfectly. Nearly all the leather used in the United States for gloves is imported from other countries. Generally it is found that animals born in high altitudes and cold climates, and those that have coarse, hairy fur, produce a leather of fine texture best suited to gloves.

The most common leather used for gloves is sheepskin. Different types of sheepskin gloves are called capeskins, mochas, degrains, suedes,· and chamois.

Fownes Bros. & Co. Photos

Skilled operators press gloves by slipping them over forms shaped like hands. This finishing process is called "laying off."

Finished gloves are carefully inspected. Only those that are perfect are sent on to stores and sold to retail customers.

Other leathers often used are deerskin, wild pigskin, and dogskin. These leathers are made in a grained finish or in a velvet finish. The grained finish has a surface that shows a rough pattern. Many pigskin, goatskin and dogskin gloves have grained finishes. Velvet-finish leathers are smooth but often have a *nap,* a surface of very short hairs. Several kinds of sheepskins and deerskin have a velvet finish. (See the article on LEATHER.)

Gloves are also made from silk, rayon, wool, cotton, and synthetic fabrics such as nylon. Fabric gloves are of two kinds, those that are knit and those that are woven. Fabric gloves are usually less expensive than leather gloves.

GLOVEMAKING IN THE UNITED STATES

The people in the American colonies wore homemade gloves until about 1750. Then a New York landowner, Sir William Johnson, invited a group of Scottish glovemakers to leave their homes and settle in the New World to make gloves. These people settled in upper New York State and called their town Gloversville. People in nearby towns also began making gloves. Today this area is still the glovemaking center of the United States, though gloves are made also in many other places.

glowworm, the larva, or young, of the firefly; see the article BEETLE.

Gluck, Christoph Willibald von

Christoph Willibald von Gluck was a German composer. (A composer is a writer of original music.) Gluck was one of the first great composers of music for opera, a play in which the words are sung and not spoken. He was born in Germany on July 2, 1714, and started to study music when he was a schoolboy. Before his time, operas were not often natural. There was very little relationship between what was happening in the story and the way the music sounded. Gluck wanted to make the music express the same emotion that the story expressed. For example, he did not think that sad music should be put in at a point in the story where a couple were dancing gayly in celebration of their engagement. This seems perfectly natural to us now, because composers make their music fit the mood of a story as a matter of course. In Gluck's day, however, they did not, and he was the first important operatic composer who used this method. Most of his operas were written about mythological characters, or ancient gods. Some famous ones were *Orpheus and Eurydice, Artaxerxes,* and *Iphigenia Among the Taurians.* Gluck died in 1787.

glucose

Glucose is a kind of sugar made from cornstarch. It is also called corn syrup. Since it costs much less to make glucose than it does to make cane sugar, glucose is used a great deal for sweetening candies, jellies and jams.

Glucose is also called *dextrose*. Pure glucose, or dextrose, is found in many plants, especially in grapes and other sweet fruits.

Our bodies also make glucose. The body cannot use most sugars as they are, and so it turns them into glucose, which can be used by the body just as it is. Starches, such as bread and potatoes, and sugars are made into glucose by the body in the course of digestion.

glue

Glue is a strong, sticky substance that holds things together. It is an adhesive; you can read about others in the article on ADHESIVES. Glue is usually made from animal bones, which contain gelatin. There are other kinds of glue, but this is the oldest kind. Marine glue is waterproof and strong, and contains India rubber or shellac instead of the gelatin from animal materials. There are liquid glues that do not become hard at room temperature, as bone glue does. Bone glue has to be dissolved and heated before it can be used, but liquid glue can be used as it comes from a tube or bottle. Isinglass is also a true gelatin glue. It is made from the bladders of fish and it is used to

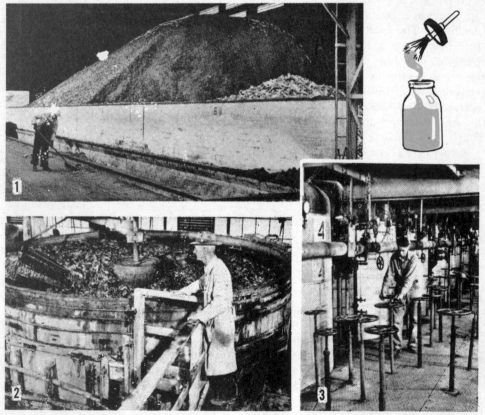

Consol. Chemical Ind. Photos

1. Bones used in making glue are stockpiled until needed. Most come from South America.
2. Bones and trimmings are treated with limewater, and then are washed in rotating mills.
3. When all the grease is out of the bones, glue is extracted in large pressure tanks.

mend glass. Isinglass is one of the oldest forms of glue.

To make glue, the bones or skin or fish substance is boiled and then steamed under pressure. This makes the glue liquor.

The liquor is drained into iron pans, where it sets into a firm jelly. The jelly is sliced into small sheets, so that the air can dry it quckly. The best glue should be a clear amber in color, and should break like glass when it is dry.

Most of the glue in America is made near Chicago, close to the big slaughter-houses from which the bones and skin may be saved for glue. Many large meat-packing companies have their own glue factories.

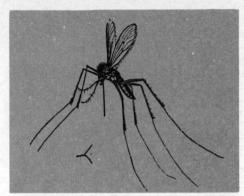

This drawing of a gnat is enlarged; the small lines show its real size.

gluten

Gluten is the part of wheat flour that will not dissolve when the wheat is washed in water. It is one of the most healthful parts of the wheat, and it is used to make a kind of bread called gluten bread, that is used in special diets for persons with certain kinds of sickness. Gluten is tough and rubbery, and has almost no taste.

glycerin

Glycerin is a sweet-tasting, white oil that is used to make such different things as dynamite, soap, paint, and plastics. It is almost as useful as water for melting or dissolving other materials. It will soak up and hold a great deal of water, too, so that substances which need to stay soft or moist may be kept so with glycerin. Some of these substances are tobacco, paper, cellophane, and some kinds of glue.

Glycerin is used a great deal in medicines and drugs because it dissolves other substances so well and forms a good base for the medicine. The vaccines used to prevent disease are often mixed in glycerin and then they stay fresh and strong for a longer time.

Glycerin is made from fats. The parts of fat are broken apart by the action of soda and brine in a process called fat-splitting. The glycerin in the fat is washed off with the watery part. If this fat-splitting is repeated several times it produces an extremely pure form of glycerin.

Some substitutes for glycerin have been discovered in the United States and Germany. The German synthetic glycerin is made from fermented beet sugar. But millions of pounds of crude glycerin are produced every year in the United States. Some of this is used in the antifreeze preparations that keep automobile radiators from freezing in the winter. It is also eaten, for glycerin is used in canning meat.

G-Man, short for government man, a member of the Federal Bureau of Investigation. See the article on FEDERAL BUREAU OF INVESTIGATION.

gnat

A gnat is a small, two-winged fly. It looks like a very small mosquito, and some kinds have a sharp bite. The buffalo gnat that attacks cattle feeds on blood as does the mosquito or the gadfly. While mosquitoes normally come out at night, the gnat flies in the daytime. The eggs of most kinds of gnat are laid in the water, and the maggots, or worms (also called *larvae*), that come from the eggs feed there without destroying fruit or other crops. However, there are gall gnats and fungus gnats that do harm plants by laying their eggs on them. In Florida human beings suffer from a disease called "sore-eye" that is carried by gnats. In England mosquitoes are sometimes also called gnats.

gneiss

Gneiss is a rock that is many millions of years old. It is usually made up of layers of quartz, feldspar, and mica, although it may contain other minerals such as hornblende or garnet. Its color depends upon the minerals found in it. The layers are not always straight and can vary in width. Gneiss is called a metamorphic, or transformed, rock because it was made from granite or from other rocks that melted and joined together again in a different form. It is a very hard rock, and for this reason it is often used for buildings and paving blocks.

gnome

A gnome is an imaginary spirit that is told about in certain fairy tales. Gnomes are supposed to live underground and watch over hidden treasures. They are usually pictured as ugly little men with pointed beards. They are gray all over. They wear long, pointed caps. You can read more about them in the article FAIRY AND FAIRY TALES.

Gnostics

The Gnostics were people who belonged to certain sects, or small religious groups, that developed about 1,800 years ago. The religious ideas of the Gnostics were called Gnosticism. These ideas came from many different places. The Gnostics adopted many Christian ideas, as well as ideas from the religions of Greece, Persia, and Babylonia.

Gnosticism taught that there are two different worlds. One is the world of goodness and light, and this is the world of God. The other is the world of evil and darkness, and this is the world that we see around us. This evil world was not made by God, but by an evil power. The Gnostics said that special knowledge was needed to overcome this power.

The Gnostics thought that only they had the knowledge that was needed to go to heaven. The Gnostics said that they had a special secret knowledge that had been given to them by Jesus and his disciples. Only Gnostics were allowed to learn this. There were many ceremonies and rites for Gnostics. They had to learn certain secret words and formulas, which they said would help them get into heaven. The Christian Church condemned Gnosticism as a heresy, or false belief, and Gnosticism died out.

gnu

A gnu is a kind of antelope. It is native to South Africa. It is as large as a medium-sized horse and has a stiff mane that stands up at the back of its neck. It has a tuft of hair on its forehead and a beard under its chin. The gnu's legs are slender. Its horns are thick at the base and curve down around the eyes before bending up. The gnu may weigh as much as five hundred pounds. Its meat is good to eat. Gnus are still found in great numbers north of the Zambesi River in Africa, but in other parts of the continent they are becoming very scarce.

goat

The goat is a graceful, sure-footed animal that lives in the mountains and rocky places in many parts of Europe, Asia, and North Africa. The goat looks very much like a sheep, and from a distance it is difficult to tell these two animals apart. The goat has a thick coat of hair that may be black, brown, or yellow, and some goats are pure white. The goat has a short tail and a beard under its chin. It has handsome, hollow horns that are flat, and twist backwards at the tips. The goat's hoofs are cloven (divided into two

British Inform. Service.

Above: A young visitor makes friends with Billy the goat on a Sunday visit to the children's zoo. *Right:* This goat is having an adventure. It is tied below deck on a cargo ship that is taking it across the sea to a new home.

Standard Oil Co.

Right: In some places, like Kodiak Island, Alaska, goats find it hard to survive. Here a member of the Fish and Wildlife Service is about to release a young male mountain goat on the Kodiak Refuge, where it is hoped that he will live to a ripe old age.

Copyright Curriculum Films, Inc.

Fish and Wildlife Service

Left: A mountain goat can be a dangerous enemy. This goat did not try to start a fight with the vicious wildcat. But its strong legs enable it to stand its ground as it gores the cat with its short, sharp horns.

These are portraits of some of the leading members of the international goat family. They include: 1. European steinbok; 2. Nubian mountain goat. 3. Bifoar goat, Africa. 4. Markhor, India. 5. Screw-horn goat. Number 6 is a kid. As much as grown-up goats differ, kid goats throughout the world resemble one another. Later the kid will change.

parts), and it can run swiftly up and down steep crags, without slipping. There are many different kinds of goats, and some of them have strange names, such as ibex, and markhor, the largest of the wild goats, that lives high up in the Himalaya Mountains of India. People have believed that goats eat everything, even tin cans, but this is not true. Goats eat grass and leaves and the bark of trees.

DOMESTIC GOATS

People have raised goats since early times. The farmers who lived in Persia about three thousand years before Jesus knew how useful goats were, and some of these people were goat farmers. Now farmers in the United States, Canada, and many parts of the world raise goats. Certain kinds of goats are raised for their milk. Goat's milk is very nourishing, and it is especially healthful for children and people who are sick, because it is easy to digest. Very good cheese is made from goat's milk, and some people eat goat meat. The skin of the goat is made into leather that is called morocco. People in factories make fine gloves and handbags and shoes of morocco leather. One of the most valuable things about the goat is its wool, which is used to make cloth. The Angora goat and the Cashmere goat have especially fine, silky hair. Farmers comb this hair from the animal's coat, and people in factories spin it into soft cashmere sweaters and scarves and other articles of clothing that are prized by people everywhere. The hair of the Angora goat is called mohair.

People in many parts of the world have had stories and legends about goats. Many people who lived on farms kept goats because they believed that a goat could find certain plants that would cure a person who was sick. People also believed that the "billy goat" (the male goat) would bring good luck, and that the female, or "nanny goat," had a magic power that could drive witches and other evil spirits away. Goats are very intelligent and playful animals, and some people keep them for pets.

goatsucker

The goatsuckers are a family of more than seventy different kinds of birds that live in many parts of Europe and the United States. These birds got their strange name because the ancient Greeks believed that they sucked the milk of goats. This is not true, but the goatsuckers have an unusual way of catching their food that explains why these early people got this wrong idea. The goatsucker has a very large mouth, and bristles stick out from the sides of this opening. The goatsucker flies with its mouth open and catches moths and other insects in the bristles.

The goatsucker sometimes searches for insects close to the ground, where goats and cattle graze. The goatsucker has brown and white and black feathers that blend with the leaves and trees, so its enemies cannot see it. The goatsucker is about ten inches long. It has a strange habit of resting lengthwise on the branch of a tree, so that it looks as if it were lying down. It does not build a regular nest. The female bird lays two eggs in a hollowed-out place under a bush. The goatsucker is sometimes called the *nightjar,* because it has a jarring call, and also because it rests during the day and flies at night.

Gobelin

The Gobelin Manufactory in Paris, France, is a factory for the making of tapestries. A tapestry is a cloth that is woven of yarns of different colors into pictures or designs. The Gobelin tapestries are famous for the beauty of the weaving. Many great paintings have been reproduced in tapestries. One of these paintings is *The Assumption,* by the Italian artist Titian.

Hundreds of years ago, a family named Gobelin started a dye business in what is now the Manufactory. In the 16th century the family began making tapestries as well as dyes. Some members of the family bought titles from the

Metrop. Mus. of Art.

Many Gobelin tapestries have historical scenes. Here, the king of France, Henry IV, greets his friend, the Duke of Sully.

king, or served in the government of France. In 1662 the business was purchased by King Louis XIV, and the firm is still controlled by the French government.

Gobi

The Gobi is a vast desert on a plateau in the heart of central Asia. The Gobi covers about 300,000 square miles, which is twice the size of the state of Montana. The waterless part of the desert covers only one-quarter of the whole area, but little grows but grass and patches of scrub anywhere in the Gobi. Most of the people who live in the Gobi are nomads, or wanderers, who move their herds of livestock about the few grassy areas. During rainy seasons when some agriculture is possible, Chinese farmers move into the eastern, more humid parts. The only important towns are located on the edge of the desert.

During World War II, supply routes between the Soviet Union and China

The camel caravan is the best way to ship goods across the vast Gobi desert. Mongolians are skilled at this hard job.

crossed through the Gobi desert. Marco Polo, the Italian explorer, crossed in the 13th century.

Some of the earliest men lived in the Gobi desert, perhaps before there were any men in Europe or the western parts of Asia. Archaeologists, scientists who study how the earliest men lived, have made some of their most important discoveries in the Gobi desert.

goblin, an imaginary spirit that plays tricks on men: see the article FAIRY AND FAIRY TALES.

God

God is the name used for the Supreme Being who made the world. He is worshiped not only in the Christian religion but also in the Jewish and Mohammedan (Moslem) religions.

There is a difference between God, spelled with a capital letter, and the many gods and goddesses that appear in the mythology or religion of ancient or prim-

itive peoples. Some of these peoples worshiped idols (statues) and even animals, thinking that they held the spirits of superhuman beings (beings that had powers greater than those of men). Where science and civilization have developed, the worship of idols and other gods and goddesses has always ended, but the belief in one supreme God has gone on.

Belief in one God is called *monotheism;* belief in many gods is called *polytheism.* Most of the early religions were polytheistic. Men were trying to understand the world around them. They saw many things more powerful than themselves. The sun brought heat and life. Terrible storms, accompanied by thunder, lightning, and great winds, destroyed many things. The mysterious forces of nature made crops grow from the soil. They looked at these things and were filled with wonder. They saw that some of these forces helped men to live and were therefore kind, but that others could destroy.

To help themselves understand these things, men imagined the forces of nature as gods. The ancient Greeks called their god of the sun Helios. Helios had great and shining palaces in the east and west (where the sun rises and sets). He had horses and chariots in which he was carried on his daily journey across the sky. Since there were many forces of nature, people had to imagine many gods. Then they had to imagine a chief, or king, of the gods. The Greeks called their chief god Zeus; the Romans called him Jupiter.

Some of the ancient people worshiped only one god. This one god was the source of all power, and he filled the universe.

The one God that most people in the Western World worship today is different from any god of ancient monotheism. The first people to accept this God were the Hebrew writers of the Old Testament. He is the only true God. He is all-good, and all-just, and all-powerful. He is the God of all men, not the god of one country. Most of all, He is invisible.

THE NAME OF GOD

In the Old Testament God is sometimes referred to by a Hebrew word of that meaning, but more often is given a personal name. It was written with four consonants: YHWH (or JHVH). The Jews came to consider the name too holy to be spoken aloud and so its pronunciation was virtually forgotten. Wherever the name occurred the Jews substituted the word *Adonai*, meaning "Lord," and so the English Bible has LORD. In the book of Exodus, in the Authorized Version of the Bible, the name is given in the pronunciation *Jehovah*, but this is not the way the Hebrews pronounce it. There is some doubt about the original pronunciation, and it seems to have varied in different places and times. A tradition that it was pronounced *Yahweh* (Jahveh) has become widely accepted. But it appears as *Yahu* or *Yaho* in some names, and can be further shortened to *Yah*, as in *Hallelujah* (Praise ye the Lord). In the Eng-lish Bible *Iah* has often been substituted for *Yahu*, as in the prophet Jeremiah's name, which appears in Hebrew as *Yirmeyahu*.

IDEAS OF GOD

By some, God has been thought of as being totally present in the world. This idea of God is called *immanence,* or an immanent conception of God. Others have thought of God as being outside the world. This is called *transcendence,* or a transcendent conception of God. The immanent view leads to what is called *pantheism,* identifying God with the world, and the transcendent view leads to what is called *deism,* making Him dwell apart from the world, taking little interest in it since creating it. The compromise is that God is both immanent and transcendent. This is called *theism* and is the general view of the Christian church.

Since men can speak about God only in human words, they have most often described Him as having human qualities, yet the whole idea of God makes it clear that His real nature may be beyond human understanding. Biblical language sometimes describes God as baring "His mighty arm" when it wants to show His power or strength, or it speaks of His eyes, hand, or mouth, to show His other qualities in human terms. This way of speaking about God is called *anthropomorphic,* meaning "in the likeness of man." An instance such as the one quoted is an *anthropomorphism.*

PROOFS OF GOD

Many great thinkers have tried to prove that God exists. Usually, Christians, Moslems, or Jews simply accept God as revealed in the holy writings of their religions. This is *belief by revelation.* Others have sought to show that even if there were no revelation, or if a man did not believe in revelation, it would be just as correct to believe in God as it is to believe that one and one make two.

Here are some of the proofs they give for God's existence: They say that there must be a reason for anything that is. In the world around us we see this sufficient reason in the cause of a thing. For example, the cause of a child is his parents and that is why the child exists. But they say, there must be a First Cause. The First Cause would not be caused by something else. It would be eternal—something that always existed and always will. This is called the argument from the First Cause.

Other arguments say that such things as the wonderful order of the stars show us that there must be an infinite Creator whose mind made this design. Or that because men think that there is a God, He must exist. Or that because nothing in the world is necessary (that is, anything in the world could not exist), there must be a necessary being or God outside the world.

But since the time of the German philosopher Kant (late 18th century) these "proofs" have been abandoned. God cannot be "proved," for all our thinking is based on comparison and He is unlike anything. If we could "prove" Him, furthermore, we would have circumscribed Him, and He cannot be circumscribed. The reality of God is experienced by people and after they have experienced it they know it exists.

Read also the articles on BUDDHISM, CHRISTIANITY, JUDAISM, and ISLAM.

Godey, Louis Antoine

Louis Antoine Godey founded the first woman's magazine in the United States. That was about a hundred years ago. The magazine was called *Godey's Lady's Book*. It contained stories and articles on subjects of interest to women, such as fashion, homemaking, and the care of children. It had many illustrations, including pictures of the latest styles in women's clothing. Louis Godey was born in New York in 1804. He became interested in newspaper work and publishing when he was still a young man. He moved

to Philadelphia and began working in a newspaper office. In 1830, he started to publish *Godey's Lady's Book*. He also published several other magazines, among them one for children. He died in Philadelphia in 1878.

Godiva

Lady Godiva was the wife of an English lord in the city of Coventry, about nine hundred years ago. Her husband's name was Leofric, and he forced his people to pay such high taxes that Lady Godiva felt sorry for them. She begged her husband to reduce the taxes, and he sarcastically said he would if she would ride naked through the streets. He thought he was safe in making this promise, but Lady Godiva took him up on it. She rode through the streets of the town on a white horse, and her long flowing hair was her only clothing. All the people of the town closed their shutters as she went by, out of respect for a great lady. All, that is, except a tailor named Tom who peeped through his window and was struck blind. To this day we call someone who spies on others a "Peeping Tom."

Godwin-Austen

Mount Godwin-Austen is the name of the second-highest peak in the world. It is also called K-2. It is in the Karakorum range of the Himalayan Mountains in the northern part of Kashmir, India.

After many years in which mountain climbers had tried to reach the top of this snow-covered mountain that rises 28,250 feet above sea level, in 1954 an Italian expedition under the leadership of Professor Ardito Desio at last succeeded. Clouds usually hide the peak, and vast glaciers make climbing very dangerous.

Goebbels, Joseph

Joseph Paul Goebbels was one of the most important men in the German government during the years from 1933 to 1945, when Germany was ruled by the Nazi Party. He was the Minister of Prop-

aganda and Public Enlightenment, and he was considered one of the greatest experts who ever lived in making people believe what he wanted them to believe. Unfortunately, what he wanted them to believe usually was not true.

Goebbels was a short, weak man who walked with a limp. He was one of the earliest followers of Adolf Hitler, the Nazi leader. As Minister of Propaganda he controlled everything that was said in newspapers, on the radio, in plays, and in motion pictures, and even everything that was said by the people of Germany themselves. He believed in a method that has since come to be called the "big lie," that is, if you tell the public something often enough they will eventually come to believe it, no matter how untrue it may be or how ridiculous it may seem at first.

Hitler depended on Goebbels to stage mass meetings and to organize festivals and parades, to build up the power of the Nazis in the minds of the German people and in the minds of people outside of Germany. Goebbels also had a program of propaganda started against the Jewish people, whom he wanted to kill or drive out of Germany. When the Germans were defeated by the Allies in 1945, Goebbels killed himself and his family.

goeduck

The goeduck is one of the largest clams in the world, and some people say that it is also the ugliest. Goeducks are found along the western coast of the United States. The shell of the goeduck is more than eight inches across, and there is a long fleshy part that sticks out between the shells. This part of the goeduck looks like a long neck, but it is called the *foot.* The foot helps the goeduck clam to breathe when it lies buried in the sand, under the water of the ocean. The goeduck eats tiny living things that it finds in the sea.

Goeduck is an Indian name that means "dip deep." The goeduck can dig two or three feet into the sand. Many people like to cook goeducks and eat them.

Goering, Hermann

Hermann Goering was the second most powerful man in the German government during the years from 1933 to 1945, when Germany was ruled by the Nazi Party. He was the only one of the high-ranking Nazis to have been an officer in World War I, which gave him a very high social position. During World War I he was one of Germany's most famous flying aces. When Hitler started the Nazi Party in 1920, Goering became one of his followers. When the Nazis came to power in 1933, Goering was put in charge of the air  force, which he built into the most powerful in the world. He was also in charge of heavy manufacturing, and one of the biggest new steel factories that Germany built was called the Hermann Goering Iron Works.

Goering was a very vain man who liked to wear gaudy uniforms. He was also a very cruel man who liked to kill animals and to see blood. He sent tens of thousands of people to death because he thought they stood in the way of his ambition, which was very great. Goering made himself very rich by using his official position, but when Germany lost the war all his wealth was taken away from him. Goering was arrested, and tried and sentenced to death as a war criminal by an International Military Court. Several hours before he was to be hanged, he killed himself with poison. It is still a mystery where he got the poison.

Goethals, George W.

George W. Goethals was the American engineer who was in charge of the  construction of the Panama Canal. The Panama Canal permits ships to cross a narrow part of Central America and get from the Atlantic Ocean to the Pacific Ocean. When the United States began to build the canal in 1907, President Theodore Roosevelt put Goethals in charge. It was considered one of the most difficult engineering feats of history, but Goethals completed it in 1914, which was even earlier than had been hoped. After that Goethals was made governor of the Canal Zone, the land around the canal, from 1914 to 1916. Goethals was born in Brooklyn, New York, in 1858, and died in 1928.

Goethe, Johann Wolfgang von

Johann Wolfgang von Goethe may have been the greatest German writer. He lived about two hundred years ago. Goethe wrote stories, plays and poems, but he is best remembered as a poet. His best-known work of poetry is *Faust,* a story about a man who sold his soul to the devil. His best-known  novel is *Wilhelm Meister,* in which he gives many of his ideas about life.

Goethe was born in 1749. When he was only 25 he wrote his first novel, *The Sorrows of Young Werther,* which made him famous overnight. The next year he was invited to visit the court of the Duke of Weimar, and he spent the rest of his life there. He became an official in the Duke's court, and he was also the court poet.

During his lifetime Goethe was considered one of the world's greatest writers, and even today his works have universal appeal. He died in 1832.

Gog and Magog

Gog was prince of the land of Magog, told about in the Bible. The Book of Ezekiel says that someday a fierce people will sweep down from the land of Magog in the north. A great army, led by Gog, will attack the land of Israel. But God will protect Israel, and destroy the invaders. The Book of Revelation in the Bible uses the names Gog and Magog to mean all the evil people of the earth, who will gather together to destroy the good people, but will themselves be destroyed at the Day of Judgment.

Gog and Magog are also characters in an old British legend. The story tells about a race of great giants. All of them were killed except for two, Gog and Magog. These two were captured, and were forced to be guards at the royal palace. When they died, statues of them were made to stand in their place. The huge wooden statues of Gog and Magog, fourteen feet high, stood for a long time in the Guildhall in London, England.

Gogh, Vincent van

Vincent van Gogh was a great Dutch painter who lived a very short life and yet is one of the most famous painters who ever lived. He was only 37 when he died. Van Gogh used a lot of oil paint on his canvases, and his pictures look as though the paint had been put on with a knife instead of with a brush. He liked to paint pictures of everyday things. Three of his most famous pictures are *Sunflowers in a Vase,* which is full of lovely shades of yellow and brown; *The Artist's Room,* a painting of his bedroom that looks like patchwork, it has so many squares of color in it; and *Wheat Fields,* which makes you feel as though you were out in a wheat field in the strong sunshine.

Sunflowers is a famous painting by Vincent van Gogh, noted for its beautiful color and masterful flower arrangement.

Van Gogh was born in the Netherlands in 1853. He was a very religious man and became a preacher to coal miners in Belgium. He did not start to paint seriously until he was about 30 years old. He taught himself almost everything he knew about painting. His brother Theo worked in an art gallery in Paris and sent Vincent to southern France to paint. Almost all of his most famous paintings were painted during the last three years of his life.

Van Gogh became mentally ill when he was only 35. In 1890 he was sure he would never be well again, and he killed himself. During his lifetime he could sell only a few of his pictures, but today one of them would cost you many thousands of dollars.

Gogol, Nikolai

Nikolai Gogol was a great Russian writer of short stories, novels, and plays. He was born in 1809. Gogol was one of the first Russians to write stories of real people in real situations. His ancestors were Cossacks, the colorful peasant-soldiers of Russia, and his first successful stories were romantic tales of these people. Gogol is chiefly remembered for his

play, *The Inspector General,* which poked fun at stuffy government officials. Gogol was worried about having this play produced for fear it would make Russian officials angry with him, but the emperor himself ordered it performed, and it has been popular ever since. It has been translated into English and several other languages. One of Gogol's greatest novels is *Dead Souls,* which tells about the unhappy lives of the serfs of Russia in olden times. Gogol died in 1852.

goiter

Goiter is a disease that occurs when the thyroid gland is not working properly. The thyroid gland is in the front of the neck. It produces a chemical called *thyroxin,* which the body needs.

KINDS OF GOITER

Simple goiter is a swelling of the thyroid gland. This happens when the body does not get enough iodine. The thyroid gland needs iodine to make thyroxin. As a medicine iodine is a poison, but a little of it in your drinking water or food is important. In places near the sea, there is usually enough iodine in the water. In other places people usually get their iodine by using iodized salt.

Exopthalmic goiter (goiter with bulging eyes) occurs if the thyroid gland makes too much thyroxin. The patient becomes very nervous and thin, and does everything so fast that he wears himself out. This disease can be corrected by removing part of the thyroid gland so that less thyroxin is produced. There are also new drugs that help this disease. See also the articles on THYROID and GLAND.

gold

Gold is one of the earth's most precious metals. It is an element, one of 103 basic substances of which everything in the world is composed. Gold is a soft metal, yellow in color. It is valuable partly for its beauty; partly because it will not rust, and most acids and other substances do not hurt it, so that it lasts a long time; and partly because it has many practical uses for which no other metal is quite as good. Gold is so valuable that for thousands of years it has been the one metal that is used everywhere and accepted everywhere as money.

Gold is usually found in gold ore, either in soil or rocks. In a few places it can simply be picked up off the ground or taken out of the ground in solid chunks called *nuggets*. When gold has been discovered, it is *assayed* to find out how much gold there is in the ore. There is a separate article on ASSAYING.

HOW GOLD IS MINED

There are two principal ways of mining gold. One is by *placer mining*, or washing it from the sand and gravel of streams. Wind and water and air have worn the gold from the rock where it once lay and carried it into the streams. There it sinks to the bottom because it is twenty times as heavy as the water. This gold may be in tiny grains smaller than grains of sand. This is called *gold dust*. Sometimes the gold is in pieces as large as good-sized pebbles. These are called nuggets. The largest gold nugget ever found weighed 183 pounds.

Placer mining used to be done by hand with a simple iron pan. The prospector, the man searching for gold, would scoop up a pan of pebbles from the bottom of the stream and fill the pan with water. Then he would shake the pan and toss out the water, with some of the pebbles. He would repeat this with more and more water until he had tossed out all the pebbles and only the gold remained. The gold had sunk to the bottom because it was heavier than the water and the pebbles.

Today powerful machinery does the work of placer mining. A hose washes great beds of gravel into a trough, and then into large baskets, which are shaken by motors to toss out the pebbles and the water.

The second method of gold mining is done just the way iron and coal are mined. That is, gold is dug out of the earth. This is called *lode mining*, because the gold is taken from great beds and veins of ore, called *lodes*, beneath the ground. Gold ore must be processed to separate the metal from the rock. This is called refining, and it is done in large plants with complicated vats and machines.

Left: Mined gold is carted from the head of an underground shaft.

Above: Huge funnels regulate the air in the underground mine.

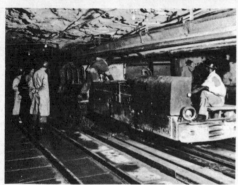

South African Tourist Corp.

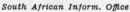

South African Inform. Office Photos

Left: Electric cars loaded with mined gold ore will move to the surface where the valuable metal will be processed. *Right:* Gold miners must be able to work in very cramped quarters.

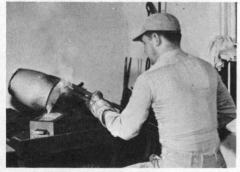

South African Inform. Office

Pan American World Airways

Left: Gold dust and nuggets are melted into bars to make shipping easier. *Right:* Weighing must be accurate. A "slight" error of only one pound could cost the shipper about $560.

Right: Panning for gold is slow work, but prospectors have made fortunes this way. Now, some people make prospecting a spare-time hobby. They go to an abandoned claim and try to find gold there. Gold is worth $35 an ounce, so some vacations can be more profitable than working.

Below: One way of washing gold from surface gravel was by using big water jets. But this dammed up many streams. Therefore, many places forbid mining gold in this way.

Sacramento Chamber of Commerce

People who work in gold refineries and in places where gold is used in manufacturing usually wear special uniforms that are kept and washed in the plant. This is because a large quantity of gold dust will collect during the day's work in the material of the workers' clothing. The gold dust is recovered by washing.

HOW GOLD IS RATED

Gold is weighed in *carats*. Pure gold, with no other metal in it, is said to be 24-carat gold. If it has 22 parts of gold and 2 parts of some other metal, such as silver, it is called 22-carat gold. The number of parts of gold out of each 24 parts determines the carat count of the metal. The symbol for carat is k, so if you see 10k on a piece of jewelry it is made of 10 parts of gold and 14 parts of another metal. Because gold is so soft, it is seldom used in its pure form.

WHERE GOLD IS FOUND

The principal sources of gold today are Canada, the southern part of Africa, and Soviet Russia's Ural Mountains and Siberia. Some very rich gold mines were found in the United States, in the far western states such as California and Nevada, and in Alaska and the Yukon Territory of Canada. When gold was found in these places it caused tremendous gold rushes. Thousands of people flocked to the gold fields and soon took most of the gold out of the ground. (There is a separate article on GOLD RUSH.) Nowadays gold mining is very scientific. It is done by elaborate machinery that belongs to big corporations and millions of dollars are invested in mining operations. There are still many prospectors, however, who search for gold in the United States and Canada where some gold ore is known to exist.

USES OF GOLD

Gold is one of the most important metals in the making of jewelry. It is also used in dental work because it makes the best possible fillings for teeth, but it is so expensive that usually other materials are used for filling cavities.

Gold can be made into sheets so thin that a pile of them an inch high would contain more than two hundred thousand separate sheets. These sheets are called *gold leaf* and are used for gilding domes and ceilings of churches and palaces, and for the gold lettering on office and store windows. Another method of gilding is by electroplating, which is putting a layer of gold over another metal. Long ago, gold plating was done by dipping an object into melted gold. In the modern method, a piece of pure gold is placed in an acid solution, along with the object to be plated. Then an electric current is passed through the solution, and this causes a very thin layer of gold to detach itself from the piece of pure gold and settle all over the surface of the other object in the solution.

GOLD AS MONEY

For thousands of years gold was made into coins. Today most countries do not have gold coins because they do not have enough gold.

In the early days of the West in the United States, gold dust was used as money. It was weighed at the time it was spent, to find out how much it was worth.

In foreign trade, settlement still is finally made in gold. When one country owes another country a large amount of money at the end of a certain period, it settles the debt by sending gold. The United States has almost nine-tenths of the world's reserve of gold used for money. This amounts to about twenty billion dollars. It is stored in an underground vault at Fort Knox, Kentucky. It is in the form of gold bars, called *bullion*. See also the article on MONEY.

Gold Coast

The Gold Coast is the southern section of the country of Ghana, in West Africa. Until Ghana became an independent country, in 1957, the name Gold Coast was applied to the entire British territory (including Ashanti and the Northern Territories) that now makes up most of Ghana. The Gold Coast section is on the Gulf of Guinea, a large section of the Atlantic Ocean, and includes the city of Accra, capital of Ghana. Gold and also diamonds, and the metal manganese, are principal products of the Gold Coast.

Golden Age

The Golden Age of a country is a period that is considered the best period in its history, especially in literature and other arts. The ancient Greeks, 2,500 years ago, spoke of an imaginary Golden Age that had happened before, but today the period about four hundred years before the birth of Jesus is considered the Golden Age of Greece. The Golden Age of Rome was about 2,000 to 1,900 years ago. During part of this period Je-

After being mined deep under the ground, gold is refined and shipped at great cost. Most of it is then returned to the bowels of the earth in deep vaults like those at Fort Knox. Any lucky prospector allowed to stake out a claim here could "mine" many billions of dollars in gold.

Ewing Galloway

sus was on earth. The Elizabethan Age in England, the period about four hundred years ago when Elizabeth I was queen, is sometimes called England's Golden Age because Shakespeare and other great writers were living and writing then.

golden calf

The golden calf was an imaginary god that some of the Jewish people set up to worship, as told in the Book of Exodus in the Bible. This book tells how Moses had just led the Jews out of Egypt, where they had been slaves, and then had gone up to Mount Sinai, where God gave him the Ten Commandments and other laws. While he was gone the people became impatient. They melted all their gold jewelry and made a small statue of a calf, which they worshiped. This broke one of the Commandments God had given to Moses, and God punished the high priest Aaron, who was Moses' brother, for permitting the people to worship the idol. When Moses found out what the people had done, he was so angry that he broke the tables, or pieces of stone on which the Commandments were engraved. He ground the golden calf to dust and mixed it with water, which he made the people drink as punishment.

Golden Fleece

In the stories the ancient Greeks told more than two thousand years ago, there was an imaginary ram, or male sheep, whose fleece or hair was made of gold. This golden ram was first heard of when it carried away two Greek children who were the grandchildren of the god Aeolus. For this Aeolus punished the ram by killing it, but its golden fleece was saved and guarded by a dragon. Later Jason and his followers, called the Argonauts, stole the Golden Fleece. You can read about this in the article on JASON.

Golden Gate

The Golden Gate is a narrow body of water that leads from the Pacific Ocean into San Francisco Bay in California. It is five miles long and one to two

Redwood Empire Assn.

The Golden Gate Bridge, one of the world's longest bridges, joins the redwood country to San Francisco. Ships heading toward the Pacific pass beneath it twenty-four hours a day.

miles wide. One of the longest suspension bridges in the world crosses the Golden Gate. It was completed in 1937. It has two towers eight hundred feet high, from which hang cables more than three feet thick. The span of the Golden Gate bridge, between the towers, is 4,200 feet long. The bridge is crossed by a six-lane roadway. At night the bridge is brilliantly lighted.

goldenrod

The goldenrod is a yellow flower that grows in many parts of North America. It is a very strong and hardy plant and can grow in dry soil, so that it brightens roadsides and many barren places where other flowers cannot grow. During the autumn months fields covered with goldenrod look like yellow carpets.

The individual flower of the goldenrod forms a crown of yellow on a green stem that grows two to eight feet high. Green leaves with sharp edges protect the bottom of the stem.

Some persons believe that the pollen of goldenrod causes hay fever, but this is not true. Goldenrod pollen is heavy and sticky, and it is not carried about by air

The male goldfinch (*left*) wears a colorful "suit" of feathers, but its lady friend's dress is not as conspicuous.

currents. What really happens is that ragweed, the pollen of which does cause hay fever, blooms at the same time as goldenrod, and thus ragweed pollen is dusted over goldenrod, asters, and other fall-blooming plants.

Golden Rule

The Golden Rule was given by Jesus in his famous Sermon on the Mount. You can find the Golden Rule in the seventh chapter of the Book of Matthew in the New Testament. Jesus told the people, "therefore all things whatsoever ye would that men should do to you, do ye even so to them." This is usually simplified in the words "Do unto others as you would have others do unto you." Men in many other religions have been credited with giving this same rule long before Jesus did, but this is not so. The Chinese teacher Confucius, the rabbi Hillel and many others said, "Do not do unto others what you do not want them to do unto you." Jesus was the only one who made the Golden Rule teach people to do kind and pleasant things, and not merely to avoid doing unkind and unpleasant things.

goldfinch

The goldfinch is a bird that looks somewhat like a canary and is about the

The goldenrod's upper stem (1) curves gently, but the lower part (2) is straight.

same size. It is yellow and has touches of black on its wing tips, the crown of its head, and the tip of its tail. The goldfinch has a beautiful song. When it flies it streaks through the air very fast in a kind of undulating, or waving, flight, and it changes its course frequently.

There are different varieties of goldfinch in the Rocky Mountains and along the Pacific coast and in Mexico. Some goldfinches visit the northeastern United States in summer. The European goldfinch has a bright red throat and is often kept in cages so that people can enjoy its singing.

goldfish

Goldfish are the most popular fish that people keep as pets. Most of them are a golden color or have some gold mixed with such other colors as red. They can be kept in almost any receptacle that holds water and they live a long time if they are properly cared for. You can read more about the care of goldfish in the article on AQUARIUM.

Until a few hundred years ago, nearly all goldfish were a dull green color, with just a trace of gold. The Chinese and Japanese began to breed the brightest-colored of them and gradually they developed the beautiful colors that goldfish have today.

There are many kinds of goldfish in many different groups and colors. For instance, a very popular kind is a goldfish with a huge, sweeping tail, called the *fringetail* or *fantail*. A rare kind of goldfish is the white one. Others have been developed with veil tails, with double or triple fins, and with huge bulging eyes.

gold rush

A gold rush occurs when gold is discovered in an unsettled territory where nobody yet owns the land. Thousands of people get there as fast as they can to find gold and make themselves rich. All kinds of people are likely to join a gold rush. Often they include criminals and dishonest or unprincipled men, so that a gold rush is likely to be a time when there is no law and order. Since the territory is unsettled, people live very rough lives, with few of the benefits of civilization. There is always a shortage of food and clothing and other materials, so these sell for very high prices. A single good meal is likely to cost a hundred dollars or so.

There have been many gold rushes in the United States. The most famous one was in California, when gold was discovered at Sutter's Mill in 1848. Most of the people got there in 1849, so they were called Forty-niners. There have been smaller gold rushes in other western states of the United States, including Colorado, Nevada, Idaho, Montana, and South Dakota.

The last big gold rush in North America was when gold was discovered in the Klondike area in the Yukon Territory of Canada. People on their way there found gold in Alaska too. This gold rush took place from 1898 to 1900. There was a gold rush in Australia in the 1850s, and in South Africa in the 1880s.

The California gold rush started after gold was found near John Sutter's Mill, shown here in 1848.

Goldsmith, Oliver

Oliver Goldsmith was a great writer who was born in Ireland about the year 1730. When he was only 19, he graduated from Trinity College in Dublin. Goldsmith studied medicine for three years but he gave up his studies to travel about  Europe, where he sometimes earned money by playing the flute. He finally settled in London, England. Goldsmith's poems, novels and plays are usually about ordinary people and are written in simple, clear language. His most famous work is a long poem called "The Deserted Village," in which Goldsmith describes a lovely little town. His novel *The Vicar of Wakefield* has always been widely read. Goldsmith also wrote plays. *She Stoops to Conquer* is a comedy that is still performed in America. In this play, the heroine, who knows that the young man her parents wish her to marry is shy with well-bred ladies, pretends for a while she is a barmaid in order to see how he behaves normally. Goldsmith died in 1774 from a fever for which he had not taken the correct medicine. Goldsmith was very generous, so he always owed money and he died poor.

Gold Star Mothers

The Gold Star Mothers are an organization of American women who had one or more sons killed in the two World Wars or in Korea. The organization has more than six thousand members. It was founded in 1928 and has its headquarters in Washington, D.C. The name Gold Star Mothers comes from the custom of placing gold stars on service flags in honor of men who were killed in war.

Goldwater, Barry

Barry Morris Goldwater was the candidate of the Republican Party for the presidency of the United States in 1964 but lost the election to Lyndon B. Johnson. Goldwater stood for the conservative group in the U.S., being opposed to the participation of the Federal Government in many cases that affect individual citizens.

Goldwater was born in Phoenix, Arizona, in 1909, the grandson of a famous Arizona pioneer who founded the first store in that state. From the time he was a young man Barry Goldwater made himself known nationally as an outstanding businessman, writer, speaker, and public official; in 1952 he was elected to the U.S. Senate from Arizona and served there until he resigned to run for President.

golf

Golf is a game played by hitting a small, hard, rubber ball with a special kind of club called a golf club. The game is played on a *golf course,* or *links,* in which there are places where a cup, or hole, has been put in the ground. This cup is 4½ inches across and 6 inches deep. Each time a player hits the ball it is called a *stroke.* He tries to sink the ball in the hole with as few strokes as possible.

A golf club is a long, thin, stick made of steel or wood, with a knob or *head* at the bottom. The ball is hit with the flat side of the head, called the *face.* The face may be straight up-and-down or tilted at an angle with the ground. Clubs with straight faces are used to hit the ball long distances. Clubs with tilted faces are used to give the ball a *loft* (that is, to hit it high into the air). A special club with a metal head, called the *putter,* is used to make the ball roll along the ground.

A full set consists of fourteen different golf clubs. Clubs with wooden heads are called *woods,* and clubs with steel heads are called *irons.* Each club has a different shaft length and a different shaped head.

Each club has a number, such as "Number One Iron." Many years ago the clubs were called by different names, such as "brassie," "spoon," "niblick," and "mashie"; now they are known by numbers.

Pa. Dept. of Commerce
Using a wood to increase his distance, the golfer swings hard to clear the water hazard.

Rubber winding (here loose) gives a golf ball bounce.

The tightly wound center is ready to be covered.

The tough, white, gloss cover makes the ball long-lived.

Arnold Palmer Co.
Arnold Palmer demonstrates the correct manner in which to shoot an iron shot.

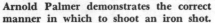

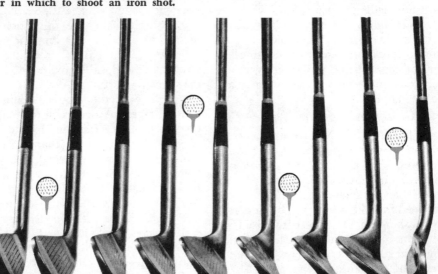

A. G. Spalding & Bros., Inc.
Irons, by number and name, from left to right: No. 1, driving iron; 2, midiron; 3, midmashie; 4, mashie iron; 5, mashie; 6, mashie niblick; 7, pitcher; 8, pitching niblick; and putter.

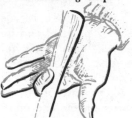

Interlocking Grip.

Canadian Govt. Travel Bureau

Deep concentration is necessary when a golfer putts. The flag is replaced when the party leaves the green.

Sand goes in every direction after the golfer finishes an "explosion" shot from a sand trap near the green.

U.S. Golf Assn.

Position of left hand.

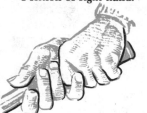

Position of right hand.

Position of both hands.

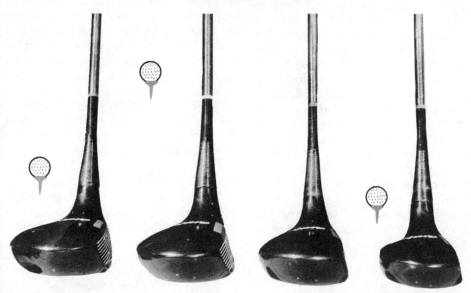

A. G. Spalding & Bros., Inc.

Golfing woods, left to right: driver, brassie, spoon, and cleek. Each wood has a different pitch to help the golfer control the distance and elevation of his shots.

THE GOLF COURSE

A golf course is a large plot of ground, specially planned and built usually with eighteen holes. Each hole is marked by a number on the flag of a long wooden stick called a *flagstick*. The hole is in a well-kept part of the course called the *putting green*. The grass on the green is cut very short. About 100 to 600 yards from the green is a mound called the *teeing ground*. Between the teeing ground and the putting green is a section of mowed grass called a *fairway*. On both sides of the fairway are usually trees, rocks, and tall grass. This is called the *rough*. It is more difficult to hit a ball when it is in the rough. Between the fairway and the green, there are usually other places where it is difficult to hit the ball. These places are called hazards, and include bodies of water and pits of sand called *bunkers* or *traps*.

HITTING THE BALL

The way in which the ball is hit with the club is called a *stroke*, or *shot*. There are many different kinds. Some shots are for distance and are called drives. To drive a ball properly, one must hit it squarely with the face of the club. If the ball is not hit squarely, it will curve off to the right in a *slice* or off to the left in a *hook*. Sometimes the club will strike the ball near the top and send it only a short distance. This is called *topping the ball*.

There are other shots that are used to bring the ball nearer or sink it into the hole. A *chip shot* is used when the ball is just off the green. It is a short, low shot. A *pitch shot* is used to bring the ball on the green and near the hole. It is a high shot with some backspin on the ball to keep the ball from rolling too far from the hole. When the ball is on the green, a *putt* is used to roll the ball toward the hole.

PLAYING A GAME OF GOLF

In playing a game of golf, a player must start on the first tee and play each hole in order, from the first to the eighteenth. This is called a *round* of golf. After sinking the ball in the first hole, he moves on to the second tee. From there he tries to sink the ball in the second hole in as few strokes as possible.

At each tee, the player places a little wooden peg into the ground. This peg has a flat top and is also called the tee. The player then places the golf ball on the wooden tee and picks out the club he wants to use. Usually he will pick out the "Number One Wood," also called the *driver*, because that club is good for distance shots. He then gets ready to hit the ball, by facing it with the side of his body toward the direction in which he wants the ball to go. He keeps his eye on the ball at all times, and places the face of his club directly in back of the ball. He slowly draws the club back until it is behind his head. He then swings the club down toward the ball and hits it with full force.

If the ball lands on the fairway, the player will next choose one of the woods or irons that will help him hit the ball on to the green. If he lands in the rough or in one of the hazards, he must choose the iron that will help him get his ball back on the fairway or on the green. If his ball is in a sand bunker he might use a special iron called a sand wedge or blaster.

When the ball lands on the green, the putter is the next club the player uses. It has a short shaft and an almost straight face that is best for rolling the ball along the green and into the hole.

THE CADDIE

In most cases, the player will go around the course with a caddie. The caddie is a boy or man who carries the clubs for the player. The caddie often helps the player to choose the right club. The caddie works for the golf course and is assigned to the player by the caddie master. The caddie gets paid for each round he caddies. Many schoolboys earn money during the summer and on week-ends by caddying.

GOATS, SHEEP AND HOGS

HAMPSHIRE SHEEP

BERKSHIRE HOG

YORKSHIRE HOG

NUBIAN GOAT

MERINO SHEEP

RYE

WHEAT

FLAX

SWEET SORGHUM

RICE

Golf is not only an enjoyable sport; when it is played on a beautiful course like this one in California, it is also a treat for anyone who enjoys lovely scenery.

Calif. Mission Trails Assn.

Each golf course has what is called *par* for the course. This is the score one of the best players is supposed to make when he is playing as well as he should. Each hole has a par. A hole that is up to 250 yards from the tee is par 3 (three strokes to get in the hole). A hole between 251 and 445 yards is a par 4. A hole between 446 and 600 yards is a par 5. Over 600 yards, the par is 6.

A *birdie* is a score of one less than par on a hole. An *eagle* is two less than par. A *hole-in-one* is a score of one stroke for a hole. To score a hole-in-one, a player must hit the ball from the tee into the hole. A *bogey* is the score a good average player should make on each hole. Usually it is one stroke above par.

GAMES AND TOURNAMENTS

Golf is usually played by two, three or four players, who go around the course together. There are two ways of scoring, called *medal* or *stroke* play and *match* play. In medal play, the player competes against everyone else on the course and the one with the lowest score for the course wins. In match play the player competes against only another playing against him. Each hole is scored separately. The player who makes the lowest score for the hole wins the hole. The player who wins the most holes wins the round.

In the United States, the United States Golf Association (USGA) governs the playing of golf. It distinguishes between amateur golfers, who cannot accept money as prizes or for teaching others to play golf, and professional golfers, who play for money prizes, teach golf, and sell golf equipment. There are separate tournaments for amateurs and for professionals, and there are open tournaments in which both may play.

Every year there are many big tournaments for professionals and for amateurs. The Professional Golfers Association (PGA) has a yearly tournament in which only professionals may play. The Walker Cup match is played between teams of amateurs representing the United States and Great Britain. The Ryder Cup match is held between the best professional golfers of the United States and Great Britain.

Golf courses are found in most country clubs where members who have paid their dues can play. At most country clubs, there is a professional golfer, or "pro," who teaches golf. There are also public courses in most large cities where you can play for a small fee.

HOW GOLF STARTED

Golf was played at least five hundred years ago in Scotland. Scottish shepherds played it by hitting a leather ball, stuffed with feathers, with the sticks they carried to herd sheep. So many people played the game in Scotland that the government stopped it. The government wanted them to practice shooting their bows and arrows instead of playing golf. With the bow and arrow they could defend their country.

This did not stop the game from being played, and by the year 1600 even the kings were playing it. This gave golf the name of a "royal and ancient game." The most famous golf club is the Royal and Ancient Golf Club of St. Andrews in Scotland. It was begun in 1754. It is the governing body of golf in the British Commonwealth.

In 1895, the first national championships were held in the United States. A few years earlier, in 1888, a group of men began the St. Andrews Golf Club in Yonkers, in the state of New York. Players were brought from England and Scotland to teach golf.

There are about four million people in the United States who play at least ten rounds of golf a year. About six hundred thousand of these people belong to golf clubs. There are more than five thousand golf courses in the United States. Men and women of all ages play golf.

Golgotha

When Jesus was to be crucified, as told in the New Testament, he was taken to a place outside the walls of the city of Jerusalem. The Hebrew name of this place was Golgotha. The Latin name was Calvary.

The word Golgotha means "place of the skull." We do not know why the place had this name, but there are many different ideas about it. There may have been a little hill there that was shaped something like a skull; or it may have been the place where criminals were executed or where there was a cemetery, and so there would be many skulls there.

Goliath

Goliath was a great and powerful giant told about in the Bible. Goliath was one of the Philistines, a people who were at war with the people of Israel. Goliath was the champion of the Philistines, and he challenged the people of Israel to send out a champion to fight alone with him. Whoever won the battle would win victory for his side. Goliath was a fearful warrior, nine feet tall, and King Saul of Israel and all his men were very much afraid. Just then the boy David happened to come to the battlefield bringing food to his brothers who were in the army. When he heard Goliath's challenge, he offered to go out and fight him, to show everyone that God would help the people of Israel. David refused to wear armor, or to carry a sword. He took only his slingshot and some smooth stones. The first stone he aimed hit Goliath in the forehead. The great giant fell down dead, and David cut off Goliath's head with Goliath's own sword.

Gomorrah, a city told about in the Bible: see the article on SODOM AND GOMORRAH.

Gompers, Samuel

Samuel Gompers was a great leader in American labor organizations. He was  born in 1850, in England. When he was still a boy his family settled in the United States. Gompers went to work in a cigar factory and he soon became a leader in the Cigarmakers' Union. From then on he devoted his life to trying to improve working conditions.

In 1886, some labor unions joined together to form a new organization of unions called the American Federation of Labor. There are separate articles about the AMERICAN FEDERATION OF LABOR and LABOR AND LABOR UNIONS. Samuel Gompers was one of the leaders in the formation of the American Federation of Labor. He was elected its first president and re-elected every year except one until he died. When World War I began Gompers helped to unite the American working people, and urged them to support the war. After the war, he helped to settle labor problems all over the world. Samuel Gompers died in 1924. Under his leadership the American Federation of Labor had grown and prospered, and American working men had been able to win better working conditions.

Goncourt, Prix de

The Prix de Goncourt is a prize that is awarded each year by the Goncourt Academy for a great work of French fiction. The academy was founded in 1900 under the will of Edmond de Goncourt. Edmond de Goncourt and his brother Jules were famous French novelists who lived and wrote together during the 19th century.

gondola

A gondola is a kind of boat. The best-known type of gondola is used in the city of Venice, in Italy. Venice has canals instead of streets, and the gondolas carry passengers from one place to another just as taxicabs do in other cities. Each gondola is pushed through the water by a man called a gondolier, with a long pole. Many of the gondoliers sing as they work.

A certain type of flat-bottomed river boat is called a gondola, and so is a flat-bottomed railroad car. The car that hangs from a dirigible airship is also called a gondola.

gong

A gong is a round metal instrument that is made of bronze, or a mixture of copper and tin. A gong looks like a shallow dish. When you strike it with a drumstick or a small, padded hammer, it makes a loud, ringing sound. The Chinese and other people of Asia have used gongs for thousands of years. They use them the way we use bells, and many temples of the East use gongs to call the people together. Oriental people like the sound of the gong in their music, and some English and French composers have written music that includes a gong. The gong makes such a clear sound that it can be heard a

Italian State Tourist Off.

Three children of Venice, wearing costumes of earlier times, ride in a miniature gondola. Venice has many canals, and people must call a gondola or other boat instead of a taxicab.

long way off, and people sometimes use gongs to call others to dinner or to a meeting.

Gonzaga

Gonzaga is the name of an Italian family that became famous about seven hundred years ago. It was a very powerful and rich family. For about four hundred years the family ruled Mantua, a large section of north Italy. Giovanni Francesco Gonzaga was the first person in the family to become rich. He added much land to that already belonging to the family. His grandson, Francesco Gonzaga, was a great soldier who married Isabella d'Este, a very beautiful and good woman. Together they helped many writers and artists. The family lost its power in 1708 after Ferdinand Charles Gonzaga had lost many wars. The land was taken over by Austria.

Good Neighbor Policy

The Good Neighbor Policy is the name given to the way in which the countries of South America and the countries of North America work together to solve their problems. Years ago, many of the countries of Central and South America did not trust the United States. They were afraid that because the United States was so large and powerful it would attempt to rule them. In 1933 President Franklin D. Roosevelt announced to the world that the United States wanted to be a good neighbor to these smaller countries. The United States would be willing to help them if they needed help but would not try to rule them or tell them what to do. Since that time all the countries of North and South America have been friendly, and in World War II all the Latin American countries except Argentina took the side of the United States. Recently the countries have held conferences, or meetings, at which they discuss what is best for all the countries. You can read about these conferences in a separate article on PAN-AMERICANISM.

Goodrich, B. F.

Benjamin Franklin Goodrich was an American businessman who founded one of the greatest rubber businesses in the world, nearly 100 years ago. He was born in 1841 and became interested in the rubber business when he was still a young man. He failed several times to make a success of the business, but continued to work hard, and finally, in 1880, he founded the B. F. Goodrich Company in Akron, Ohio. He died in 1888.

Goodyear, Charles

Charles Goodyear was an American inventor. His most famous invention was a way of making rubber that is hard, strong, and able to stretch in all kinds of weather. He was born in New Haven, Connecticut, in 1800. After finishing public school, he went to work in his father's hardware business. His father was

Goodyear Tire and Rubber Co.

Charles Goodyear holds the first piece of vulcanized rubber. The pot in which he accidentally made his discovery is still steaming on his kitchen stove.

Chicago Park District

The yellow goslings are hatched in June. Their parents then teach them to find food, swim, and fly. In a few months the young geese are sent out on their own.

an inventor of farm machinery, and Charles helped him with many of his inventions. However, when his father lost all his money because of bad business management, Charles had to find other ways of making money. He tried to find a way to make rubber that would not crack or become sticky when the weather changed. The rubber then being used would melt in the summer and freeze in the winter. Goodyear worked for ten years trying to make rubber that would not spoil. Then, in 1839, he found what he was looking for. One day he accidentally dropped a mixture of rubber and sulfur on a hot stove. When he scraped off the mixture, he found that the rubber could be stretched more easily and was much stronger. What was more important, it did not spoil in winter and summer. Heating a mixture of rubber and sulfur is called *vulcanization.* It is named after Vulcan, god of fire in the religion of the ancient Romans. Vulcanization is used to make most of the rubber in the world today. Goodyear began to manufacture rubber products by vulcanization, but many people used his invention without paying him for it, and when he died in 1860 he had very little money. The Goodyear Tire and Rubber Company, which was formed in 1898, was named after Charles Goodyear but he did not start it.

goose

A goose is a waterfowl similar to the duck in many ways, but larger and with a longer neck. Geese live in all parts of the world, on lakes, ponds, and rivers. They have webbed feet and are good swimmers. They also are powerful fliers, and some can fly as fast as sixty miles per hour. You can read about domestic geese, which are raised for their meat and for eating weeds in gardens, in the article on POULTRY.

Wild geese are migratory, which means they move in flocks from north to south in the fall, and back again in the spring. They fly higher than any other migratory bird. They are very noisy and honk constantly when they fly. A type of Canadian goose is called the *honker,* because it is even noisier than most geese. Like wild ducks, geese are game for hunters.

Laws have been passed to protect them and sanctuaries have been established where they can safely stop to feed during their migrations.

Wild geese live on roots of plants they find in marshy fields, rather than from water plants as ducks do. They usually do not breed until they are 3 years old. They build their nests on an island or a mound in shallow marshy water. They mate for life, and can live from twenty to thirty years. Ganders, the male geese, protect their families and will fiercely attack enemies, such as the fox.

gooseberry

The gooseberry is a berry used in preserves and in desserts such as pies. It grows on a thorny bush that is found in England, northern Europe, the northern part of the United States, and other places. The shrubs grow wild in most places, but in England they have been carefully cultivated for more than four hundred years, and they yield a large, sweet, plumlike fruit that can be eaten right off the bush. As the fruit ripens its color changes from green to purple. It has many seeds. The gooseberry grown in other parts of the world is usually bitter on the bushes.

Gooseberries make a tasty jam that is a favorite treat of English children.

gopher

A gopher is a small animal that spends most of its life underground. It lives in the western part of North America. It is seven to fourteen inches long, and is gray, tan, or brown in color. A gopher does not see very well, because it seldom comes out during the daytime and does not need good sight in the underground darkness. Gophers are rodents, or gnawing animals, and are related to rats, beavers, and squirrels.

Gophers live alone, and make tunnels

The gopher's long, hard claws enable it to dig underground tunnels, through which it gets to the roots it feeds on.

or burrows in which they live. Each gopher's house contains several storage compartments for food to be eaten during the winter, when it would be hard to find the plant roots and bulbs that gophers live on. The gopher has a strange way of carrying its food home. It has two fur-lined pouches or pockets on the outside of its cheeks, and it fills these pockets with the food it wants to store or with materials for its nest. That is why it is often called a pocket gopher.

Male and female gophers live in separate burrows, and never associate with each other except at mating time. If one gopher meets another in a burrow they sometimes fight until one is killed. Baby gophers are born in the late spring. There are from one to nine in a litter, and they are only about an inch long when they are born. When the young gophers are two months old, they leave their mother's home to build their own tunnels and houses.

Farmers of the western part of the United States and Canada find gophers a pest, because they eat the tender roots of many crops. Minnesota is called the Gopher State, because so many gophers used to live there.

Gordian knot

The story of the Gordian knot is told in Greek mythology, the stories the ancient Greeks told about their gods. According to the story, an oracle (one who could see the future) had foretold that the people of a country called Phrygia would get a strong king to solve their troubles. This king would arrive in a wagon. One day a poor peasant named Gordius brought his wagon to the market place, and the people made him their king. He was so grateful for this good fortune that he dedicated his wagon to the greatest of the gods, called Zeus. The pole of the wagon was fastened to the yoke for the animals by a very complicated knot. The oracle also foretold that the man who could loosen this knot would be ruler of all Asia. Alexander the Great came to the city and very simply cut the knot with one blow of his sword. He then declared that he had fulfilled the prophecy. Modern students of history doubt very much that Alexander cut the true Gordian knot; they think that he cut through a copy of it. It is true that he did go on to conquer Asia.

Gordon, Charles William

Charles William Gordon was a Canadian minister who was best known by his pen name, Ralph Connor. Under this name he wrote many novels about his life as a missionary in the lumbering country of the Northwest Territory of Canada. Among the best known of his books were *The Prospector, Corporal Cameron,* and *The Sky Pilot.* Gordon was born in Ontario, Canada, in 1860. After he became a minister, he was sent as a missionary to the Northwest Territory for three years. He lived with the lumbermen, and his books were based on his experiences during this time. Later he became minister of St. Stephen's Church in Winnipeg. He died in 1937.

Gordon, Chinese

Charles George Gordon was a famous British soldier. He is often called *Chinese Gordon* because of his many years of service in China, and sometimes is

called *Gordon Pasha* because of his military service in Egypt. He was born in Woolwich, England, in 1833, and was graduated from the Royal Military Academy when he was about 20 years old. He went to China and took part in the capture of Peking. Later, he helped the Chinese forces to defeat the Taiping rebels.

In 1873, the khedive, or ruler, of Egypt asked Gordon to become governor of the Sudan, which is south of Egypt. Several years later he returned to England, only to be called back to the Sudan again to help the khedive. He was besieged at Khartoum for ten months by rebel forces. Gordon was killed by the rebels only a few days before new troops arrived to help him. It is said that his head was cut off and taken to the chief of the rebel forces as a trophy.

Gorgas, William Crawford

William C. Gorgas was a very famous doctor who became surgeon general of the United States Army. The surgeon general is the chief medical officer of the Army. Gorgas was born in 1854, and when he was a young boy he had two ambitions, to be a soldier and to be a doctor. So  he studied medicine and then entered the Army Medical Corps. While stationed in Texas, he became ill with yellow fever. He recovered and was immune to the disease from then on. After the Spanish-American War, about fifty years ago, Gorgas was made sanitation officer in Havana, Cuba, which was then occupied by American soldiers. Within a short time he permanently rid the city of yellow fever. He was promoted to colonel for this work.

In 1904, Gorgas went to Panama, where the United States government was building the Panama Canal. The land was very unhealthful and many workers were dying of yellow fever and other diseases. Gorgas knew that yellow fever was carried by a certain kind of mosquito, so he immediately set about draining the marshes and swamps, and putting screens on the doors and windows of the houses. His work rid the Canal Zone of yellow fever and made it possible to finish the canal. From 1914 to 1919 he served as surgeon general. Gorgas died in 1920. He is now in the Hall of Fame.

Gorgon

The Gorgons were three fearful-looking women in Greek mythology, the stories the ancient Greeks told about their gods and goddesses. The Gorgons had coiled snakes on their heads instead of hair; they had sharp claws and huge teeth. They were named Stheno, Medusa, and Euryale. They were so horrible-looking that anyone who looked at any of them was instantly turned to stone. Medusa was killed by a Greek hero named Perseus, who killed her while looking at his polished shield as he chopped off her head. Because he did not have to look directly at her, he was not turned to stone as many other heroes had been. He took the head of Medusa to the temple of the goddess Athena as an offering, or gift, because Athena had given him the polished shield that saved his life.

gorilla

Gorillas are the largest of all the apes. A male gorilla may be as much as six feet tall and weigh four hundred pounds. A gorilla is an enormously powerful animal, and other beasts of the jungle usually leave gorillas strictly alone. The gorilla, however, never seems to attack other animals deliberately, and is peaceful unless threatened. Gorillas live mostly on fruits and vegetables.

Gorillas live in family groups, with one adult male, one or two females, their babies, and a few half-grown gorillas. They travel from place to place, and

Am. Mus. of Nat. Hist.

A large male gorilla pounds his chest. The jungle of the Congo is a rather hot place for him to wear such a heavy fur coat.

make camps for the night as they go. They never live with other families, as baboons do.

There are two kinds of gorilla. The black mountain gorilla lives in the mountain forests of central Africa. The lowland or coast gorilla is iron-gray in color, and it lives in the damp rain forests in the western coastal section of equatorial Africa. Both are covered with hair everywhere

Baby Mambo of the Bronx Zoo gets a rubdown with baby oil in the zoo nursery. The little gorilla seems to be ticklish.

Standard Oil Co.

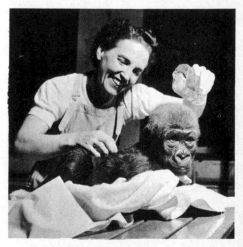

on their bodies except the face, the palms of the hands, and the soles of the feet. They have a strangely human look, but their arms are so long they reach to the middle of the legs when the animal stands upright. Gorillas lumber about on all fours most of the time. See also the article APE.

Gorki

Gorki is the name of one of the most important industrial cities of Russia. It is also one of the oldest cities in Russia, and has often been called the birthplace of the Russian empire. Gorki used to be called Nizhni Novgorod, but the name was changed to honor the great Russian writer, Maxim Gorki. The city is about 260 miles east of Moscow, the capital of Russia, at the point where the Oka and Volga Rivers meet. About 930,000 people live in Gorki. They are mostly workers in the iron and steel factories of the city, or in the automobile factory that is one of the largest in Russia.

The city is divided into two parts. The upper part of the town is where the historic cathedrals, the fortress called the Kremlin, and a government palace are located. The lower part of the city, near the river, is the industrial area. Gorki is also an important commercial town. In the Middle Ages, more than six hundred years ago, great fairs were held here.

Gorki, Maxim

Maxim Gorki, whose real name was Alexei Maximovich Peshkov, was born in Nizhni Novgorod, Russia, in 1868. He became so famous as a writer that in 1932 the city was renamed Gorki in his honor. Gorki supported himself from the age of 9, and he traveled all over Russia and Europe, working at all kinds of jobs and meeting many kinds of people. He published his first story in a Russian newspaper. He used the name of Gorki, which means "the bitter one," because he was bitter that so many people had to live in poverty and despair.

Gorki became a journalist and started writing short stories, plays and novels that became popular all over the world. Some of these are *The Lower Depths, Twenty-six Men and a Girl,* and *Mother.* The people he wrote about best were those he had met on his travels: the poor, the tramps, the unfortunates. He wrote with great force and sadness about their unhappy lives. He gave a broad picture of life in Russia and discussed the many problems people had to face. Gorki supported the Bolshevik revolution and became head of the propaganda bureau, but ill health forced him to go abroad in 1922. He returned to Russia and died there in 1936.

goshawk

The goshawk is a large, handsome bird that lives in many parts of the United States, Canada, and Europe. It is about two feet long, and is blue-gray in color, with a white stomach and gray stripes across its underpart. The goshawk has flashing red eyes and a white streak above each eye. Like all members of the hawk family, the goshawk eats other birds. It also catches rabbits and squirrels, and will swoop down on barnyards and kill chickens.

The goshawk builds a strong nest made of sticks and mud, high up in the trees of pine forests. Every year the goshawk builds a new nest, and the female lays white or pale blue eggs. People in Europe taught captive goshawks to bring the rabbits, or other animals it caught, back to them, and this became a popular sport called *falconry.*

Goshen

Goshen was the name of a territory given by Pharaoh to the Israelites, the Jewish people who had come to Egypt from Israel. There is some question as to the exact location of Goshen, but from the description of it in the Bible it is believed to have been outside of Egypt. The land was very good in Goshen, and all things grew well there. Today people think of the land of Goshen as a place of good things.

Gospel

Gospel means "good news." Christians have used the word for hundreds of years to mean the good news that Jesus Christ, the savior of mankind, had come to earth as promised in the Bible. A preacher is said to "preach the Gospel." Usually we use the word to mean any of the first four books of the New Testament, the books of Matthew, Mark, Luke, and John.

All of these Gospels were written during the first century A.D., which means they were written within less than a hundred years of the time when Jesus was actually on earth. Scholars have considered that each of the four Gospels has a slightly different message. St. Matthew tells of Jesus the preacher who preached the Sermon on the Mount. St. Mark tells a simple story of Jesus' life on earth. St. Luke shows Jesus as founder of the Christian Church. St. John shows Jesus as the Son of God, the spiritual inspiration of men.

The first three Gospels, Matthew, Mark, and Luke, are called the *synoptic* Gospels. *Synoptic* comes from Greek words meaning "the same eyes." The synoptics, as though seen through the same eyes, tell much the same story. The Gospel of Saint John is not so much a biography, or story of Jesus' life, as it is an interpretation of his life.

A "Harmony of the Gospels" is an arrangement of them so that each is shown to tell the same story as the other. The word *harmony* means "agreement." *Harmonics* is the study of the Gospels in such a way as to show that they agree with one another.

Gothic

Gothic is a style of architecture, the design and construction of buildings. The Gothic style came into use in Europe in the Middle Ages, about eight hundred years ago, and developed out of a growing love of beauty and a widening interest among the people in religion. Gothic architecture was originally used for churches, but gradually its style was copied for other types of building.

The pointed arch is a main feature of Gothic architecture. As you can read in the article on ARCH, the Roman arches of earlier times had been rounded with very thick walls and small windows if any. The architects wanted their churches to have more windows to let in sunlight. To have more windows they had to make the walls higher and straighter. The pointed arch gave them the straighter walls that they wanted but they were not as strong as the rounded arch. So they invented the *flying*

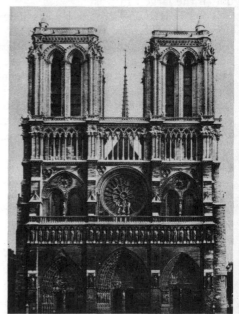

French Govt. Inform. Service

Many tourists visit the early Gothic Cathedral of Notre Dame in Paris. Spires should top the two towers, but the beautiful cathedral has never been finished.

The interior of the Exeter Cathedral in England is a beautiful example of medieval Gothic architecture.

British Railways

buttress. The flying buttress is a stone pillar that is propped against the wall to support it.

One of the most famous Gothic churches is in Paris. It is the cathedral of Notre Dame, and it was built almost eight hundred years ago. It has beautiful stained-glass windows showing scenes from the Bible, and a lovely round window called a "rose window" that looks like a blossoming rose. There are many churches in the United States that are built in the Gothic style. St. Patrick's Cathedral and the Cathedral of St. John the Divine in New York City are two of the finest Gothic churches in America.

Goths

The Goths were a Germanic or northern people who lived hundreds of years ago in what is now southern Sweden. From there they slowly moved down across Europe, conquering any tribes who tried to stop them. About three hundred years after Jesus was born they reached the borders of the Roman Empire. Rome at that time controlled most of the civilized world. The Romans fought the Goths for many years. As the Roman Empire became less powerful, more and more of the Goths tried to cross its boundaries. In the year 36 the Goths divided into two groups. One group, called the West Goths, or Visigoths, crossed the Danube River and were allowed to settle in the Roman Empire. The other group, called the East Goths, or Ostrogoths, remained behind.

The Romans did not treat the Goths well at first, and the wars continued. The most famous leaders of the Visigoths were two kings named ALARIC; you can read a separate article about these kings. After about thirty more years of war, during which the Visigoths invaded the city of Rome, they moved west to what is now Spain and southern France. Here the Goths founded a kingdom that lasted more than three hundred years. It was finally conquered by the Moors.

The Ostrogoths later came down into Italy and conquered a large part of the Roman Empire, where they ruled for about 35 years. This kingdom was finally taken back by the Romans.

The Goths were fierce and bold fighters. They were not as civilized as the people they conquered, but they were good rulers. They let the conquered people keep their own laws and religions and customs. Often the Goths settled down in the conquered regions, adopted the customs of the empire, and lived in peace with the people they had conquered. They later accepted the Christian religion. Many of the people living throughout southern Europe are the descendants of these northern people.

Gould, Jay

Jay Gould was an American financier and railroad owner who became very rich and powerful. He was extremely clever, but his business methods were not always according to the highest standards. He was born in Roxbury, New York, in 1836. He was a rich man before he was 20. In 1869, Gould and a man named James Fisk tried to buy up all of the gold in the United States. The government stepped in to prevent this so they did not succeed, but their activities caused a great stock market panic that was called the Black Friday Panic. Gould started to buy railroads soon after he moved to New York City, and by 1880 he owned nearly one tenth of all the railroads in the United States and controlled the Western Union Telegraph Company. He died in 1892.

Gounod, Charles

Charles Francis Gounod was a famous French composer, a writer of music. He was born in Paris in 1818. He is best known for his operas, which are plays in which the characters sing the parts instead of speaking. His most famous opera is *Faust,* the story of a man who sells his soul to the devil, and how he is punished for it. He also composed an opera about the story of *Romeo and Juliet.* Gounod wrote a great deal of church music. One of his best-known religious works is *The Redemption,* an oratorio, or music for chorus and soloists. During the Franco-Prussian War, Gounod lived in England. While he was there he founded the Gounod Choir, which was a chorus of men's and women's voices. Gounod died in St. Cloud, France, in 1893.

gourd

Gourd is the popular name for a group of plants that bear hard-shelled fruits of many different shapes. The shells are used as decorations, drinking cups, bowls, and dippers. Some plants of the gourd family may be eaten. Pumpkins and the different kinds of squash that Americans like to eat are members of the gourd family.

Non-edible, ornamental gourds grown along fences or on the ground make a colorful addition to the garden in the fall.

Gourds were used as dippers, drinking cups, and bowls by the American Indians long before the white man arrived in the New World. In many American homes small gourds are used as table decorations. They are usually bought at a fruit market and varnished or shellacked to preserve them. This type of gourd cannot be eaten. They make attractive decorations because of their odd shapes and pretty colors. They may be orange, green tan, or cream colored, and a few are green on top and orange below. Some are about the size and shape of a large pickle; others are round and the size of a large apple. Many have thick round bumps on them like warts. The larger gourds are about the size of a small pumpkin. One kind of gourd from which dippers are made is about fifteen inches long and is shaped like a dipper, with a long stem for a handle and a round end that forms the bowl when the top is cut off. The gourd is picked and allowed to dry until the seeds rattle inside it. They cannot be used for hot liquids but serve very well for cold liquids and will last for many years.

gout

Gout is a painful disease of the joints. It is a form of ARTHRITIS, about which there is a separate article. Gout attacks a small joint (usually the big toe), which becomes hot, swollen, and red. The area becomes so tender that even the weight of bedclothes is painful. Attacks of gout usually begin in the night and last from three days to a week. Often there is fever as high as 103 degrees.

Gout is brought on by something in the body that causes too much uric acid to form in the blood. This results in chalky deposits in joints such as the toes. Women usually do not have to worry about getting gout; nineteen out of twenty cases are men, most of whom are over 35. Gout was very common in Europe in the 18th and 19th centuries. It was once known as the "rich man's disease," probably because acute attacks are sometimes brought on by overindulgence in rich food and drink. The best thing to do for gout is to keep the infected joint warm and at a level higher than the rest of the body. Doctors may also prescribe large doses of baking soda and water, or a drug called *colchine.*

government

Government is the organization set up to keep people from doing harm to each other or to the society in which they live, and to help them lead safe and comfortable lives. There have been many different forms of government throughout the ages, and most of them have benefited the rulers more than the people who were governed. But every American's idea of a good government is what Thomas Jefferson expressed in the Declaration of Independence:

"We hold these truths to be self-evident, that all men are created equal, that they are endowed by their Creator with certain unalienable rights, that among these are life, liberty and the pursuit of happiness.—That to secure these rights, governments are instituted among men, deriving their just powers from the consent of the governed.—That whenever any form of government becomes destructive of these ends, it is the right of the people to alter or to abolish it, and to institute new government, laying its foundation on such principles and organizing its powers in such form, as to them shall seem most likely to effect their safety and happiness."

FORMS OF GOVERNMENT

Beginning with the early Greek thinkers, men have considered and studied different forms of government and tried to decide which is the best one. The great philosopher Aristotle divided governments into three classes: autocracy, aristocracy, and democracy. AUTOCRACY is government by one man; ARISTOCRACY is government by a special group of people who are considered the best people; DEMOCRACY is government by all the people. There are separate articles on these. There are innumerable ways in which these forms of government can be set up, and men have given them dozens of different names. A few of these are: Oligarchy is government by a small group; it is like aristocracy, except that in an aristocracy the governing group holds its position by some special privilege such as inheriting it. Plutocracy is government by the very rich. Theocracy is government by priests; this was quite usual in ancient civilizations.

Left: In a democracy, the people tell the government what to do. *Right:* But in a dictatorship, the government has all the power and tells the people what they must do.

In the world today there are two main forms of government: democracy and dictatorship. Dictatorship as we have known it is government by a single man or a single political party. You can read about it in the articles on COMMUNISM and FASCISM.

FORMS OF DEMOCRATIC GOVERNMENT

Most of the countries that we call democracies today use either of two systems: the system used in the United States, and the parliamentary system. The United States system is called a system of "checks and balances," because there are three branches of government and none of them has supreme power. They constantly check and balance one another. These branches are the *executive*, the *legislative*, and the *judicial*.

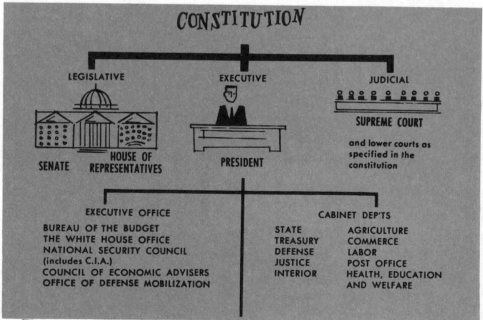

The government of the United States is organized under three branches—the legislative, executive, and judicial. Governments of other nations may be organized differently, but all have branches or departments like those of the United States government.

The legislative branch is the Congress, with its Senate and House of Representatives. It decides what should be done, by passing laws. The executive branch consists of the President, his Cabinet, and all the government departments and their employees. It carries out the laws made by the legislative branch. The judicial branch consists of the various Federal courts. It judges whether the laws are proper laws, and whether any of them are being violated.

These three branches depend on each other because each one limits the authority of the others so that no one of them can become too powerful.

The parliamentary system is different in one particular way. Parliament is the lawmaking body, as Congress is, but it has both legislative and executive powers. The President of the United States and the Prime Minister, or Premier, of a parliamentary country are different because the President is not a member of Congress, while the Prime Minister is a member of Parliament and is the chairman of its executive committee. Nearly every democratic country in the world except the United States follows the parliamentary system. The states of the United States follow the same system as the federal government.

CONSTITUTIONS

A constitution is the basic principles that underlie all the laws and all the acts of any of the branches of government. The United States and many other countries have written constitutions, and no member or division of the government may do anything that violates this basic set of laws. There is a separate article on CONSTITUTION. In Great Britain there is no written constitution, so that any act of Parliament becomes a part of the constitution. However, there are certain basic principles and policies that it would be as impossible for the British Parliament to violate as it would be for Congress to violate the United States Constitution.

In the United States, the Federal government makes laws, maintains defense, issues money, and cares for natural resources.

LOCAL GOVERNMENT

Every group of people, no matter how small, needs some form of government. In the home, the parents are the government, although happy family life requires that there be a certain amount of democracy, with each member having some say in decisions affecting him. In the town, the city, the county, and the state or province, there must be local government to handle matters that do not affect people outside that particular community. Towns and cities have mayors or city managers, as the executive branch, and councils or

State governments in the United States make local laws, and maintain courts, police, schools, health services, and roads.

assemblies to pass laws (often called *ordinances*). Counties have officials such as sheriffs and judges and clerks. States and provinces have more elaborate systems that are very much like a national government.

government ownership

When a country finds that certain things are too large and important for one person or group of persons to own and operate, these things are often put under government ownership. In the United States certain great forests and parks, post offices and the postal system, the Panama Canal, all atomic-energy resources, the Tennessee Valley Authority system of dams and water power for electricity, the Grand Coulee Dam, the Hoover Dam and other great public works belong to the government. They are all supposed to be operated by the government for the benefit of all the people. State, county, or city governments in the United States operate such things as the public schools, some highway systems, subways, sewers, and electric-light and gas systems.

Some people in the United States believe that the national government should own and operate many more works or industries; others believe the government already owns too many things.

In many countries of Europe, governments own and operate the railroads, the telephone and telegraph systems, radio, coal mines, and banks. In England, under the Labour Party, the government took over the railroads, the mines, and the public-health system. This was done by what is called *nationalization,* the taking over by the nation of what had been owned or operated by private citizens or firms.

At one time United States companies owned many oil wells in Mexico, but the Mexican government *expropriated* them, or took them over to operate itself with the promise of paying the owners for the value of the wells and property.

Under communism as in Soviet Russia, the government owns almost all land and natural resources, and either owns or controls all business, industry, and agriculture. Under socialism, the government also owns many things. (There are separate articles about COMMUNISM and SOCIALISM.)

Government Printing Office

The Government Printing Office is a branch of the United States Congress. It prints the documents and records of the United States government. It was started by Congress almost a hundred years ago. One of the most important things that is printed by the Government Printing Office is the Congressional Record, which tells what Senators and Representatives are doing. The office also publishes many other books and pamphlets that are ordered by Congress or other departments of the government. Many of these publications can be bought from the Government Printing Office. There are about fifty thousand publications available. They deal with everything from how to take care of a baby to how to grow corn. You can obtain information and catalogs by writing to the Superintendent of Documents, Government Printing Office, Washington 25, D.C.

governor

A governor is an attachment used to keep an automobile or truck or elevator or train from moving too fast. It is attached to the engine and slows it down when it reaches a certain speed. The usual type of governor is called a *flyball governor.*

This governor has a shaft with two steel balls that move outward when the shaft turns. These balls are on hinged arms that are held down by a spring. This spring is measured so that an exact amount of pressure is needed to open the

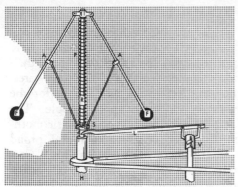

The parts of a governor: Shaft (H), governor shaft (P), balls (F), arms (A), spring (R), slide valve (S), lever (L), and valve (V).

spring. When the arms push the spring open and move up the shaft, a lever attached to them shuts off the fuel to the motor, or makes brakes go on. As the car moves, the shaft of the governor turns. The faster the car goes, the faster the shaft turns. As the shaft turns faster, centrifugal force moves the balls outward, and pulls the arms up. If the car is going too fast, the arms move up strongly enough to push the spring open. This makes the car slow down until the shaft also slows and the arms come down again. There is a separate article about CENTRIFUGAL FORCE.

governor

Governor is a title used by the heads of various governments and organizations.

In the United States, the head or chief executive of the government of each state is called the Governor. His position is almost exactly like that of the President of the United States, because the state governments are modeled after the United States government. He can sign or veto laws passed by the state legislature, and he can pardon persons convicted of crimes. He is commander-in-chief of the state's militia, or own army, and he can appoint the heads of the various departments that run the state government. Each state decides what other powers the Governor has, and what his term of office shall be. The term of office is two years in some states and four years in other states. In some states the same man cannot be re-elected as Governor.

Many countries appoint men called Governors to run their colonies and possessions. The President of the United States appoints a Governor for the Virgin Islands and other U.S. territories.

Governor-General

Governor-General is a title used in Canada, Australia, and other dominions that are members of the British Commonwealth of Nations. A dominion governs itself but recognizes the British king or queen as its king or queen. The Governor-General lives in the dominion as personal representative of the king or queen. In the government of the dominion he has the same power that Queen Elizabeth II has in Great Britain. This is not very much power, because the Prime Minister and cabinet, who represent the Parliament, actually run the country, but the Governor-General has a great deal of influence.

Most often the Governor-General of a dominion has been a member of the British royal family or a high-ranking nobleman sent from Great Britain, but in 1952 for the first time a native Canadian, Vincent Massey, was appointed Governor-General of Canada.

In India, when it was a part of the British Empire, Viceroy was the title of the man in the same position as the Governor-General in dominions.

Governors Island

Governors Island is a small island in New York harbor, less than a mile from the tip of Manhattan. It was bought from the Indians more than three hundred years ago by the Dutch settlers. Later, when the English occupied New York, it was used by the English governors, and this is why it is called Governors Island. Several forts were built on the island, and until 1965 the island was headquarters of the U.S. Army's First Corps Area. In 1966 it became a base for the U.S. Coast Guard.

Goya, Francisco

Francisco José de Goya y Lucientes was a famous Spanish artist and designer. He is best known for his drawings and etchings of bullfights and of warfare, which he made seem very real. He was born in Aragon, in Spain, in 1746. His family was very poor, and he too would probably have been poor if it had not been for a priest who saw him drawing on walls. The priest was impressed by his talents and found a patron, or wealthy man, to help Goya. Goya painted many portraits of Spanish royalty and society, and later produced many religious paintings. Most of his work was designed to show the stupidity, greed, cruelty, and other defects of men. When he was an elderly man he left Spain because he disapproved of the government. He died in Bordeaux, France, in 1828.

Gracchi

Tiberius Gracchus and Gaius Gracchus, together called "the Gracchi," were brothers who lived in Rome more than two thousand years ago. They were statesmen and reformers, and fought for the farmers and other poor people. The Gracchi were brought up by their mother, Cornelia, an intelligent and proud woman. There is a story that when Cornelia heard all of her rich friends boasting about their gorgeous collections of jewelry, she pointed to her two boys and said "*These* are my jewels." After fighting in Africa, Tiberius, the elder brother, returned to Rome and became a tribune —one of the rulers who were supposed to protect the common people from the nobles. He was very popular with the people, especially because he persuaded the assembly to pass a law limiting the amount of land any one person might hold and providing that the land left over should be rented to the poor at a very low rental.

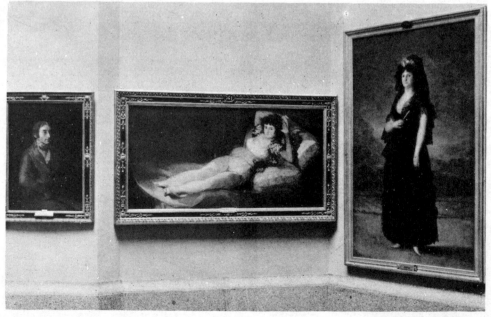

Spanish Tourist Office

Many famous people asked Goya to paint their pictures. The portrait of Queen Maria Luisa on the right is very true to life. These paintings are in the Prado Museum, Madrid.

Graces

The Graces were three goddesses in Greek mythology, the stories the ancient Greeks told about their gods and goddesses. The Graces controlled the gifts of beauty, elegance, and charm. They were named *Aglaia,* which means brightness; *Euphrosyne,* which means joyfulness; and *Thalia,* which means bloom. They lived on Mt. Olympus with their father, Zeus, king of the gods, and their mother, Eurynome. The Graces are usually associated with the Muses, nine sisters who were goddesses of the arts. Many artists have made statues of the three Graces standing together and holding hands.

grackle

The grackle is the largest of the American blackbirds. It makes its home in the eastern part of the United States and in some parts of Canada. The grackle is sometimes called the *crow-blackbird.* It is usually about one foot long, although some of these great birds are about eighteen inches long. The males are black, and in the sun their feathers shine with green and blue color. The female is a pale grayish-brown color. Grackles build their nests of grass and reeds in swampy marshes, on or close to the ground. The female lays pale blue or greenish eggs with brown spots on them. The grackle has a hoarse cry that is unpleasant to hear. Grackles are very useful because they eat many insects, but they can also be a pest to farmers because they are fond of corn.

graduation, the receiving of a certificate or diploma from a school or college. See the article COMMENCEMENT.

Grady, Henry W.

Henry W. Grady was an American newspaperman and speaker. He was born in Athens, Georgia, in 1850, and he studied at the University of Georgia. In 1879, after the end of the Civil War, Grady bought part of the Atlanta *Constitution,*

The grackle has a graceful shape, but its harsh cry very often makes it unwelcome, especially in the early morning.

a newspaper he helped make famous. In editorials in the newspaper and in many speeches, he worked hard to help the North and South make up their differences after the war, and to help the South rebuild its life and industry. His greatest speech was "The New South," made in 1886 in New York. Grady died in 1889.

grafting

Grafting is joining a part of one plant to another so that the two plants will unite and grow. Grafting usually gives the farmer new or better plants. Usually a bud or a small branch, called the *scion,* is grafted onto a growing plant or tree which is called the *stock.* The scion and the stock do not have to be the same kind, but they do have to be very closely related and in the same plant family. Grafting a pear variety on another pear variety, an apple on another apple, and so on, gives the best results. You cannot graft an apple and a peach. If an apple scion is grafted on a pear stock,

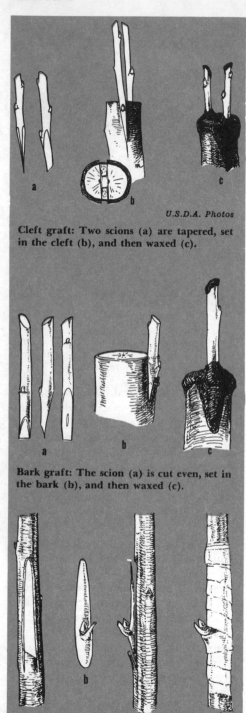

Cleft graft: Two scions (a) are tapered, set in the cleft (b), and then waxed (c).

U.S.D.A. Photos

Bark graft: The scion (a) is cut even, set in the bark (b), and then waxed (c).

Bud graft: The wood is exposed (a), the bud (b) set in place (c), and wrapped (d).

the scion will keep on growing as an apple even though it is nourished by the pear stock.

If you peel off the bark of a twig in early spring you will find a thin layer of plant tissue inside the bark. This is the cambium, and the graft is successful only if the cambium layers of both scion and stock are touching each other. Usually a graft is tied in place to keep the cambiums joined and then covered with a special grafting wax to prevent the graft from drying out. Sometimes the trunks or branches of two closely related plants growing close to each other will get pressed tightly together, and a *natural* graft will be made when some of the bark gets worn away and the two cambium layers unite. Natural grafts have been made by farmers for more than two thousand years, and the first man who tried it probably had seen one in the field and got the idea of making one like it himself.

The chief use of grafting is to grow new trees of a kind that do not easily reproduce their kind by seed or that would not root easily when a piece of branch is planted. When a new tree is wanted, a very young tree that grows easily from seed is taken for the stock. Then most of the top is cut off, and a scion, or twig, from the desired tree is grafted on. This kind of grafting is also used if the farmer wants to grow a tree where the soil or climate is not suitable for it. Here he uses a tree that grows well in the soil and climate as the stock, and then grafts the kind of tree he wants onto it.

Sometimes a farmer will have a fairly old tree that produces a kind of apple he does not like. He will cut back most of the branches and graft onto them scions of a kind of apple he does like. When you graft this way, or "top-work a tree," as it is called, you will get fruit quicker than if you wait for a young tree to begin bearing fruit. Sometimes grafting is used for novelties, such as one apple tree that has five different kinds of apples grafted on to it.

There is a separate article about the great scientist, Luther BURBANK, that tells how he experimented with, and produced, many new plants by grafting.

Doctors sometimes are able to graft skin onto people who have been badly burned. See the article PLASTIC SURGERY.

Graham, Billy

Billy Graham is the most successful evangelist of modern times. He was born in Charlotte, North Carolina, in 1918, and his full name is William Franklin Graham. He became a Baptist preacher after acquiring college training in theology, and he delivered sermons on radio, later on television, and in revivals attended by tens of thousands wherever he traveled throughout the world, urging his listeners to make "a decision for Christ." Also he has written much for newspapers, magazines, and books, and has produced many evangelical films. See EVANGELIST.

grain

Grain is the seeds of certain plants, such as wheat, oats, corn, barley, and rice. These seeds are made into flour at mills, or they are used as cereals; sometimes they are fed to animals. Bread, which is made from grain, has been called the "staff of life" because it contains so many important elements which the body needs for growth and health. There is gluten, which is a tissue builder; and starch and fat, which provide heat and energy. Grain also contains certain vitamins and minerals.

grain elevator

A grain elevator is a large bin in which grain is stored until it is needed. Many farmers harvest their grain at the same time, and some of it must be stored for later use. The elevator is a series of bins set close together, with machinery for lifting the grain, for weighing, cleaning, and drying it, and for unloading it again. Long ago grain elevators were made of wood covered with a layer of bricks, but today they are made of fire-

J. Schlitz Co.

This grain elevator holds 3,500,000 bushels of grain. It is the second-highest building in the state of Wisconsin.

proof materials such as steel or concrete.

The farmer sends his grain to the elevator in cargo ships, or by freight train, or in large trucks, and the first job is to get it unloaded. There are two ways of getting the grain up to the top of an elevator. The first way is with a machine consisting of a long circular belt with buckets attached. The grain is scooped into the buckets and the belt carries them to the top where they are emptied. At some elevators the unloading is done in another way. There is a long tube that works like a vacuum cleaner, sucking up the grain with a long nozzle.

At the top of the elevator the grain is cleaned, weighed, and dried, and there it stays until some big mill needs grain. Then it is unloaded and shipped to where it is needed. Some of the biggest elevators can hold up to ten million bushels of grain, as in Duluth, Chicago, and Minneapolis.

grammar

Grammar is the science of the forms of words used in a language. Many things affect the form of the word to be used. These include NUMBER, PERSON, GENDER, TENSE, and CASE, about which there are separate articles.

Sometimes the whole study of language is called grammar. The grammar you study in school may include things that are not really grammar, such as *syntax*, which is the study of how words should be arranged in a sentence, and *rhetoric*, which is the study of the choice of words. There are separate articles on SYNTAX and RHETORIC.

Very often your intelligence, as well as your education and family background, will be judged by the grammar you use, so it is important to learn and use correct grammar.

ENGLISH GRAMMAR

English grammar is easier to learn than the grammar of most other Indo-European languages (the family of languages to which English and other European languages belong). The changes in the form of a word are called *inflections*, and a word has a certain inflection according to its use. The English language has few inflections, and the only words that change their form according to the way they are used are nouns, pronouns, and verbs. These are called PARTS OF SPEECH, and you may read more about them in a separate article.

The pronouns have the greatest number of grammatical forms. The sentence "He sees me and I see him" shows one way in which pronouns change their forms. *He* and *him* stand for the same person, and *I* and *me* stand for the same person, but they have different forms when they are used differently.

The noun in English has only three forms: a form to show that it is one thing, or singular; a form to show that it is more than one thing, or plural; and a form to show that it owns something, or posses-

sive. Both the singular and the plural forms can be made possessive. Thus we say: dog, to mean one animal; dogs, to mean more than one animal; dog's, to mean that one animal owns something; and dogs', to mean that more than one animal owns something. There are some irregular nouns in English that do not form their plurals by adding "s" to the singular. Such a noun is *man,* the plural of which is *men,* or *deer,* the plural of which is also *deer.*

The verb in English has six tenses. Each of these has a special form. Most verbs do not change their form within any tense except the present and then only after he, she, it, or a noun. We say *I see* and *you see,* but we say *she, he,* or *it sees.*

Some irregular verbs follow no such pattern. The verb *be,* for example, changes form in all three persons of the present tense, and is conjugated *I am, you are, he, she,* or *it is.*

GRAMMAR IN OTHER LANGUAGES

In most Indo-European languages there are more inflected forms than there are in English. The Latin language, for example, has six different forms for each verb in the present tense, and ten different endings for each noun. In French, most words are either masculine or feminine and often the form of the word depends on which it is. Ancient Greek had more than a hundred forms for verbs.

In many languages the adjectives also change their form according to their use, and nouns have special endings to be used after certain prepositions or to be used instead of prepositions. The English language was once a highly inflected language, too, but gradually it dropped most of the inflections.

grampus

The grampus is a large animal that lives in the sea. It is the largest member of the dolphin family and is related to the whale. Though it lives in the water, it is not a fish but a mammal. This means that the females bear their children alive and nurse them. The grampus is sometimes more than twenty feet long. It has powerful jaws armed with sharp teeth, and it hunts and roams the sea in packs of more than forty, seeking its food. It will eat anything, even man, and is sometimes known as "the killer of the sea." The killer grampus can swallow dolphins, great tuna fish, or seals whole. Its characteristic round head and glistening black back are signs for other fish to get out of the way. The grampus can be found in all waters of the world, but it is more common in the colder regions.

Granada

Granada is a region in southern Spain. It was once an independent kingdom but is now a province in modern Spain. Granada is also the name of its capital, a city of about 157,000. Most of the people are farmers or raisers of livestock. There is very little industry in the region, which borders on the Mediterranean Sea.

Granada has had a long history. About a thousand years ago most of Spain was ruled by Mohammedan peoples from Arabia and Africa, and Granada was a separate country in Spain. It was called an emirate, and the prince who ruled it was called an emir. In the city of Granada is the most famous of all the palaces built by Mohammedan rulers, the Alhambra. In 1492 the Spanish king and queen, Ferdinand and Isabella, drove the Moors out of Granada. There is a story that the last emir of Granada, after he had been forced to leave the city, looked back on it from a hill near by. There were tears in his eyes because he had lost the city to the Spaniards, and his mother said to him, "Do not weep like a woman for that which you were unable to defend as a man."

Gran Chaco

The Gran Chaco is a large area of land in South America. The Gran Chaco has no large cities or industries, but a

Spanish State Tourist Office Photos

Above: A view of Granada from a tower window of an ancient castle.
Below: Granada's Alhambra, six hundred years ago the palace of Moorish kings.

terrible war was fought to control it. Two South American nations, Bolivia and Paraguay, fought bloody battles for more than eight years to gain possession of the Gran Chaco. They both claimed the land on account of old Spanish land grants. Moreover, Bolivia wanted the Gran Chaco, which is on the Paraguay River, in order to have a route to the sea. A treaty was signed in 1935 ending the war, and giving most of the Gran Chaco to Paraguay, but giving Bolivia a strip of land leading to the Paraguay River, so that Bolivia could ship goods to the sea.

Grand Alliance

The Grand Alliance is the name given to the group of nations including England, Holland, Brandenburg and the Duchy of Savoy, which joined together to fight Louis XIV of France. Louis XIV had wanted to make his empire larger by taking over other lands, and the nations of the Grand Alliance went to war against him to prevent this. The war, which began in 1688, lasted for nine years. It ended in the Treaty of Ryswick, in which Louis lost many of his earlier conquests.

Grand Army of the Republic

The Grand Army of the Republic, or G.A.R., was an organization of veterans who served in the Northern army during the Civil War. It was started in Decatur, Illinois, more than 85 years ago. The purpose of the founders was to bring together the men who had fought to save the republic; to take care of the dependents of the soldiers who had died; and to protect the laws and Constitution of the United States. The G.A.R. was the first organization to celebrate Memorial Day in the northern part of the United States.

Every year the G.A.R. would meet, in "encampments," and discuss matters of national interest. The G.A.R. had its largest membership about seventy years ago, when t' ere were more than 400,000 members. It held its final official meeting in 1949.

Grand Banks

The Grand Banks is a large area of shallow water near the coast of Newfoundland. The Banks begin on the southeastern tip of Newfoundland and curve around the coast for about two hundred miles, sometimes extending more than 250 miles into the Atlantic Ocean. The water of the Grand Banks ranges from 50 to 1,000 feet in depth.

The Grand Banks is one of the best fishing areas in the world. The most important catch is cod, which swim in large schools, or groups. The fishermen of many different nations travel to the Grand Banks to catch these fish with nets and hooks. However, the fishermen must face many dangers from icebergs, storms, and fogs. Thick fogs are frequent; they are caused by the warm air from the Gulf Stream meeting the much colder air of the Labrador current, which passes by the Grand Banks.

Grand Canal

There are several canals in the world that have the name of Grand Canal. Two of the most famous of these are the Grand Canal in Venice and the Grand Canal in China. You can read more about Venice's Grand Canal in the article on VENICE.

The Grand Canal in China is the oldest and longest canal in the world. It was started about 2,400 years ago and took almost two thousand years to build. It is a thousand miles long and runs from north to south through the two Chinese cities of Chinkiang and Tientsin. It connects two of China's main rivers, the Yangtze and the Yellow Rivers. The canal was originally built to make transportation easier between the Yangtze River and the North China Plain.

Grand Canyon

The Grand Canyon, in the state of Arizona, is the most famous canyon in the world. The word *canyon* comes from

1. Grand Canyon is the home of many Hopi Indians, and there is a Hopi House on the south rim of the canyon. Here a brave rests before taking part in one of the age-old Hopi dances. On his lap rest the traditional feather headdress and mask. In his hands is a dried gourd. When he shakes it, the seeds inside will keep time with the drums.

2. This Indian-style building houses a modern photographic studio for tourists.

Feature Service Photos

3. The Colorado River cut the Grand Canyon out of solid rock. When the sun catches the many-colored cliffs of this scenic spectacle, the visitor is impressed with the grandness of nature.

4. Grand Canyon rocks look as if they were left behind by a careless giant. The flat top of the cliff on the opposite side of the canyon gives a good idea of the original flat plateau into which the Colorado River began to cut ages ago.

U.S. Dept. of the Interior

T.W.A.

a Spanish word that means "hollow," and the Grand Canyon is a tremendous hollow in the earth. It is more than two hundred miles long, and in some places it is about eighteen miles wide at the top, while other parts are only about four miles wide.

The sides of the Grand Canyon are straight walls of rock. If you stand at the top, you can look down and see a tiny silver thread of water about a mile below. This is the mighty Colorado River. For millions of years the flowing water of the river has worn away the rock and earth and made this gigantic hollow in the earth's surface. You can read about the way this happened in separate articles on EROSION and COLORADO RIVER.

The sunlight and shadows fall on the towering peaks and crags and deep hollows of the canyon, and show the brilliant red, green, blue and white colors of the rock. As the light changes, the rocks glow and change colors. People come from every part of the world to visit the Grand Canyon. About fifty years ago, the United States government turned about a hundred miles of the Grand Canyon into a national park. In 1932, almost two hundred thousand acres adjoining Grand Canyon National Park were set aside by the national government and named Grand Canyon National Monument. You can read more about these in the separate article on NATIONAL PARKS.

Scientists have studied the rocks of the Grand Canyon, and they have learned many important things about how the earth was formed. The Grand Canyon was first visited by Spanish explorers more than four hundred years ago.

Grand Coulee Dam

Grand Coulee Dam is one of the largest dams in the world. It is on the Columbia River in the state of Washington. It is a tremendous dam, 4,173 feet long and 550 feet high. It was completed in

To the many Indians who live in the Grand Canyon region this impressive view is just an everyday affair. The Indians shown here make beautiful handwoven rugs and shawls.

Feature Service

Bureau of Reclamation

Grand Coulee Dam, as viewed from Crown Point in Washington State Park, shows how man can harness a great river and use it for electric power and farm irrigation.

1942, and provides power for industry and water for irrigation.

Grand Coulee has electric generators inside it. As the water goes through the dam it turns big paddle wheels, which turn the generators. The Grand Coulee Dam generates more electricity than any other dam in the world.

This dam is also a very important source of water for farmers. Most farmers in Washington do not have to worry about dry spells, because the water that is stored behind the Grand Coulee Dam is enough to cover ten thousand acres of land with a foot of water.

grand jury, people chosen to decide whether a person who has been accused of committing a crime should be tried in court. See the article on JURY.

Grand Rapids

Grand Rapids is an important city in the state of Michigan. It is on the Grand River and gets its name from the river rapids near the city. Grand Rapids is often called the furniture capital of America because the designing, manufacturing and selling of furniture is one of its main industries. Grand Rapids has a population of more than 197,000 people. Many of them work in various branches of the furniture business. Others work in plants that make metal and paper products, and in the shipping and packing businesses. The city was settled in 1877.

Grand Remonstrance

About three hundred years ago in England, during the reign of Charles I, there was a great struggle for power between the king and the Parliament. Charles thought that he should have sole power to rule the country, but Parliament was always getting in his way by passing legislation that he did not like, or refusing to give him money that he wanted.

From 1629 to 1640 Charles ruled without any Parliament. Then he formed a new one, which came to be called the Long Parliament because it lasted nearly twenty years. For a short time it did what Charles wanted, but then, in 1641, it passed a measure called the Grand Remonstrance, which set forth a list of things that the people considered very unfair. The king pretended to accept this measure, but he did not like it and tried to arrest five leaders of Parliament who had voted for the Grand Remonstrance. This made Parliament and the people so angry that it led to civil war in England, and Charles I was put to death.

Grange

The Grange is an organization of farmers that was founded in 1867 by a United States government clerk named Oliver H. Kelley. *Grange* is a word that had been used in England for many years; it means "farm." Kelley called his organization the National Grange of the Patrons of Husbandry, but soon everyone just called it the Grange. Kelley founded the Grange to try to help farmers learn more modern methods so that they could make better livings for themselves and their families. The movement spread very quickly, and by 1875 there were more than 800,000 Grangers in the Midwest. It became so strong that it was able to get laws passed for the farmers' benefit. These were called Granger laws, and they set rates that the railroads could charge for hauling produce.

The Grange continues to be very helpful to its members. Any adult member of a farm family may join, and there are special groups for children under 14. When there are problems to be solved, the members discuss them at meetings and sometimes send representatives to Congress to present their opinions and requests. There are lectures at the meetings, but there is fun too, with parties, dances, and picnics. Sometimes Grangers get together to buy things they all need,

such as feed or machinery, because it is cheaper to buy in large quantities. The Grange has members all over the United States, but it is strongest in New York, Pennsylvania, Ohio, New Jersey, and New England.

Grange, Red

Harold E. Grange was one of the greatest American football players. He was three times named an All-American, and is a member of most of the All-Time All-American teams that have been chosen. Many experts rank him second only to the late Jim Thorpe as a backfield star. Grange played under the famous coach Bob Zuppke at the University of Illinois in 1923, 1924, and 1925, and then left college to become a professional football player. He played until 1935 for the Chicago Bears and the New York Yankees, and has been elected to many all-time professional teams. Grange was nicknamed the "Galloping Ghost," and his number, 77, was famous throughout the country while he was playing. His greatest single game was played against Michigan in 1924. He scored four touchdowns in the first twelve minutes, on runs of 90, 60, 45 and 55 yards. Later in the same game he ran for one more touchdown, and passed for still another.

granite

Granite is a kind of very hard rock. It is usually gray, but there is also a great deal of red granite. Scientists believe that it was formed millions of years ago when the liquid rock of the earth's crust cooled and hardened. It is usually found deep under layers of other kinds of rock, but in many places it has been brought to the surface of the earth by the kind of terrific upheaval that created the mountains of the world long before man or animal life existed. Many mountains are almost solid granite. Thousands of years ago in Rome and Egypt granite was used for buildings and monuments. Granite takes a very high polish and is still used as a building stone by modern man.

ULYSSES S. GRANT

Ulysses Simpson Grant was the eighteenth President of the United States. He was the head of the Union, or northern, forces during the Civil War. There have been several American generals who became President, but Grant and Dwight D. Eisenhower are the only ones who were graduates of West Point. When Grant became supreme commander of the Union Army in March of 1864, the war had not been going well for the North. It was not until Grant assumed command that the tide turned definitely in favor of the Union. The war was won thirteen months later.

Even in his triumph, Grant was generous and considerate of the defeated Confederate forces. General Robert E. Lee, head of the Confederate Army, was treated with the utmost courtesy. The Confederate soldiers were allowed to keep their horses, instead of being forced to surrender them, because they "would be needed for spring plowing."

In the first presidential election after the Civil War was over, Grant was elected President by a large majority, in November, 1868. He was re-elected in 1872, again by a large majority. During his administration, there was a great deal of difficulty within the government. Some of the officials he appointed were not honest and used their government jobs to make money for themselves. This was done without Grant's knowledge, but it created a bad impression of the administration.

Ulysses Grant was a short, heavy-set man with a black beard. He was a stern military commander, but in private life he was gentle, kind, and extremely fair.

HIS EARLY YEARS

Ulysses Grant was born in Point Pleasant, Ohio, on April 27, 1822. His father was a farmer, and his mother's maiden name was Hannah Simpson. Although Grant was originally named Hiram Ulysses Grant, the registration office at West Point made a mistake, and entered his name on the academy's list of students as Ulysses Simpson Grant instead. He found it easier to change his name than to change West Point records. When he was twenty-one, he was graduated from West Point as a second lieutenant, with a commission in the regular army. Three years later, the war with Mexico broke out, and Grant was assigned to duty there. He received two promotions in recognition of his war service, and when peace came he was a captain. In 1848, when he was 26 years old, he married Miss Julia Dent of St. Louis, Missouri. He remained in the army as a captain until 1854, and at that time it seemed that there was not much prospect of a good future for him in the army. He resigned his commission and retired to civilian life in Galena, Illinois. He believed that he was through with the army for good. He tried farming, did a little real-estate operation, and worked

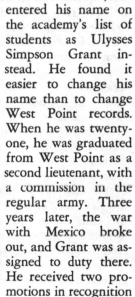

selling leather goods, without much success in anything.

GRANT AS A SOLDIER

When the Civil War started in 1861, Grant immediately offered his services to the government. He was ready to do anything that might be needed, and at which he could be useful. At that time no one knew of his great gifts of leadership, but his offer to serve was welcome. He was appointed colonel of the 21st Illinois Volunteer Regiment. He took whatever duty was given to him, and never tried to get any special favors or easy jobs. Grant never tried to build up his reputation by looking for publicity, but went about his work quietly and efficiently, doing his job well. In fact, Grant did it so well that President Lincoln very soon noticed what a capable officer and soldier he was and promoted him to brigadier general.

He commanded his troops in a long series of battles. At the battle of Belmont, Maryland, the horse on which Grant was riding was shot. Grant was unhurt, however. Shortly afterward he was sent to the Kentucky-Tennessee area to fight under General H. W. Halleck. Grant's forces took Fort Henry on the Tennessee River in the early part of February, 1862, and a few days later attacked Fort Donelson on the Cumberland River near Nashville, Tennessee. It was here that he made the famous speech that gave him the nickname of "Unconditional Surrender" Grant. The general defending Fort Donelson asked what terms Grant would give them, and Grant replied: "No terms other than an unconditional and immediate surrender can be accepted . . ." The capture of this fort was an important victory for the Union Army, and it was the beginning of General Grant's fame as a commander.

About two months after the capture of Fort Donelson, Grant was camped at Pittsburg Landing in the southern part of Tennessee, near the Mississippi border, on the west bank of the Tennessee River. The Confederates attacked him there, and he was slightly wounded in battle. It was not a severe wound, however, and it did not keep him out of the fight. He went on to the Battle of Shiloh, a few miles away, after his men had driven the Confederate army back. Victory at Shiloh gave the Union forces control as far south as Vicksburg, Mississippi. Vicksburg surrendered on July 4, 1863.

Grant's next important step was to attack the Confederate army in the Battle of Chattanooga, in eastern Tennessee. His victory there, in November, 1863, drove the Confederates out of the state.

By this time, Grant was a great public hero. Congress presented him with a special medal in recognition of his skill as a commander, and President Lincoln gave him full command of all the Union forces. On March 9, 1864, he took over his new responsibility, and the people of the country felt that the North could not lose the war with General Grant in command of the army.

General Grant conducted a long and bitter fight against the Confederate Army led by General Robert E. Lee, and it was not until April 9, 1865, that he was able to force the surrender of Lee at Appomattox Courthouse, Virginia.

HOW HE BECAME PRESIDENT

Grant was the hero of the day, and he was generally given credit for having won the war. For the next Presidental election, in 1868, the Republican party nominated him for President and the people elected him with a large majority of votes in his favor. The Democratic candidate that year was Horatio Seymour.

During his first years as President, Grant succeeded in convincing Congress that the South was being harshly treated in some respects. He was as popular as President as he had been as a general of the army. He succeeded in correcting some of the injustices that Johnson's Congress had voted into law. An important achievement was the Amnesty Bill, which gave back the civil rights of all people in the

South except a few Confederate leaders. The Fifteenth Amendment to the Constitution was ratified during his first two years in office. This was the amendment that gave all citizens the right to vote, regardless of whether they were white or Negro, or whether they had once been slaves.

President Grant also succeeded in reducing the national debt during his term of office. The cost of the Civil War had been high, and the country was deeply in debt when he became President. The public showed its appreciation of Grant's original administration by electing him for a second time in 1872, when he defeated Horace Greeley, the famous publisher and journalist.

HIS LATER YEARS

After his second term was over, Grant and his family made a trip around the world, visiting many foreign countries. People in foreign countries were not well acquainted with Americans at that time, and his trip did a great deal toward showing them what Americans were like. He was welcomed by the highest officials and rulers of every country he visited, and given the highest honors a visitor could receive.

When Grant returned to the United States at the end of the tour, an influential group of Republicans tried to nominate him for the Presidency for a third time, but there was then a very strong feeling against a third term for any President and he was not nominated.

Grant retired to private life and attempted to conduct a banking business in New York City, but he was unsuccessful. He did not have the kind of experience that is needed in banking, and also he was badly cheated by several people whom he had trusted. They took advantage of his fine name and great reputation in order to make fortunes for themselves. Soon he had lost all his money, and it was necessary to do something in order to provide for his family.

N.Y. Dept. of Parks

Grant's Tomb is a majestic monument to a great, courageous, and beloved figure.

When it became known that the great general and ex-President was poor, the entire country sympathized, and the sentiment was so strong that Congress introduced a bill to award him a pension of $5,000 a year. He asked to have the bill withdrawn, however, and Congress felt that it must do as he wished in this matter.

It was then that Grant started to write his personal life history, in which he included complete stories of all the battles in which he had taken part. He called it his "Personal Memoirs," and worked very hard to finish it. It was extremely difficult, because at this time he was in almost constant pain from cancer of the throat. He finished his book, however, and it is considered by many people to be one of the best military biographies ever written. It brought about half a million dollars to his family, although the general himself did not live to enjoy his painfully earned money. He died at Saratoga, New York, on July 23, 1885.

Grant's Tomb, on Riverside Drive at 123rd Street in New York City, is a famous monument. It is 150 feet high and 90 feet square. It was built by money contributed by the public, and cost $600,000. Grant's body was removed from the temporary tomb in which it had been placed and transferred to the monumental tomb where it remains. The transfer took place on April 17, 1897, twelve years after his death. The body of Mrs. Ulysses Grant was placed there also when she died.

MRS. ULYSSES S. GRANT

Julia Dent Grant was born in 1826, the daughter of Judge Frederick Dent, of St. Louis. She was married to Grant in August, 1848, and they had three sons and one daughter. Mrs. Grant outlived her husband by seventeen years. She died in 1902 and was buried in the same tomb as Grant, in New York City.

granulation

Granulation is making into grains. Ordinary table sugar is an example of a substance that has been granulated. When the sugar is taken from the sugar cane (or sugar beets), it is in the form of a very thick syrup. This heavy syrup is slowly heated and mixed, until all of the water is driven out of it. Then all that is left is the tiny white grains of sugar, which is the form in which we get it from the grocery store. We say that the sugar has been granulated.

Doctors often find a different kind of "grain," called a *granule,* on a wound or sore that has become infected and has begun to heal. The forming of these granules is also called granulation. The granules are made of capillaries (tiny blood vessels) and other parts of the flesh. Eventually they will form a scab.

grape

The grape is a fruit or, more exactly, a berry, that grows in bunches on a vine.

It is one of the oldest plants known to man and grows in almost every country in the world. It is one of the principal crops of France, Italy, Spain, Germany, and the United States, especially in California.

There are many different varieties of grape, but only a few dozen are widely grown. The most important species (kind) of grapes is the *vinifera* or Old World grape, and most of the grapes grown in the world are of this type. The second most important species of grape is called *labrusca* or New World grape. It can be recognized easily because unlike the Old World grape, its skin slips off easily but the seeds stick to the fleshy part. It is grown in many parts of America.

Grapes may be eaten fresh but some Old World varieties are dried first. Dried grapes are called *raisins* or *currants*. Grapes may also be used to make grape juice and wine. The most common grapes used for eating fresh are the yellow Thompson Seedless, the most important grape grown, the red Tokay, the Malaga, the Ribier, and the Muscat. The Thompson Seedless and the Muscat are also used for raisins, as are the tiny Black Corinth grapes. Wine is made from the Pinot, Riesling, Mission, Madeira and Muscat grapes, and grape juice from the Concord grape.

Grapes grow well where the winter is not too cold and where there is a long, warm summer that enables the plants to ripen their fruit slowly. This kind of climate is often found near lakes and oceans, and grapes may be planted on nearby hillsides. The soil must be fertile and care must be taken to keep insects and disease away. Grapevines must be carefully pruned each year and the vines are often grown on trellises or tied to stakes.

A good grapevine may live more than fifty years and will produce large quantities of grapes, the amount depending on the variety and where and how it is grown.

1. Dark purple grapes, sun-ripened on the vine, are being picked for shipment to fruit markets all over the United States.

2. Grapes raised on the rolling hills of California may also be allowed to dry in the sun. Then they become sweet raisins.

3. Many different beverages are made from grapes. Some are served in special glasses that best bring out their flavor.

Grapefruit tastes sharp and refreshing, and contains lots of healthful Vitamin C.

grapefruit

The grapefruit is a juicy, round, yellow fruit that belongs to the same family as lemons and oranges and limes. The grapefruit is one of the largest of the citrus fruits. The grapefruit gets its name because it grows in bunches, as grapes do, but it is many times larger than the grape. Most grapefruits weigh about four or five pounds. The grapefruit first grew in Asia, and the Spanish people began to grow grapefruit in the West Indies and Florida hundreds of years ago. Now people in California, Italy, and many tropical countries raise grapefruit.

People have discovered new ways to improve the grapefruit in the last fifty years. Now you can buy grapefruits that are much larger and have more juice, and do not have any seeds. Fifty years ago people had to use sugar on grapefruit, but now many grapefruits are sweet enough to eat without adding sugar. Some of them have a pink flesh that is especially sweet and juicy. The juice of the grapefruit is canned and frozen and is a very popular breakfast drink. See also the article CITRUS FRUITS.

graph

A graph is a special kind of picture that can give you a quick idea about different sets of numbers. There are several kinds of graphs, but the main purpose of all of them is to tell a story about numbers easily and clearly.

There are some things that all graphs have. A graph must have a title that tells what the graph explains. A graph must also have a scale, which is somewhat like a ruler.

The scale shows you in regular units of measurement the difference between the things that are being explained on the graph. Every good graph depends on accurate number facts. Sometimes number facts are called statistics. Only when the statistics are accurate, and have been written down in regular order in what is called a *table of numbers,* can you make a good graph. Sometimes a table of numbers has numbers that are too large or too uneven to be compared with each other easily. In these cases, the numbers must be rounded off. This means that they must be brought to the nearest even set of numbers that can be entered on the graph. For example, the number 104 might be made 100, or the number 489 might be rounded off to 500. In this way the figures can be shown in terms of hundreds, which make them easier to understand quickly. Because of this, however, a graph should never be taken as completely accurate. It is meant to give only an approximate idea about number facts.

LINE GRAPH

A line graph is a very good way to show what happens over a period of time. A line graph is drawn on paper that is marked with small squares. Suppose you wanted to show how the population of your town has grown in the last fifty

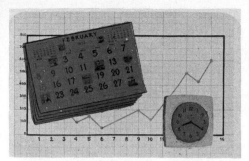

The main purpose of any line graph is to show what happens over a period of time.

years. Across the bottom of the graph, you would mark off the years. Each square might represent one year. Along the left side of the paper, up and down, you mark off the number of people. Each square might stand for one thousand people. Then, you would make dots on the graph to show how many people there were in your town in each year. When you connect the dots, you have a line that shows how the population has changed from year to year. When a person is sick, the nurse may make a line graph of his temperature. Then the doctor can see at a glance if the patient's fever went up or down.

CIRCLE GRAPH

A circle graph is another good way to tell a number story. Circle graphs are used to show the relation of the parts of a thing to the whole thing. For example, suppose you wanted to make a graph that shows how a family spends its money;

The circle graph shows the changing relationship between parts of a whole.

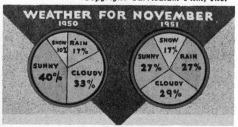

how much of the family income is spent for food, how much for clothes, how much for entertainment, and so on. You divide the circle into sections. Suppose the income is $5,000 and you divide the circle into 50 parts. Each section stands for $100. If the family spent $500 for food, you would mark off five parts to form a section representing food. Finally the circle would show, by the size of the sections, about how much your family spent for each thing.

PICTOGRAPH

A pictograph is very useful when you want to show things in round numbers. If you wanted to show how many children were enrolled in schools in the United States in 1960, you could make a picto-

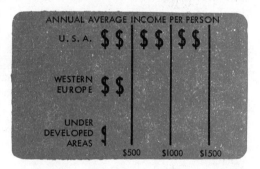

The pictograph uses symbols to dramatize statistics. The dollar signs contrast incomes of people in different places.

graph. On the graph you would place tiny pictures of children. Each picture would stand for one million children. If you placed three figures next to ages five to thirteen, you would know that three million children of those ages were enrolled in school in 1960. In a pictograph you have to count the symbols (the little figures) and multiply by the scale (each figure stands for one million children) to find out the number information.

BAR GRAPH

A bar graph, like a line graph, is made on paper with small squares on it. If you

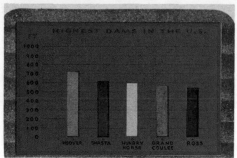

A bar graph makes it quite simple to measure by scale and to compare amounts.

wanted to show the number of workers in the factories in your town, you could make a bar graph. Across the bottom of the graph you make a scale of numbers that are rounded off. Then on the vertical lefthand side of the graph, you label the kinds of factory in your town, such as chemical and plastics and automobile factories. Then you can use your scale to mark the approximate number of men who work in each of these factories. A person who looks at the bar graph can tell, without having to measure, which kind of factory employs the most men. When you want to compare several number facts, a bar graph is a clear way to do it.

graphic arts

The graphic arts are the use of any kind of drawing, writing or printing to create something beautiful. The designing of beautiful books has come to be considered as much one of the graphic arts as ENGRAVING and LITHOGRAPHY, which were once considered the principal graphic arts. There are separate articles about these.

graphite

Graphite is a pure form of carbon. It is black or grayish black, soft and greasy, and it has a shine like a metal. Graphite is a good conductor of electricity and does not burn easily or melt even at high temperatures. Because of its resistance to great heat it is often used for *crucibles,* the vessels or pots in which metals are melted. It is very important as a lubricant and is often used where large flat surfaces must rub against each other. Locksmiths sometimes blow powdered graphite inside locks to lubricate them, instead of using light oil which dries out and becomes sticky. The black grease used to lubricate the gears of automobiles is often a mixture of heavy petroleum oil and powdered graphite. The pencils that most students use in school do not really contain lead but a mixture of clay and graphite. Soft pencils that write very black contain a larger amount of graphite than hard pencils. The more clay that is mixed with the graphite, the harder the pencil, and the lighter it writes. Graphite is dug out of the earth as are coal, iron, and other metals or minerals. It is mined in the states of Nevada, Michigan, Rhode Island, Alabama, and North Carolina in the United States, as well as in Great Britain, Europe, parts of South America, and Ceylon in southeast Asia.

graphology, the study of handwriting in the belief that it reveals something about the writer's character and personality: see the article on HANDWRITING.

grass

Grass is the most important family of plants in the world. There is hardly a place in the world where some form of grass does not grow. This family of plants has many members, ranging in size from the inch-high grass on your lawn to the tall stalks of bamboo that grow to be over a hundred feet high. Because it is such a varied family, it has many uses.

THE CEREALS

All cereals are grasses. Cereals include wheat, corn, rice, rye, oats, and barley. Most of the farmed land in the world is used for raising one or another of these cereals. They are used primarily for food, either for man or animals.

Grass has many uses. Animals graze in meadows; humans make foods from cereal grasses and enjoy relaxing or playing on grass-covered ground. Even the soil itself is helped by grass, which has complex roots that hold the earth together and prevent dangerous erosion.

Wheat is the most important single crop. It has been known to man for more than five thousand years, and he has grown it wherever he has gone. It is a fairly easy crop to grow, but without proper care it dies out in a few years. The main use of wheat is in making "the staff of life," or bread.

Rice has been almost as important a crop as wheat, and today it may feed even more people, for it is the chief cereal of India, all of East Asia, Japan, and the South Pacific islands including Indonesia; also it is a big crop in the United States.

Corn (that is, *maize* or *Indian corn*) is important in the Americas as a vegetable and grain for bread, but also as food for animals bred for meat. In England, "corn" means "wheat." It is believed that today's corn, or maize, has been refined over the centuries from a plant first found in North America and used by American Indians long ago. In some parts of North America it is used more than wheat.

Oats are not nearly as important as a cereal as they used to be. The main use of oats was to feed horses, but with the invention of gasoline and diesel engines, the number of work horses has greatly decreased. Oats are a very sturdy grain which will grow on fairly rocky soil where there is not too much sunshine. These qualities make oats very popular with people living in cool, rather barren places, such as Scotland. Oatmeal is considered the "national food" of Scotland. The usual yield of oats is 15 bushels per acre.

OTHER GRASSES

The kinds of grass that grow lower to the ground are valuable for feeding animals. These grasses do not include clover, which belongs to another family. Sometimes these grasses are used for fertilizer, when they are plowed under the ground.

Grass is also very important when used as hay. This is a dried grass that is used for food during the winter months when the animals cannot get green grass. The most important hay crop is a grass called alfalfa. Other grasses used in hay-making are timothy, wild hay, blue grass, and the stalks of the cereals after the grain has been removed.

There are many other uses for grass. Most of these other uses depend upon the particular qualities of the grasses and the region in which they are used. Bamboo is used in the southern Asiatic countries for making everything from houses to writing paper. Other grasses are used for weaving baskets and mats. There is almost no limit to the things that can be made of grass.

GRASS AS A DECORATION

The members of the grass family that we are most familiar with are the grasses that make our lawns and gardens beautiful.

There are many different kinds of lawn grass. Some are used for their color, while some are selected because of the soil to be used. The best way to find out what kind of grass to plant is to have the soil inspected by an agricultural expert. He will find out what kinds of grass may grow in your soil, and then you may se-lect the particular color you want. Some grasses are much more dense than others; some grow very tall, while some stay very close to the ground and never have to be cut at all. These things should be considered when choosing your grass.

There are two ways to plant a lawn. One way is to "seed" it. The grass seed is bought at a hardware or garden store. The ground is dug up and very carefully raked. Then the seeds are planted. Strips of burlap, or some other cloth, are placed over the seeded area to keep the birds from eating the seeds and to keep the rain from washing them away. If the lawn is carefully watered and not disturbed, in a few weeks the first blades of grass grow up through the burlap.

Another way to start a lawn is to buy strips of sod, or earth which has grass growing in it already. These strips of sod are placed on the ground, watered, and allowed to grow into the soil. This is a much surer way of growing a lawn, because the grass has already started growing and does not need as much care as the seeded lawn.

There are many things that can happen to a lawn to make it die, but usually if a lawn is well watered and taken care of, it will remain healthy. Sometimes a lawn will turn brown in spots. Usually this means that it has not been getting enough water. If careful watering does not make the brown spots turn green again, it is necessary to dig up the spots, rake them out, and either plant more seed or lay a piece of sod down.

When something happens to the lawn that you cannot seem to prevent, the best solution is to have an expert look at it. You may be doing something wrong, and the expert will be able to tell you how to correct it. Most garden stores have men who know all about lawns and can help you out.

grasshopper

The grasshopper is an insect that lives in almost every part of the world.

Am. Mus. of Nat. Hist.

The wingless grasshopper found in many southern states looks harmless enough, but does lots of damage when it sets out to eat its way through a crop.

It is a great jumper and with its strong back legs can hop very quickly from one place to another. When they are full-grown, grasshoppers have wings, and some kinds fly hundreds of miles in search of food. They travel in swarms, and in earlier times people reported flights of grasshoppers so huge that they blotted out the sun. Grasshoppers feed on all kinds of plant, and are a great pest to farmers because they destroy the crops. About eighty years ago, grasshoppers east of the Rocky Mountains, especially in the states of Kansas and Nebraska, destroyed hundreds of millions of dollars worth of grain. Farmers now have good ways of killing grasshoppers, mainly by spraying their crops with poisons.

There are many different kinds of grasshopper, but all of them belong to either of two main groups: those that have short feelers on top of their heads, and those that have long feelers. Grasshoppers make various kinds of sound. They do this by striking their wings together, or by rubbing their hind legs against their wings. The most common of all grasshoppers is the short-horned insect that makes a noise that sounds like a steady hum.

gravel

Gravel is made up of small pieces of rock. Some gravel is made by the action of rivers and oceans. This kind usually has pebbles that are round in shape because the waters of the rivers and oceans have tumbled them around and over each other for hundreds of centuries. The very tiny chips of stone that are knocked off by this action form the sand that is found on beaches and riverbanks.

A special kind of gravel that is not round is found in deposits in the earth, where it was formed in ancient times when ice covered large areas of the earth. This gravel is dug out in many of the northern states of the United States.

Gravel is very important because it is used in building roads and in making concrete. The United States produces about three hundred million tons of gravel every year.

gravitation or gravity

Everything in the world attracts every other thing in the world—that is, it pulls every other thing to it. This attraction is called *gravitation,* or "the force of gravity."

Larger things have a greater pull than smaller things. That is why we do not see such things as tables, chairs, stones, or other things coming together just because they are standing near each other. They are not large enough for us to notice their pull. The earth, sun, moon, and planets are constantly pulling on each

No matter where a person stands, gravitation pulls him toward the center of the earth. But the pull is stronger for an Eskimo near the North Pole than for a Chinese farther away from it.

other. The planets turn around the sun because the sun is larger than any of them and pulls them toward it.

The gravitational pull you are most familiar with is the pull of the earth on you. If you jump into the air, you will always come down again to the ground. The reason is that the earth is pulling you down. *Gravity* means "heaviness." Because the earth is so much larger than you are, its pull on you is much greater than your pull on it. When you stand on a scale, the earth pulls your body to the scale. The amount by which your body is pulled down is called your weight.

The earth acts somewhat as a magnet does with a piece of iron. It makes rivers and streams run downhill. The closer something is to the center of the earth, the more it will be pulled down, so the more it will weigh. If something weighs a thousand pounds on top of a mountain about 14,000 feet high, it will weigh one pound more if it is brought down to sea level.

The farther you are from the earth the less you will weigh. If you weigh 100 pounds on earth, you will weigh only 25 pounds 4,000 miles away. If you were on the moon, you would weigh only 17 pounds. The reason is that the moon is so much smaller than the earth, and pulls you down less than the earth does. If you were on the sun you would weigh almost 3,000 pounds, because gravity on the sun is much stronger than the earth's.

SPEED OF FALLING OBJECTS

Because gravity's pull is greater as a weight comes closer to the center of the earth, a falling body increases its speed as it falls. This increase in speed is called acceleration of gravity and it is constant, which means it is always the same. The rate of acceleration is *16 feet per second per second;* that is, at the end of every second the falling object is going 16 feet per second faster than it was at the end of the previous second.

Suppose a ball is dropped from a high place. At the moment that it is dropped, it is not falling at any speed. At the end of a second it is falling at the rate of 16 feet per second. At the end of two seconds it is falling at the rate of 32 feet per second; after three seconds at the rate of 48 feet; and so on. In the first second it will have fallen 8 feet; in the next second 24 feet, making 32 feet in all it has fallen; in the third second 40 feet, making 72 feet in all. Therefore the number of feet a falling object has traveled in a given number of seconds is the square of the number of seconds, times 8. An object that has fallen for four seconds has a speed of 64 feet per second and has fallen 128 feet (4^2 or $4 \times 4 = 16 \times 8 = 128$).

If a one-pound and a two-pound weight are dropped from the same height, the force of gravity is greater on the two-pound weight, but the two-pound weight is also pulling on the earth with a greater force than the one-pound weight. This cancels out the extra gravitational pull of the earth, and the weights fall with the same acceleration. The fact that things of different weight fall with the same acceleration was first proved by the Italian scientist Galileo, more than 350 years ago.

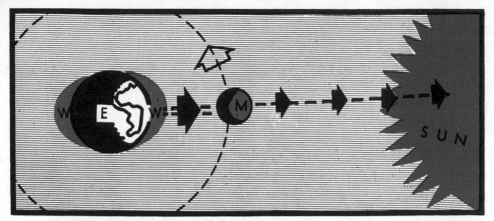

The gravitational attraction of the moon (*M*) causes every shore line (*W*) on earth (*E*) to have two high and two low tides daily. The moon attracts water facing it; at the same time it pulls the hard surface of the earth, thus causing a high-tide water bulge on the opposite side of the earth. Tides rise and fall as the earth spins. Twice a month the sun and moon combine their gravitational pulls to make a very high tide (as diagram shows).

The English scientist Sir Isaac Newton first explained the way gravitation works more than 250 years ago. His explanation is called the Law of Universal Gravitation. He discovered that the pull of the sun on the planets, and the pull of the earth on things on its surface, are alike and can be explained in the same way.

The law of gravitation says that the pull between two things depends on how large they are and how far apart they are. The larger they are, the greater the pull; the closer they are, the greater the pull. With the law of gravitation, many things can be explained. One of the most interesting is the rising and falling of the tides in the ocean. A tide is a movement of water in or out from the shore or beach. At high tide the water comes in toward the beach; at low tide it goes out from the beach. The law of gravitation tells us how this happens. The moon is constantly going around the earth, due to the earth's gravitational pull. But the

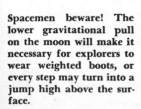

Spacemen beware! The lower gravitational pull on the moon will make it necessary for explorers to wear weighted boots, or every step may turn into a jump high above the surface.

moon is also pulling on the earth. It pulls on both the water and the land, but the water moves more easily than the land. The pulled-up water soon reaches the shore and makes a tide there. This is called high tide. When the moon has moved away from that part of the earth, the water settles back and we have low tide. The pull of the sun on the earth also causes tides.

Although Newton explained the way gravitation worked, he did not know how one body could pull another without touching it. This is called action at a distance. In 1916 the scientist Albert Einstein wrote a new explanation of gravity called the theory of relativity. He said that things did not pull on each other through a distance. The reason why a little body moves toward a heavy body, as do the planets toward the sun, is that the heavy body is in a downhill part of space. Because it is heavier it makes more of a dent in space than the lighter one. According to Einstein's theory, light would have to travel through these dents in space when it comes from the sun to the earth. This would cause it to be bent. In 1922, during an eclipse of the sun, scientists observed that light was bent, and

Standard Oil Co.

A gravity meter measures the pull of gravitation on substances beneath the earth's surface and so can show how much they weigh.

part of Einstein's theory was proved. Thirty years later Einstein published another theory in which he tried to explain other kinds of motion, such as movement of electricity and light, by gravitation.

Gray, Asa

Asa Gray was an American botanist who was born in New York in 1810. A botanist is a man who studies plant life, but Asa Gray did more than this. He wrote about his work so clearly that his books are still of great value. He became a professor of natural history at Harvard University, and became such an authority that the city in which he lived, Cambridge, Massachusetts, became a center for botanical study. He traveled a great deal and made friends everywhere. Charles Darwin was one of these friends. Gray died in 1888 after receiving many honors.

Gray, Elisha

Elisha Gray was an inventor with a sad story. He was born in Ohio in 1835, and he put himself through college by doing carpentry. His interest in electricity led him to make many inventions of telegraph equipment and appliances. He worked especially hard on a way of sending the human voice over wires from one place to another. When he succeeded, he went to the patent office in Washington to register this invention. But someone else had come there a few hours earlier with a similar invention; it was Alexander Graham Bell, and his invention was the telephone. Gray died in 1901.

Gray, Thomas

Thomas Gray was an English poet who lived about two hundred years ago. He was considered by some critics to be the greatest English poet of his century. He was born in 1716. His father was a cruel man, and finally Thomas's mother left him and supported her son by herself. She sent him to school and then helped

Left: Sightseers admire the view from a pleasure craft nosing its way through the waters of Australia's Great Barrier Reef. *Right:* Coral on the reef forms striking patterns.

him to travel to Europe. Gray was a very quiet and gentle man. He spent most of his life in Cambridge, England, where he went to school and later became professor of modern history. His most famous poem is the "Elegy Written in a Country Churchyard," but he also wrote many odes, and a number of poems that children like, such as the one about his favorite cat. Gray died in 1771. A famous story about the "Elegy Written in a Country Churchyard" is that the British commander James Wolfe recited the poem before the attack in which his army took the city of Quebec from the French. At the end of the poem Wolfe said to his men: "Gentlemen, I would rather have written those lines than take Quebec."

grayling

The grayling is a beautiful fish that lives in the cool rivers of Europe and Alaska, and in the waters of Montana and Michigan, in the United States. The grayling has a slender, gracefully curved

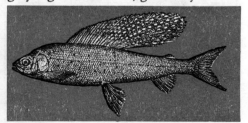

The grayling, an artful dodger of hooks and bait, challenges a fisherman's skill.

body and large fins. It is a bright blue, rose, and green color, though the graylings that are found in the United States are not as bright or as large as the European graylings. The American grayling weighs about two pounds, and the grayling of Europe weighs about four pounds. The grayling is a very lively fish. It has a small mouth, so it is difficult for fishermen to hook it. The meat of the grayling tastes very good, and people consider it a great delicacy.

greasewood

The greasewood is a plant that grows in the western part of the United States, where the soil is dry. The greasewood plant grows from four to eight feet tall, and it has deep roots that often reach far beneath the ground to buried streams. The greasewood can survive for very long periods without any rain at all. It has small, thick leaves that make a good food for cattle and sheep. The wood of the greasewood is hard and yellow. It is often used as firewood.

Great Barrier Reef

The Great Barrier Reef is the name of the largest coral reef in the world. A coral reef is built up by millions of tiny sea animals, and you can read about how it is formed in the article about CORAL. The Great Barrier Reef is off the northeastern coast of Australia, and it is more than 1,200 miles long. It ranges in width from less than one mile to several miles. At some places it is more than a hundred miles from the coast; at other places it may lie only ten miles from the coast. The Great Barrier Reef has rocky ridges that rise sharply from extremely deep waters. It is very dangerous to ships during a storm, because they may be blown onto the reef and break apart and sink. If a ship is able to pass into the water that lies between the reef and the mainland, it is then protected from the high waves and winds of the open ocean.

Great Basin

The Great Basin is a large area in the United States covering most of the state of Nevada and parts of the neighboring states of Utah, Idaho, Oregon and California. It is shaped like a triangle and is called the Great Basin because it has no rivers flowing out of it. It is rimmed by the Sierra Nevada Mountains on the west side and by the Wasatch Range of the Rocky Mountains on the east. In the Basin are mountains 5,000 to 7,000 feet high, and hundreds of broken ridges, some of which are 12,000 feet high. Death Valley, the lowest place in North America, is in the Great Basin, as are the Great Salt Lake, near which the settlers called Mormons built homes, and the Mohave and Carson Deserts.

The climate is dry and few plants grow, but the Great Basin has rich mineral deposits. Many thousands of years ago, two great lakes called Bonneville and Lahotan covered most of the northern part of the Basin. The Great Basin was named by the explorer John Frémont.

Great Bear Lake

The Great Bear Lake is in northwestern Canada, near the Arctic Circle. It is 12,000 square miles in area. It is frozen over most of the year, and ships can sail there for a few weeks in August and September only. Pitchblende, an ore

from which uranium and radium are taken, was discovered there in large amounts in 1930, and the largest town on the lake was named Port Radium.

Great Britain

Great Britain is one of the British Isles and by far the largest one. It has 88,619 square miles. Historically this is divided into England in the south (51,-356 square miles), Scotland in the north (29,794 square miles), and Wales in a small southwestern section (7,469 square miles). From 1707 until 1927 Great Britain was the official name of the country that included these three sections of the island and that ruled the tremendous British Empire. Since 1927 ,the official name has been the United Kingdom of Great Britain and Northern Ireland. In speaking of either Great Britain or the United Kingdom, people ordinarily use simply the name Britain or the name England, which for two thousand years has been the most important of the British countries. The history of Great Britain is usually called English history, and you can read about it in the article ENGLAND.

Great Circle

A great circle is the largest circle that can be drawn around a sphere or any ball-shaped object. The equator, the imaginary line that runs around the "center" of the earth, is a great circle. Every point on a great circle is exactly the same distance from the center of the sphere.

The great circle is extremely important in navigation. Though it is the longest line that can be drawn around a sphere, it is the shortest distance between any two points on the sphere. A navigator wanting to get from one place to another on a ship finds the great circle that runs through both of those points and follows that as his course.

Some great circles are already drawn on the globe so that you do not have to imagine them. The circles passing through the North and South Poles, called *meridians,* are great circles.

There are other circles that are drawn around the globe, passing through the meridians. These are called *parallels.* The equator is the only parallel that is a great circle.

In certain places a ship cannot follow a great-circle course because it may lead over land or into dangerous waters. In that case, it follows a course as close to a great circle as possible. This is called a *composite course* and is the one used by most ships.

Airplanes are usually able to follow a great-circle course without too much trouble. In flying from the United States to China, airplanes may soon be able to follow a great-circle course over the North Pole instead of flying over the Pacific Ocean. This great-circle course is really the shortest way, though it looks longer on a flat map.

Great Commoner

The Great Commoner was a name first given to William Pitt, who was Prime Minister of England about two hundred years ago. Before Pitt's time, most of the leaders of England had come

Mrs. Ada Carliss

Their strength makes great Danes dangerous enemies and very useful watchdogs.

from the House of Lords and were of noble birth. Pitt was called a "commoner" because he was a member of the House of Commons, or the elected body of the English Parliament, the lawmaking body of Great Britain. There is a separate article about William PITT.

William Jennings BRYAN, an American, was also called the Great Commoner. There is a separate article about him.

great Dane

A great Dane is a giant among dogs. It is one of the largest and most powerful breeds of dog in the world. Strangely enough, it did not come from Denmark but from Germany. The hunters who lived in Germany about four hundred years ago wanted a powerful, brave dog that had the strength and courage to hunt wild boars—the most dangerous of all game animals in Europe. The great Dane was developed for that purpose, and it proved to be everything that the hunters had wanted in a dog. Today in both Europe and America great Danes are kept as watchdogs, as pets, and for hunting. They are good pets because they are usually gentle and affectionate.

A great Dane stands about 20 to 24 inches high at the shoulders, and usually weighs between 95 and 120 pounds. The most common color is light tan, but great Danes are sometimes also black, brindled (light tan with narrow black stripes), and white with black patches. Its coat is smooth and short and its tail is long and thin. Its ears are long, but some owners clip the ears to make them stand up in sharp little points. The great Dane has a large, noble-looking head, and a squarish muzzle.

Great Eastern

The *Great Eastern* was one of the most famous steamships ever built, and the largest of its time. It was called the "Great Iron Ship," and it was planned to be a luxury ocean liner; but from the day it was launched in 1858 until it was finally abandoned thirty years later, it had one misfortune after another. Men were killed in building it, it was damaged by storms at sea, and its owners lost great sums of money on it. The *Great Eastern* was almost 700 feet long, driven by sails, paddles (like the Mississippi river boats), and screws (under-water propellers such as modern steamships have). After its failure as a passenger ship, it was used for cable-laying and was the ship that laid the successful Atlantic cable, which you can read about in the article CABLE.

Great Lakes

The Great Lakes are a group of five large lakes in the central part of North America, between Canada and the United States. Ever since they were discovered by French traders nearly three hundred years ago, they have been very important to the commerce and trade of North America. Iron ore, coal, wheat and other foods are among the products carried in ships on the Great Lakes.

Vast quantities of goods are carried across the Great Lakes. The canal at Sault Ste. Marie carries more tonnage in a year than the Suez and Panama canals combined.

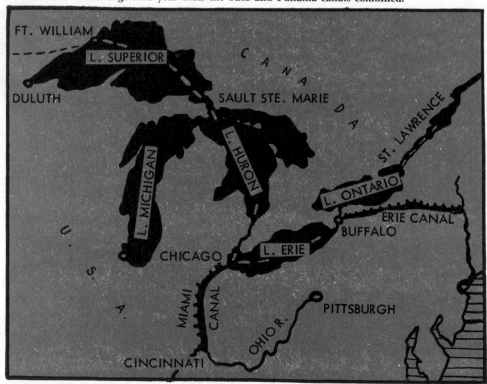

The Great Lakes are the largest group of lakes in the world. They are Lake Superior, Lake Michigan, Lake Huron, Lake Erie, and Lake Ontario. Some people remember these names by remembering that their initials spell the word HOMES. Lake Michigan is the only one that lies entirely within the United States; all of the others are partly in the United States and partly in Canada. On the Canadian side, all the great lakes are in the province of Ontario. The most important Canadian lake port is Toronto. On the American side the Great Lakes stretch all the way from Minnesota to New York. The most important ports are Duluth, Minnesota; Milwaukee, Wisconsin; Detroit, Michigan; Chicago, Illinois; Toledo and Cleveland, Ohio; Erie, Pennsylvania; and Buffalo, New York.

The total area of the Great Lakes is about 94,000 square miles, nearly as large as the state of Oregon. Lake Superior is the largest. It has an area of 31,820 square miles, about the size of North Carolina. Lake Ontario, with an area of 7,540 square miles, which is about the area of New Jersey, is the smallest.

The Great Lakes are all connected with each other, so that boats can travel all the way from Lake Superior in the west to Lake Ontario in the east. Some of the natural connections between the lakes were too shallow or too rough for ships to travel, so deeper channels or canals were built. The Sault Ste. Marie Canal connects Lake Superior to Lake Michigan and Lake Huron. Nearly all of the iron ore from the great Mesabi Range in Minnesota is shipped through this canal and across the Great Lakes to the steel mills of Indiana, Ohio, and Pennsylvania. Lake Erie and Lake Ontario are connected by the great Welland Ship Canal, which by-passes Niagara Falls. The first of the Great Lakes canals was the ERIE CANAL, about which there is a separate article. It was built in 1825, to connect Lake Erie with the Hudson River. The Great Lakes are connected to the Mississippi River and the Gulf of Mexico in the south through the Chicago-Illinois River Canal.

The Great Lakes are connected with the Atlantic by the St. Lawrence Seaway. The Seaway makes it possible for sea-going ships from all parts of the world to sail all the way inland as far as Duluth, Minnesota. It was created by deepening the passageway from Lake Superior to the Atlantic. The work, a joint project of the United States and Canada, took five years and was completed in 1959.

From April to December there is heavy traffic on the Great Lakes. After that ice forms and navigation of any kind becomes impossible.

There are many summer resorts on the Great Lakes. The greatest inland naval training center in the world, the Great Lakes Naval Training Center of the United States Navy, is on the Illinois side of Lake Michigan, north of Chicago.

Great Plains

In the western half of the United States is a great stretch of level, treeless, grassy land that is known as the Great Plains. The Great Plains run from the Rocky Mountains in the west to the Missouri Valley in the east, and from Canada in the north to Texas in the south. Parts of ten states are in the Great Plains: Texas, North Dakota, South Dakota, Nebraska, Kansas, Oklahoma, Colorado, New Mexico, Wyoming, and Montana. Before the white men came, this area was the home of many American Indian tribes that came to be called the PLAINS INDIANS. You can read about them in a separate article. There are a few rivers flowing eastward through the Great Plains, but there are not enough to irrigate the entire section, and therefore the Plains farmers depend a good deal on rain. When the summers are very dry, the wheat is very low.

The grazing lands of the Great Plains is called the *range*. This is a word that has been made famous in many American

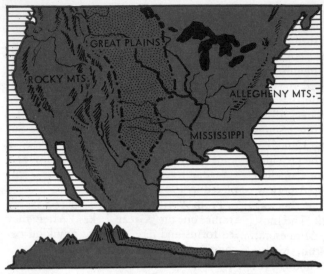

Left: **Much of the wheat and cattle in the United States come from the Great Plains. The dotted part of the section-through shows how the plains rise gently until they suddenly end in the great peaks of the Rocky Mountains.** *Right:* **The tough pioneer shown in this old picture crossed the Great Plains to the Rockies, where he trapped the plentiful game.**

cowboy songs such as "Home on the Range." On the range the cowboys live and work and have their rodeos, where they ride bucking broncos and rope wild steers.

During the days of the pioneers, more than a hundred years ago, people crossed the Great Plains in covered wagons looking for places to settle and build their homes. They traveled for months over

the flat, treeless country, enduring many hardships. Often they could not find water to drink. In summer they had no protection or shade from the burning sun, since there are no trees on the Great Plains. They were frequently attacked by bands of wild Indians. But the pioneers were brave people, and they kept on going until they found places to build their homes.

Great Pyrenees

The Great Pyrenees is one of the largest dogs in the world. It is a very old breed of working dog that has been known in Europe for nearly four thousand years. It is still used to pull sleds and dog-carts in Europe, to guard flocks of sheep, and as a watchdog in general. Long ago the shepherds of the Pyrenees Mountains, between France and Spain, had a saying that one Great Pyrenees was worth two men as protectors of a flock.

Few wild beasts dare to attack sheep guarded by a Great Pyrenees.

E. V. Crane

The Great Pyrenees has been called a "mat dog" because of its habit of curling up like a door mat outside its owner's home.

Great Pyrenees do not mind the cold, even in midwinter, because their coats are extremely thick and heavy. They stand about 27 to 32 inches high at the shoulders and weigh about 100 to 125 pounds. They are always white. They are shaggy-looking dogs and very much resemble St. Bernards in general size and shape.

Great Salt Lake

The Great Salt Lake is a shallow lake in Utah, near Salt Lake City. It is all that is left of an ancient inland sea called Bonneville Lake that gradually dried up. The lake varies in size from year to year, but it averages about 75 miles long and 50 miles wide, and its average depth is about 12 feet. The water of Great Salt Lake is more than five times as salty as ocean water; it is so salty that only one kind of animal, a small shrimp, can live in it. This is because the lake has no outlet, and as the water dries up, the salt is left behind. Because of its saltiness it is almost impossible for a swimmer to sink. This is one of the reasons that the summer resort of Saltair, on the northeast shore of the lake, is so popular. On the west side of the lake are flat, salt wastelands called Bonneville Flats, where many auto races take place. These flats are like a great beach made of salt instead of sand. The salt in the Great Salt Lake is extracted from the water and used in industry.

Great Slave Lake

Great Slave Lake is one of the largest lakes in all of North America. It is in the Mackenzie District of the Northwest Territories of Canada, and it lies in a beautiful forest. Great Slave Lake is more than 11,000 square miles in area, or 1,000 square miles larger than Lake Erie. The two chief rivers that flow into Great Slave Lake are the Hay and the Slave Rivers. It is drained by the Mackenzie River at its west end. The lake is frozen over for nearly eight months of the year. From July to October, when the ice has melted, the great logs that have been chopped down by lumberjacks in the forests around the lake are floated down to the Mackenzie River. Then they are taken to sawmills, where they are cut into lumber. Great Slave Lake is a favorite spot for fishermen and for hunters and trappers of fur-bearing animals.

Great Smoky Mountains

The Great Smoky Mountains are a part of the North American range called the Appalachian Mountains. They lie on the border between North Carolina and Tennessee. The Great Smoky Mountains get their name from the fact that their peaks are usually hidden in a cloud mist. They are among the highest of all the Appalachian range. The highest peak of the Great Smoky Mountains is Clingmans Dome, which rises 6,642 feet. Part of the Great Smoky Mountains is a national park that is run by the United States government. It was established in 1930. More than one hundred kinds of tree grow on the Great Smoky Mountains. There is fishing for trout in the mountain streams and hiking along part of the famous Appalachian Trail. There are museums in which there are relics of the early pioneer days and of the Indians.

Great Wall of China

The Great Wall of China was a high wall of earth and stone that stretched from the northeastern coast of China on the Yellow Sea to the high mountains in the west. It was more than 1,500 miles long, and so wide that columns of soldiers could march on its top as if on an elevated highway.

The Chinese built most of the Great Wall during the reign of the powerful Chinese emperor, Shih Huang-ti, more than 2,500 years ago. He ordered the wall built to keep out the fierce horseback-riding tribesmen who were invading his country from the north. It was about 25 feet high, and every 200 to 300 yards there were towers as high as 40 feet. In these towers sentries were stationed. For many years this barrier kept the invaders from entering China. About seven hundred years ago, however, most of the tribes of the north had been united under the leadership of a great warrior named Genghis Khan. He was able to break through the wall with his army and soon conquered most of China. A large part of the Great Wall of China is still standing.

grebe

The grebe is an unusual bird that lives in many parts of Europe, the United States, and South America. Grebes are water birds, and they are excellent divers, but they are not strong flyers. Their legs are set far back on their bodies, so that they can dive swiftly and well. The grebe has webbed feet, short, rounded wings, and almost no tail. It is usually brown with a shiny white underpart. One of the kinds of grebe found in the United States has a long, slender neck. This bird builds a very strange nest. It gathers clumps of waterweeds and floats these on a lagoon or some sheltered body of water, and on this clump the female lays its white eggs. Then the parent birds cover the eggs with more weeds until they are hidden. The heat of the decaying weeds keeps the eggs warm until they are

Walt Disney, Inc.
A grebe builds its own houseboat, floating its waterweed nest in a quiet lagoon.

ready to hatch. The young birds come out of the shell covered with downy feathers, and they are striped with black and brown and white colors. The parent grebe will often carry the young bird on its back. When the parent senses danger, it will tuck the baby under its wing and dive beneath the water. During the mating season, the grebe grows a special tuft of feathers, and performs many complicated ceremonies. People use the feathers of grebes to decorate hats.

Greco, El

El Greco, which means "The Greek," was a great painter who lived more than three hundred years ago. His real name was Kyriakos Theotokopoulos.

El Greco was born on the Greek island of Crete, probably in 1541. He went to Venice to study painting with the great artist Titian. After studying there for a few years he went to Spain in 1577 and stayed there until his death, in 1614.

El Greco's paintings look as modern as if they had been painted yesterday. All of the figures are very long and thin, as if they had been made in modeling clay and stretched. One of his most famous paintings is called *Toledo.* It is a scene from a hillside, with the Spanish city of Toledo in the distance and dark thunderclouds overhead. He also did two paintings called *St. Jerome as Cardinal.* In them St. Jerome has a small, thin head and a long, straggly beard, and he wears a heavy pink robe that weighs down his shoulders. One of them is in the National Gallery in London, in England, and the other is in the Frick Collection, in New York City.

There are several paintings by El Greco in the United States, including a beautiful picture of St. Francis in the museum at Detroit, Michigan.

Greece

Greece

Greece is a country in the southeastern part of Europe. It is a peninsula, that is, it is surrounded on three sides by water. It sticks out into the eastern end of the Mediterranean Sea, and there is another small sea that extends up the eastern shore of Greece, between Greece and Turkey, called the Aegean Sea. The Aegean Sea is almost like a bay of the Mediterranean. The area of Greece is about 51,000 square miles, which is about the size of Alabama, but more than 8,000,000 people live there, which is more than twice as many people as there are in Alabama. Greece has been torn by wars and poverty for many years. The people of Greece have always been artistic, beauty-loving, and warmhearted. Thousands of years ago, Greek architects and sculptors created masterpieces that have endured to modern times and have been an inspiration to artists for centuries. Greece is one of the oldest countries in the world. Greek civilization began more than three thousand years ago.

THE PEOPLE WHO LIVE THERE

The people of Greece are descended from ancient peoples who settled the land at least five thousand years ago. Although many invaders have entered Greece, and groups of them remained, the people who live there now are almost the same as those original Greeks of ancient days. They speak a similar language, and they still have the same type of features and general appearance.

Most Greeks have black hair, and they usually have what people call "olive" complexions. That is, their skin is rather dark, not pink-and-white the way the skin of English people often is. They are friendly people, and hospitable to travelers. If you should travel through the countryside, you would often be invited into the homes of farmers along the way to have a bite to eat and a glass of goat's milk.

HOW THE PEOPLE LIVE

Most of the people of Greece live in small villages and farming communities. There are only a few large cities in the entire country. Athens, Piraeus, and Salonika are the largest cities, and they seem very much like any large city in the United States or Canada. Athens and Piraeus are in the eastern central part, and Salonika is in the northeast.

Until recent years Greece had few modern conveniences. There is very little coal in the country, and coal used to be needed for nearly all electric-power plants. There were few paved roads, and travel inside the country was by donkey cart or on horseback. Since World War II, the Greeks have built several hydroelectric plants (which use water stored behind dams to turn electric generators).

Ewing Galloway

Athens, the capital of Greece, is a city of contrasts. Scattered among modern buildings are ancient ruins 2,400 to 3,000 years old. Mount Lycabettus in the distance is 909 feet high.

Ewing Galloway

Piraeus is the chief harbor in Greece. Vessels of all sizes leave here with goods that are destined for every country in the world. Piraeus is also the most important Greek manufacturing city.

Now most places, even the villages, have electricity. Telephone and telegraph lines connect all parts of the country. Railroads connect all the cities except in the northwestern region, and many of the roads have been paved.

Most of the people make their living by farming, raising sheep, and quarrying marble. There is not much rain in most parts of the country, and sheep need less food and water than cows. The favorite meat of the Greek people is lamb, and the fleece of the animals provides wool for clothing.

Although the soil is poor, and there is very little rain, the farms of Greece produce enormous quantities of food. In the south there are all kinds of fruit and tobacco, grapes for wine, and olives. Greek olives and Greek olive oil are shipped all over the world. The farms of the northern part of Greece grow cereal grains and produce large quantities of wheat, barley, and maize. Greece also exports textiles, iron, copper, zinc, lead, and other minerals.

The Greeks have been seafaring men for thousands of years, and today Greece's merchant marine is one of the largest in the world and many of the men earn their livings as seamen.

Most village life centers around the church. The people are Christians, members of the Greek Orthodox Church. Whenever there is an important event in a village, you will find the people gathered around the church. It is the center of their social as well as their religious life.

All children must go to school from the time they are six until they are twelve, even if they live in the very smallest of towns. After the age of twelve, they no longer go to school, but they can attend schools in the larger cities and towns if they want to. For many hundreds of years, Greek children did not have to go to school, and most people could neither read nor write. Today, however, four out of five people are literate (can read and write).

WHAT KIND OF PLACE IT IS

There are a great many mountains in Greece. Some are over 9,000 feet high. The most famous mountain is Mount Olympus in the northeast part of the country. The ancient Greek gods were supposed to live on Mount Olympus.

Greece has many rivers, but they are often too shallow for navigation. Many of the rivers in the southern part of the country are so shallow that in summer they dry up completely. There are many small lakes in the northern part.

Greece includes many islands in the seas that surround the peninsula. There is one large island, Crete, off the southeast coast. There are other island groups that are part of Greece in the Aegean Sea (the Dodecanese), others in the Mediterranean Sea, off the west coast (the Ionians), and still others around the southern tip of Greece, in the Aegean (the Cyclades, Lesbos, Samos, and Khios).

The mainland of Greece is divided by a natural channel called the Gulf of Corinth. The northern part of Greece is separated from the southern part (which is also called the Peloponnesus) except for a narrow strip of land called the Isthmus of Corinth.

Greece has a climate very much like that of other Mediterranean countries. Near the seashore the weather is mild, with very little snow or frost. In the mountains, the winters are long and cold.

About one-fifth of the land is covered with forests. There are pines, firs, and oaks, and the lumbering business produces resins and turpentine for export as well as for use in the country itself.

HOW THE PEOPLE ARE GOVERNED

Greece is a constitutional monarchy. The king is head of the country but a parliament (the House of Deputies, with 300 members elected by the people) makes the laws and a premier is head of the government. In 1964 a young king, 24-year-old Constantine, succeeded his father, King Paul. In 1965 Constantine disagreed with the premier, George Papandreou, leading to some riots by Papandreou's supporters, but the king won.

All adults may vote in Greek elections, including women since 1953.

In tiny Greek villages hidden away in the mountains many people still live much as their ancestors did centuries ago.

Ewing Galloway

Monks on Mount Athos, the chief center of Greek monasteries, prepare to sound a bell, calling all to prayer.

Ewing Galloway

CHIEF CITIES OF GREECE

The leading cities of Greece, with 1961 populations, are:

Athens, population 627,564 (with suburbs, 1,688,832), the capital and largest city.

Salonika, population 373,635, the second-largest city, in the northeast.

Piraeus, population 183,877, the third-largest city, often considered part of Greater Athens.

GREECE IN THE PAST

The history of Greece goes back for thousands of years. The earliest recorded history of Greece starts in 776 B.C., and the highest point in ancient Greek civilization came in about 450 B.C. After that, the expanding Roman Empire overshadowed Greece, and it finally became almost a minor Roman colony, or province. Greece was a part of the Roman Empire until the time of the Crusades in the 13th century. Then the Turks started their campaign to conquer smaller countries. By the beginning of the 1400s, Greece had been conquered by the invading Turks and remained under Turkish control for nearly four hundred years. Then a strong patriotism rose up in Greece, and in 1821 a revolution started, very much in the same way that the American Revolution had started. England and France helped Greece to throw off the Turkish rule, and the war was over in 1829. Greece was once again a free country, and at that time the people decided they wanted to be ruled by a king. They did not surrender their love of personal liberty, and in 1844 they made the king agree to a constitution.

In the 1890s and early 1900s, Greece fought in the Balkan Wars (see the article on BALKANS) and won more territory. In World War I, from 1914 to 1918, Greece was on the side of the Allies (Great Britain, France, Russia, and later the United States), but there was not much fighting in Greece.

During World War II, Greece tried to remain neutral but the Italians invaded Greek territory. The Greeks fought with bravery that all the free world admired, but when the mighty German army joined the fight against Greece the Greeks were helpless. Their country was occupied by German troops until the end of the war.

After the war, Greece found itself surrounded by countries that had come under the control of Russia and were ruled

The shaded section of the map shows the great empire conquered by the Greek soldiers of Alexander the Great. They brought civilization to the "outposts" of the old world.

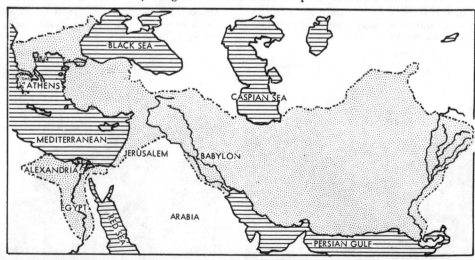

1. A Greek shepherd stands with his flock at the foot of Mount Olympus, in ancient Greek religion the home of the gods.

2. Many Greek peasant women still bake bread in large outdoor ovens.

3. Greek women show that they can use their heads after picking grapes.

4. A devout monk sitting under a grape arbor watches the quiet hillside.

5. No noisy traffic disturbs Greek country girls spinning wool behind their house.

by Communist governments. These countries tried to cause a revolution in Greece, but they were unsuccessful. The United States helped the Greek government with supplies and money, and by sending Army officers to advise the Greek Army.

In 1952 Greece joined the North Atlantic Treaty Organization (NATO), and in 1954 Greece, Turkey, and Yugoslavia formed a military alliance. From 1955 to 1959, however, relations with Turkey, and with the United States and Britain, were strained when Greek Cypriots on Cyprus, a British colony, demanded union with Greece and fought a guerrilla war. Peace was restored in 1959 and Cyprus was made a republic.

ANCIENT GREECE

The history of Greece goes back a very long time. There were civilized people and big cities there more than 2,500 years ago, long before there were any cities or civilized people in North America. At that time the Greeks did not have a single government, as a single nation. Instead they lived in separate city-states. A city-state was like a little country controlled by one powerful city. Each had its own kind of government, its own laws, and its own army. Sometimes one city-state would make war on another and conquer its people. In this way some city-states grew large and powerful. The Greek city-states also grew by sending out groups of pioneers to form settlements in new places. These new settlements were called colonies, and they were supposed to help their mother cities in war and in trading with other people; but sometimes a colony would revolt from its mother city and become independent. Greek colonies were started in places all around the Mediterranean Sea, and some grew into large and important city-states themselves. After a time there were Greek cities not only in Greece and on many islands in the Aegean Sea, but in Asia Minor (that part of Asia that is now Turkey) and in the lands we now call Sicily, Italy, southern France, and Spain. However, the two richest and strongest Greek city-states, Athens and Sparta, were on the Greek peninsula, the main part of the land we call Greece today. There are separate articles on ATHENS and SPARTA in other volumes of this encyclopedia.

WHAT THE CITIES WERE LIKE

The early Greeks lived in low houses made of mud brick. Most of the houses had no outside windows, and there was nothing along most of the streets but blank walls. The streets themselves were just wide enough for two or three people to walk between the houses. After a rain the streets would be full of mud, because there was no pavement. But the houses were very pleasant inside. They were built with their rooms arranged around courtyards open to the light and air. Most houses were only one story high, but the biggest had two stories and several courtyards, one leading into another. Often there would be one courtyard for the men and boys of a family and another one for the women and girls.

The public buildings in a Greek city were large and beautiful. Most of them were temples to the gods. The Greeks worshiped many different gods, as you can read in the article on MYTHOLOGY. The articles on ATHENS and ACROPOLIS tell more about the Greek temples. Nearly every city had an acropolis, or fortified hill, to which all the people could go if they were attacked by an enemy.

Another kind of public building that you would have found in an ancient Greek city or near it was the open-air theater. The Greeks would build a theater by putting a stage at the bottom of a narrow valley and arranging stone benches in circles on hillsides surrounding the stage. The Greeks loved to go to their theaters to watch stage plays. At Athens the people held a big contest every year for authors and actors, and all the men of the city would spend several days watching and judging the plays. The winners of the contest would get valuable prizes and become famous all over Greece. AESCHYLUS, SOPHOCLES, EURIPIDES, and ARISTOPHANES were authors of prize-winning plays, which many people today think are some of the greatest plays ever written. You can read about these authors in separate articles.

In every Greek city you would have found a public market place, called the *agora,* where the people bought all the things they needed in daily life. Around the sides of the agora, which was a big open area, there were booths where craftsmen sold their wares and farmers from the countryside brought their produce. Here the citizens would come to meet their friends and to gossip, as well as to buy and sell. The agora was one of the most important places in an ancient Greek city, for it partly took the place of newspapers, radio, and television in our modern world. In the agora, an ancient Greek could hear the latest news or exchange opinions with his neighbors about political affairs.

ANCIENT GREEK ATHLETICS

The Greeks loved athletic contests of all sorts. Every four years the best athletes from all the city-states would meet at a place in southern Greece called Olympia. There the athletes competed against each other in many different kinds of contests. Today we call these contests the Olympic Games. The athletes who won in the Olympic Games were treated like heroes in their home cities. The Greeks considered the Olympic Games so important that they measured time in four-year periods between Olympic Games. They called these periods *Olympiads,* and they would say that something happened in the first year of the tenth Olympiad, or the second year of the eleventh Olympiad, and so on.

PHILOSOPHY, SCIENCE, AND LEARNING

Ancient Greece was the center of science and learning. Greek thinkers were the first to solve many of the mysteries of such sciences as mathematics, physics, and natural history. There is a separate article about the GREEK LANGUAGE AND LITERATURE, which in some ways has not been surpassed in 2,500 years. ARCHIMEDES, EUCLID, SOCRATES, PLATO, and ARISTOTLE are among the early Greeks whose wisdom gave the world much of what it knows today.

ANCIENT GREEK WARS

The ancient Greeks fought many wars. Sometimes the city-states fought among themselves, but the most bitter battles were against the Persians. Persia was then a great empire in Asia Minor, the territory across the Sea of Marmara and the narrow straits. Two great Persian kings, first Darius and later Xerxes, tried to conquer Greece but both failed. The Greeks are still proud to remember the battles of MARATHON and THERMOPOLAE, about which there are separate articles.

There is also a separate article about ALEXANDER THE GREAT, who spread the great learning and civilization of Greece to Asia and northern Africa. Alexander was a king of Macedon, a Greek country that had become so strong that it ruled all of Greece in the year 337 B.C. (about 2,200 years ago), when Alexander became king. Alexander set out to "conquer the world" and almost succeeded. Wherever his armies went, they taught the people Greek ways.

Less than two hundred years later, the Roman empire and not Greece had become the most powerful nation on earth. The Greeks were conquered by the Romans, and became a colony of Rome. Many of the best-educated men in Greece were captured in warfare and became slaves of the Romans. Yet in the long

1

Ewing Galloway

Remains of the great Greek past:

1. A sculpture of the Greek goddess Athena.
2. The medieval section of Athens.
3. An old Greek wine pitcher in the form of a head.
4. The temple of Victory, a great classic building.
5. The Academy in Athens where Plato taught.
6. A pair of silver bracelets ending in lion's heads, which were made in the 5th century B.C.

Royal Greek Embassy Photos

2

5

Metropolitan Museum of Art

3

6

Ewing Galloway

1. A ruined theater at the foot of the Acropolis. The magnificent Parthenon is on top of the hill.

2. An ancient Greek vase showing a battle scene.

3. Pillars carved of marble 2,300 years ago to represent servants of the gods watching over Athens.

4. The Erechtheum, temple of the chief gods of Athens, one of the world's most beautiful buildings.

T.W.A.

run Greece "won" over the Romans. They taught the Romans their skill in art and literature. When Rome fell to Germanic invaders, about 1,500 years ago, the capital of the Roman Empire moved to Greece and for a thousand years the Greeks kept Roman civilization alive in the BYZANTINE EMPIRE, which was actually a Greek empire. There is a separate article about it.

Finally, in the year 1453, the Byzantine capital, Constantinople, fell to the Turks and the history of ancient Greece was ended.

GREECE. Area, 51,843 square miles. Population (1964 estimate) 8,510,000. Language, Greek. Religion, Greek Orthodox. Government, constitutional monarchy. Monetary unit, the drachma, 30 to $1 (U.S.). Flag, navy blue ground quartered by white cross. Capital, Athens. Greek name, Hellas.

Greek fire

Greek fire was a liquid that could float on the surface of water and burn with a hot flame. It was used years ago by the defenders of the Greek city of Constantinople against enemy ships. Constantinople was a fortified city on the Bosporus, the narrow strait that connects the Black Sea with the eastern end of the Mediterranean Sea. It was a great center of Greek Christian civilization and was constantly being attacked by the Moslems. Greek fire was used successfully in the year 673 against Moslem ships that sailed close to the walls of Constantinople in an attempt to land troops. The defenders poured their secret liquid on the water and then threw blazing torches into it. The fierce flames burned some of the Moslem ships and forced others to flee.

Greek language and literature

The Greek language belongs to the Indo-European family of languages, the same family that English and nearly all other European languages belong to. Among these languages, Greek is unique (the only one of its kind) in several ways. It was the first Indo-European language to produce literature, and though the early Greek literature was written thousands of years ago it remains among the greatest—perhaps it is the greatest—ever written. Greek was the first language in which there were words for the profound ideas of the greatest thinkers, and today we often use a Greek word to express an idea because no other language has such a word. Greek is the only one of the ancient languages that has lasted without great change into the present day. Old English, French, Spanish, German, and other languages have changed so much in a thousand years or less that speakers of the modern languages cannot understand them. Greek has changed so little in thousands of years that it can still be read by those who know modern Greek.

Greek today is the native language of only about ten million people, but in some ways it is more an international language than any other. Nearly all scientists and scholars use it. Through the Near East, people of different countries can speak to one another in a form of Greek that all of them know. For hundreds of years all well-educated men in England and other European countries learned Greek in school.

Greek had a great effect on modern English, because it had a great effect on Latin. Many words and forms in the Latin language were taken from the Greek. English, in turn, took these words and forms from Latin.

The ancient Greek language was quite complicated compared to English, or even compared to modern Greek. There were many inflections, or changes in the sound and spelling of a word depending on how it was used in a sentence. Differences in meaning were often shown by pitch accent (the tone in which the word was spoken) as well as by stress accent (pronouncing one syllable louder than others, as we do in English). Many of these complications have been dropped from modern Greek.

There are two forms of modern Greek. One is called Romaic, and is the usual spoken language. The other is called neo-Hellenic (new Greek) and is used more often in writing. It is more like the ancient Greek language, but is simplified.

According to the legends of the Greeks themselves, a king named Hellen founded the Greek people. He left his kingdom to his oldest son, Aeolus, while his son Dorus and his grandson Ion founded other kingdoms. The early Greek languages were accordingly called Aeolic, Doric, Ionic, and Attic (a branch of Ionic). Scholars recognize other branches of the Greek language, for example Achaean and Cyprian. The Minoan language, spoken on the island of Crete four thousand years ago, is now recognized as a form of early Greek.

The Greek alphabet is worth learning even by those who do not learn the language. It is much used in mathematics, physics, and other sciences. For example, the first two Greek letters, *alpha* and *beta,* are used to name the alpha rays and beta rays known to atomic science. The letter *pi* is important in mathematics. Most of the twenty-four letters of the Greek alphabet were developed into letters of the English alphabet that we use.

GREEK LITERATURE

Greek literature may be divided into three periods. The oldest period, which includes the classical Greek literature of the greatest writers, began almost three thousand years ago and lasted until about a thousand years ago. Then, about the year 529, the Byzantine period began. During the Byzantine period, the capital of the Roman Empire was the city of Constantinople, which formerly had been called Byzantium. The Byzantine period lasted until the year 1453, when Constantinople was captured by the Turks. After that the period of modern Greek literature began.

The first great Greek literature was the poetry of Homer. His great works were the long poems called the *Iliad* and the *Odyssey.* Homer is supposed to have lived sometime between 1044 B.C. and 850 B.C.—about three thousand years ago. No one knows if he ever actually lived, or if he wrote either or both of these poems, but they are as great as any poetry ever written.

Almost all of the early Greek literature was poetry. Sappho, a woman who lived on the Greek island of Lesbos, and Alcaeus, a man who lived on Lesbos at about the same time, wrote great poetry about six hundred years before the time of Christ. They wrote in the Aeolic branch of the Greek language. Pindar, who lived about a hundred years later in Boeotia, a region on the Greek mainland, wrote some of the greatest Greek poetry in the Ionic branch.

The greatest of the ancient Greek literature was the Attic literature. It was written in Athens, the city-state that was the center of the region called Attica. Between four and five hundred years before the time of Christ, Aeschylus, Sophocles, Euripides and Aristophanes wrote their plays, and Herodotus and Thucydides wrote the first histories. In the next century, between 400 B.C. and 300 B.C., great scientific writing was produced. Plato and Aristotle wrote books of philosophy (general knowledge) and Euclid wrote his books on geometry. No other country or age has produced greater literature.

Greece was conquered by Rome in 146 B.C., but Rome adopted the Greek culture instead of replacing it. The greatest writers of Rome followed the Greek style in literature. The Roman emperor Marcus Aurelius wrote in Greek, and other great Greek literature was produced in Rome by Epictetus, a Greek slave.

During the Byzantine period there was a great deal of Greek literature written, but none of it did much more than imitate the literature of the ancients.

Modern Greek literature, for some hundreds of years, also followed the ancient style. In the last fifty years it has become more like the modern literature of other countries.

The New Testament is one of the great works written in Greek. In the main it was written in the classical style, but parts of it use the conversational Greek used in the time of Christ.

Greek Orthodox Church

The Greek Orthodox Church is the church to which most Christians living in Greece belong. There are branches of this church in other countries near Greece, and in countries, such as the United States, where many people of Greek descent live. The church is also called the Eastern Orthodox Church.

In most of their beliefs, members of the Greek Orthodox Church agree with Roman Catholics, but they recognize the patriarch (archbishop) of Constantinople as their leader instead of the Pope of Rome. They usually say the Mass according to the Byzantine rite (which means the prayers are different from those used by the Roman Catholics, and that in Communion the communicants receive both bread and wine). Parish priests of the Greek Orthodox Church are allowed to marry, but there are many monks who never marry. The most famous Greek Orthodox monastery is Mount Athos, pictures of which are included in the article on GREECE. A beautiful large church, the Saint Sophia Greek Orthodox Cathedral, was built in Los Angeles during the 1950s. The most important contributions for building this church were made by the Skouras brothers, motion-picture executives.

There are almost 3,000,000 members of the Greek Orthodox Church living in North and South America.

Greeley, Horace

Horace Greeley was one of the most famous American newspapermen of about a hundred years ago. He founded the New York *Tribune* and developed it into the leading paper of New York City.

Greeley was born in New Hampshire in 1811. His father was a farmer, and Horace did not get very much education. When Horace was about 20, he went to  New York City to seek his fortune. He arrived with only one suit of clothes and no money. He worked in the printing trade, and then began to write for weekly newspapers. In 1841 he started the New York *Tribune,* and he was its editor for thirty years.

Greeley also became active in politics. He was a good friend of Abraham Lincoln, and helped him to become President. Greeley wanted to be President but was unable to get the nomination. In 1872 he was nominated but was defeated in the election by Ulysses S. Grant. He died soon after the election.

Greeley lived in the days when the United States was growing up and spreading out, and advised, "Go West, young man, go West."

Greely, Adolphus

Adolphus Washington Greely was a great American explorer and soldier who made a famous expedition to Greenland and other arctic regions. He was born in 1844 in the little town of Newbury, Massachusetts. When he was seventeen years old, Greely enlisted in the army. He fought bravely during the Civil War and, though he was very young, he was made a major. In 1881, Greely was chosen to lead a government expedition to the Arctic. Greely set out with 25 men and provisions for three years. They made many valuable discoveries. The expedition set out for the return trip in 1883, but it was stranded for the winter. All but six men died before a relief ship arrived. Greely wrote an exciting book about his adventures in the Arctic. Greely also set up important telegraphic communications for the United States in Cuba, Puerto Rico, and Alaska. He spent most of his life in the Signal Corps of the Army, and he became a major general. Greely died in 1935. He received the Congressional Medal of Honor, which is the highest honor a military man càn get.

Green, Hetty

Hetty Green was one of the world's richest women, but she hated to spend her money. She dressed very shabbily, and wore newspapers pinned around her instead of underwear to keep her warm in winter. She was born in 1835 in New Bedford, Massachusetts, where her father had amassed a great fortune. Her name was Henrietta Robinson, but she was always know by the nickname Hetty. She married Edward Green and had two children, but her chief interest was in managing and increasing her fortune. She was a very able trader in the Stock Exchange. She spent most of her time in Wall Street buying and selling stocks, and she had money invested in real estate and many other businesses. But rich as she was, she never got over her miserliness. She died in 1916 after a quarrel with a friend's cook over the price of the meat being served.

Green, William

William Green was an outstanding leader of United States labor organizations. Green was born in 1873, and went to work in the coal mines when he was quite young. He soon became interested in labor unions and became first a member and then an officer of the United Mine Workers. For a while he served in the senate of the state government of Ohio, but afterwards he returned to his union work. He became an officer of the AMERICAN FEDERATION OF LABOR (usually called the A.F. of L.), which is an organization of labor unions about which you can read in a separate article.

In 1924, when the first president of the A.F. of L. died, Green was elected president. He was re-elected to that post many times, and held the office until he died. Green thought that the government should keep out of union affairs, but during World War II, he cooperated with the government by preventing strikes in war industries. He died in 1952.

Greenaway, Kate

Kate Greenaway was an English artist and writer who was born in London about one hundred years ago. Her father was an engraver. When she was still very young, he taught her to draw and also sent her to art school. When she grew up, Kate Greenaway began to draw pictures to go with stories for children. She is most famous for the pictures she made to go with "Mother Goose" and the "Pied Piper of Hamelin." Books that have Kate Greenaway drawings in them are very much valued now. Kate Greenaway also wrote many stories and poems for children. She was born in 1846 and died in 1901.

Greenback Party

A greenback is a piece of paper money. The paper in it has no value, so paper money is simply a promise of a government to pay. A government is supposed to have gold or silver with which it can redeem (buy back) its paper money when anyone wants it to, but during wars, when governments have to buy large quantities of war materials, a government often prints extra paper money as a way of borrowing from the people. Then, after the war, the government stops spending so much. It tries not to print more paper money than it can afford to.

During the Civil War, the United States government printed a lot of paper money, which people called "greenbacks." After the Civil War it stopped. This hurt many farmers who had been selling their produce to the government. For this reason the Greenback Party was formed in

1874, nine years after the Civil War ended. The Greenback Party wanted the government to keep on printing extra paper money and spending it so that they could get good prices for their crops. The party lasted only fourteen years, and did not succeed in electing a President or in persuading the government to print more greenbacks.

Greene, Nathanael

Nathanael Greene was an American patriot of the Revolutionary War.

Greene was born in Rhode Island in 1742. At that time the Colonies still belonged to England, but Greene was one of the people who thought they should be independent. As soon as the fighting began in 1775, he joined the army. He began as a private, but through his good work in every job, he rose to be a major general. Greene had many different assignments in the war. For a while he held the post of quartermaster-general, who is in charge of getting clothing and such things for the soldiers. He was president of the court-martial board that sentenced to death the British spy, Major John André. Later he was sent to the South, after the American army there had been defeated, and he managed to reorganize the broken army.

Greene did not win any great victories in the South, but he managed to drive the English out. Not long after the war was over, Greene died, in 1786.

Greenfield Village

Greenfield Village is a copy of an early American village. It was built in 1929 in Dearborn, Michigan, by Henry Ford. Some of the buildings are copies of buildings famous in American history. Others are the very buildings used by famous people and moved there especially for visitors to see. Thomas A. Edison's workshop is there, as are the house where Noah Webster lived, the house where Luther Burbank was born, Stephen Foster's home, the shop where the Wright brothers made the first airplane, and other old, interesting things. There are a number of shops, most of them working, that show early ways of making flour, cider, cloth, pottery, and many other things the early settlers made for themselves.

greenhouse

A greenhouse is a building that is mostly glass windows and a glass roof. Plants, fruits and vegetables are grown in it. The building itself is not colored green. The many green things that grow inside of it give it the name of greenhouse. The glass protects the plants inside from the cold and wind, and, at the same time, lets in the sunlight necessary for them to grow.

During the cold winter months a greenhouse is usually heated by a furnace. The temperature is checked carefully to see that it is not too hot or too cold. Care is also taken to see that there is enough moisture in the air inside the house so that the plants do not dry up and die. The plants are watered and cared for just as if they were out in the open air. They are sprayed to protect them from bugs and

U.S. Dept. of Agriculture

An electrically heated hotbed with removable glass cover is enough to start early plants for the average home garden.

A greenhouse like the one at the right with an aluminum base is a great asset for any home gardener. Though small, it enables him to have cheerful flowers in his home all through the long winter months.

Lord & Burnham

other harmful insects and to guard them against plant diseases.

In a greenhouse plants can be grown during any season of the year. Some plants may be grown entirely in greenhouses, while others are begun there and then moved or transplanted outdoors during the warm months. Greenhouses may be small, with sides only a few feet long, or they may be so large that they spread over several acres. In large greenhouses, tractors and other farm machinery are often used to work the soil.

Many rich families have private greenhouses. These are often called *conservatories.* Large cities also have greenhouses, in parks called botanical gardens. These greenhouses are often used to grow plants that would not ordinarily grow in cold climates. Such plants, called tropical plants, are raised in greenhouses called *hothouses,* where the temperature is kept very high.

One of the most important uses of a greenhouse is in growing plants out of season. This is called *forcing.* Many of the vegetables and fruits that you eat in the spring and summer were started in the winter in these forcing houses. Tomatoes, cauliflower, peppers, cabbages, sweet potatoes, cucumbers, grapes, and other fruits

and vegetables are often planted in the winter in a forcing house. When spring comes, they are moved outdoors into the fields, where they are ready to be picked many weeks earlier than they would otherwise. Some vegetables, such as radishes, lettuce, and spinach, may be grown entirely in a greenhouse until they are ready to be picked.

HOTBEDS

Sometimes very small greenhouses, called *hotbeds,* are used by farmers and gardeners to start vegetables and fruits. A hotbed is a wooden frame set into a hole in the ground. It is about two feet deep and about three feet square, and is covered with a glass window. Manure or some other fertilizer is put into the hole, about 20 inches high. Then a layer of soil is put over the top. Seeds are planted in the soil and are watered. The window lets in the sunlight and keeps the seedlings warm. Heat made by the decaying fertilizer also helps the seeds sprout faster. Soil is usually banked against the sides of the wooden frame to prevent the heat from escaping.

Greenland

Greenland is the largest island in the world, with an area of about 827,000

Royal Danish Inform. Service

Greenland became part of the Danish commonwealth in 1953, with the right to elect its own representatives to parliament.

The old Eskimo woman is a grandmother many times over. She still wears her hair in a traditional knot, once the height of fashion among Greenlanders.

The world's best sledge drivers live in Greenland. Here, a hunter prepares his dogs for a trip.

In some places the ice has receded, and between desolate mountain tops are fertile sheltered valleys.

Greenland children, like those everywhere, listen eagerly as teacher describes foreign countries.

The church in Godthaab, South Greenland's growing capital city, is still the community center.

Royal Danish Inform. Service

Summer clothes in Greenland must be warm, because even in July the temperature does not go much above fifty degrees.

The Greenland housewife keeps her kitchen neat. She has no modern appliances, but the weather gives her a "deep freeze," just outside the kitchen door.

Large ships call only at Greenland's main settlements. Small schooners supply the outposts.

Greenland Eskimos, like American Indians, find this the best way to carry babies on long trips.

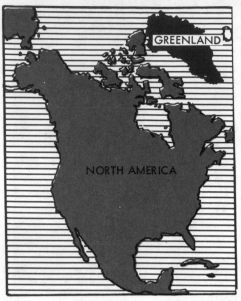

stations, which proved to be very important.

Shortly after the end of World War II, the United States finished a great air base at Thule, a town on the northwest coast. The air base, which is called Blue Jay, cost more than three hundred million dollars to build. The United States has promised to help Denmark protect Greenland in time of war.

Since Greenland lies within the Arctic Circle, it is very cold. The temperature is below zero for more than half the year, and during parts of the long winter there is almost no sunlight. The island was discovered by a famous Norse explorer, Eric the Red, nearly a thousand years ago. He founded a colony of Norsemen there, but they died or left. Most of the people today are either native Eskimos or Danish settlers who have gone to Greenland within the last few hundred years. The people speak Danish or a language called Greenlandic, which is an Eskimo dialect. Most of the people of Greenland make their living by fishing, sheep-herding, and growing vegetables in the summer. There are many minerals in Greenland. The most important are cryolite, which is used in making aluminum; graphite, which is used in the "lead" of pencils; and lignite, which is a fuel similar to coal.

GREENLAND. Area, 827,300 square miles. Population (1964 estimate) 37,000. Largest island on earth. Government, integral part of Denmark.

square miles. (Australia is more than three times as large but is considered a continent.) Greenland is a part of Denmark though it is 2,000 miles away. It lies almost entirely within the Arctic Circle, off the east cost of Canada. The interior of the island is covered by a sheet of ice more than 1,000 feet thick and is surrounded by high mountains, so the people of Greenland live along the coast. Greenland has a population of only about 37,000.

Most of the people in Greenland live on the west coast, which is divided into two provinces. Godthaab is the capital of South Greenland and Godhavn is the capital of North Greenland. Each of these provinces has its own parliament, or ruling body, and Greenland sends its representatives to the Danish parliament which is headed by a Danish official.

Greenland is very important from a military point of view. It provides the shortest air route from North America to many parts of Europe and Asia. Planes can fly directly from Greenland across the North Pole. During World War II, the United States got permission from Denmark to build military and air bases in Greenland. It also set up weather

Green Mountains

The Green Mountains are a part of the great North American mountain range called the Appalachian Mountains. The Green Mountains stretch from Quebec in the north right through Vermont and into Massachusetts. Most of the Green Mountain range is in Vermont. The state called itself Vermont because *vert mont* means "green mountain" in French. We know Vermont as the "Green Mountain State."

None of the Green Mountains is very

tall, but they are very rugged and not easy to climb. The highest peak of the Green Mountains is Mount Mansfield, in Vermont, 4,393 feet high. The Green Mountains are covered with fir and pine trees, and are green the whole year round. The Green Mountains are very beautiful and are popular with vacationists.

Marble and granite are dug from many quarries in the Green Mountains. Some Green Mountain farmers make maple sugar from the sap of the maple trees.

Before the American Revolution, a group of men who lived in the western section of what is now Vermont banded together under the name of the Green Mountain Boys to defend their territory against colonists in New York State, who wanted to make it a part of New York. Later, the Green Mountain Boys fought against the British in the American Revolution. You can read about this in the article about their leader, a patriot named Ethan ALLEN.

Greenwich Observatory

The Greenwich Observatory was built in London, England, about three hundred years ago, to fix the exact time of day by observing the sun and stars. The purpose of the observatory was to help British ships at sea. It is extremely important for navigators to know the exact time, as you can read in the article on NAVIGATION. In 1954 the observatory was moved away from Greenwich, be-

British Inform. Service

Greenwich Observatory used to be in London, England, but was moved to this castle because the brightness of London's lights and the haze of industrial smoke hindered meteorological observation.

cause the smoke and the lights of London made it hard for the scientists to see the sky. The observatory is now in a castle about sixty miles from London.

The Greenwich Observatory has always been controlled by the British Navy. It was founded in 1675 and the first buildings were designed by the famous English architect Christopher Wren. In 1884 all the countries of the world decided to accept Greenwich time as the standard, but several of them, including the United States, now have their own observatories.

Greenwich Village

Greenwich Village is the name of a section in New York City. Many artists and writers have lived there. People who visit New York often like to walk through Greenwich Village, with its narrow winding streets, its many art and curio shops, and the outdoor art exhibits that are often held in or near "the Village." Washington Square, a small park where New York's famous Fifth Avenue begins, is considered the heart of Greenwich Village.

Gregory

Gregory was a name borne by sixteen Popes of the Roman Catholic Church. The last Pope Gregory died in 1846. Three of them were especially famous. Gregory I, known as Gregory the Great, was born about the year 540 in Rome. He came from a noble and rich family, and for a while he was a civil official of Rome. But Gregory decided to devote his life to religion, and he became a monk. In 590, all the people and priests of Rome chose Gregory to be Pope. He did not want the position, but finally he had to accept it.

As Pope, Gregory was a strong and powerful leader of the Roman Catholic Church. In the Church, he ruled with a strong hand, especially over the churches in Italy. He encouraged the growth and spread of monasteries, and sent a monk, Augustine, to England to convert people there, the Anglo-Saxons. He also insisted on reforms within the Church. The Gregorian chant, which is a form of church music, was developed in his time and named for him. Gregory was not only the head of the Church, but because of social and political conditions he was also in many ways the ruler of Italy. He was the first Pope to have great power outside the Church. Gregory I died in 604.

Gregory VII became Pope in 1073 and changed his name from Hildebrand to Gregory VII. He made many reforms in the Church and made the position of Pope more important than that of any other ruler. Once he forced the Holy Roman Emperor, who opposed him, to beg forgiveness. You can read about their quarrel in the article on HENRY, Holy Roman Emperor. In the end, Gregory lost his power and was forced to leave Rome. He died in exile, in 1085.

Gregory XIII became Pope in 1572. He is best remembered for having revised the calendar. The calendar we use today is called the Gregorian calendar. He was born in 1502 and died in 1585.

gremlin

A gremlin is an imaginary being, like a fairy or an elf. Gremlins are thought to be about a foot high and to cause much trouble. In World War II, when something went wrong with an airplane in a mysterious way, pilots jokingly blamed it on gremlins.

grenade

A grenade is a small bomb that is thrown by hand or fired from a rifle. The French first called the bomb *pomegranate,* because the first grenades looked like the pomegranate fruit. Grenades were first used more than three hundred years ago. Soon special groups of soldiers called *grenadiers* were formed to use them. The grenadiers wore high, brimless hats called *shakos,* which could not get in the way when the grenade was whirled about the head in throwing. After about a hundred years the grenade went out of use, and it did not reappear until World War I. Today the United States Army uses a grenade that is marked off into small squares. It is made to explode three to five minutes after a safety pin has been pulled out. The grenade can be fired from a rifle as far as two hundred yards, and when it explodes it bursts into pieces that act like bullets.

grenadier

A grenadier was originally a soldier who carried and threw grenades. He was chosen for his special strength. Because the first grenades were exploded by gunpowder fuses, the grenadier had to carry something to light the fuse. This was a piece of punk which held a spark for a long time, and was called a *slowmatch.* When modern grenades were invented, there was little need for a special soldier because anyone could now throw grenades. The title of grenadier came to be used for members of certain special regiments of soldiers, such as "The Queen's Own Grenadiers" in England.

Grenfell, Sir Wilfred Thomason

Sir Wilfred Thomason Grenfell was a great English doctor who did more than any other person to help the fishermen and Eskimos of Labrador and Newfoundland, in Canada. He was born in 1865. Grenfell went to Labrador in 1892, and he spent more than forty years in this lonely country, where he worked to make life healthy and happy for the people who lived there. Grenfell traveled from

one place to another, taking care of the sick. He built hospitals and schools, and orphanages where children who had no parents could receive good care. He built libraries and stores and meeting halls. Every year, Grenfell traveled by boat to all the centers he had helped to set up. The ship he used was the first hospital ship, fully equipped to take care of sick people. Everyone loved and respected Grenfell, and the English government made him a knight in appreciation for his great work. Grenfell wrote many books about his experiences. One of them is called *Forty Years for Labrador,* and it is the story of his exciting life. Grenfell died in 1940.

Gretna Green

Gretna Green is a village in Scotland, just north of the English border. For more than a hundred years, many couples eloped, or ran away to be married, to Gretna Green. In England people who wanted to be married had to post a public notice of their intentions and then had to wait a certain length of time after that before the wedding ceremony could take place. These notices were called *banns* and were usually read in church. In Gretna Green no waiting period was necessary, and many couples who did not want to wait, or whose parents objected to their marriage, went across the border and were married there. In 1856 a law was passed that at least one member of the couple getting married had to live in Scotland for three weeks before the ceremony, so the runaway marriages were stopped. Any place where couples can get married quickly is sometimes called a "Gretna Green."

Grey, Albert

Albert Henry George Grey was a Governor-General of Canada. He was born in 1851. His grandfather, Earl Grey, had been Prime Minister of England, so it was quite natural for Albert Grey to go into politics. After he received his education in Trinity College, at Cambridge University, Grey was elected to Parliament, and he held many important positions in the English government. In 1895, Grey was given the responsible job of governing Rhodesia, a new British colony in Africa. Then, in 1904, he became Governor-General of Canada, and did many things to help the farmers and workers to have better working conditions. He died in 1917.

Grey, Edward

Edward Grey was the British foreign minister in 1914 when World War I broke out. Probably no man tried so hard to prevent the war as he did. Grey was born in 1862. He came from a famous family and was trained for government service.

Grey was a very sincere and honest man, and when it seemed to him that the Germans were preparing for war he tried to discourage them. He persuaded France and Russia to stand together with England, and he even tried to get the United States to join them. But the war began, and Grey resigned. He is remembered for his statement about World War I: "The lamps are going out all over Europe; we shall not see them lit again in our lifetime."

After the war Grey became ambassador to the United States, and he continued to fight for peace by helping the League of Nations. Grey was made a knight, and later Viscount of Fallodon, by the British government. He died in 1933.

Grey, Lady Jane

Lady Jane Grey was an English girl who for nine days was queen of England. This was about four hundred years ago. Jane Grey never wanted to be queen of England, but she was a great-granddaughter of King Henry VII and her ambitious father-in-law, the Duke of Northumberland, made her queen so that he could control England by controlling her. This was in 1553. The English Parliament would not let him do this, because Princess Mary was the oldest child of King Henry VIII. Mary became queen and Lady Jane Grey was beheaded in 1554, when she was only 17 years old.

Jane Grey's whole life was short and tragic. Her parents forced her to marry Lord Guilford Dudley, a man she did not love, before her sixteenth birthday.

Grey, Zane

Zane Grey was an American writer who wrote many popular stories about the days when men were settling the West and life was rugged and wild. Grey was born in Zanesville, Ohio, in 1875. He studied dentistry at the University of Pennsylvania, and became a dentist in New York City. Among his most popular novels were *Riders of the Purple Sage* and *The Vanishing American.* Many of his exciting books were made into movies. Grey died in 1939.

greyhound

The greyhound is one of the oldest breeds of dog in the world. It can run faster than any other breed, and people have used greyhounds in hunting for over four thousand years. Although greyhounds are very gentle, even-tempered dogs, they are not usually kept as family pets, but more often are used for hunting hares or for racing. Many hundreds of years ago, only people with titles, such as princes, dukes, or earls, kept greyhounds. It is regarded as the dog of royalty.

A greyhound stands about 28 to 30 inches high at the shoulders, and it weighs

Pennyworth Kennels

The swift and graceful greyhound is one of the few dogs that hunt by sight instead of tracking prey by smell.

about 65 pounds. It has a long, thin tail. The coat is short and smooth, and you can see greyhounds in almost any dog color. The name has nothing to do with the dog's color. You will recognize the breed by the fact that it appears gracefully curved on the underside. This is because the chest is roomy and powerful, and the hips are slender, with slim hindquarters that enable the strong legs to run swiftly without tiring quickly.

Grieg, Edvard Hagerup

Edvard Hagerup Grieg was a Norwegian composer, or writer of original music. Grieg was born in the city of Bergen, Norway, in 1843. When he was a young man Grieg traveled in Germany, Denmark, and Italy, where he studied different kinds of music. Then he returned to his own country and wrote beautiful songs and pieces for the piano and violin. Grieg loved the folk music of the Norwegian people, and many of his compositions are based on their simple tunes. Henrik Ibsen, the great Norwegian playwright, asked Grieg to write some music to go with his play, *Peer Gynt.* The music that Grieg wrote, the *Peer Gynt Suite,* is among his most famous works. Grieg died in 1907.

griffin

The griffin was an imaginary monster in stories told by the Greeks and other ancient peoples thousands of years ago. The griffin had the body of a lion, the head and wings of an eagle, feathers all over its back, and a long, serpentlike tail. This monster was almost ten times as big as a lion. In the stories, the griffin drew the chariot that carried the sun across the sky. The griffin knew just where to find buried treasures, and it built its nests out of gold. Hunters were always fighting with the monster to reclaim the gold.

Griffith, D. W.

David Wark Griffith was one of the first men to make motion pictures. He was both a director and a producer. In 1915 he produced a full-length motion picture that set the standard for every motion picture that has been made since. This film was called *The Birth of a Nation* and was a story of the American Civil War and the years after it. It is considered to be one of the best motion pictures ever made.

Griffith was born in Kentucky in 1875. As a young man he acted in plays and motion pictures. He was rich and famous when he died in Hollywood in 1948.

King, a champion wire-haired pointing griffon, is lively and intelligent.

griffon

The griffon is a tiny dog with a turned-up nose and large, round eyes, kept as a pet both in Europe and America. There are different types. One is called the *Brabancon*. It has smooth, short hair like a Boston terrier. Another is called the *Belgian griffon,* and it has wiry hair, with a little, rough beard on its chin. Some puppies in a litter may be the smooth-haired type, and some may be the wire-haired type.

A griffon is a very small dog, standing only about 9 to 11 inches high at the shoulder. Some are even smaller. Usually they weigh about 9 pounds, but can weigh as little as 6 or as much as 12 pounds. Their tails are clipped short just after they are born.

The wire-haired pointing griffon is a

hunting dog that has been known in the United States and Canada only since 1900. It was developed by a Hollander, E. M. Korthals, when he wanted to breed a new type of sporting dog.

It is a medium-sized dog, with extremely wiry hair that makes an effect of eyebrows and a mustache on the dog's face. It is about the size of a boxer, or slightly smaller. The color is usually gray and tan. The tail is usually clipped when puppies are a few days old.

Grimm, Jakob and Wilhelm

Jakob Ludwig Grimm and Wilhelm Karl Grimm were brothers who lived in Germany more than a hundred years ago. They are best known for the collection of folk tales, or stories that had been handed down among the German country folk for many years. This collection, now called *Grimm's Fairy Tales,* was first published in 1812. Both Jakob and Wilhelm Grimm were great scholars in the study of language. Jakob Grimm worked out a rule to determine the way in which sounds change from one European language to another. This rule is called

N.Y. Pub. Library

The Grimm Brothers, Wilhelm (*left*) and Jakob (*right*), wrote many delightful tales, but others were "grim" indeed.

Grimm's Law and is very important.

Grimm's Fairy Tales was first written down in very scholarly language but it was later rewritten and became popular all over the world. Recently the stories have been criticized because some of the characters in them are so cruel, but they are still very popular with both children and adults. Wilhelm Grimm was born in 1786 and died in 1859. Jakob was born in 1785 and died in 1863.

grinding

Grinding is another name for rubbing or scraping. It is done with special materials called ABRASIVES, about which you can read in a separate article. Rubbing something with a piece of sandpaper is a kind of grinding.

Most grinding is done by machines. These have wheels that are made from abrasives or that have strips of abrasives cemented on their edges. The wheels are on a shaft, or long rod, which is turned by a motor. Pieces of a material are held against the turning wheels, to be smoothed, polished, sharpened, or made into different shapes. This is called turning. The earliest grinding machine was the grindstone, which is turned by hand. It is used to sharpen axes, knives, and other tools. The lathe was the first motor-driven grinding machine, and most grind-ing machines are patterned after it. (You can read more about the LATHE in a separate article.)

There are many types of grinding machines and each has a special use. They often are very large, the size of a large table or even larger, and must be securely attached to the floor so they do not move around and spoil the grinding operation. Some machines are able to grind off one-thousandth of an inch of surface or even less. These are called *precision grinders*. A *centerless grinder* is used to make perfect cylinders and ball-shaped pieces, such as billiard balls or the little metal balls that are used in ball bearings. Hollow cylinders can be smoothed and polished by grinders called *external* and *internal grinders*. An external grinder is a wheel that smooths the outside of the cylinder. The cylinder is usually placed on a turning shaft and automatically pressed against the revolving grinding wheel. Sometimes the grinding wheel is hollow so that the cylinder can be slipped inside of it and smoothed by the abrasive on the inside of the wheel. Internal grinders are wheels that smooth the insides of hollow cylinders. The grinding wheel is just small enough to slip inside the turning cylinder. Special grinding machines called *universal grinders* are used for both internal and external grinding.

GRINDING

ABRASIVE WHEEL

WORK

The grinder gives the steel roll a high polish.

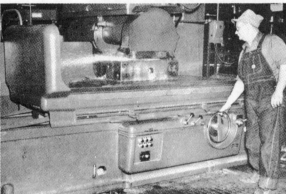

Above: A special machine grinds an almost invisible part of a watch. *Right:* A tool and cutter grinder sharpens a broach used for shaping metal surfaces. *Below left:* A grinder smooths the threads of a "worm" for a washing-machine wringer. *Below right:* Sparks fly as the grinder comes down on the top of a die block.

Grinding wheels must often be cleaned and smoothed off. This is done by metal star-shaped wheels or by diamond stones. These remove pieces of metal dust and other unwanted material from the grinding wheels.

grippe, a disease that is like a very bad cold, and is very easy to catch from another person: see the article on IN-FLUENZA.

grits

Grits is ground-up kernels of corn that has been dried and bleached white. Throughout the southern part of the United States it is eaten as a vegetable in much the same way that potato is eaten in the North. Grits is usually boiled in water and looks very much like breakfast cereals such as Cream of Wheat. It may also be cooled until it hardens; it is then sliced and fried before it is eaten. Fried grits is usually eaten for breakfast, and is served with syrup and butter. Sometimes the corn is not ground up and the whole dried kernel is cooked and served. It is then called *hominy.*

grizzly bear, one of the largest and fiercest of all bears: see the article on BEAR.

grosbeak

The grosbeak is a bird. Its name means "heavy beak," and several birds with thick bills are known as grosbeaks, but the name is most often used for a kind of finch. The grosbeak is a small or medium-large bird. It is a singing bird and lives in pine woods in Europe and North America.

One kind is the cardinal grosbeak, which is also called the *Virginia nightingale.* It lives in the eastern part of the United States. The male bird, or cock, is bright red and has a beautiful song. The female is more modest in her coloring and her song is not as beautiful as the male's.

Grosbeaks have bills that are good for breaking seeds. They are helpful to man because they eat seeds of weeds that grow around gardens and crops.

Grotius, Hugo

Hugo Grotius was a great Dutch scholar who lived from 1583 to 1645. He  is best known as the author of the first book ever written on international law, which is the rules of conduct for countries in their dealings with one another. Grotius was an official of the Dutch government for a while but then he became involved in a religious quarrel that was going on in Holland and was sentenced to life imprisonment. With the help of his wife, he managed to escape by hiding in a trunk that was carried out of the jail. He made his way to France, and it was there that he wrote his famous book. It is called *De Jure Belli et Pacis,* which means "Concerning the Laws of War and Peace." Most people interested in systems of international law and world government have used many of Grotius's ideas.

Groundhog Day, February 2, the day on which the groundhog is supposed to come out of his burrow: see the article on CANDLEMAS.

ground squirrel

Ground squirrels are squirrels that live on the ground, and not in trees like other squirrels. Like all squirrels, the ground squirrels are rodents. Mice, rats, and other animals that have special teeth used for gnawing are called rodents. There are different kinds of ground squirrels, including the chipmunk and the prairie dog. Ground squirrels often live in large groups together in their underground burrows. When winter comes, they creep into their burrows and sleep until the warm weather returns. The animal that is usually called a ground squirrel has short legs and short ears. Its tail is bushy. Ground squirrels eat green plants and seeds and also many insects. They are found in most parts of the United States, except for the east coast.

ground water

Ground water lies below the surface of the ground and feeds all wells and springs. Solid rock is very rare below the ground; in most places the rock has openings in it ranging from tiny pores to enormous caverns. Water that falls on the ground drains into these openings in the rock. Ground water flows "downhill" underneath the surface of the earth, just as streams above the surface flow down mountainsides. Sometimes it can be gotten out by pumping. It also flows out from springs on hillsides. Sometimes water is forced out of the ground under great pressure, and it may furnish most of the water found in some brooks and rivers. A very large spring in the state of Florida, Silver Springs, gets its supply from ground water.

Ground water is very important in farming and also in industry. Farmers use it to water their crops during periods when no rain has fallen. It is used in industry because it is a fairly steady supply of water, and it is available even when there has been no rain. It is especially useful in industry for cooling machines, because it is cool when it comes from the ground. When it is used to cool things, the water is usually pumped out of the ground into the machine and back into the ground so that it may be cooled and used again.

grouper

A grouper is an ocean fish that is related to the sea bass family. It is a good food fish, and is very popular with sport fishermen. There are many kinds of grouper, ranging from small to very large. The most usual kind found in American waters is the red grouper, which is about two feet long and has a red snout that blends into pink on the head. The red grouper is found in the Atlantic Ocean from Virginia to Brazil. Other kinds of grouper grow to be as much as twelve feet long and weigh up to five hundred pounds. Groupers of different kinds have different colors, usually greenish-gray or orange-brown. Even the smaller varieties have very large mouths, and they feed on shellfish and other fish.

grouse

A grouse is a wild bird that looks like a young hen. Grouse are game birds, that is, hunters shoot them because they are good to eat. The grouse has a plump body and a small head. It is chestnut-brown in color. Some species, called ptarmigans, turn white in the winter, making it difficult to see them in the snow. These grouse are found in Scandinavia and in other very cold parts of the world, such as Siberia, Alaska, and Newfoundland. Closely related to this kind is a red grouse that lives on the moors in the British Isles and feeds on heather, a bushy kind of flower. This is the kind that is hunted a great deal in England and Scotland. The ruffed grouse is found in America. The male bird can drum on a log, a sound that is heard in the woods in the spring. The sage grouse and the blackcock have drum "tournaments" in the spring. They have a

To attract a mate, the male ruffed grouse whirs his wings, producing air vibrations that sound like the beating of a drum.

special grounds for it and they all gather there to compete in the tournament. Still other kinds of grouse are the blue grouse or pine hen, which lives in forests of pine and other cone-bearing trees, and the sharp-tailed grouse and the prairie chicken, which live in the prairies.

growth

Any living thing, whether it is a plant or an animal, becomes larger as it becomes older, and this is called *growth.* A time comes when it stops growing but continues to become older, and then it is said to have reached *maturity,* or to have become *adult.* Many plants do not stop growing. They continue to grow throughout their lives, but they reach a point at which they grow more slowly. Some animals, too, continue to grow, but do so more slowly.

Scientists know a great deal about how things grow. They do not know why things grow. Especially they do not know why things stop growing.

In a separate article you can read about the CELL, the basic unit of life, of which all living things are made. Each type of living thing is made of cells of its own kind. Most cells have the ability to absorb food and turn it into other cells. As long as a living thing is growing, it is always making more cells than there were before. After it stops growing, it makes

Rate of growth differs. Baby deer can walk in a few hours, bamboo may grow a foot a day, and a chick hops right out of its egg. But human babies creep for months before they walk. Giant redwoods grow slowly, but may live 3,000 years, and the turtle may not be fully grown until a hundred years after it leaves its egg.

new cells to replace some of the ones that are constantly dying.

THINGS THAT AFFECT GROWTH

A living thing inherits from its parents the fact that it will grow to a certain size in a certain length of time. In human beings this means that tall parents are likely to have tall children. Members of certain races will be taller than members of other races. Men will usually be taller and heavier than women, but women are likely to grow somewhat faster during their early years.

Certain GLANDS, about which you can read in a separate article, affect growth. The pituitary gland is sometimes called the "growth gland." If it is not working

properly, a person may turn out to be a dwarf, and if it is doing too much work it may make a giant.

Good food and a proper amount of heat, as well as sunlight, are necessary to proper growth. A child who does not have a good nourishing diet may not grow as rapidly or as tall as he would if he were properly fed.

HUMAN GROWTH

It is not possible to say exactly how much a human child should grow in any particular year. Too much depends on how large the child will finally be, based on heredity and other things. It need not be a cause for worry if a child does not seem to grow rapidly. There are many cases in which rapid growth is delayed and then occurs during adolescence.

A girl will usually grow faster than a boy until she is 12 or 13 years old. At these ages she may be taller than a boy who is some day going to be considerably taller than she is. After the girl and boy are both 13 or 14 years old, the boy will grow faster than she does, and will overtake and pass her.

A baby will usually grow about ten inches in its first two years. It grows faster in its first years than it ever will again. During its third year a child will grow about four inches, or a little less, and for each of its next six years it will grow about the same. A girl's rate of growth will slow down when she is about 9 years old, and a boy's when he is about 11 years old.

Because they are eating better and more nourishing food, and are aided by scientific knowledge that tells what foods are best to eat and that also has stamped out many diseases, Americans are becoming taller in every generation. Between World War I and World War II the average height of men in the armed forces went up from a little under 5 feet 8 inches to a little under 5 feet 9 inches.

The mind grows along with the body. During the period when the body is grow-

63 INCHES
57 INCHES
53 INCHES
49 INCHES

7 YEARS   9 YEARS   11 YEARS   14 YEARS

60 LBS. 58 LBS.   70 LBS. 68 LBS.   85 LBS. 81 LBS.   120 LBS. 112 LBS.

The growth of most boys and girls follows this pattern, though there are many exceptions.

ing, the mind becomes better able to understand. This ability in the mind does not depend on the size of the mind in the same way that the strength of the body depends on its size.

Because human beings are constantly learning, it is not possible to say how much of an increase in mental capacity is due to greater maturity and how much is due to the person's increased knowledge. See also the article on INTELLIGENCE.

Gruenther, Alfred M.

Alfred Maximilian Gruenther, as general in the United States Army, held some of the most important positions in the defense of his country during World War II and since. He was born in Platte Center, a small town in Nebraska, in the year 1899, and was graduated from the United States Military Academy (West Point) in 1919. He was a regular army officer for nearly forty years. When he was promoted to major general during World War II he was the youngest man in the United States Army to have so high a

rank. Later he was advanced to full general's rank. He was chief of staff under General Eisenhower and then under General Mark Clark in World War II. Then he was chief of staff to Eisenhower in the "SHAPE" organization (Supreme Headquarters, Allied Powers Europe) in Paris, France. In 1953, when Eisenhower was President of the United States, Gruenther became Supreme Commander of SHAPE. In 1957 Gruenther retired from the Army and became president of the American Red Cross. In 1965 he retired as Red Cross president.

grunion

A grunion is a small fish that is found in large numbers in the Pacific Ocean along the western shores of the United States. The largest grunion may grow to 7 inches, about the length of a pencil. The grunion's spawning, or egg-laying, habits are unusual. The female grunion lays its eggs only at high tide. Great schools of grunion rush in to very shallow water after the highest tide. The female wiggles backward into the sand, lays its eggs, and quickly moves out to sea. After two weeks, the eggs are hatched and the baby grunion are washed out to sea by the next high tide. When the fish come in to lay eggs at some beaches, hundreds of people gather to catch them and fry them for eating.

Guadalajara

Guadalajara is the name of a city in Mexico, and of a province and its capital city in Spain. The Mexican city of Guadalajara is the capital of the state of Jalisco, which is on the western coast of the country. It is the second-largest city in Mexico. About 590,000 people live there, just about as many as live in San Antonio, Texas. Guadalajara is a very modern city, but it also contains many beautiful old buildings that date back more than three hundred years. There is a fine art museum and an excellent university in Guadalajara. The city is fa-

Mexican Govt. Railway System

The government palace in Guadalajara is one of its many lovely buildings.

mous for the lovely pottery and glassware made by the people who live there. Guadalajara was first settled about four hundred years ago, in 1542.

The province of Guadalajara in Spain is in the central part of the country, not far from Madrid, the capital city of Spain. It is in the section of Spain called New Castile. More than a thousand years ago, most of Spain was controlled by Moslems from Africa, who were called Moors by the Spaniards. The Moors called this section *Wad-al-hejarra,* which means "valley of stones." One of Spain's most important rivers, the Henares River, flows through Guadalajara. The countryside is very fertile and good for farming, but is rocky and stony in parts. A great battle in the Spanish Civil War (which lasted from 1936 to 1939) was fought just outside of the city of Guadalajara, capital of the province.

GUADALAJARA, MEXICO. Population (1959 estimate) 589,900. Capital of Jalisco state.

Guadalcanal

The name of Guadalcanal has joined other names famous for American heroism, such as Valley Forge, Gettysburg, and Belleau Wood. Guadalcanal is one of the Solomon Islands in the southwest Pacific Ocean. Here, during World War II, the United States Army, Navy and Marine Corps fought a fierce and desperate battle with the Japanese. On August 7, 1942, twenty thousand Marines landed on Guadalcanal. They soon captured Henderson Airfield, but on August 9 the Japanese navy sank four cruisers that were protecting the landing of supplies and ammunition. For months the Marines, who were reinforced by the Army, fought the Japanese in the dense, steaming jungle. The Japanese put more troops on the island and counterattacked, but the Americans held on. In November there was another battle between the two navies near Guadalcanal. This time the United States won, and the Japanese were

The Guadaloupe fisherman (*left*) wears a hat that will protect him against the sun. The housewife (*right*) is shown against a background sketch of one of the small island harbors.

now no longer able to control the seas and land more men. In February 1943 the Japanese admitted that they were defeated and left the island. Guadalcanal was the first great American land victory of the war.

Guadalupe Hildago, Treaty of

The Treaty of Guadalupe Hildago was the agreement that ended the Mexican-American War in February, 1848. This war was fought principally over Mexico's refusal to let Texas join the United States. In the small town of Guadalupe Hildago, which is near Mexico City, it was decided that the United States would get the great piece of Mexican land out of which were made the states of California, Nevada, Utah, most of New Mexico and Arizona, and parts of Wyoming and Colorado. Texas was allowed to join the United States and its boundary was fixed at the Rio Grande. The United States paid Mexico fifteen million dollars, and agreed to pay claims that American citizens had against Mexico.

Guadeloupe

Guadeloupe is the name of a group of small islands in the West Indies, and is also the name of the largest island in the group. These islands belong to France. About 300,000 people live there, nearly all of them Negroes. Most of the people live on the largest island. The principal town of Guadeloupe is Basse-Terre, a city of about 12,000 on the western coast. The next largest island is called Grande-Terre, with the chief town of Pointe-à-Pitre, which has a population of about 26,000. The islands are fertile and the people grow sugar, coffee, cocoa, and bananas, and make rum. The climate is hot and damp, and often there are terrible hurricanes. Christopher Columbus discovered Guadeloupe in 1493 and the French settled it in 1635.

Guam

Guam is one of the Marianas Islands in the western Pacific Ocean. It is an important United States air and naval base because of its central location near Japan, China, the Philippine Islands, New Guinea, and Hawaii.

Guam is a small island with forest-covered mountains and fertile valleys. The climate is warm and pleasant, and many of the 72,000 people who live there work on coconut plantations or grow coffee, cacao, sugar, or rice. About a third of them are natives called *Chamorros,* and most of the others are of Spanish descent. The people speak English and Spanish.

Guam was discovered by the Spanish explorer Ferdinand Magellan in 1521, and it belonged to Spain until the Spanish-American War when the United States took it over. At the beginning of World War II it was attacked and captured by Japan. Near the end of the war the United States recaptured it and began to rebuild the ruined capital city of Agana, the naval base at Apra, and the airfield. Now the people of Guam are citizens of the United States and they elect their own government except for the governor, who is appointed by the President of the United States.

guan

A guan is a bird that looks somewhat like a turkey, but is smaller. It has a red throat without feathers and a fleshy red bag hanging at its throat. A guan is about thirty inches long, half of which is tail feathers. Its body is shiny reddish-green in color. The female guan has a border of white on the top of her head and along her chest. Guans are restless, noisy birds and fly up in the trees when they are alarmed. They roost in trees at night and make their nests on branches. Guans live in the American tropics, but some are found in Texas. In South America they have been domesticated for a long time.

guanaco

The guanaco is a wild animal that lives in South America. It belongs to the camel family, but is a good deal smaller than a camel and has no hump. It is related also to the llama, alpaca, and vicuña, which are other South American members of the camel family. The guanaco stands about four feet high at the shoulder. It has a curved neck and long slender legs. There are bare patches on the hind legs where the short tail curves down. The long beautiful hair of the guanaco is used to make a fine wool. It is fawn-colored on top of the body and white underneath.

Guanacos live in herds of from six to thirty. They are very shy and difficult to get near, although they can be tamed quite easily. The Indians of Patagonia in South

The guanaco is at home high up in the Andes Mountains of South America.

America hunt them as food. The Indians also use the droppings of the guanaco for fuel, and its hide for clothing and tents. The puma, a kind of large wildcat, attacks the guanaco and feeds on it almost entirely. Guanacos live in the southern half of South America, from Peru to Cape Horn. The guanaco goes to a special place to die. There are great heaps of bones in these burial grounds of the guanaco.

guano

Guano is used by farmers as a fertilizer, which is a substance that keeps soil enriched. Guano is the waste matter of many kinds of sea birds, which leave deposits on the islands where they live. All the biggest deposits of guano are found in tropical areas, such as the west coast of South America and some islands in the South Pacific Ocean. The country of Peru was the leader in the production of guano and Peruvian farmers have used guano as a fertilizer for centuries. However, the best deposits have been used up, and guano has been replaced by synthetic, or man-made, fertilizers, or by fertilizer made from fish.

guaranty or guarantee

A guaranty is a promise to pay another person's debt, if he does not pay it himself. Suppose a person wants to borrow money from a bank, but the bank is not sure he will be able to pay it back. The borrower asks a rich friend to give the bank a guaranty. The rich friend then signs an agreement to repay the loan if the borrower does not. The person who borrows the money is called the *principal.* The rich friend who signs for him is called the *guarantor.* (In some cases he is called a *co-signer,* because he and the borrower both sign a note, or promise to repay the loan.) The bank cannot collect from the guarantor unless it has already tried to collect from the borrower and the borrower has failed to pay.

A guaranty is also spelled *guarantee,* but usually the word guarantee means a different kind of promise. This is a promise made by someone who manufactures or sells some kind of merchandise. A seller of vacuum cleaners may guarantee that the vacuum cleaner will work properly for at least a year. If it breaks down during the year, the seller will repair it or replace it without charge. A seller of cloth may guarantee that it will not fade. If it does fade, he will replace it or give back the money. Nearly all advertised merchandise has some kind of guarantee behind it.

A *title guaranty* is a special kind of guaranty in real estate (lands and buildings). When you buy real estate, the seller gives you an official paper, called a *deed,* which you record in a town or county office. A title guaranty company will make a *title search* for you, tracing back all the deeds ever recorded on that land. The record may go back hundreds of years. If the company finds that everyone who ever sold the land had a legal right to sell it, the company will give you a *title insurance* policy, which assures you that you own the land.

guardian

When a child's parents are dead, or are unable to take care of him properly, a guardian may be appointed for him. A judge, in a court of law, appoints the guardian. The legal duties of the guardian are very much like those of parents. The guardian must make sure the child is properly fed and clothed and cared for in other ways, and the child must obey the guardian as he would his parents. The guardian manages any money or other property that belongs to the child, and must report regularly to the judge as to how he has managed it. The judge has the right to appoint a guardian for any child, even if its parents are alive, but this seldom happens unless the parents are neglecting or abusing the child. When the parents have died and have made a will asking that some particular person be appointed as guardian, the judge will usually appoint that person, but he does not have to. Usually the guardianship does not end before the child is 21 years old.

Guardians are sometimes appointed for persons who are mentally or physically unable to take care of themselves or to manage their own business affairs. This kind of guardian is called a *trustee.*

Guarnieri

Guarnieri was the name of a family of violin-makers who lived in the city of Cremona, in Italy, and made some of the finest violins of all history. Their violins are called Guarnierius violins. The first violin-maker in the family was Andrea Guarnieri, who was born about 1626. The greatest of all the Guarnieris was Giuseppe, who was born in 1683 and died in 1745. He was known as *"del Gesù"* (*Gesù* means Jesus) because he marked all of the violins he made with a cross and the letters IHS, which is a Greek abbreviation for Jesus. Three or four of the del Gesu Guarnierius violins are considered by experts to be the finest ever made.

Guatemala

Guatemala

Guatemala is a small country in Central America. It is about the same size as the state of Tennessee, but has more people than Tennessee. It has the largest population in Central America, with more than four million people. For a brief period in 1953 and 1954 Gautemala was often in the news because it fell under the control of a Communist government, but later in 1954 the Communist government was replaced by a more democratic one.

Guatemala extends through Central America, with a seacoast on the Pacific Ocean on the west and a shorter seacoast on the Caribbean Sea on the east.

WHAT KIND OF PLACE IT IS

A volcanic mountain range cuts through the center of Guatemala. This mountain area, called the highlands, covers most of Guatemala except for a strip of jungle about thirty miles wide on each coast, and a large plain in the north called El Petén.

Along the coast, where it is low and flat, the climate is uncomfortably hot and damp, and very few people live there. In the highlands it is cooler the higher you go, and the weather is usually like spring.

The only seasons in Guatemala are the dry season from November to May and the rainy season from May to November. Because of the better climate in the highlands, only one Guatemalan out of every two hundred lives in the northern plain, though that region covers one-third of the nation.

There are more than thirty volcanoes in Guatemala, many of them more than 10,000 feet high. Some still erupt and spill their molten lava down the mountainside without much warning. Many cities and villages have been destroyed in this way. Earthquakes also occur often. However, the people come back to live in the highlands, because when the lava cools it makes excellent soil and fine coffee trees will grow there.

Many rivers flow down from the mountains, especially toward the Pacific Ocean. Ships cannot sail these rivers, but their waters are used to irrigate farm lands during the dry season. Ships can sail down the important Motagua River, which empties into the Atlantic Ocean. Guatemala has three large lakes, Izabal, Petén-Itza, and the beautiful Atitlán.

Many useful trees grow in the low jungle sections. Bananas are the most important, and the chicle, from which chewing gum is made, is widely grown. Mahogany for furniture, the huge ceiba for kapok to stuff mattresses, chinchona for the medicine quinine, and even camphor trees, are found in the jungle. In the Petén region there are jaguars, pumas (a

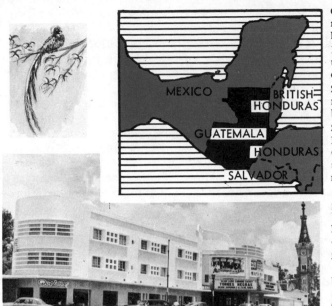

Guatemala (black area on map) has many mountains, large farms, and cities.

1. Hollywood movies are popular in Guatemala City, the country's capital.

2. Violent earthquakes have ruined many of Guatemala's beautiful old buildings.

3. Guatemala City has many lovely parks. The Roman Catholic Cathedral is the center of the Church to which most Guatemalans belong.

4. Tourists and rich coffee growers enjoy the resorts and beautiful sights of Antigua. Many of them visit the church of Our Lady of Mercy.

5. Spain ruled Guatemala until 1821, and the Spanish built imposing buildings such as this Palace of the Captains-General in Antigua.

Guatemala Nat'l Tourist Bureau

kind of wildcat), crocodiles and many other wild animals. There are more than nine hundred kinds of bird. It is against the law to kill one kind, the quetzal bird. The quetzal has brilliant green and red plumage and a crested head. Guatemala has made this bird the national emblem, like the eagle in the United States, and they call their dollar bills quetzals.

THE PEOPLE OF GUATEMALA

Guatemala was originally settled by the Mayas, one of the most intelligent and industrious Indian tribes in America. The Spaniards came, bringing with them European religon, art, styles of dress, and language. The Indians learned from the Spaniards but also kept their own customs. More than half the people in Guatemala are pure-blooded descendants of the original Maya race. The rest are either Spanish or a mixture of Spanish and Indian. A person having both Spanish and Indian blood is called a *ladino*. Wherever

you go you will see both native Mayans and ladinos.

In the large cities, especially in Guatemala City, the capital, you may see men and women wearing the same style of clothing as in New York or Paris, but you will also see the bright-colored native dress. In the cities the people speak mostly Spanish and some English, but as you go to more isolated places you hear more of the native language spoken.

Almost all the people in Guatemala are farmers. On the cool mountain slopes they grow coffee, and in the coastal jungles they find chicle and grow bananas. The bananas are rushed to Puerto Barrios, where refrigerated ships wait to take them to the United States and Canada.

To the Guatemalan, the most important crop is corn, and it is grown everywhere. It is used in many tasty dishes, such as *tamales,* and to make corn meal. The people also raise and eat many strange fruits, such as the mango, papaya, and anona.

The Guatemalans used to scoop out the fruit of a large gourd and use the shell to make a musical instrument called the marimba. Now the marimba looks like a large xylophone and it is the national instrument of Guatemala.

The schools in Guatemala are good, and all children must attend. After kindergarten there are usually separate schools for boys and girls, and some-

Guatemala Nat'l Tourist Bureau Photos

Visitors to Guatemala are often awed by its mighty volcanoes and by the strange rocks found in its caves and grottos. They can also admire traces of the old civilization of the Mayan Indians.
1. In 1902, the Santa Maria volcano wiped out an entire village.
2. Mayan Indians carved their hieroglyphics on large slabs of stone.
3. Limestone drippings made a statue of a "mother and child."

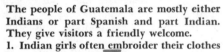

Guatemala Nat'l Tourist Office Photos

The people of Guatemala are mostly either Indians or part Spanish and part Indian. They give visitors a friendly welcome.

1. Indian girls often embroider their clothes with colorful figures.

2. An Indian mother may carry her baby on her back and the wash on her head.

3. Many visitors to Guatemala bring home rugs and shawls hand-woven by the Indians.

4. High volcanoes surround Lake Atitlán.

5. People rest in the hot afternoon sun.

6. Family prayers start and end the day.

times the children wear uniforms. The excellent San Carlos University of Guatemala, founded in 1676, is one of the oldest in the New World.

HOW THE PEOPLE ARE GOVERNED

The Republic of Guatemala is divided into twenty-two departments, which are like states in the United States. Its government is similar to that of the United States, with a legislature to make laws and a President elected by the people. Citizens must be over 18 to vote. The judges are appointed by the legislature, and the governor of each department is appointed by the President. A new constitution adopted in 1956 guarantees freedom of the press, of speech and assembly, and the protection of workers. All men between 18 and 50 must serve in the army or air force.

CHIEF CITIES OF GUATEMALA

Guatemala City is the capital. It is the largest city in Guatemala and in all of Central America, with a population of about 374,000. It is the business, political, educational, and transportation center.

Quezaltenango, with 36,000 people, is the second-largest city. It is in the center of the important farming area.

Puerto Barrios is one of the most important ports on the Caribbean Sea, chiefly exporting bananas. Its population is about 20,000.

GUATEMALA IN THE PAST

The Mayan people probably settled in Guatemala about three thousand years ago. They went there from Mexico. They made a fine civilization, with great advancements in agriculture, astronomy, and arithmetic, but they were no match for the Spanish explorers in warfare. The first Spaniards, commanded by Pedro de Alvarado, arrived in the year 1523, not long after Columbus discovered the New World.

The Spaniards were greatly outnumbered, but they would help one tribe fight another, and by dividing the natives they weakened them. Finally, in a hand-to-hand battle between the great Indian chief Tecum Uman and Alvarado, the Spaniards won, and the Mayas became a conquered people.

One of the most dramatic episodes in Guatemalan history occurred after the death of Alvarado, who had become governor. His wife, Doña Beatriz, who called herself "The Unfortunate One" because of his death, wanted to become the new governor. On September 9, 1541, she became the first and only woman ever to head a government in the New World under the Spanish administration. That night a great flood of very hot water burst out of a nearby volcano, Agua, and swept over the capital, Ciudad Vieja, destroying the entire city and killing hundreds. One of those killed was "the unfortunate" Doña Beatriz. The city was never rebuilt.

Guatemala remained under Spanish rule until 1821, when most of Spain's American colonies rebelled. In the years that followed many men tried to seize power, but few were outstanding until Justo Rufino Barrios became president in 1873. He ruled for twelve years, in which time he established a department of education, built highways and railroads, encouraged the planting of coffee, cacao, and bananas, and tried to get all the Central American nations to unite into one country. Barrios is often called the Lincoln of Guatemala. There are statues of him everywhere and the seaport Puerto Barrios bears his name.

The government of Guatemala has had many changes and revolutions throughout its history. During World War II Guatemala fought on the side of the Allies.

GUATEMALA. Area, 42,042 square miles. Population (1964 estimate) 4,305,000. Language, Spanish. Religion, mainly Roman Catholic. Government, republic. Monetary unit, the quetzal, worth $1.00 (U.S.). Flag, a blue, a white, and a blue vertical stripe, with coat-of-arms in center stripe.

The guava's fruit makes fine preserves; the tiny blossoms smell delightful.

guava

Guava is a tree that bears a sweet-tasting fruit used in making jellies, jams, and preserves. It can also be eaten fresh. The guava fruit is shaped somewhat like a pear and is about the size of a hen's egg. The guava plant grows mostly in the West Indies, but it is cultivated by a few fruit-growers in the warm parts of the United States. It grows to a height of fifteen to thirty feet. It has smooth, light green, egg-shaped leaves, and fragrant white blossoms.

Guelphs and Ghibellines

The Guelphs and the Ghibellines were two opposing groups in Europe about eight hundred years ago. Each group was named for the family at the head of it. The Guelphs were named for a German family named Welf, from which came many later kings of European countries. The Ghibellines were perhaps named for Waiblingen, a possession of the Hohenstaufens, a German family from which came several emperors of the Holy Roman Empire. In Italy, these names were spelled Guelph and Ghibelline.

For several hundred years the two groups were rivals for power, and each group had its share of successes.

Guiana

Guiana is a stretch of land on the northeast coast of South America. It is between the two largest rivers of that continent—the Orinoco and the Amazon Rivers. It is also bordered by the countries of Venezuela and Brazil. The climate of Guiana is always extremely hot, although there is heavy rainfall throughout the year. Deeper inside the Guiana country there are hills and mountains. The highest mountain is Mount Roraima, 8,640 feet high. Many hundreds of years ago, the native Indian population of Guiana was defeated in a war with the Dutch. Later on, the French and English took over part of the land. See FRENCH GUIANA, BRITISH GUIANA (now GUYANA), and SURINAM (Dutch Guiana).

guided missile

A guided missile is a flying device, carrying an explosive charge, that is like an aircraft except that it carries no men but is steered by radio equipment that it carries and that can be controlled by ground crews or by automatic machinery inside the guided missile. In World War II there were no true guided missiles, though the German V-2, used in the last months of the war, was a forerunner of the guided missile (see FLYING BOMB). Since World War II every big country has developed guided missiles, most of them carrying "atomic warheads" (an atomic or hydrogen bomb as the explosive part of the missile) that can destroy big cities and kill all the people in them.

Guided missiles are grouped into classes, depending on how they are launched and what their targets are:

Ground-to-ground (or surface-to-surface). This type of missile is launched from the attacking country and is aimed and guided so as to hit a target on the ground, for example a city, in the enemy country. Guided missiles launched from ships or submarines are placed in this class.

Ground-to-air (or surface-to-air). A missile launched from the ground and designed to seek out and destroy an attacking aircraft or missile sent by an enemy.

Air-to-ground (or air-to-surface). A missile launched from an airplane toward targets on the ground or sea.

Air-to-air. A missile launched by an airplane toward an attacking airplane or missile.

BALLISTIC MISSILES

A true guided missile is distinguished from a *ballistic missile,* which is always of the ground-to-ground type and aimed when it is launched, just as a shell from a cannon is. Ballistic missiles are grouped in two classes, called by the initials of their names: The ICBM, or Intercontinental Ballistic Missile, which must be able to travel under its own power and strike a target 5,000 or more miles from its launching point; and the IRBM, or Intermediate Range Ballistic Missile, which is a similar device but is designed to strike targets only 800 to 3,000 miles from its launching point. An ICBM may have a speed ranging from 600 to 14,000 or more miles per hour. Nearly every artificial satellite has been developed from an ICBM. The Russian sputniks have resulted from their experimental ICBMs. In the United States, the Army, Navy and Air Force have independently developed guided and ballistic missiles, but since 1957 the Air Force has been given the chief responsibility and the Air Force base at Cape Canaveral, Florida, has been the chief base. Missiles developed in the United States have all been given names. The Army's ground-to-air "Nike" (named for the Greek goddess of victory) and ground-to-ground "WAC Corporal" missiles were the earliest put into operation. The Army's "Jupiter" and Navy's "Vanguard" powered the first successful American artificial satellites.

DESIGN AND OPERATION

Some guided missiles are called "glider" missiles, because they are launched from planes and depend partly on the power of gravity and the impetus given to them by the speed of the plane to carry them to their targets; but nearly all modern guided missiles are propelled by ROCKET power (about which there is a separate article) or have rocket boosters to start them, after which jet engines take over. The missiles may look like rockets or like medium-sized airplanes with short wings. Each missile carries, besides its warhead, electronic equipment by which it guides itself or can be guided by a control room on the ground. There are several methods of guiding the missile:

1. By radar, which registers in the missile the position of the target. The radar either guides the missile to the target or sends a radio message back to the control room, which then steers the missile by radio. But radio signals can be jammed by an enemy transmitter.

2. By an electric eye in the nose of the missile. This will guide the missile to anything that the beam of the electric eye strikes. However, enemy planes or missiles can drop obstructions that will meet the beam of the electric eye and send the missile astray.

3. By following a radar beam from the ground, which will intercept enemy aircraft or missiles. This is the favored method for ground-to-air missiles used in defense of cities and military targets.

4. By being preset so that a telescope takes bearings from the stars and sends back radio signals giving its position, so that a control unit can guide the missile by radio. This is the favored method for long-range missiles.

5. By a heat-seeker, an electronic device for measuring heat. There are devices so sensitive that they respond to the heat of planets or stars. A heat-seeker directs a missile to any source of heat; it may be the smokestack on a ship or factory.

All these methods have certain disadvantages. Radio signals can be jammed; radar signals end at the horizon; heat guided missiles may strike unintended targets.

USE OF GUIDED MISSILES

The guided missile is acknowledged to be the principal weapon of future war-

Douglas Aircraft

Air Force Photos

1. The Nike, a guided missile used against attacking aircraft, is launched into the air from ground batteries that can be moved from one place to another by truck, rail, or airplane. The Nike, like most other guided missiles, has fins to stabilize its flight (keep it from wobbling).

2. Takeoff of the Thor, an IRBM with a 1,500-mile range, in a test at Cape Canaveral, Florida. The Thor is powered by a rocket using a liquid fuel. It delivers a thrust of 135,000 pounds, fifty times that of the Nike.

3. Test launching of the Atlas ICBM, which has a range of more than 5,000 miles, at Cape Canaveral. The Atlas's three rocket engines may deliver a thrust up to 400,000 pounds and a speed up to 14,000 miles per hour.

4. One type of guided-missile operation: Radio-control station (C) guides missile through radio-control receiver (R). Oxygen (O) mixing with fuel (F) provides rocket power through exhaust (E) and nozzle (N). Warhead (W) explodes on hitting target.

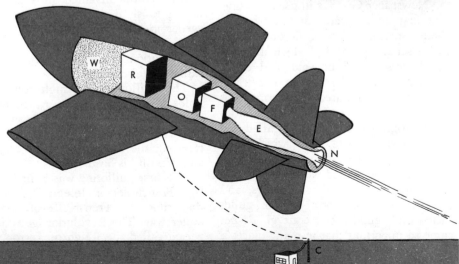

fare, and to be so deadly a weapon that it is hoped no major war can start because every country must fear total destruction from the guided missiles of its enemy. The United States has sought security by establishing throughout the world launching bases for guided missiles and by building aircraft carriers to carry planes capable of launching guided missiles, plus submarines and cruisers (some of them atomic-powered) that can approach an enemy coast by sea and launch guided missiles. In 1954, the U.S. Air Force spent only 10% of its procurement funds on guided missiles; in 1959 this had risen to almost 50%.

Missiles like the Titan and the Atlas have proved accurate within two miles at distances of 5,000 miles and can travel as far as 9,000 miles. Plans are on the drawingboard for super-rockets that will thrust 100-ton satellites into orbit or 50-ton satellites deep into space.

guild

Guilds were organizations of merchants and skilled craftsmen during the Middle Ages, hundreds of years ago. The labor unions of our time grew out of these guilds, and some unions, such as the Newspaper Guild, still use the name. The first guilds were formed by merchants in the cities of Europe. These guilds set the prices for which different merchandise could be sold, and established customs and rules for fair trade.

About seven hundred years ago, groups of these guilds in several European cities joined together in a league called the HANSEATIC LEAGUE, about which there is a separate article. About two hundred years later, the skilled workers or craftsmen, such as goldsmiths, weavers, and bakers, began to form similar guilds called craft guilds. The craft guilds became so important that in many places a person could not work at his trade unless he was a member of the guild. Each

guild decided how its trade would be run, what materials should be used, and what things the workers should make. Anyone who wanted to become a member of a guild had to follow very strict rules. You can read more about them in the article on APPRENTICESHIP.

guillemot

The guillemot is a small sea bird about the size of a raven. It lives on fish and dives into the ocean to get them. Guillemots are numerous along rocky coasts of the northern oceans near the Arctic. They lay their eggs on ledges facing the sea. The egg of the guillemot is much thicker at one end than at the other, so that it cannot roll off the ledge. When the wind blows the egg it spins around instead of rolling. Each pair of guillemots produces one egg a year. The parents take turns lifting the egg onto their webbed toes and warming it with their feathered legs. Guillemots can be made into pets and become intelligent and entertaining companions.

guillotine

The guillotine is a machine for capital punishment, that is, for killing criminals who have been sentenced to death. It was invented in France but machines similar to it had been used earlier in other countries of Europe. In our time most countries use hanging, electrocution, or the gas chamber for capital punishment.

The guillotine is a high frame that holds a heavy knife blade. At the foot of the frame the condemned person places his head on a block. When a spring is released, the knife blade falls very fast and cuts off his head.

The first guillotine was built in 1792 by a French doctor, Joseph Guillotin. At that time the French Revolution was under way. The Revolution grew into a period called the Reign of Terror when noblemen, members of the royal family, and any real or imagined political enemies of the government were put to death, sometimes after an unfair trial, or even no trial at all. The king and queen of France, Louis XVI and Marie Antoinette, died on the guillotine.

Guinea

Guinea is a republic on the west coast of Africa. Formerly a part of French West Africa, it became an independent country in 1958. The name Guinea is also applied to the region in which this country lies, a vast area along a coastline of about 1,500 miles on the Gulf of Guinea, which is part of the Atlantic Ocean. A small part of this region is Portuguese Guinea, a possession of Portugal.

The Republic of Guinea has an area of 96,865 square miles, which is about the size of the state of Oregon. Its population is about 3,500,000. The capital is Conakry, an important seaport on the Atlantic, a city of about 113,000 people. Almost all the people of Guinea are Africans of the Negro race. They speak a Sudan Negro language and, in the cities, French. Many of the people are Christians (chiefly Roman Catholics) but still more follow native religions. Most of the people are farmers, the soil being very fertile, and their principal crops are bananas and coffee; but there is mining of iron ore and bauxite (aluminum ore), about 1,-500,000 tons of ores being shipped through Conakry each year. Nearly all the land belongs to the natives. The climate is tropical—hot all year around, with a rainy season in the summer. There are some mountains (the highest being 6,000 feet), in which are the sources of the Niger and Senegal Rivers.

The territory that is now the Republic of Guinea was claimed as a French colony in 1882. During the seventy-five years that followed, France did much to raise living standards in Guinea, which became one of the most prosperous parts of Africa. In 1958 the French premier Charles de Gaulle offered independence to any French overseas territory that wished it, and while all other territories chose to remain associated with France, the principal political leader in Guinea, Sekou Touré, favored independence and the people supported him by an overwhelming vote. Guinea then joined the United Nations. Touré became the first President of Guinea and followed a pro-Communist policy.

GUINEA. Area, 96,865 square miles. Population (1964 estimate) 3,420,000. Government, republic. Capital, Conakry. Monetary unit, Guinea franc. Flag, vertical bars of red, yellow and green.

guinea fowl

Guinea fowl are birds that are like chickens but smaller, and are considered very good to eat. Unlike chickens, they like to roost, that is, go to sleep on the branch of a tree or some other perch. They live in flocks, and they lay their eggs on the ground. Guinea fowl are usually black-and-white striped, but some of the males of the wild guinea fowl have long, colorful tails and fancy, bright-colored head feathers.

guinea pig

The guinea pig is a small rodent, or gnawing animal, related to the rat and the squirrel. The guinea pig is not a kind of pig at all. Another name for it is the *cavy*. It is about six to ten inches long, and it can be brown, black, white, or a mixture of tan and white.

Guinea pigs are very important to science. They are used for testing medi-

N.Y. Zoological Society
Guinea pig

cines and reaction to diseases. There are two reasons for this. The first is that the guinea pig breeds so fast. A female guinea pig gives birth to a new litter, or group of newly born animals, about every ten to twelve weeks, and there may be four to twelve animals in a litter. Another reason is that in many ways the guinea pig's reaction to drugs and bacteria that cause diseases is the same as the reaction of a human being.

guitar

A guitar is a stringed musical instrument. It is shaped somewhat like a violin but is much larger. It has six strings stretched over the sound box and up a long neck. Plucking these strings with the fingers or with a plectrum or "pick" produces the sound. Along the neck are steel ridges called frets. Holding any string down against a fret with the fingers will change the note it will play when plucked. The guitar has become one of the most important instruments in dance bands, where it has replaced the banjo.

The guitar most used today comes from Spain and has six strings. Three are silk covered with wire, and three are cat-gut, which is tough string made from the insides of certain animals.

The Hawaiian steel guitar is played by Hawaiian musicians. This guitar is not made of steel. It is called a steel guitar because a small steel bar is held against the strings when the guitar is being played. The steel bar gives the music of the guitar a wailing sound.

Guiteau, Charles

Charles Guiteau was the man who killed President James A. Garfield. Guiteau was a lawyer in Chicago, and in 1880 he went to Washington, D.C. He spent a great deal of time trying to get himself appointed to a government job. He especially wanted the job of United State consul in Marseilles, France. But no one paid any attention to him, and this made him very angry. He shot President Garfield on July 2, 1881, in the waiting room of a railroad station in Washington. On September 19, the President died from the wound. Guiteau was hanged in June 1882, in the District of Columbia jail.

Gulf Stream

The Gulf Stream is like a river of warm water that flows through the At-

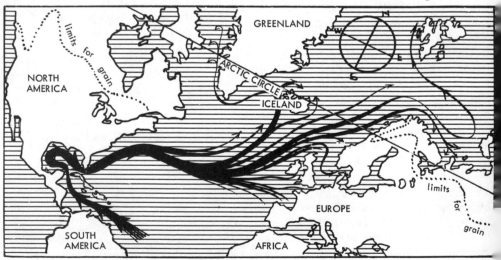

The Gulf Stream rises in the Gulf of Mexico from equatorial water drifts coming from South America. It flows around Florida, then north and east.

lantic Ocean. The Gulf Stream is about fifty miles wide and about two thousand feet deep. It begins in the Gulf of Mexico and flows through the Florida Straits and up the east coast of the United States as far as Nantucket Island. Then the Gulf Stream heads east into the Atlantic Ocean, where it merges with another great current called the North Atlantic Drift. The Gulf Stream flows at a rate of about four miles an hour in the Gulf of Mexico. The temperature of the water in the Gulf of Mexico is about eighty degrees. The Gulf Stream cools off as it flows north and east, but its warm water helps to keep the land along the American shore much warmer than it would be otherwise and it also helps to keep the British Isles warm. In Florida the deep blue color of the Gulf Stream can be seen from the shore. Many large deep-sea fish live in the Gulf Stream, and it is a popular fishing ground.

gull

A gull is a long-winged, grey-white bird that lives at the seashore. Gulls sometimes float almost motionless in the air over harbors and along stretches of beach. With their powerful, graceful wings they use the least amount of motion to fly. Gulls can be seen in large numbers along most shores, floating in the water as most ducks do. From a distance they look like ducks.

Gulls belong to the tern family. They are known all over the world, but they are most familiar in Arctic and temperate climates. There are a hundred different kinds of gull. Most of them live near the sea, and so are called sea gulls. In size gulls may be 20 to 30 inches long. In color almost all gulls are grey on top and white underneath, so that if you look up at them from the ground they are almost invisible against the sky. The young are usually brown, and some gulls remain brown, spotted with white. Others have large black markings. The roseate gull of the Arctic is a beautiful shade of

Margot L. Wolf

A soaring gull is one of the most graceful creatures in the world.

pink; it is sometimes called "the rose that blooms unseen," because so few people have come across it.

Sea gulls have many remarkable habits. They have almost unbelievable endurance and have been known to follow ships far out to sea and even cross oceans in flight. In some places they feed on clams, and since they cannot break the clam shell with their bills they fly up and drop it on a rock to break it open. Gulls breed in colonies on islands. When the young are hatched, they are covered with down. They are able to walk but they are dependent on their parents until they can fly. While gulls are breeding they feed on the young and the eggs of other birds that are nesting near them. A full-grown gull is a scavenger, which means it feeds on refuse cast off by ships or washed up on the shores by the sea. This habit makes them useful to man.

gum arabic

Gum arabic is a kind of gum used in making perfumes, medicine, candies, and mucilage. The mucilage on postage stamps and envelope flaps is made from gum arabic, but it is mixed with sugar to prevent it from cracking. Gum arabic is very pleasant smelling and therefore it is used as a base for perfumes. Sometimes

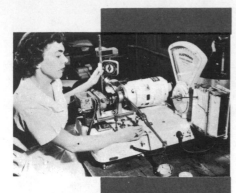

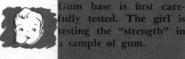
Gum base is first carefully tested. The girl is testing the "strength" in a sample of gum.

A "clarifier" removes impurities from gum base, which now looks like lava from a volcano.

American Chicle Co. Photos

In the coating room, flavor is added to thousands of Chiclets in a rapidly revolving drum. Next they are packaged.

it is used on textiles to give them a sheen. Gum arabic comes from the sap of the acacia tree, which grows in the northwestern part of Africa. For this reason it is sometimes known as *gum acacia*.

gum chewing

Chewing gum is a pliable substance that is given a sweet or other agreeable flavor and chewed for its taste and also because it helps some people to be less nervous. Chewing gum as it is known today was first made in the United States, less than a hundred years ago, but chewing for pleasure had been known long before that, for hundreds or even thousands of years.

Many people had chewed the sap of the spruce tree and paraffin waxes in the same way that they chew gum today. Even the most primitive people chewed grasses, berries, and tree barks for pleasure. Although many people think that gum chewing is an unattractive habit, some doctors say that it is helpful because it aids digestion, relaxes tension, and helps concentration.

Chewing gum is particularly popular in the United States, where the people spend $264,000,000 on gum each year. The making of chewing gum has become a major industry, and one of the tallest buildings in the United States, the Wrigley Building in Chicago, was built with the money earned from the sale of gum.

HISTORY OF CHEWING GUM

Chewing gum was first sold in 1869, in Jersey City, New Jersey. It was made by Thomas Adams, a merchant and inventor, and his son, Horatio. This gum was made from chicle, which is the latex from the sapodilla tree. This tree grows wild in southern Mexico and Central America.

Adams had been experimenting with chicle to see if he could use it as a substitute for rubber, but he had had no success. One day he saw a little girl buying some paraffin chewing wax and remembered that he had chewed the chicle during his experiments with it. That night he and his son rolled the chicle into round balls, packed it in boxes, and put it on sale in a nearby drugstore. This first chewing gum was successful from the very start. Soon after this Adams started a large plant in Brooklyn, and within a few years several other companies built plants to make gum. The original Adams' Sons Chewing Gum Company later joined other companies and became the American Chicle Company, one of the largest chewing-gum companies.

The first chewing gum was unflavored. The first flavoring to be used in it was licorice. Peppermint was used as a flavor soon after that. Dr. Beeman, a Cleveland pharmacist, started to put pepsin into gum as an aid to digestion. As more and more companies began to make chewing gum, more and more flavors were used. The round balls of gum were replaced by pencillike sticks and finally by the flat slab form that gum is made in today.

Scientists working for the chewing-gum companies discovered that other gums added to the chicle made the gum smoother and finer. Most modern chewing gums are made from newly developed plastics, but some are made from a combination of several gums. Gutta siak, a sap obtained from trees that grow in Malaya, is one of the most commonly used gums. Bubble gum is made of a different plastic, one that is tougher and more elastic.

HOW CHEWING GUM IS MADE

Today chewing gum is made in modern factories with modern machines. If plastics are used, they are extruded, or forced through an opening, to form a long, flat bar that is cut into "sticks"; the flavoring is added when the plastic compound is mixed.

When gums are used, they are "cooked," or heated until they are "runny." Then the mixture is sweetened, usually with corn syrup, or sugar, and the flavors are added.

A machine called a kneader fixes the mixture into a velvety texture. Then the mixture is rolled on a rolling belt until it is the proper thickness. As the gum is being rolled it is sprinkled with powdered sugar.

Knives mark off widths and lengths in patterns, and then the gum is sliced into squares before it is cut down into individual sticks. Candy-coated gum, such as Chiclets, is rolled in thicker widths, broken into squares by machines, and coated. The coating is polished by another machine.

The wrapping and packing of chewing gum is also done by machine. The paper in which the gum is wrapped is moistureproof and sealed airtight so that none of the freshness and flavor of the gum can escape. The individual packages are packed in boxes and shipped to all parts of the world.

USE OF CHEWING GUM

Most people like to chew gum. They feel that it makes them more relaxed, and they enjoy the taste. Some people are able to concentrate harder when they have gum to chew. Many students believe that they do better work on examinations if they chew gum.

During World War II many of the soldiers chewed gum to relieve the tension when they were on duty. The Army also found that gum chewing relieved the soldiers' thirst. Many athletes find that they are calmer if they are chewing gum during a big contest. Factory workers with dull jobs like to chew gum, too, for it relieves some of their boredom.

Many airlines give gum to their passengers to relieve the discomfort in their ears that is caused by varying air pressures. In the same way, the chewing of gum may relieve the temporary deafness that comes with a bad cold. People also chew gum, particularly chlorophyll gum, to make their breath sweeter.

There are certain rules that everyone who chews gum should follow. It is not good manners to chew gum in public

The story of gunpowder in the United States follows the story of the E.I. du Pont de Nemours Company. When Eleuthère du Pont came to the United States from France, he discovered, while hunting, that American gunpowder was inferior.

President Thomas Jefferson studied du Pont's plans for a gunpowder mill and approved of them. Jefferson felt that the United States should not have to depend on European manufacturers to fill the need for good gunpowder.

places, such as in school or on the street. The person who chews gum should keep his mouth closed and should chew quietly. Most young children like to blow bubbles with bubble gum, but they have to learn to be careful that they do not get gum on themselves and on their clothing. Gum should always be thrown away wrapped in a paper of some sort so that it will not stick to anything, as it is very hard to remove from any surface.

gum tree, a tree that gives off a resin or gum of some kind: see the articles on EUCALYPTUS and SWEET GUM.

gun

A gun is a weapon that fires bullets or explosive shells. There are separate articles on the different kinds of gun. *Pistols* and *revolvers* are small guns that can be fired with one hand. *Rifles* are weapons that are fired from the shoulder. They have twisted grooves inside the barrel, so that the bullet spins as it flies through the air. This spinning keeps the bullet on a straight course, just as the spinning of a football does when it is thrown properly. *Shotguns,* which are also fired from the shoulder, shoot shells containing many tiny bullets that fly in many directions. Shotguns are often used for hunting animals. *Machine guns* fire a

continuous stream of bullets. *Cannon* are large guns that are used by the artillery.

Most guns today are loaded with cartridges at the breech, which is the end where the trigger is. (See the article on AMMUNITION.) The first guns were invented about seven hundred years ago. Modern guns are of all sizes, firing bullets less than a quarter of an inch in diameter, or shells 18 inches in diameter. Big guns have been built to fire shells a distance of 75 miles.

gunboat

A gunboat is a small warship that is used for patrolling rivers and coasts. About 150 years ago, President Thomas Jefferson ordered the building of a fleet of gunboats for the navy, each carrying one large gun. These ships were not designed for sailing on the open sea, and they could not do much to protect the Atlantic coast from the British during the War of 1812. Gunboats were used by the North on the Mississippi River during the Civil War, and they helped capture control of this river for the Union. In 1937, there was a crisis between Japan and the United States, when Japanese planes sank the American gunboat *Panay* near Nanking, China. Gunboats are similar to the small cutters that are used by the Coast Guard.

Workmen in the United States soon learned to produce an excellent gunpowder. At first, charcoal, saltpeter and sulfur were kept in open barrels and mixed in simple scales. For a long time, frequent explosions made the job dangerous.

Many new kinds of explosive were developed in the nineteenth century. Lammot du Pont (standing) discovered an important new blasting powder. It helped construction workers to "move mountains" as the United States grew.

guncotton

Guncotton is an explosive made by treating cellulose fibers, such as cotton, with nitric acid. It is a form of nitro-cellulose. Guncotton was discovered during the 1890s and was one of the first materials used to make "smokeless powders," which replaced gunpowder as the principal explosive used in firearms. Guncotton looks like fine, very white, fluffy cotton such as that used to spin thread for cloth. Read also the articles on AMMUNITION, EXPLOSIVES, and NITROGEN.

The early du Pont saltpeter refinery was very small. The square building on the right was the drying room for refined saltpeter. Other buildings of the early mill were badly damaged by a great explosion in 1890.

gunpowder

Gunpowder is an explosive made of sulfur, saltpeter and charcoal ground up and mixed into the form of a powder. Its color is such a dark gray that it is almost black. When set on fire, it explodes and so can be used in firearms, as you can read in the article on AMMUNITION. It is believed that the Chinese were the first people to use gunpowder. They used it mostly in fireworks. When Europeans learned about it, they saw it could be used to fire missiles much harder than the catapults they had used before. The first cannons were used about 650 years ago. They changed the entire method of warfare.

The size and shape of the tiny grains of which gunpowder is made up are im-

E.I. du Pont de Nemours & Co. Photos

A laboratory room, built to create ideal low-humidity conditions for the easy firing of gunpowder, enables a scientist to test the effectiveness of different kinds of gunpowder. The scene is Northwestern University in Illinois.

portant, because space must be left between them so the fire can enter. For a long time no one knew much about this, and sometimes the guns loaded with gunpowder would burst. The gunner had to know just how to "ram" the powder into the gun so it would not go off too fast. This was hard to learn, and gunners who knew how to pound the powder into the gun just right were highly paid.

HOW IT WAS MADE

When gunpowder was first made, it was ground in holes cut in logs. Then special machines were made to do this work. It was very dangerous because a small spark would cause the gunpowder to go off, killing the workmen. So many men were killed in England making gunpowder for use in hunting that a law was passed against this kind of factory. About three hundred years ago people learned to make gunpowder into a kind of cake by wetting it. After this it was ground, and the gunpowder worked better and was safer.

In those days guns were smooth inside. When it was learned that grooves inside the guns made them shoot straighter, a new kind of gunpowder was needed. This was because the grooves kept the cannon balls from being driven out of the gun as fast as before. The old kind of gunpowder exploded very fast and when the ball did not leave the gun quickly the gun would burst. General Thomas Rodman of the United States Army found a way to make a gunpowder that would not do this, and soon armies all over the world began using it.

In the early days of gunpowder not much could be made because it was hard to find enough saltpeter (which is also called niter).

Later large deposits of nitrate, which is used in making saltpeter, were found in Chile, but for most uses gunpowder has been replaced by smokeless powder and other explosives, as you can read in the article on EXPLOSIVES.

Gunpowder Plot, a conspiracy to blow up the British houses of Parliament in London, on November 5, 1605. See the article on Guy FAWKES.

guppy

The guppy is a tiny fish that is popular in home aquariums because it is an easy fish to breed. Male guppies grow to be about three quarters of an inch long, and their bodies have bright patches of red and yellow, violet, orange, and black. The female is about twice as large as the male, and it is a pale greenish-gray. The female guppy can have from fifteen to fifty live babies about once every month.

Guppies live in the warm waters of streams and ponds in South America, and they have been taken to almost every tropical part of the world. The little guppy is a very useful fish. It eats mosquito eggs, and for this reason it has been bred in many places. Scientists have learned many important new things from their study of the guppy.

The guppy was named in honor of Dr. R. J. Guppy, a scientist who lived in the West Indies and who first took guppies to the British Museum in London, England.

Gurkha

A Gurkha is a warrior of Nepal, a mountainous country in Asia between India and Tibet. Gurkhas are Hindus by religion.

The Gurkha regiments were part of the British Army in World Wars I and II and they were famous for their strength, bravery, and independence. In addition to a rifle, a Gurkha always carries a *kukri*, which is a heavy, curved knife. The Gurkhas used to say that when a kukri is drawn from its scabbard, it must draw blood before it is returned.

gurnards

Gurnards are small fish that seem to walk on the ocean floor. Actually, they are using their fins as legs. Other kinds of gurnard are flying fish that jump from the water and glide through the air for short distances. There are not many of the flying gurnards. Most kinds of gurnard are small, reaching a length of one foot. They are found mostly in the warmer waters, including some shores of the Atlantic Ocean. Other fish of the gurnard family are found in the Indian Ocean. The gurnard is also known as the *volanda*.

Gustavus

The name Gustavus has been borne by six kings of Sweden, and several of them were outstanding rulers and great leaders of their people.

Gustavus I, called Gustavus Vasa, was born in 1496. In his time, Denmark ruled Sweden, but some Swedish people wanted their country to be independent. Gustavus Vasa was a great leader in the war against Denmark, and when Sweden won its independence, he was elected its first king. He ruled until his death in 1560.

Gustavus II, known as Gustavus Adolphus, was a very great general. He was born in 1594. In his time, the countries of Europe were almost constantly at war, and Gustavus made his army one of the best in Europe and led it to many great victories. Gustavus II was also a great king at home. He reorganized the government, and helped the country to grow more prosperous. Gustavus was killed in battle in 1632. He is still remembered as Sweden's greatest military hero.

Gustavus V was born in 1858, and became king in 1907. He was a very democratic king, and was always most interested in the welfare of his country. When he became king, he would not have any great coronation, or crowning ceremony, because he thought it would be a waste of the country's money. He managed to keep his country peaceful in both World Wars.

Gustavus loved tennis, and even when he was past 80 he played a good game. When Gustavus died in 1950, he was 92 years old and had ruled for 43 years.

Gustavus VI, the son of Gustavus V, was born in 1882, and became king when his father died. Gustavus VI visited the United States twice before he became king, in 1926 and in 1938.

Gutenberg, Johannes

Johannes Gutenberg was a German printer who lived more than five hundred years ago in the city of Mainz. He was the first man to print a book from movable type. He was born about 1400. At that time books were printed by carving a complete page on a block of wood and printing from it. The block of wood was useful only for printing that particular book. Gutenberg made movable type—each letter was a separate block. It could be rearranged any number of times for printing different books.

The first book Gutenberg printed was a Bible that came to be known as the Gutenberg Bible. He probably printed it over the course of several years between 1445 and 1455. Sometimes this Bible is called the Mazarin Bible, because the first one ever found was owned by Cardinal Mazarin of France, who died in 1611. Other copies have been found since then. The Gutenberg Bible is now the most valuable book ever printed, and one or two sheets from a Gutenberg Bible have been sold for hundreds of dollars. Gutenberg printed many other books before he died in 1468. There is a Gutenberg Museum in Mainz and many statues of him have been erected in Germany.

gutta percha

Gutta percha is a thick rubberlike substance that is used to protect submarine cables, and to coat electrical equipment. Dentists also, use gutta percha, to make temporary fillings for cavities, in teeth. At one time golf balls were made entirely of gutta percha, but now they are made of rubber with a covering of gutta percha.

There are two things that make gutta percha very useful in all of these different ways. It is waterproof, and when you heat gutta percha it becomes soft so that it can be easily molded into any shape. Then it hardens quickly as it cools.

Gutta percha comes from the trunk and leaves of large evergreen trees that grow in Malaya, other Asiatic countries and South Sea Islands, and some parts of South America. The natives gather the thick green leaves and chop them to obtain the sticky juice. Sometimes they cut down the tree and make deep rings in the bark, and the gutta percha oozes from these rings. As it comes out, gutta percha looks like thick milk.

Gwyn, Nell

Nell Gwyn was an English actress who lived about three hundred years ago. She was born in 1650 and her parents died when she was very young, so she had to earn her own living. At first she did this by selling oranges near the theaters of London. A theater director noticed her beauty, her fiery red hair, and her good humor. He trained her for the stage when she was only 15. Her sense of humor and natural, unspoiled manner made her popular with audiences. She was a favorite of King Charles II, and though her behavior would not be considered moral today, she remained famous until her death in 1687.

gymnasium

A gymnasium is a place where people perform exercises and play certain games. It can be either indoors or outdoors. A gymnasium is built for such games and sports as basketball, handball, volleyball, boxing, wrestling, and badminton. Some gymnasiums are so large

that they have room for tracks for races or for indoor baseball. Gymnasiums also have rings and bars and other equipment for gymnastics.

Gymnasium is from a Greek word meaning "to exercise," and gymnasiums existed as far back as ancient Greek times, when men used to go to a spacious arena for a variety of athletic games and contests. In Europe the word *gymnasium* is often used to mean a high school.

gymnastics

Gymnastics is a form of physical activity for developing the body by means of exercise. Another term for gymnastics is *physical culture.* People usually perform gymnastics in a gymnasium, a place for exercise. However, gymnastics can also be done at home.

There are many kinds of gymnastics. One kind is performed without the use of any equipment, or apparatus. This includes such body exercises as push-ups and sit-ups. However, most kinds of gymnastics are performed with the aid of light apparatus or fixed apparatus. Some forms of light apparatus are clubs, weights called dumbbells, and balls. Fixed gymnastic apparatus includes bars to swing on, and other equipment such as horses, bars, rings, ropes, and mats. All of these are used to strengthen the arms, legs, and the upper part of the body.

Gymnastics as a whole is used for the improvement of muscles, for physical coordination, and to keep the body fit. Most schools require a program of gymnastics and there are gymnastic contests where the performers compete for style and form.

gypsum

Gypsum is a mineral that is very important to man for a number of uses. Sheets of gypsum are sometimes used as ready-made walls for homes. Builders mix gypsum with cement so that the cement will not harden too quickly. Gyp-

National Gypsum Co.

Gypsum miners work in cramped quarters as their rotary drill cuts into the rock.

sum also is an ingredient of many kinds of plaster. In fact, gypsum is sometimes called *plaster rock*. When gypsum is heated to remove the water from it, it becomes *plaster of Paris,* a plaster that can be molded easily and is used by sculptors, and also by doctors to make plaster casts.

Gypsum is found all over the world in many forms. A fine, delicately col-

Gypsum is used in making the plaster that the worker is spreading on the wall.

National Gypsum Co.

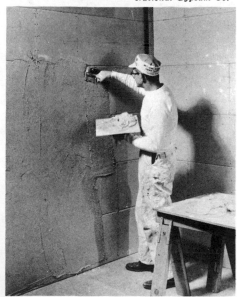

ored gypsum is called *alabaster,* which is used to make beautiful statues and vases. It is translucent (light can be seen through it). Another type of gypsum is called *satin spar,* from which certain kinds of jewelry are made.

Gypsum is one of the softest minerals found in the earth. It is so soft that it can be scratched with the fingernail. It is usually white or gray. The United States is the leading producer of gypsum.

gypsy

Gypsies are a group of people who have wandered through parts of Europe

Ewing Galloway

Many modern gypsies live in villages, but they still enjoy the gay dances and music of their wandering ancestors.

for hundreds of years. Many of them now live in American countries. No one is sure just where the gypsies came from, but very likely they once lived in India, because their language, called *Romany,* is somewhat like the languages of northwestern India. They call themselves *Rom,* which in gypsy language means "man."

About a thousand years ago, gypsies began to appear in northern Asia, traveling on foot or in wagons. Later they spread to North Africa and Europe. More of them stayed in the Balkan countries, such as Rumania, Bulgaria, and Hungary, than anywhere else.

For hundreds of years almost no gypsies had any permanent home. They

Left: Fortunetelling is a famous gypsy art. In a dark room lit by a single candle, the customer crosses the gypsy's palm with silver. Then the gypsy "reads the future" in the cards.

Ewing Galloway Photos

Right: Gypsies love holidays and fairs, where they can join in the singing and dancing. They put on their brightest dresses and decorate their carts in anticipation of merrymaking.

Left: In Spain, gypsies are welcome visitors at holiday festivities. Everyone knows that they will bring their guitars and violins, and that the graceful gypsy girls will whirl and stamp their feet in time to their clicking castanets.

Right: While dancing, the gypsies seem wild. But when the dance ends, the girls remain motionless, and their bright shawls hang in flowing curves from their shoulders.

wandered in wagons and camped out. They are a colorful and interesting people. Most of them are rather small, with light-brown skin, very black hair, beautiful dark eyes, and extremely white teeth. Gypsies, especially the women, wear bright-colored clothes, and both men and women often wear large earrings. Many of the women read palms, tell fortunes, and sell books on magic. Horse-trading used to be the main work of the gypsies, but they have had to change to other occupations, such as keeping stores in countries where they are allowed to own buildings and land. In Russia, Poland, and Hungary, many gypsies are musicians. They are especially good at playing the violin, and some great writers of music, such as Franz Liszt and Johannes Brahms, have used gay gypsy tunes in their compositions. The gypsies are known as good dancers, and gypsy girls used to be hired to entertain with their dances.

The gypsies' unsettled way of living has created prejudice against them in many places. In some parts of Europe they were driven out.

During the present century they have changed greatly. Many gypsies have settled in cities. They still keep to themselves, as they did earlier, but less than before. They still have their own language, but they also have learned the languages of the countries in which they have settled. Before World War II there were between two million and four million gypsies in the world. Since World War II there are fewer gypsies, because many were killed by the Germans when the Nazis controlled Germany.

gypsy moth

The gypsy moth is a destructive insect found mostly in the New England states of the United States. Its original home was Europe. While it is in the caterpillar stage and looks like a worm, it eats leaves and does great damage to trees. Many millions of dollars have been spent by the government in trying to wipe out or control the gypsy moth, but it continues to do great damage. It likes best to feed on the leaves of oak, birch, apple, alder, poplar and willow trees, but after such trees have been stripped of their leaves the gypsy moth caterpillars will feed on almost any tree.

gyroscope

The gyroscope is a kind of top. Like other tops, it spins. Originally, like other tops, it was only a toy. Then, because a man named Elmer Sperry had a brilliant idea for putting the gyroscope to practical use, it became one of the most important of all scientific instruments. Control of airplanes, bombsights and some kinds of guided missile are only a few of the scientific advances that have been based on the gyroscope.

Take any kind of top, and spin it in an upright position. As long as it is spinning fast, it will remain upright on its point, even though you know it would fall over if it were not spinning. As it begins to spin slower, it will lose its tendency to stand upright. It will gradually lean to the side until it topples over completely. Obviously, it stood upright because it was spinning and for no other reason.

Now spin a top in an upright position on a plank of wood that you can pick up and tilt to the side. While the top is spinning fast, pick up the plank and tilt it slightly. The top will not tilt with it. It will remain upright. If you tilt the plank enough the top will slide off, but it will continue to spin in its upright position until it slides off, and if it falls to the floor and is still spinning fast it will still be upright.

The scientific principle behind this can be explained as follows:

Imagine a straight line drawn from the bottom point, or spike, of the top straight up through it. While the top is spinning, this line is the *axis* on which it is rotating.

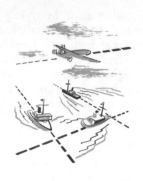

Sperry Gyroscope Co. Photos

1. In its simplest form a gyroscope is a toy that tends to stay upright when it spins.
2. When the flywheel on the axle supported by the inner ring of the gyroscope is spinning, no matter how the base is turned, the inner ring always will lie in the same position.
3. Sperry's first gyrocompass used a gyroscope to make a compass of great accuracy.
4. The top of a ship's radarscope must always show what is in the north. A gyrocompass does this automatically, and the navigator reading the radar cannot be misled.
5. The gyrocompass, shown with its housing removed, is a highly complex mechanism.
6. The master compass on a large ship determines the readings of small repeater compasses.

1. The air-driven Attitude Gyro is used in airplanes. The ball remains still. If the plane climbs, dives, or tips right or left, the markers on the gyro's face move around the ball, and show the plane's attitude or position.

2. Most airplanes have gyromagnetic compasses, which always point to the magnetic north.

3. The aircraft radio direction finder gives the pilot automatic compass readings. It also shows him the direction of north as recorded by a gyromagnetic compass.

Sperry Gyroscope Co. Photos

A spinning object will resist any tendency to change the direction of its axis of rotation. The faster it is spinning, the greater its resistance will be.

Consider an aircraft instrument that is supposed always to show a line that is level with the surface of the earth. Connect this instrument with a top that is kept spinning at high speed. The nose of the plane may point up or point down; the wings may tilt to the left or tilt to the right; but as long as that top is spinning, the instrument will always be level because the spinning top will not permit its axis of rotation to be changed.

That is the principle on which "gyro-" instruments, such as the gyrocompass and the gyrostabilizer and others, are based.

HOW THE GYROSCOPE IS MADE

They used to sell gyroscopes in five-and-ten-cent stores for a quarter; they still sell them for a dollar or a little less. Any one of these ten-cent-store gyroscopes will show you how a gyroscope works.

There is a wheel, called the flywheel, and through the center of the wheel runs a shaft, or bar of metal. The ends of the shaft are mounted in a ring. The ring is attached to a base. The flywheel can spin on the shaft; the ring can turn on the base; the base itself can be put in any position.

Start the flywheel spinning, then turn the ring or the base, or both, in any direction. The shaft (which is the axis of rotation of the spinning flywheel) will continue to point in the same direction.

The first serious use of the gyroscope was in the year 1818, when a spinning gyroscope was used to show why the earth keeps the same position as it rotates around the sun.

One great bar to serious use of the gyroscope was that it was so hard to keep it turning. This problem was solved about a hundred years ago when the electric motor was invented.

In 1910, Sperry founded the Sperry Gyroscope Company in Brooklyn, New York, to make navigation instruments based on the principle of the spinning top.

USES OF THE GYROSCOPE

There is at least one gyrocompass on every ship of every navy in the world, on most commercial vessels, and on many airplanes. The gyrocompass makes use of the fact that a gyroscope always points very steadily in the same direction. The gyrocompass is more accurate than the magnetic compass, because anything made of iron or steel will cause a magnetic compass to be wrong, but nothing changes a gyrocompass as long as it is spinning properly.

Some ships have their gyrocompasses connected to an electric motor that steers the ship. This arrangement is called a gyropilot. Whenever the ship veers a little off its course, the gyropilot causes the motor to turn the ship's rudder and steer it back onto its course.

The gyrostabilizer is a much larger instrument. One Italian ship has two gyrostabilizers that together weigh 660 tons. These devices make use of the steadying effect of the gyroscope. They are very heavy gyroscopes installed in the bottom of the ship to keep it from rolling. When a ship starts to roll in one direction, the gyrostabilizer shifts weight to the other side, making the ship stay level. This makes the voyage much more comfortable for the passengers and reduces strain on the ship.

H or h

The letter H is the eighth letter of the alphabet. It can be traced all the way back to the earliest writing known to man, in Egypt thousands of years ago. In the Hebrew language, in which much of the Bible was written, the letter was called *cheth,* which means "fence." The ancient Greeks took the same letter and called it *eta.* At first the Greek eta was an *aspirate,* which means a heavily breathed sound used before or after another sound, as in the English word *hope.* Later the Greeks expressed the aspirate, or rough breathing sound, by a sign somewhat like an apostrophe turned backwards. *Eta* then came to have a sound somewhat like the *a* in *fare.* The Romans, however, borrowed the earlier aspirate sound, and in English the H often has the rough breathing sound as in *hope,* but may have no sound at all, as in the word *hour.* In English the letter H can be joined with other letters to give sounds for which there is no single letter in our alphabet. We find these sounds in such words as *chop, shun, gherkin,* and *thin.*

At the top of the page, at the far left, you can see the Egyptian symbol, called a hieroglyph, from which the H came. Beside it is the Hebrew *cheth.* At the right of the capital H you can see the early Greek *eta.* You can easily see how much it is like our own H. At the right of that is the German "black-letter" capital H, used in many German books.

Read also the article ALPHABET.

Haakon

Haakon is a name of several kings of Norway. The one we know best is Haakon VII, who became the first king of Norway as we know it today. He was always well loved by his people, but especially so after his heroism in World War II. In 1940 Norway was one of the first countries attacked by the Germans. They struck without warning, and seized three seaports and the capital city of Oslo. Norway was unprepared and had no chance against the strong German armies, but King Haakon and his government refused to give in. They fled from the capital and

King Haakon VII

declared war against Germany. At last Haakon was forced to flee from his country. He went to England and set up a government-in-exile there, working hard to encourage and help his people. As soon as the Germans were defeated, in 1945, Haakon returned to Norway.

For hundreds of years Norway was united with Denmark and Sweden, or sometimes with only one of these two countries. During this period Norway was independent but had no king of its own. In 1905, the Norwegian people decided to break off their union (at that time with Sweden) and elect their own king. They chose Prince Charles of Denmark, a son of the king of Denmark.

Prince Charles was born in 1872 and was married to a daughter of the king of England. When Charles was elected to the throne of Norway, he chose for his official name an old Norwegian name and was crowned as King Haakon VII in 1906. He died in 1957, at the age of 85, and his son became king as Olav V.

habeas corpus

Habeas corpus are two words from the Latin language meaning "you may have the body." They have a legal meaning that is very important to liberty. Under the constitutions of the United States and other English-speaking countries, a person may not be imprisoned without a hearing before a judge. If a person is imprisoned without a hearing, his lawyer may get a writ of habeas corpus from the court. This writ, or order, means that the person must immediately be brought to court and unless the police can show good reason why he is being held he must be released.

The writ of habeas corpus has been a part of the law in England for hundreds of years. When the American colonies gained their freedom and wrote their constitution, the right of habeas corpus was put into the Bill of Rights, which is the first ten amendments to the Constitution.

habit

A habit is a need or desire to do something time after time, and to do it in the same way each time. A person may have a habit of rubbing his cheek when he thinks. Every time he is trying to solve a problem or decide something, he will rub his cheek. There are habits in speaking, such as saying "You see" many times when explaining something. *Doodling* is a kind of habit. A person doodles when he scribbles or draws with a pencil on paper while he is talking or thinking.

Habits that hurt the body, such as smoking too much or drinking too much, and habits that annoy other people, are called *bad habits* or *petty vices*. People who have them often try to give them up, but sometimes the desire to do them has become so great that this becomes very difficult. In these cases, the difficulty is in the mind and not in the body. That is, giving up the bad habit would not cause actual pain in the body. Dangerous drugs, however, can cause a kind of habit called *addiction*. When an addicted person stops taking the drug, he suffers actual pain and should be under a doctor's care. It is still necessary to give up the drug habit or die within a few years.

Certain habits become automatic. We do them without being conscious of it; that is, without thinking about it. Examples are swallowing when we eat and drink, and bending our knees when we walk. The special name for this kind of habit is *conditioned reflex.* There is a separate article on REFLEX.

hackberry

The hackberry is a tree of the elm family. It grows in North America. It is not as tall a tree as the elm, and has straighter branches and smaller leaves. The hackberry is sometimes called the *sugar-berry* or *nettle* tree. Its fruit is like a small black cherry, and it is good to eat. The wood of the hackberry is soft and coarse-grained; it is not strong enough to be very useful as lumber.

Hadassah

Hadassah is the name of a large organization of American Jewish women. It began in 1912 and was named for a Jewish heroine (see ESTHER). These women are Zionists; they believe that the Jewish people should have a homeland in Palestine. Both before and after 1948, when the state of Israel was founded in a part of Palestine, Hadassah did many things to help the people in that country. Hadassah founded hospitals for the sick. It also started health centers and clinics, where mothers could learn how to take good care of their children. An important part of Hadassah's program is called Youth Aliyah. This works to give orphans and needy children a permanent family home and an education. It also sets up schools to help young people learn how to earn a living.

There are about 320,000 women in the United States who belong to Hadassah, and they have chapters in forty-eight states. The headquarters is in New York City.

haddock

The haddock is an ocean fish. It is one of the most important food fish along the eastern coast of the United States. The haddock is related to the cod, and it is caught by fishermen in the same places as cod, all along the New England coast, and along the Grand Banks of Newfoundland, off the northeast coast of Canada. It usually weighs three or four pounds, and rarely is found heavier than fifteen pounds. The fish is eaten fresh, or dried and smoked. Smoked haddock is called *finnan haddie,* which is what the people of Scotland called it when they invented this way of preparing and eating haddock. Haddock is also caught on the other side of the Atlantic Ocean, around Great Britain and in the North Sea.

Haddock swim in schools (in large groups). They feed on invertebrate, or spineless, animals on the bottom of the ocean. They lay their eggs in the late winter or early spring, depending on how far south they may be and how warm the water is.

Hades

Hades is a word now used to mean about the same thing as Hell, a place where the souls of bad people go after death. To the ancient Greeks, more than two thousand years ago, it meant a place where the souls of all dead people, good or bad, went. It was not especially a place of punishment, but it was very gloomy and unpleasant. The king of Ha-des was the god Pluto, or Dis. His kingdom was bounded by the river Styx and guarded by Cerberus, a fearful dog with three heads. The souls of the dead had to pass through Erebus, a place of complete darkness, on their way to Hades. In some stories, there was a god called Erebus who ruled over this gloomy place.

Hadrian

Hadrian was an emperor of Rome when it was the greatest empire in the world. He lived about a hundred years after the time of Jesus. Hadrian was a very good ruler, and during his reign he had many beautiful temples and palaces built. His villa near Rome was a magnificent place that covered several square miles. It included a the-

ater, a stadium, a palace, several temples, and many other buildings. Its ruins can still be seen, and many of its fine statues are now in museums in Rome. Hadrian visited Britain, which was part of his empire, and there he had built a fortification called Hadrian's Wall. This wall was almost 75 miles long, running across the narrow part of the island of Great Britain. It was built in the years 122 to 124. The bits of it that are left today show that it must have been six feet high and eight feet thick. Every mile or so there were towers built for lookouts. Along the wall were roads, and camps for soldiers. The whole defense system is considered one of the best of ancient times.

Hadrian also built a mausoleum, or tomb, which has since been rebuilt and is now called the Castle of Saint Angelo. It is 230 feet across and the ancient concrete foundations are 300 feet square. The burial room and passages underground are just as they were in Hadrian's time, but the rest of the building has been very much changed through the centuries.

Hadrian was born in the year 76 and died in 138.

Haeckel, Ernst

Ernest Haeckel was a German biologist, that is, a scientist who studies living things. He was born in 1834, and he lived and taught for most of his life in the city of Jena. In Haeckel's time, Charles Darwin had just developed his theory of organic evolution, which says that new kinds of animals develop from changes in older kinds. Haeckel agreed completely with this theory, but he carried it so far that not even Darwin would have agreed with a great many of the things he said. Haeckel wrote a great many books and scientific papers. He died in 1919.

Hagenbeck, Carl

Carl Hagenbeck was a German who had the most famous collection of wild animals of all time. He was born in 1844. He got the idea for his career from watching his father, who had made a hobby of collecting and training animals. Carl toured Europe with his animals and in 1893 he brought a collection of more than one thousand of them to the United States to be shown at the Columbian Exposition, or World Fair, being held at Chicago. The tricks he taught his animals were very popular with the people who came to his shows, and they gave American circus men many ideas for wild animal acts. Hagenbeck stayed for a while in the United States, and joined his show with that of another man, named Wallace, to make the Hagenbeck-Wallace Circus, which became famous throughout he country.

In Hamburg, a big city in Germany, Hagenbeck thought up and built a new kind of zoo, where the animals live in surroundings that are like their natural homes, and are kept in only by deep ditches instead of bars. This idea is now being used in some of the biggest zoos in the United States, such as the New York Zoological Gardens and the Brookfield Zoo in Chicago. Hagenbeck died in 1913, but other members of his family carried on his work.

Hague, The

The Hague is one of the most important cities of the Netherlands. Though the city of Amsterdam is the official capital, The Hague has long been the city where the principal government offices are, and the Dutch parliament meets there. The Hague is also famous as the seat of the INTERNATIONAL COURT OF JUSTICE, about which you can read in a separate article.

The Hague is the third-largest city in the Netherlands (after Amsterdam and Rotterdam). About 600,000 people live there. The city has many fine gardens and parks and is criss-crossed by many canals. It is close to the sea, and nearby are many popular seaside resorts. It also has many historic buildings that

Netherlands Inform. Office

The queen arrives in a gold carriage to open the parliament at The Hague.

go back to important events in Dutch history.

The Hague was founded more than seven hundred years ago, in 1247, by Count William II of Holland. It was called *'s-Gravenhage,* which means "hedge of the counts," and that name is still used, even though the hedge that bounded Count William's castle and land is no longer there. Until 1948, The Hague was the home of the Dutch kings and queens.

Much of The Hague was destroyed by bombs in World War II, especially the remains of the great forest there in which the Dutch counts used to hunt. The people have since repaired much of the damage and have built new parks.

THE HAGUE, NETHERLANDS. Population (1960 estimate) 606,000. Founded in 1247.

Haig, Douglas

Douglas Haig was the highest-ranking officer in the British army at the end of World War I. He was born in 1861 in Scotland, and started his military career as a young man. In 1918, when the Germans started their last desperate drive and almost captured the city of Paris, Haig was commander of the British armies in France. Little by little he pushed the Germans back and finally won the last big battle of the war. At that time Haig was a field marshal, the highest rank in an army. After the war he was made an earl. He formed the British Legion, which is an organization of veterans somewhat like the American Legion. He also started the custom of selling poppies to raise money to help veterans. Haig died in 1928.

hail

Hail is little pebbles of ice that sometimes fall in showers from the clouds just before a thunderstorm, in very warm weather. Usually a shower of hailstones makes lots of noise, but does little damage. However, hailstones are sometimes as big as eggs, or even bigger,

Unations

Haile Selassie, Emperor of Ethiopia.

and then they can be very dangerous. The life story of a hailstone is interesting. It starts as a drop of ordinary rain water that is caught in a thundercloud blown up into the sky by a sudden blast of wind. The higher the raindrop goes the colder the air gets, until finally the raindrop is frozen into a tiny speck of ice. Now other blasts of wind catch the frozen raindrop and start blowing it up and down, all over the thundercloud. One moment it is whizzing through a pocket of warm, wet air, which coats it with water. The next moment it is zooming through another air pocket that is bitter cold and instantly freezes the water. In this way, little by little, a hailstone is built up. If the winds are fierce enough to keep the stone up in the air for quite a long time, it may grow as large as a baseball or a small grapefruit.

Haile Selassie

Haile Selassie is the name of a man who became emperor of Ethiopia, a country in Africa, in 1930. Five years later he became famous throughout the world because of his brave resistance to Italy's efforts to conquer his country. He personally led his armies in battle, even though they were armed only with swords and spears against the Italian cannons and tanks. In 1936 he made a very stirring speech to the League of Nations, begging them to help his country against the invaders. This speech was so moving that it was recorded, and many people have bought phonograph records of it.

The League of Nations would not help Haile Selassie, and the Ethiopians were defeated. Selassie escaped and fled to England. In 1941, after Italy had entered World War II as an ally of Germany, England flew Selassie back to Africa to encourage his people to fight the Italians. When World War II was over the Italians had lost and Selassie was emperor again. After the war Selassie continued his efforts to modernize and improve his country. He introduced schools, hospitals, electric lights, a European police sytem, and motion pictures. In 1954 Selassie came to the United States, where he was received by President Eisenhower and was a guest at the White House.

Haile Selassie traces his descent from King Solomon and the Queen of Sheba. His official title is the "Conquering Lion of Judah," and another of his titles is Negus, which means about the same thing as "emperor." His çapital is the city of ADDIS ABABA, about which you can read in a separate article.

hair

Hair is a thin, threadlike outgrowth of the skin. It is found on all mammals, which means all animals that (like human beings) bear living offspring and nurse them. No kind of animal except mammals has hair, but hair is more or less the equivalent in mammals of the feathers of birds and the scales of reptiles.

An ordinary hair consists of a *shaft* and a *bulb*. The shaft is the part we call the hair; that is, the part that grows outside the skin. This shaft is rooted deep in the skin in a tiny *follicle,* or hole in the skin. The bulb of the hair grows in this follicle, and is supplied with blood from blood vessels that grow around it.

The shaft of the hair is composed of a horny layer of scales, called the *cuticle.* You can feel these scales by pulling a hair the wrong way between your fingers. Under the cuticle there is another horny layer called the *cortex,* and in the center is a core called the *medulla.* The hair grows from the roots, not the ends. The individual cells of which the hair is made form at the root and push the older cells outward. A hair will live from two to four years. When an old one falls out, a new one grows from the same follicle. Hair will continue to grow unless the follicle is destroyed.

Hair grows on all parts of the human body except for the palms of the hands and the soles of the feet. Mostly it grows on the scalp, the eyebrows, the edge of the eyelids, the pubic area, the chin, cheeks, armpits, chest, and entrance of the nose and ears. The hair generally grows in a slanting direction, because of the way the follicles are placed in the skin. Sometimes these follicles are placed differently in certain parts of the scalp, and then they form a "cowlick," in which the hair grows in a different direction from the rest of the hair on the scalp. This can usually be corrected with constant brushing. When we say that our "hair stood on end" with cold, or fright, or surprise, it can be literally true, because at such times tiny muscles in the skin may contract and cause the hair to stand up almost straight.

COLOR OF HAIR

Hair grows in different shapes. It is never really round, but straight hair is the most nearly round. Curly hair is slightly flattened. Kinky hair is very flat, like a ribbon, and has a groove along its length; it is believed that the tight twist of kinky hair is because the fibers are pulled tightly along this groove.

Hair also grows in different colors, and the color is determined deep in the root by an oil that is transmitted to the hair as it grows. The color also depends on many tiny air spaces in the hair. These reflect light and thus make the hair appear darker. Color and thickness of hair are related to color of skin and eyes. For example, blond hair is usually very thin, or fine, and people with blond hair usually have light skins and blue eyes; black hair is usually thicker, and people with dark hair usually have dark eyes and an olive skin. Gray hair is due to a lack of coloring pigment, which usually comes with age. But grayness of the hair has nothing to do with its health; gray hair is often stronger than hair that still has its color. Age and worry and illness can cut down the making of the coloring matter in hair and turn it gray. Since the nutrition of hair is provided through the blood, the general state of a person's health has a great deal to do with the condition of his hair. Persons who have been ill for a long time or who have had an improper diet will lose the shiny, healthy gloss of their hair. Baldnesss can be caused by poor circulation of blood in the scalp, or by neglect of the scalp, dandruff, and other conditions that reduce the nutrition of the hair; but there is evidence that the tendency to baldness is inherited.

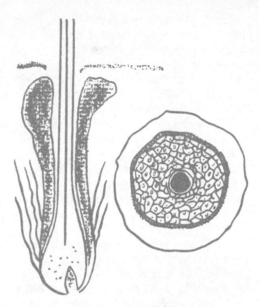

On the left, the bulb and shaft of a hair growing through the follicle. On the right, a cross-section of a hair showing cuticle, cortex, cells, and medulla.

ANIMAL HAIR

Animal hair is of even more varieties than human hair. There are the short, stiff bristle of the pig; the long, silky hair of the Persian cat; and the tight, curly hair of the Karakul sheep, from which fur coats are made. It may vary a little in structure, but it is all hair.

In animals the principal function of hair is protection from the weather. The long fur of many animals keeps them warm in winter, and in the hot weather it insulates their bodies against the heat. As the warm season nears, most animals lose some of their fur. This is called shedding, and you have probably seen it happen to a dog or cat in the spring.

Animal hair is used for many things. The bristles of pigs are used to make brushes of all kinds. The pelts of many kinds of animal provide fur garments for human beings. The hair of rabbits, beavers, and other animals is used to make felt. Horsehair and the hair of oxen is used as stuffing for cushions and mattresses. Camel's hair makes fine cloth, and the hair of Angora goats is used for beautiful shawls and sweaters. Human hair is made into wigs, and into hairpieces for women to use if they want their hair to look longer for some particular new style.

HAIRDRESSING

Ever since prehistoric times hair has been considered an ornament to human appearance. The curl and the color of hair have always been important to people. The ancient Assyrians, a people who lived around the Mediterranean Sea in Biblical times, wore wigs if they were bald. They dyed their hair different colors, and wore ornaments in it. The men even curled their beards as well as their hair, and sometimes braided the hair and beard together. The Persians also dyed their hair, and used perfumed oils and ointments in it, but they preferred simple ways of wearing it. It was cut shorter and worn close to the head.

In ancient Egypt the ruling class wore their hair high on top of the head, combed straight back and held with a wide, stiff band. Later the Egyptians had different styles. Cleopatra, the most famous queen of Egypt, wore her black hair in a long, simple frame about her face.

Greek women were the first to wear a hair style that has been popular from time to time ever since. This style frames the face with short curls and bangs across the forehead, and the long hair is gathered at the back of the head and worn in a tight knot high above the neck. Greek children wore their hair long until they were about 18; then they cut it off and sacrificed it to one of their gods, usually to Apollo. Young girls cut their hair off before they were married. The men of Greece wore their hair short, and slaves were not allowed to have long hair. The first known hairdressers were Greek. There was so much demand for their services that hairdressing became an industry.

Until about 2,200 years ago (about the year 300 B.C.) the Romans wore their hair long. Then a man named Ticinius Mena brought the first barber from the island of Sicily to Rome. Later, Roman women wore elaborate hair styles. They got false blond hair from captured women of the Germanic peoples, and braided it into their own. The North European races had long, coarse, blond hair, which they wore long and bound up behind the head. Short hair among these Celtic and Germanic peoples meant that the person was a servant, or was in disgrace for breaking a law, because criminals and slaves had their hair cut off.

During the Middle Ages, which lasted until about six hundred years ago, hair styles became simpler. Generally the men wore short hair and the women long braids. About three hundred years ago, however, King Louis XIV of France changed this style. He was a very short man, and he wore a towering wig to make him look taller. The fashion spread to all the people, men and women, of the upper classes in France. Elaborate wigs were worn by all the people at the court. These wigs were built high in waves and curls, and powdered to give a soft effect around the face. This fashion continued until the Revolution in France, and finally disappeared. However, for women it returned about a hundred years later, in the reign of Queen Victoria of England, and elaborate structures of real and false hair again were worn, but without the powder. Today wigs are worn only by the higher members of a court of law in some European countries.

MODERN STYLES

After World War I, another big change took place. Women had worn their hair long, with or without wigs or false hair, for hundreds of years. In the 1920s they began to cut it off, and the fashion of bobbed hair began. Today most women wear their hair short.

Late in the 1920s, women started to have permanent waves in their hair. A permanent wave is a way of curling the hair so that it will stay curled for months or until it grows out. About the time of World War II, "home permanents" were developed. Women could give themselves permanent waves as easily as they could put their hair up in curlers. Ways were found to cut the hair so as to bring out even a slight natural wave.

Women have always known that it is important to care for their hair. They have treated it to keep it from becoming dry and brittle, and they have tinted or dyed it to hide the grayness that is a sign of age. Brushing and combing the hair regularly are aids to healthy hair.

The girl to the left shows her very popular hair style. The girl wearing earrings displays an evening style created with a hairpiece. The model to her right is not using a hairpiece. The girl with bows in her hair is wearing a style not seen as often as the others on this page. The girl to her right has a short, easy-to-comb style.

Photos: Clairol

Haiti

Haiti is a small American country on an island in the West Indies. The island is also called Haiti, though the present custom is to call it Hispaniola, and formerly it was called Santo Domingo (Spanish for Saint Dominic). The island is the first place Christopher Columbus landed when he discovered America in 1492.

Haiti is one of two independent republics on the island. The Republic of Haiti is on the western side. It is about the size of the state of Maryland, with an area of about 10,000 square miles, but its population of four and a half million is much greater than the population of Maryland. The other independent country on the island, the Dominican Republic, is about twice as large as Haiti. There is a separate article on the DOMINICAN REPUBLIC.

The Republic of Haiti is one of the most densely populated regions in the Americas. Most of the people live on small farms. Because of its steady climate, which is very pleasant, Haiti has become a very popular place for vacations.

Off Haiti's northwest coast is the island of Tortuga, which was once famous as a hideaway for pirates. Haiti has some mountains, and many fertile plains where the farming is done.

THE PEOPLE OF HAITI

When Columbus landed on Haiti in December, 1492, it was inhabited by Arawak Indians. The Spaniards enslaved them. The Indians could not stand the labor they were made to do, and soon died out. The Spanish then brought in African Negroes to be slaves. So many were brought in that today most of the people are Negroes or a mixture of white and Negro blood. Of course, slavery has been against the law for many years.

The official language is French, but most of the people speak a mixture of French with some African words and some Spanish words. Nearly all the people belong to the Roman Catholic Church.

The Negro people have also kept some of their African traditions and are said to

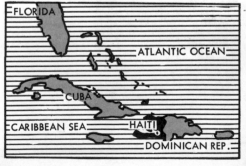

practice voodoo, which is a modified survival of some ancient African religion. Some of this has been made up just for the tourists.

WHAT THE COUNTRY IS LIKE

About four-fifths of the island of Haiti is covered by mountains with heavy forests. The most important ranges are the Massif du Nord, the Massif de la Sele, and the Massif de la Hotte. Between these are the fertile plains, such as the Plaine du Nord, Artibonite, Central, and Cul-de-Sac. The plains are watered by many streams. The most important river is also called the Artibonite. The climate is tropical (very hot and rainy) and changes very seldom. Trade winds from the northwest make the island a pleasant place.

The main crops of Haiti are coffee, cotton, and sugar. There are forests of very fine woods, such as mahogany, cedar, rosewood, and oak. Haiti has many minerals, including silver, copper, iron, sulfur, iridium, manganese, and bauxite (from which aluminum is made). Not much has been done to get them out of the ground, but bauxite is now being mined. Haiti has very few factories.

THE GOVERNMENT

According to its constitution, Haiti is a republic in which the people elect a president and a National Assembly of 67 members, which makes the laws. There is a cabinet (heads of departments) to conduct the government's affairs. But the way Haiti has really been governed is very different. For almost all its history as an independent nation, Haiti has been ruled either by a dictator or by a group (junta) of military men. There have been no really free elections. As a result, politicians and rich men who bribe them are very rich but most of the people of Haiti are very poor.

Education is free and children, according to law, must attend school. But this law is not enforced and almost 90 percent of the people cannot read or write.

The capital and largest city of Haiti is Port-au-Prince, population 200,000. It is also the chief seaport and has excellent natural harbors. The University of Haiti is located there.

The second-largest city of Haiti is Cap-Haïtien, called Le Cap by the people. It has a population of 25,000. Two interesting things to see there are the citadel La Ferrière, a huge fortress and the Sans-Souci palace.

Gonaïves is another port city, about 70 miles from Port-au-Prince. It is a historic town because the independence of the Republic of Haiti was proclaimed there.

HAITI IN THE PAST

Much of Haiti's history is made up of wars, revolutions, and assassinations. France gained control of the island in 1697. By 1789 there were many people who were free and who had money but who had no political rights. They asked for equality of political rights, and the French Assembly granted these, but the French landlords in Haiti did not like the grant and started trouble. These landlords, called colons, asked the English to help them against their mother country, France. In 1793, the English took possession of the island. It seemed that France had lost everything, because part of the island was held by the English and another part was held by the Spanish.

Then Haiti's most famous historical figure, Toussaint L'Ouverture, decided to help France. He was an amazing man with great personality. He was a Negro and had been a slave for forty years. Because of this he found it easy to enlist help from the natives. In a short time he drove both the English and the Spanish from the island. The French government rewarded him by making him a major general and appointing him governor of Haiti. In 1795, Spain gave its part of the island, called Santo Domingo, to France.

Later on, the French emperor Napoleon was afraid that Toussaint was becoming too powerful, and sent a French-

Pan American Airways Photos

Haiti has the oldest civilization in the western world, because Columbus founded the first settlement in 1492. Its many beautiful buildings contrast the old and the new, and its high mountains and fertile valleys provide dramatic scenery.

1. The cathedral in Port-au-Prince.

2. A stupendous mountain-top fortress.

3. The peaceful lagoon at Port-au-Prince. The boat has a patchwork sail.

4. One of Haiti's outdoor markets.

5. The Gaiety Hotel, with typical Haitian balconies and "gingerbread" decorations.

Haiti Nat'l Tourist Office Photos

Haiti is the home of voodoo, a magical religion followed in the rural area. The people enjoy strange and haunting music and wild dancing.

1. A typical Haitian orchestra.

2. A barefoot sword dancer performing by the sea.

3. A dance of happiness and joy, by a couple discovering love.

4. A dancer wearing typical Haitian calf length trousers.

5. Voodoo drums decorated with magic symbols.

man, General Leclerc, to be the new governor. A large army came with Leclerc in case of trouble. There were a few small battles, but Toussaint was tired of fighting and surrendered. He retired to one of his plantations, but Leclerc had him arrested and sent to France. Leclerc was afraid Toussaint might again rouse the natives. Arresting him was a mistake. The natives became very angry, and in 1802 they rebelled again, under the leadership of General Dessalines. They were successful, and on January 1, 1804, Haiti proclaimed its independence. One of the first laws passed by General Dessalines abolished slavery.

Since that time there have been many revolutions and assassinations. In 1915, United States Marines went in after the murder of President Guillaume Sam. The Marines remained in Haiti from 1915 to 1934, during which time the island received many benefits from the United States. There were revolutions in 1945, 1949, and 1956. The last revolution was followed by a period of chaos and a military junta assumed control. Then a new president, François Duvalier, was elected in 1957. In 1964, Duvalier had himself named president for life.

HAITI. Area, 10,714 square miles. Population (1964 estimate), 4,551,000. Government, republic. Languages, French and Creole. Religion, Roman Catholic and pagan. Monetary unit, gourde (20 U.S. cents). Capital and largest city, Port-au-Prince.

hake

The hake is a fish that is valuable as a food. It is somewhat like the cod and the haddock. It is sometimes called a *codling* or a *whiting*. Hake fishing is an important industry. The hake can be eaten fresh or it can be eaten after it has been preserved by salting. The salted hake is called "boneless cod." The air bladders of hake are dried and used to make isinglass. The hake is found in the Atlantic Ocean along the eastern coast north of Virginia; it is also found in the Pacific Ocean. It lives in deep water and feeds on herring and other small fish.

Hale, Edward Everett

Edward Everett Hale was an American writer and clergyman who lived about a hundred years ago. He is best known for a story he wrote, "The Man Without A Country." He was born in Boston in 1822, and was the nephew of Nathan HALE and of Edward EVERETT, about whom you can read in separate articles. Edward Everett Hale entered Harvard College at the age of 13. After graduation he became a minister. For forty-five years he was pastor of the South Congregational Church in Boston. He spent much of his life trying to help others. He was opposed to slavery, and he believed that every American child should have the chance to be educated. Toward the end of his life he became chaplain of the United States Senate. Hale died in 1909.

Hale, Nathan

Nathan Hale, an American hero of the Revolutionary War, was executed  by the British as a spy. Hale was born in 1755 and was graduated from Yale College at the age of 18. He began a career as a teacher, but two years later the outbreak of the Revolution caused him to join the army as a captain. His first exploit was the capture, with only one other man, of a provision ship from under the guns of a British man-of-war. Hale divided up the prize goods among his fellow American soldiers.

In 1776 he was assigned to a dangerous spying mission. After the American retreat from Long Island, General Washington needed to know what the British were going to do next. Hale disguised himself as a Dutch schoolmaster, passed easily through the British lines, and made notes and drawings of the information

Washington wanted. But he was seen and recognized by a relative who was a supporter of the British side. This relative betrayed him to the British, and he was seized and taken to the mansion where General Howe had his headquarters. There he was held all night in a greenhouse. Under questioning he freely admitted that he was an American officer and a spy. The next morning he was taken out to be hanged, without even a trial. He went to the gallows bravely, and just before he was executed he made a famous statement: "I only regret that I have but one life to lose for my country."

halftone, a method of printing a picture: see PHOTOENGRAVING.

halibut

The halibut is a large ocean fish. It is one of the most important food fish on the eastern and western coasts of the United States. At one time there were a great many of them off the east coast, but now the fishermen have to go up to the waters off Newfoundland and Iceland to catch them. Off the west coast halibut is very abundant, and there the halibut industry is second in importance only to the salmon industry.

The halibut is the largest of the flatfish. The flatfish swim flat in the water, and have both eyes on the upper side. The upper side of the halibut is grey-brown, and the underside is white. Halibut weigh as much as 400 pounds. One caught off the coast of Sweden weighed 750 pounds.

The meat of halibut is white, rather dry, and very good to eat. It is usually

The halibut's large mouth and sharp teeth make him a danger to other, smaller fish.

Nat'l Film Board
The Nova Scotia legislature meets in the stately Province House in Halifax.

served in steaks. Halibut liver oil is rich in vitamins A and D. The fish are caught with hook and line. Fresh fish, often herring, are used for bait.

Halifax

Halifax is the capital and largest city of the province of Nova Scotia, in Canada. It is a peninsula (an arm of land sticking into the ocean) on the southern coast of Nova Scotia. Halifax is the most important seaport in Nova Scotia and has one of the finest harbors in the world. It is especially important during the winter months, because the waters never freeze and ships can come and go easily.

More than 93,000 people live in Halifax. Many of them work in factories that build ships and make clothing and furniture. Some of them work in the large oil- and sugar-refining plants, and others are fishermen. Two Canadian railroads run to Halifax, and there is a fine airport.

Halifax has many historic buildings. One of them is St. Paul's Church, which was built in 1750 and is the oldest Anglican Church in Canada. There are three colleges. There is also a great fort, built about 150 years ago.

Halifax was founded in 1749 as a British naval base. This was very useful to the British during the Revolutionary

War. During World War I and again in World War II, Halifax was a great naval base from which fighting men were sent to all parts of the world.

HALIFAX, NOVA SCOTIA. Population (1967 estimate) 99,372. Capital of Nova Scotia. On the Atlantic Ocean.

Hall, Charles M., an American inventor who developed a method of manufacturing aluminum, in 1886. See the article on ALUMINUM.

Hall of Fame

The Hall of Fame is a building on the grounds of New York University in the Bronx, New York City, in which are bronze busts (sculpture showing the head and shoulders) of great Americans. A tablet below each bust gives interesting words that were written or spoken by that person. The building itself is in the shape of a half-circle colonnade, or covered walk with pillars that support the roof. Anyone may suggest the name of an American to be included in the Hall of Fame, but the person must have been dead for at least 25 years. Then a group of about one hundred outstanding men and women from all over the United States make the final choice. Elections are

MEN AND WOMEN IN THE HALL OF FAME

1900		1930
John Adams	William Tecumseh Sherman	Matthew Fontaine Maury
John James Audubon	John Greenleaf Whittier	James Monroe
Henry Ward Beecher	Emma Willard	James McNeill Whistler
William Ellery Channing	1910	Walt Whitman
Henry Clay	George Bancroft	1935
Peter Cooper	Phillips Brooks	Grover Cleveland
Jonathan Edwards	William Cullen Bryant	Simon Newcomb
Ralph Waldo Emerson	James Fenimore Cooper	William Penn
David Glasgow Farragut	Oliver Wendell Holmes	1940
Benjamin Franklin	Andrew Jackson	Stephen Collins Foster
Robert Fulton	John Lothrop Motley	1945
Ulysses Simpson Grant	Edgar Allen Poe	Sidney Lanier
Asa Gray	Harriet Beecher Stowe	Thomas Paine
Nathaniel Hawthorne	Frances Elizabeth Willard	Walter Reed
Washington Irving	1915	Booker T. Washington
Thomas Jefferson	Louis Agassiz	1950
James Kent	Daniel Boone	Susan B. Anthony
Robert Edward Lee	Rufus Choate	Alexander Graham Bell
Abraham Lincoln	Charlotte Saunders Cushman	Josiah Willard Gibbs
Henry Wadsworth Longfellow	Alexander Hamilton	William Crawford Gorgas
John Marshall	Joseph Henry	Theodore Roosevelt
Horace Mann	Mark Hopkins	Woodrow Wilson
Samuel Finley Breese Morse	Elias Howe	1955
George Peabody	Francis Parkman	Thomas J. Jackson
Joseph Story	1920	George Westinghouse
Gilbert Charles Stuart	Samuel Langhorne Clemens	Wilbur Wright
George Washington	James Buchanan Eads	1960
Daniel Webster	Patrick Henry	Thomas Alva Edison
Eli Whitney	William T. G. Morton	Edward A. MacDowell
1905	Alice Freeman Palmer	Henry David Thoreau
John Quincy Adams	Augustus Saint-Gaudens	1965
James Russell Lowell	Roger Williams	Jane Addams
Mary Lyon	1925	O. W. Holmes, Jr.
James Madison	Edwin Booth	Sylvanus Thayer
Maria Mitchell	John Paul Jones	Orville Wright

held every five years. The first one was held in 1900. There is room for 100 busts. By 1960, 89 men and women had been elected to the Hall of Fame.

Hallowe'en

Hallowe'en is the night of October 31. Traditionally it is a time for playing pranks, but actually it is the day before a holy day, All Saints' Day. This holy day was once called All Hallows or Hallowmas, because *hallow* meant "saint." Therefore Hallowe'en means the eve (night before) All Hallows day.

The legend of Hallowe'en is that the evil spirits and witches go out and celebrate that particular night because the next day, when the saints are honored, they had better be in hiding. In earlier times there were many superstitions connected with Hallowe'en. Robert Burns wrote a poem called "Tam o' Shanter," in which he describes the goblins and ghosts that travel about on Hallowe'en.

Modern children celebrate Hallowe'en with all sorts of pranks. They dress up in disguises and go about to neighbors' houses saying, "Trick or treat." This means that the householder must give them a treat of candy or cake, or the children will play tricks on him. The traditional colors of the day are orange and black, and Hallowe'en parties are decorated with witches flying on broomsticks, and black cats, and pumpkin jack o'lanterns. The children play special games such as bobbing for apples.

hallucination

A hallucination is imagining something that is not there. The most common kinds of hallucination are seeing or hearing things that are not present, but a person having an hallucination may feel sure that he is feeling, or smelling, or tasting something when he is not. Hallucinations occur in the mind. They are most common in persons who are men-

Standard Oil Co.

When the masked "goblin" comes to the door on Hallowe'en, the people inside must treat, or he will play "terrible" tricks.

tally sick, but normal people who are under great strain or who have high fever may also have hallucinations. Hallucinations are different from mirages, which are caused by tricks of light. You can read about MIRAGES in a separate article.

halo

A halo is a ring of light around something. In painting, it is a bright circle that frames the head of Jesus or the Virgin Mary or the saints, and is put there to indicate their holiness.

The word *halo* is also used by astronomers to describe the bright circle that is sometimes seen around the sun or moon. This halo is usually reddish in color at the inner edge and violet on the outer edge. Sometimes long spokes of light can be seen extending out from the moon or sun to the circle of light; at other times two circles can be seen, one inside the other.

Halos are caused by ice crystals or other tiny particles in the earth's atmosphere that interfere with the light.

Metropolitan Museum of Art

Frans Hals liked good food and good company, and often made them the subject of his paintings. *Merry Company* is a good example of his light-hearted work.

Hals, Frans

Frans Hals was a Dutch painter who lived about three hundred years ago. His most famous painting is *The Laughing Cavalier,* a portrait of a jolly Dutchman in the costume of the time. Hals was born in 1580, and lived at the same time as another great Dutch painter, Rubens. Hals painted rich merchants and influential ministers, but he also painted poor people, such as fishwives and wandering players.

Hals had a family of ten children, and he supported them very well until about 1652. Then things started going badly with him, and at last his possessions were sold at auction to pay his debts. Hals' paintings were not considered of much value until two hundred years after his death in 1666. Then they started to bring enormous prices at auction, and many of them are prized possessions of great museums. His painting *The Smoker* is in the Metropolitan Museum, New York City.

Halsey, William Frederick

William Frederick Halsey became famous in World War II as an admiral of the United States Navy. His doggedness in battle won him the nickname of "Bull" Halsey.

Halsey was born in 1882 in Elizabeth, New Jersey, and he graduated from the Naval Academy at Annapolis in 1904. When war broke out against Japan in 1941, Halsey was a vice-admiral. In October 1942 he was made commander of the Allied fleets in the South Pacific, and he won several victories over the Japanese near the island of Guadalcanal. In 1944 he became commander of the U.S. 3rd Fleet, and his aircraft carriers helped defeat the Japanese in the Battle of the Philippine Sea. He was promoted to admiral of the fleet, the highest rank in the Navy, in 1945, and he retired the same year. He died in 1959.

ham, the meat from the upper part of a hog's hind leg, that is eaten after it has been salted and smoked: see the article on MEAT.

Haman

Haman is a character in the Bible who is remembered mainly because he was hanged on the gallows he had intended for another man. His story is told in the Book of Esther. Haman was the favorite minister of King Ahasuerus of Persia at a time when the Jews were being kept in captivity by the Persians. Everyone used to praise Haman except a Jew named Mordecai, and in revenge Haman decided to have all the Jews in Persia killed. He persuaded the king to agree by telling him lies about the Jews. But the king's wife, Esther, was the niece of Mordecai. She told the king the truth about Haman's plot. Thus the Jews were saved, and Haman was hanged on the gallows he had built for Mordecai. Every year there is a Jewish festival, the festival of Purim, in memory of Esther's saving the Jews.

Hamburg

Hamburg is a city on the Elbe River, in West Germany. Seagoing ships sail up the Elbe and make Hamburg the largest port in Germany. About 1,800,000 people live there. Many of them work in the great shipyards and docks, and others work in factories that make rubber, cloth, and chemicals.

Hamburg has a wonderful system of canals and bridges and tunnels that make it easy to travel from one part of the city to another. This is very important, because supplies must be carried to the warehouses and docks to be shipped to other places. Many young men and women go to the University of Hamburg, and others attend several technical and medical schools. There are also many concert halls. The great composers Brahms and Mendelssohn were both born in Hamburg, and the first German opera house was built there almost three hundred years ago.

Hamburg was founded more than one thousand years ago, when the great emperor Charlemagne built a mighty castle where the city of Hamburg now stands. In the year 1241, Hamburg and the port city of Lübeck made an agreement to help protect each other's business interests. This was the beginning of the famous HANSEATIC LEAGUE, which you can read about in a separate article. Hamburg became the most powerful city in the League. About four hundred years ago it was made a free city, with the power to make its own laws. Because it was such an important port, Hamburg was bombed very heavily during World War II. More than half of the city was destroyed, and many people lost their lives.

HAMBURG, GERMANY. Population (1961 estimate) 1,836,000. On Elbe River.

Hamilcar

Hamilcar was a great general of Carthage, a city that created a great empire more than two thousand years ago.

German Tourist Bureau

The city hall of Hamburg is built on the banks of the Alster River.

Carthage was on the coast of North Africa, near where the present city of Algiers is. At that time the Romans as well as the Carthaginians were trying to found great empires. They fought a series of wars against each other until the Romans finally won and destroyed Carthage.

In several of these wars Hamilcar was the leader of the Carthaginian forces. He failed to win the island of Sicily from the Romans, but he conquered all of Spain and made it into a province of Carthage. He was killed in battle in Spain when he was 42 years old. His campaigns were continued by his famous son HANNIBAL, about whom you can read in a separate article.

Hamilton

Hamilton is a city in the southern part of the province of Ontario, in Canada. It is on Lake Ontario, at the western end of the lake, and is built at the foot of a mountain. Over 298,000 people live in the city of Hamilton. They work in automobile and steel factories and in cotton and knitting mills, and some make typewriters and tobacco products. Hamilton was once separated from Lake Ontario by a sandbar, but more than a hundred years ago a channel was cut through the sandbar, making Hamilton a lake port. Hamilton has several beautiful churches and McMaster University. Dundern Castle, in Dundern Park, is a museum with exhibits of many things of interest in Canadian history.

HAMILTON, ONTARIO. Population (1967 estimate) 298,121. County seat of Wentworth County. Settled in 1813.

Hamilton, Alexander

Alexander Hamilton was one of the greatest of the early Americans. He  served with distinction in the Revolutionary War as a fighter and as aide-de-camp and secretary to General Washington. He was one of the most active and successful supporters of the Constitution, and he became the first Secretary of the Treasury of the new United States.

Alexander Hamilton was born in the West Indies in 1757. He was sent to the Colonies in America at the age of 15, and later studied at King's College, which later became Columbia University. When he was only 17 he made a speech supporting the Colonies' cause against England.

Two years later, in 1776, Hamilton joined the army and was made captain of artillery. He served with such bravery that he came to the attention of General Washington, who made Hamilton his secretary, with the rank of lieutenant colonel.

After the fighting was ended, Hamilton left the army and became a lawyer. He built up a good practice in New York City, and became a member of the Continental Congress, which had been set up by the Articles of Confederation. He was a member of the convention that drafted the Constitution, and he did more than almost anyone else to get it accepted by the states. He did this especially by his writings in the Federalist Papers. These were a series of essays written by Hamilton, James Madison, and John Jay. Hamilton thought up the idea and wrote about fifty of the essays, which were published in New York newspapers and copied by papers in many other places.

Hamilton was appointed Secretary of the Treasury by President Washington, and when the first Congress under the new Constitution held its first sessions, Hamilton presented it with a complete program for the financial operation of the nation. He wanted the government to establish a national bank, to raise taxes, and to set up high tariffs, or duties, on goods imported from abroad.

A great many people did not like his program of strong Federal control, and this led to the formation of the first two political parties, the Federalists, led by Hamilton and John Adams, and the Anti-Federalists, led by Thomas Jefferson. Hamilton was able to achieve establishment of the Bank of the United States, but his other proposals on taxes and tariffs were strongly opposed. However, by the time he retired as Secretary of the Treasury in 1795 he had given the United States a very good financial (money) policy. Some experts think Hamilton was not only the first Secretary of the Treasury but the greatest.

After his retirement Hamilton returned to the practice of law in New York City, but he still held great political power. In 1796 John Adams was elected President, and Hamilton helped Washington to write his Farewell Address.

When the United States seemed on the verge of war with France in 1798, President Adams appointed General Washington commander-in-chief, and Hamilton as his second in command. On the death of Washington in 1799, Hamilton succeeded him as commander-in-chief, but the army was soon disbanded.

Hamilton and Adams had begun to disagree, chiefly over how much power Hamilton should have as leader of the Federalist Party. In the election of 1800, Hamilton's influence was responsible for the election of Thomas Jefferson as President and Aaron Burr as Vice President, even though Jefferson belonged to the opposite political party.

In 1804 Burr ran for the office of governor of New York. Hamilton had spoken against him in party meetings, calling him unreliable. When Burr was defeated in the election, he blamed Hamilton and challenged him to a duel. The two men met at Weehawken Heights, in New Jersey. Hamilton did not fire a shot, but Burr wounded Hamilton, who died the following day. He was only 47.

Hammarskjold, Dag

Dag Hammarskjold was the second Secretary-General of the United Nations, from 1953 until his death in an air crash in Africa in 1961. He was born in Sweden in 1905. He became an expert in the field of economics, dealing with problems of business, money, and trade. Hammarskjold held  many posts in the government of Sweden, and he represented his country in many international conferences. In 1952 and 1953, Hammarskjold was one of the Swedish representatives at the United Nations.

hammerhead, a fierce shark that has a hammer-shaped head: see SHARK.

Hammerstein, Oscar

Oscar Hammerstein is the name of two men who have contributed greatly to American music. The first Oscar Hammerstein was born in 1847 in Berlin, Germany. He came to America when he was 16 years old. He invented a machine for spreading tobacco leaves and this made him a fortune. Then he devoted his time and money to promoting music in the United States. He built several theaters and opera houses in New York City, and brought entire companies of singers from Europe to produce operas.

His nephew, Oscar Hammerstein II, became one of the outstanding American writers of the librettos (spoken words) of musical plays. He was born in New York City in 1895 and studied at Columbia  University. In several of the most successful musical plays since 1943, beginning with *Oklahoma!*, Hammerstein wrote the words and Richard Rodgers the music. These include *Oklahoma!*, *Carousel*, *South Pacific*, and *The King and I*. Previously, Hammerstein had written the words to music by Sigmund Romberg and Rudolf Friml, and to Jerome Kern's music for *Show Boat*. Hammerstein died in 1960.

Hammond

Hammond is a city in northwestern Indiana, on Grand Calumet River, near Chicago, Illinois, and near Lake Michigan. In 1960, the population of Hammond was 111,698. Hammond has factories that make soap, farm tools, and railroad cars. Printing also is an important industry. Hammond was founded in 1851.

Hammond, John Hays

Hammond is the name of two prominent Americans, father and son, both named John Hays Hammond. The first John Hays Hammond was a mining engineer who developed mines in many parts of the world. He was born in 1855. After working for the United States government as a mining expert, he went to Mexico and later to South Africa. During the Boer War in 1895, Hammond was captured by the Boers and sentenced to death. Later he was released upon payment of $125,000 to the Boers. Hammond was special ambassador from the United States when George V was crowned king of Great Britain in 1911. Later he returned to the United States and lectured at many universities. He died in 1936. His son, John Hays Hammond, Jr., was born in 1888. He became an electrical engineer and an inventor. Among his important devices was a radio-directed torpedo that he made for the United States Navy. He also invented devices to improve telegraph and telephone equipment, and was a pioneer in developing remote control for rockets and airplanes. He holds more patents than any other inventor of our time—about nine hundred, in the United States and other countries.

Hampton Roads

Hampton Roads is a channel, or water passageway, in Virginia. Three rivers—the James, the Nansemond, and the Elizabeth—meet there, and flow together through the channel into Chesapeake Bay. Hampton Roads is a very fine harbor, and the four cities on its shores are large and busy ports. These four cities are Newport News, Portsmouth, Hampton, and Norfolk. Hampton Roads and the city of Newport News are best known in the United States because one of the most important bases of the United States Navy is there. It is the headquarters for the Atlantic fleet.

Hampton Roads is famous in American history because of important events that took place there during the American Civil War. One was the battle between two warships, the *Monitor* and the *Merrimac,* in 1862. The *Monitor* fought for the North, and the *Merrimac* for the South. It was the first battle in history between two iron-covered ships. The other famous event was the Hampton Roads Conference, which took place in February, 1865. The North and the South were still fighting, but some people hoped that the leaders on both sides might be able to agree about ending the war. So President Abraham Lincoln met with some of the southern leaders on a ship in Hampton Roads. They talked for several hours, but the southern leaders would not agree to what Lincoln wanted, so the conference did no good. The South went on fighting a little longer but surrendered in April, 1865.

hamster

A hamster is a little animal that is related to the mouse. The hamsters that are kept as pets in the United States have furry brown or gray bodies about six inches long, and stubby tails only about half an inch long. They have broad heads and round ears, and in their cheeks are large pouches where they can hold food the way squirrels do. Other kinds of hamster grow as large as rats or guinea pigs.

Some hamsters are albinos, which means their bodies are almost pure white and their eyes are pinkish.

Hamsters build their homes underground and have several rooms for different uses. One room is used as a storeroom where the hamsters store corn for use during the winter. Animal homes that are dug in the ground like this are called burrows. In the winter, hamsters go into their burrows four or five feet deep in the ground, and close the entrance. They spend several months down there, sleeping and living on the food they have stored.

Hamsters are full of fight and can be quite ferocious for their size. The males fight for the females. Female hamsters have several litters of young during the year. There are about twelve baby hamsters in each litter. They are blind at birth. As soon as they are old enough they are turned out to build their own burrows. Hamsters feed on roots, fruits, and grains. They also eat lizards and insects. The hamster itself is the prey of foxes, dogs, cats, and other animals.

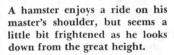

A hamster enjoys a ride on his master's shoulder, but seems a little bit frightened as he looks down from the great height.

Copyright Curriculum Films, Inc.

A small hamster makes a very interesting pet. It can be kept in a cage or box with enough earth and leaves in it so that the hamster can dig a hole and hide. The box should be kept very clean. Careful feeding is important.

Hamsun, Knut

Knut Hamsun was a Norwegian writer of novels. He was born in 1859, and he started writing stories while he was working as a shoemaker. When he was young he came to America, where he was a street-car conductor and a farm worker. He wrote mostly about poor people. His most famous book was *Growth of the Soil*. This book won him the Nobel Prize in 1920. After World War II the Norwegian government said Hamsun must go to prison for helping the Germans when they took Norway. But he was an old man then, and he was not sent to prison, but he had to pay a large fine. He died in 1952.

Hancock, John

John Hancock was an American patriot and one of the leaders of the Colonies' fight for independence. He was the first signer of the Declaration of Independence, and he signed with such a bold hand that we use his name to mean any signature. If someone says "I put down my John Hancock," he means he has signed his name to something important.

Hancock was born in 1737 in Massachusetts. He was graduated from Harvard College at the age of 17. His uncle was a merchant, and Hancock entered his business and later inherited it with a large fortune when his uncle died. Since he was a businessman, he was especially opposed to the Stamp Act and other taxes that the British levied on the colonies.

In 1774 a Continental Congress was called in Philadelphia, with representatives of eleven of the American colonies present. John Hancock was president of the Congress, and Samuel Adams was a delegate. You can read more about Samuel ADAMS in a separate article. Hancock and Adams worked so hard for the cause of freedom that they were called outlaws by General Thomas Gage, the commander of all the British troops in America.

General Gage was so eager to arrest Hancock and Adams that on April 18, 1775, he sent British troops out of Boston to look for them. Paul Revere's famous ride was made chiefly to warn Adams and Hancock that the British soldiers were coming to get them. A battle began at Concord, and it started the Revolutionary War. In the confusion of the battle, Hancock and Adams escaped. Later, when General Gage was still trying to make peace with the colonies, he offered a pardon to everyone but Adams and Hancock, whom he considered too dangerous to allow freedom. However, he never caught either of them.

Hancock was appointed the first major-general of the Massachusetts militia, and took part in much of the fighting in Rhode Island. He was a brave and clever officer. After the war he was elected the first governor of Massachusetts, and he was president of the state convention that ratified the national Constitution. Hancock remained governor of Massachusetts until his death in 1793.

hand

The hand, and especially the thumb, are among the greatest advantages besides the brain that human beings have over dumb animals. No other animal has a thumb that can be used with the fingers to form a sort of pincers. This makes the hand the most useful tool in nature. It enables men to do things that no other animal can do.

The human hand is composed of five digits, the four fingers and the thumb. The bones of the fingers are called *phalanges*. There are three phalanges in each finger and two in the thumb. There are five bones called *metacarpals* in the palm of the hand, and eight bones called *carpals* in the wrist. These bones are connected by muscles and nerves that get their directions from the brain. There are more nerves receiving messages from the brain in the tips of the fingers than anywhere else in the body. For this reason we think of the sense of touch as being centered chiefly in the fingers. Most of the movements of the hand are made without our

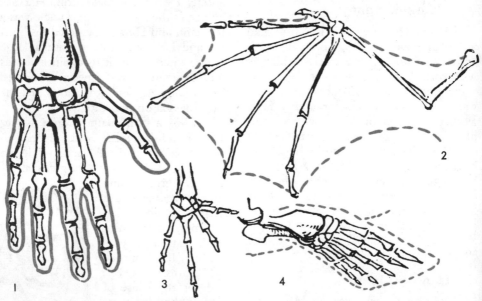

The human hand (1) is more highly developed than the "hand" of any other animal. But other animals do have similar bone structures at the lower end of their forelimbs. The bat's wing (2), the frog's forefoot, (3) which it often raises while sitting, and the seal's flipper (4) all resemble the human hand. But none of them has a thumb, the most important finger.

Handball may be played either on a one-wall court (1) or a four-wall court (2). The server (3) bounces the ball and then hits it against the wall. His opponent (4) must hit the ball on the first bounce back against the wall, then the server returns, and so on, until one of them misses. There are few games that make greater demands on the players' endurance.

even realizing it. The hand and the brain work so well together that the hands' ordinary movements are almost automatic.

The right hand is operated by the left side of the brain, and the left hand is operated by the right side of the brain. Most people are right-handed, that is, they use their right hand with greater ease than their left hand. A few people are left-handed. There are different ideas about what causes left-handedness. Some say it is inherited. All agree that left-handed children should not be forced to use the right hand if it is difficult for them.

The hands show certain things about a person that make him different from any other person, even the members of his own family. Fingerprints, the marks made by the fingertips, are different in every person. Handwriting is also different with each person.

handball

Handball is a game played by hitting a small rubber ball with your hand. Your object is to hit it against a wall so that your opponent cannot return it (hit it back against the wall) on the first bounce at least. When your opponent has hit the ball against the wall, your object is to return it on the first bounce at least.

There are two forms of handball, one-wall handball and four-wall handball.

One-wall handball is played on a place, called a court, that is 20 feet wide and 34 feet long. A wall 16 feet high is at one end of the court. It is the same width as the court. A line 16 feet from the wall is drawn across the width of the court. This is called the *service line*.

One player stands by the service line, bounces the ball once, and hits it against the wall with the palm of his hand. He is called the *server*. On the serve, the ball must strike the wall without a bounce ("on the fly"). It must bounce back so that it passes over the service line on the fly. The other player must then hit it before it bounces, or after one bounce, so that the ball strikes the wall on the fly and stays within the court. The ball is hit by one player, then by the other, until one of them is unable to return it to the wall on the fly, or hits it out of the court. If the server does not return it, he loses the right to serve. If the other player cannot return it, the server gets one point. The first player to get 21 points wins the game. If the score is tied at 20 to 20, the first player to get two points more than the other wins the game.

In four-wall handball, the court is 46 feet long and 23 feet wide. It is surrounded by three walls 23 feet high and a back wall 10 feet high. The rules are the same as for one-wall handball, except that the ball may be hit off any of the walls or off a combination of them.

In one-wall handball, "first bounce" means a bounce off the floor. In four-wall handball it means a bounce off the floor or any wall.

When two persons play, it is "singles." When four play, two against two as partners, it is "doubles."

Handball may be played indoors or outdoors. It is a very strenuous game and helps to develop the muscles in your arms and legs. Thin leather gloves are often worn by the players to protect their hands. In the United States, there are handball courts in most playgrounds and gymnasiums. Men, women and children of all ages play the game. Tournaments are held to find out who is the best handball player. Once a year a tournament is held in the United States for the world's championship. People in the United States began to play handball in about 1882, but the game is very old and was first played eight hundred years ago in Ireland.

handcrafts

Handcrafts are the skills that we use in making things with our hands. Sometimes we call handcrafts "arts and crafts." Handcrafts often require the use of tools and other equipment. These tools may be as simple as the hammer and screwdriver or as elaborate as a workshop with electric drills and lathes. What is important about handcrafts is not the tools but the skill and imagination that are used in making things. The American Indians, who have made some of the best and most beautiful arts and crafts objects, had very few tools to work with.

Handcrafts, or arts and crafts, are taught in many schools and in recreation centers and summer camps. Doing handcrafts, of course, is quite different from doing arithmetic or spelling, and this is exactly why they are taught. They give children a chance to work with their hands and to make things from their imaginations. Handcrafts are also taught to people who are recovering from physical or mental illnesses because this gives them a chance to occupy themselves and take their minds off their troubles. This is called *occupational therapy*. Blind people are also taught some crafts, such as weaving and basketry. There are many grownups who do arts and crafts work as a hobby. They find it relaxing to work with their hands after spending their days at a business or profession.

Some of the most popular handcrafts are woodworking, leatherworking, metalworking, pottery, printing, bookbinding, weaving, basket-making, puppet making, making objects out of paper, and soap carving. Some of these crafts

X-acto, Inc.

Above: Making "wampum" of Indian beads.
Right: Shaping clay for a pottery bowl.

Standard Oil Co.

are discussed in separate articles (such as MODELMAKING). Here we will give a few simple projects to work at in some of the crafts.

MAKING A WOVEN BASKET

There is a separate article on BASKETS in another volume of this encyclopedia. Here is one way to make a woven basket:

A good material for weaving a basket is rattan. This comes from a vine which is grown in the Philippine Islands. Round rattan reed is graded by numbers ranging from 00 (very fine) to 9 (heavy).

In the weaving of rattan baskets the reeds that form the skeleton framework are called *spokes,* while those that pass in and out, thus filling in between the spokes, are called the *weavers.*

Rattan should always be moistened before it is used, but it should never be put into hot water and should not be soaked for more than half an hour. The reeds to be used as spokes should be cut to the proper lengths and tied together in bundles before wetting; those to be used as weavers should be coiled and tied before being wet. The basket-maker should keep his fingers moist by dipping them occasionally into water.

In making a rattan basket from five to eight inches in diameter, it is advisable to use No. 4 reed for the spokes and No. 2 reed for the weavers. The basket-maker takes four spokes in each hand, and, pressing these flat so that they lie beside one another, he places the four spokes held in the right hand upon the four held in the left hand. The groups of

Handweaver and Craftsman   British Inform. Services

Weaving on a loom, making baskets and hand-tooling metal are three old handcrafts.

The most popular material for a hand-craftsman to work with is wood, whether he whittles a stick or carves a statue.
1. Printing with a wood block is a good rainy-day occupation for children.
2. A sharp cutting tool helps anyone carving a figure out of wood.
3. Making marionettes is a handcraft that takes great skill and patience.
4. A hand-carved jewelry box is a gift that any woman would appreciate.

X-acto, Inc., Photos

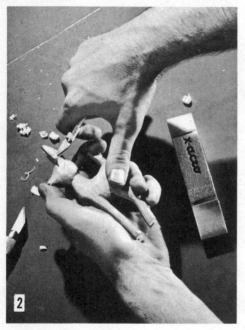

four reeds each are now made to cross each other at right angles, the point of intersection being midway from end to end on each group of reeds. A half-length spoke is now placed beside one group of four, and the weaving is begun. The weaver reed passes over and under each of the four groups of spokes in turn, until all the spokes are held securely in place. The next step is to separate the spokes and pass the weaver over and under each spoke in turn.

When the *start,* as this work is called, has reached a diameter of five or six inches, a new spoke is inserted beside each of those already in position except the last. The weaving of the basket is then carried on to completion. If the sides of the basket are to turn up abruptly the spokes will have to be bent. They may be tied together at their ends to keep them bent until the turn is made. To finish the rim,

bring each spoke around the two following it and into the basket, moistening the reeds, pulling them into place, and pressing them tightly down upon the basket.

MAKING A CLAY BASKET

Pottery is the craft of making objects out of clay, which are then made hard by heat. There is a separate article on POTTERY in another volume.

Pottery objects can be made on a *potter's wheel,* or they can be made by the *coil method.* The project described here uses the coil method because it does not require much equipment. The clay for this project can be obtained from a craft supply shop.

FORMING THE VASE

The vase is made by building with clay coils rolled between the hands and the desk top. First protect the desk with a sheet of linoleum, a board, or a piece of heavy paper. A pasteboard disk having the same diameter as the base of the proposed vase is used as a guide in starting. This is covered with coils of clay wound around in a spiral and pressed firmly together to form a disk about one-fourth of an inch thick.

The building of the walls is also accomplished by this spiral arrangement of coils, which are welded together by being pressed firmly against the ever-growing wall. If the walls become unsteady because of their moist condition and the weight of the clay, the work should be set aside until it becomes leather-hard; then building may be continued. Before continuing, the rim formed by the last coil should be cut squarely off with a knife and a thick mixture of *slip* (clay and water mixed to the consistency of thick cream) should be applied with a brush.

When the vase has been entirely built it is allowed to dry out somewhat. Then it may be scraped and carefully "trued" with a knife and finally finished with sandpaper.

DECORATING

If you wish, you may add a decoration to the outside of the vase. The design is scratched on by means of the sharp point of a wire nail before the clay is thoroughly dry. The parts to be colored are brushed over with slip and the color is applied immediately. Colors may be obtained at a paint or drug store. Yellow ocher is used for yellow-red, red oxide of iron for red, and black oxide of copper for black. The colors, in powder form, are mixed with liquid glue and are painted upon the slightly moist clay in the form of a thick paste. It is a good idea to scratch the surface with a pin or piece of broken window glass before painting the clay. This will help the paint hold to the clay surface.

FIRING

In firing (baking) pottery it is not necessary to use a real kiln. An iron kettle placed in an open fire of wood can be used. This method is similar to that employed long ago by the American Indians. The kettle will keep the burning embers from falling upon and breaking the dishes. It should have an iron cover. The heating and cooling should be gradual; the kettle should be kept at a red heat for at least an hour.

MAKING A COPPER TRAY

A copper tray is easy to make. The only special equipment needed is a hammer with a ball-shaped striking end, which is called a *ball-peen hammer,* and a pair of metal snips or shears.

Cut out of sheet copper a circle ¼ inch larger in diameter than the plate is to be. Beat the edges of the tray with a hammer, causing the metal to become somewhat thicker at the edge. Beat down the depression in the plate using a block of wood as an anvil. To do this, first draw a line with compasses where the depression is to start; then hold the plate on the end of a block of wood and beat it down over the edge of the block with a hammer, along the pencil line.

If the plate is to have a deep impression, it will be necessary to "anneal" it, because it will become hard while being beaten. This is done by heating it to red heat in a gas or other flame, and then cooling it quickly in water.

If desired, the brim of the plate may have a border decoration etched on it. The design for this is painted on with asphaltum varnish, as are all parts of the plate that are not to be etched. The whole is placed, when the varnish is dry, in a solution of one part nitric acid and two parts water, in a stoneware or glass dish. The acid will, in a few minutes, begin to eat away or etch the metal that has been left bare.

After the metal has been etched deep enough (which will take anywhere from thirty minutes to three hours, according to the depth desired), take the tray out of the acid and remove the asphaltum varnish by soaking the tray for about an hour in turpentine or a solution of lye. Then the varnish can be wiped off.

Handel, George Frederick

George Frederick Handel was a famous composer who was born in Germany but made his biggest reputation in England. He wrote *The Messiah* and other great oratorios that lovers of music still know and hear every year. An oratorio is a sacred story with music, played by an orchestra and sung by soloists and a chorus.

Handel was born in Halle, Germany, in 1685. He became organist in the cathedral at Halle as a young man, and also played the violin in the Hamburg orchestra. When he was 20 his first two operas were performed in Hamburg with great success. He spent some time in Italy, and in 1710 became musical director to the elector, or king, of Hanover, which was a country in Germany. Four years later this elector became King George I of England. Handel went to England and lived there the rest of his life. He wrote many more operas, but the English people did not care much for them. Then he turned to writing oratorios, which became popular at once. Besides *The Messiah,* the story of the life of Jesus that he wrote in 1742, Handel is also known for the oratorios *Israel in Egypt* and *Samson.* Handel also wrote music for orchestras and an anthem for the coronation of George II. This anthem is played at the crowning of every English king and queen. Handel died in England in 1759.

handwriting

Handwriting is writing by hand with a form of letter called script. The word is not used for making capital letters, which we call printing, even when it is done by hand.

The script in which most people write developed long after the forms of the letters used for printing books and carved inscriptions, even though handwriting came long before mechanical printing. First there were capital letters only, but in the days before printing all books had to be copied by hand and the original capital letters were inconvenient, because before making each one you had to lift the pen from the paper. Therefore people gradually began to develop forms of the letters that would run together easily and could still be read. These letters are called *cursive,* which means "running along."

STYLES OF HANDWRITING

Most handwriting slants to the right. When instead it slants to the left it is called *backhand.*

Unless the letters are fairly carefully formed, they are hard to read. Many systems have been devised to make handwriting easier to do and at the same time easier to read. There are also many ways to teach handwriting. You can read about them in the article on PENMANSHIP.

The art of very beautiful handwriting is called *chirography*. Chirographers used to make up personal calling cards, wedding invitations, and many other forms that now are usually engraved or printed. Many diplomas and other such documents are still written by hand. Such a document is said to be *engrossed.*

Some people insist that you can tell about a person's character from his handwriting. They call this the art of *graphology.*

AUTOGRAPHS

A handwritten signature is called an *autograph,* and many people collect the autographs of famous persons. Usually they have the autographs written in autograph books, but sometimes they have them on cards that they trade with other autograph collectors.

Most genuine autographs are collected by young people who live in big cities where the stars actually appear. You can get autographs by writing for them, but there are so many requests that the celebrities do not have time to write them all and often the ones they send are printed or are signed by someone who imitates their signature.

There always have been collectors of the autographs of famous men and women of history. The most valuable autograph in the United States is that of Button Gwinnett. He was a signer of the Declaration of Independence from Georgia, but there are very few letters or other papers that he signed. Some people collect the autographs of signers of the Declaration of Independence, and they cannot complete their sets without one of the Button Gwinnett signatures. That makes a Gwinnett signature cost a lot.

Autographs of famous men and women are usually sold by the same dealers and stores that sell stamps to stamp collectors and coins to coin collectors. The values of various autographs are listed in catalogs.

HOLOGRAPHS

Handwriting sometimes has a special meaning in law. If a person writes a will in his own handwriting it is called a *holograph* will, and sometimes the courts will accept this will while they will not accept a will that was simply signed. Handwriting experts are often able to study handwriting and know definitely if a person did or did not write something, even if he tried to disguise his handwriting. Such experts have solved many crimes, including the crime of FORGERY, about which you can read in a separate article.

Handy, W. C.

William Christopher Handy is the name of one of the greatest American composers, or writers of original music. He is called the "father of the blues," and his most famous songs are of the type called blues. He also wrote down for the first time some of the Negro spirituals that are most popular today. In many cases he wrote the words as well as the music for his songs.

W. C. Handy, as he is usually called, was a member of the Negro race. He was born in Alabama in 1873, only a few years after the Negroes had been freed from slavery. His father had been a slave but became a preacher. W. C. Handy went through high school and attended college, and then taught music in a southern college for Negroes. When he was 35 years old he formed a band to play in Memphis, Tennessee. A few years later, E. H. Crump, who later became the most powerful political figure in Tennessee, was running for an office in Memphis and asked Handy to write a campaign song for him. The song Handy wrote, now called the "Memphis Blues," has since become famous.

Southern Negroes had been singing *blues,* or sad songs, for many years, but Handy was the first man to use them as a serious musical form. His first song, the "Memphis Blues," was stolen from him by a southern publisher, because Negroes still had few legal rights in the South, but later Handy regained ownership of it. His most popular song, written a few years later, is the "St. Louis Blues," and both the words and music are considered classic. After that song was published, Handy moved to New York City and founded his own publishing firm, which has been very successful ever since. He wrote down and published many spirituals that he remembered from his boyhood, among them "Steal Away to Jesus."

In middle age Handy lost much of the use of his eyes, and later he became totally blind, but he continued to write music and to manage his publishing business, which made him rich as well as famous. He died in 1958.

Hanging Gardens of Babylon

The Hanging Gardens of Babylon were a marvelous structure built in the ancient city of Babylon, more than 2,500 years ago. Babylon was the capital of a great empire in Asia. The Hanging Gardens were built by King Nebuchadnezzar, about whom you can read in the Bible, in the Book of Daniel. The land around Babylon was flat and dry. Nebuchadnezzar's queen, who came from a land of mountain scenery, was homesick. That is why the gardens were built.

The Hanging Gardens were really a kind of roof garden such as you might see on a penthouse in a modern city. They were laid out on a sort of square building that rested on arches and pillars. The pillars were hollow and filled with earth, so that the roots of the trees could have room to grow deep down into them. Masses of soil were laid on the flat roof and arranged into terraces one beneath the other. Waterfalls tumbled from one level to the next. The flowers and vines grew over the edges of the terraces so they seemed to be hanging there.

A force of men was at work constantly

pumping water up to the gardens from the nearby Euphrates River. The gardens were threaded with walks, and people came to sit there in the coolness under the palm trees and enjoy the flowers, which were imported from foreign lands.

The Hanging Gardens could be seen for miles around the level countryside. From a distance they looked like a tower, narrow at the top and broad at the base. They were so wonderful that they are still called one of the Seven Wonders of the Ancient World. The ruins of the Hanging Gardens of Babylon can still be seen.

Hankow or Wuhan

Hankow, or Wuhan, formerly called also Wuchang, is a large city in the central part of China. It is situated on the great Yangtze River. Hankow is sometimes called the "Chicago of China," because, like Chicago, it is a very important manufacturing center and easy to reach by boat and train. Boats can sail from Hankow down the Yangtze River for six hundred miles, to the East China Sea. More than two million people live in Hankow. They make cloth and cement and chemicals, and they ship tea, cotton, and many other things from their city to many places in China and other countries. About one hundred years ago, a treaty was signed that stated that other countries could begin to trade in Hankow, and the city grew very fast. Most of the business was carried on in the European section of Hankow, where there were many banks. The Japanese held Hankow from 1938 until 1945; then in 1949 the Communists took control of the city, and renamed it Wuhan.

HANKOW, CHINA. Population (1959 estimate) 2,150,000. On Yangtze River.

Hannibal

Hannibal was the greatest general of Carthage, a city that created a great empire more than two thousand years ago. Carthage was on the coast of North Africa, near where the city of Algiers is today. At that time the Romans as well as the Carthaginians were trying to found great empires, and fought a series of wars against each other. Hannibal lived about two hundred years before the birth of Jesus. His father was HAMILCAR, another great general, about whom you can read in a separate article. When Hannibal was only 9 years old, he went with his father on an expedition to conquer Spain. Hannibal swore an oath that he would always fight the Romans, and when his father was killed he took up his campaign.

Hannibal's greatest campaign was an invasion of Italy, in which he almost conquered Rome. He marched his army and a big supply train, in which the heaviest loads were carried by elephants, across the Pyrenees Mountains. Then he faced the towering Alps, barring his way into Italy. He made this almost impossible crossing in fifteen days, battling all the way against barbarian tribes, snow, and storms. At first he won many victories in Italy. One of his most famous victories was the Battle of CANNAE, about which there is a separate article. But finally the Roman general Fabius defeated him. Hannibal had to give up and go back to Carthage.

The Romans continued to win battles from Carthage, and at last Carthage had to submit to a peace that included the payment of heavy taxes to Rome. Hannibal made reforms that enabled Carthage to pay these taxes, but the Romans still considered him dangerous and demanded that he surrender to them in person. Hannibal took refuge with the king of Bithynia, a country on the Black Sea, and when this king was about to turn him over to the Romans, Hannibal poisoned himself.

Hannibal was a just ruler, and was usually merciful to his enemies. He is still considered one of the greatest military leaders of all time.

Hanoi

Hanoi is the capital city of North Viet Nam, in southeast Asia. It is on the Red River, and it is a very busy port and railroad center. More than 600,000 people live in Hanoi. Many of them work in rice mills, and in factories where they make fine wool and beautiful silk cloth. Others make chinaware, matches, and leather products. There is a modern part of the city that has a large university, many fine buildings, and a beautiful park. In the old part of the city there are many ancient temples and narrow, winding streets. In 1954, the Communists in the northern part of Viet Nam took control of Hanoi from the French, who had made the city the capital of their colony, French Indo-China. Before that, the city had been occupied by Chinese, who ruled the country thousands of years ago.

HANOI, VIET NAM. Population (1960 estimate) 638,600. Capital of North Viet Nam.

Hanover

Hanover is the capital of the state of Lower Saxony, in West Germany. This territory was occupied by the British, after World War II. Hanover is situated on the Leine River. It is an important manufacturing center, and it has several large technical schools. About 570,000 people live in Hanover. Many of them work in factories, where they make automobile tires, machinery, and iron and steel. The city of

N.Y. Public Library

Hannibal lost many of his troops because of the terrible cold and dangerous climb when he crossed the Alps into Italy.

Hanover is about eight hundred years old. During World War II more than half of the city was destroyed. Since then the center of Hanover has been completely rebuilt and is now one of the most modern cities in Germany.

There was formerly an independent German kingdom of Hanover, and the city of Hanover was its capital. The family of kings who ruled Hanover was called the House of Hanover. The official title of the king was *elector,* because he was one of the German kings who elected the Holy Roman Emperor. In 1714 the Elector of Hanover became also the king of England under the title of George I, and you can read about the Hanover kings of England in the article GEORGE, KING OF ENGLAND. In 1871, when the German Empire was formed, Hanover became part of it, and after World War II it became part of the province of Lower Saxony in West Germany. While West Germany was occupied by the Allied powers, Hanover was in the British zone.

HANOVER, GERMANY. Population (1961 estimate) 576,100. Capital of province of Lower Saxony. On Leine River.

Hanseatic League

The Hanseatic League was a group of cities in Europe that had an agreement to trade with one another, about seven hundred years ago. The agreement was made by the merchants in these cities.

At that time great changes were taking place in Europe. For hundreds of years, the noblemen in their castles had controlled all the European countries. Then cities began to grow, and as they became larger they also became more important and more powerful. The merchants began to do business on a bigger scale, but they faced great obstacles, such as pirates at sea, and very high customs duties (or taxes on goods brought into other countries). So these merchants formed guilds, or trade associations, to protect themselves. As the merchant guilds grew stronger, they began to be competition

for each other, and so groups of guilds joined together into organizations called *hanses.* At last the hanses joined together into a league, called the Hanseatic League.

The Hanseatic League at its strongest period included 85 towns. It made wars and dictated the terms of treaties. At one time, in 1370, it was so strong that Denmark agreed not to name any king without the consent of the Hanseatic League. The League owned and operated ships, and kept armed forces to protect the interests of its members. For many years it was the ruler of trade on the Baltic and North Seas.

The Hanseatic League was very powerful for about two hundred years. Then, as new nations arose, and the seas and roads were better protected, the League gradually lost its powers. Member groups dropped out, and during the 1500s the League went out of existence.

Hansel and Gretel

Hansel and Gretel is the name of an opera written for children, but people of all ages enjoy it. An opera is a play in which all the conversation is sung instead of spoken. *Hansel and Gretel* was written

Hansel and Gretel want to eat the gingerbread house right down to the ground, but the wicked old witch has other plans.

by a German composer named Engelbert Humperdinck. He based his story on the fairy tale of the same name. The opera is most often performed at Christmas.

STORY OF THE OPERA

The story is about a brother and sister named Hansel and Gretel who are sent into the woods by their stepmother to find strawberries. They lose their way and meet a witch, who persuades them to go with her to her house made of gingerbread. The witch tries to make them climb into an oven so that she can make gingerbread of them, something she has done to many other children. But Hansel and Gretel are too wise for the witch. They put her into the oven instead. The witch's spell is broken, and all the rows of gingerbread children turn back into living boys and girls, who go back to their homes singing happily.

Hanukkah

Hanukkah, or *Chanukah,* is a Jewish holiday that falls every year about the same time as Christmas. It is called the Festival of Lights because, every evening of the eight days of the holiday, candles are lit. Jewish families keep candlesticks in their homes that have places for eight candles. One candle is lit the first evening, two the second, and so on until the eight days are over. Gifts are also exchanged during Hanukkah. This holiday has been observed by Jewish people throughout the world for more than two thousand years.

Hapsburg

Hapsburg is the name of one of the most important royal families of Europe. For nearly seven hundred years they ruled various countries of Europe, including Spain, Holland and Hungary, but their principal possession was always Austria and later the combined country of Austria-Hungary. For many years members of the Hapsburg family were the Holy Roman Emperors. The emper-

An additional candle is lit for each day of Hanukkah, an eight-day Jewish festival.

ors were elected, but it became a habit to elect a Hapsburg.

The name Hapsburg, which is also spelled *Habsburg,* comes from the name of the family's castle, Habichtsburg, meaning "hawk castle." This castle was in Switzerland.

harakiri

Harakiri is the name of a way of committing suicide, formerly used by the Samurai (warrior) class in Japan. When a Japanese man felt that he had been disgraced, or that he had failed to do his duty in some way, he used to believe that the only honorable way he could make up for his failure was by killing himself. This he did by committing harakiri, or stabbing himself in the stomach with a dagger. Years ago there were even special jeweled daggers for committing harakiri. The custom has been abandoned in recent years.

Harbin

Harbin is a city in Manchuria, which is a vast region in northeast China. Until about seventy years ago Harbin was an unimportant little village, but in 1896 China gave Russia permission to build up the town as a trade center, and it became one of the most important cities in eastern Asia. In 1924 China took control of Harbin again, in 1932 the Japanese captured the city, and during World War II the

Russians took it from the Japanese and returned it to China. While the Chinese Communists were fighting their national government in 1948 they took Harbin and it was one of their most important cities until they finally gained control of the entire country. Today more than a million and a half people live in Harbin. It is the trade center of central Manchuria, and an important railroad junction.

HARBIN, MANCHURIA. Population (1965 estimate) 1,552,000. Capital of Singkiang Province.

harbor

A harbor is a sort of small bay into which ships can sail and be safe from winds and storms while loading and unloading goods. Some harbors are natural, and some are made by man.

A good harbor should be about fifty feet deep, so that ocean-going ships can sail in safely. The bottom must be hard and firm so that anchors can hold, even in storms. Usually an artificial, or man-made, harbor has two or more breakwaters, or sea walls. A breakwater breaks up heavy ocean waves. Most breakwaters are made of broken stone and concrete, which is dumped by the ton into the harbor until the wall is high enough. Some harbors have such natural breakwaters as sand bars, coral reefs, and islands.

Among the world's best natural harbors are those in New York City, San Francisco and Seattle in the United States. Important artificial harbors have been built in Los Angeles and in several cities on the Great Lakes.

THE NORMANDY INVASION HARBORS

The most unusual artificial harbors ever built were used by the Allied forces to invade Normandy, in northern France, during World War II. Huge, floating breakwaters were made in Great Britain, towed in sections across the English Channel, and put together on the French side. They turned open beaches into harbors where big ships could unload tanks, artillery, locomotives, and other heavy equipment.

Furness Lines

The Statue of Liberty greets liners and freighters steaming into New York harbor.

WARREN GAMALIEL HARDING

Warren Gamaliel Harding was the twenty-ninth President of the United States. He served from March 4, 1921, until his death in office on August 2, 1923. Calvin Coolidge, who had been Vice President, became President when Harding died.

Warren Harding was one of the most handsome presidents the country has ever had. He was a tall, well-built man, with gray hair that was almost white. He had a friendly smile and most people liked him. He enjoyed the social life of Washington and the interesting events that are part of a President's life.

As President he did not demonstrate a great deal of executive ability. After he had appointed a man to an important office, he usually paid no further attention to what that man did. This was unfortunate, because several of the people he put in office proved to be greedy and dishonest. Harding's administration earned the reputation of being one of the weakest in the history of the United States. Many people believe that when Harding finally realized how poorly he had controlled his appointed officials, the shock was too much for him and broke his heart with shame and disappointment. Some people thought that this had a great deal to do with the fact that he was unable to fight off the pneumonia that caused his death in 1923, when he had been President less than two and a half years.

HIS EARLY YEARS

Warren G. Harding was born near Corsica, Ohio, on November 2, 1865. His father was a farmer and a country doctor. Harding went to public school, and attended Ohio State Central College in Iberia, Ohio. He studied law, but after finishing college he taught school for a time and then got a position on the *Daily Star,* a newspaper in Marion, Ohio. He married a young widow in 1891, when he was twenty-six years old. She was five years older than he was, and her maiden name had been Florence Kling.

When Harding bought the Marion *Daily Star,* a few years later, his wife helped him run the paper.

Harding was a fine public speaker, and his friends urged him to go into politics where the ability to speak is important. Harding agreed to run for office, and in 1900 he was elected to the Ohio state senate, where he served for two terms. In 1904 he became lieutenant governor of Ohio, but was defeated when he ran for governor in 1910. In November of 1914 the people of Ohio elected Harding to the United States Senate. As a senator he voted for the bill that enforced the Prohibition Amendment. This was the law that made it illegal to sell or transport alcoholic liquors within the United States. He also voted for the "Woman's Suffrage" Amendment, which gave women the right to vote.

HOW HE BECAME PRESIDENT

In the Republican Convention of 1920, there were three powerful groups of delegates, each with its favorite candidate. One group wanted to nominate General Leonard Wood, one wanted Senator Hiram Johnson of California, and a third wanted Governor Frank O. Lowden of Illinois. Several ballots were taken and each of the three men received about the same number of votes on each ballot. Each man and his backers refused to drop out.

After the ninth ballot, a group of the top men in the Republican party left the convention hall and went to a hotel room to discuss what should be done. In this "small, smoke-filled room" they decided that they would use their influence to nominate Harding.

Very few people had ever heard of Senator Harding of Ohio. He had never done anything startling or unusual, but he at least had not done anything that made people dislike him. Also, he had always been a good, solid Republican. He spoke well, and he made a good appearance. The men in the hotel room knew they could get the tired convention delegates to nominate Harding instead of one of the three leading candidates.

Not only did the convention accept him, but the people of the country elected him with a large majority. The defeated Democratic candidate was James M. Cox, and Cox's running mate, as the candidate for Vice President, was Franklin Delano Roosevelt.

After Harding became President, he called the first great international conference of important representatives from countries all over the world to discuss the reduction of armaments. You can read more about this in the article on DISARMAMENT.

In one of Harding's speeches, he advised a return to "normalcy." At that time, there was no such word in the English language. When Harding used the word, it was incorrect. He should have said "normality." However, the fact that a man who became president of the United States had used the word made other people use it also, so Harding was responsible for adding a word to the English language.

During the Harding administration the Teapot Dome oil scandal made headlines, and his administration has always been associated with it in the memory of the public. The Teapot Dome oil fields near Caspar, Wyoming, were government property, but the Secretary of the Interior, Albert Fall, leased them to private operators. Several people were sent to prison for defrauding the government, which rightfully should have received all the profits from this oil land. The entire episode was a great scandal and it hurt the Republican Party.

Harding thought that he might help his party if he travelled about the country and talked to people everywhere, so he toured the United States, taking an extra trip up to Alaska at the same time. On the way back he became ill with pneumonia and died in San Francisco on August 2, 1923. He was buried in Marion, Ohio.

MRS. WARREN G. HARDING

Mrs. Florence Kling De Wolfe Harding was born in Marion, Ohio, on August 15, 1860. She was the daughter of a hardware merchant who later became a banker. She had been married once before, to Henry De Wolfe, by whom she had one son. At the time of her marriage to Warren G. Harding, she was 31. Mrs. Warren Harding died on November 21, 1924.

hardness

Hardness is a way of describing the degree to which a substance can resist being scratched by another substance. There is a scale for measuring how hard any particular material is. This scale is called Mohs' Hardness Test, and it rates the hardness of minerals by numbers from 1 to 10. The higher the number, the harder the substance. The scale is as follows:

1. talc	6. feldspar
2. gypsum	7. quartz
3. calcite	8. topaz
4. fluorite	9. sapphire
5. apatite	10. diamond

Any substance in the world can be rated by comparing it with substances on this scale. The numbers show where each one rates in hardness, but it does not show how much harder each one is than the next. The fact that apatite is rated 5 and diamond is rated 10 does not mean that diamond is twice as hard as apatite. The scale only shows that each substance is harder than the one before it, and provides a convenient way to express the hardness of all substances by comparing them with those on the scale.

Hardy, Thomas

Thomas Hardy was an English writer of novels and poems. He lived about a 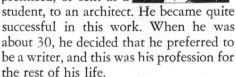 hundred years ago, having been born in 1840. His father planned for him to be a designer and builder of churches, so as a boy Hardy was apprenticed, or sent as a student, to an architect. He became quite successful in this work. When he was about 30, he decided that he preferred to be a writer, and this was his profession for the rest of his life.

Hardy's first successful novel was *Far from the Madding Crowd,* which was published in 1874. After that he wrote a series of books about the people of his native region, which was called Wessex. The most famous of these were *The Return of the Native* and *Tess of the D'Urbervilles.* Later Hardy turned to writing poetry and short stories. He came to be considered one of the greatest of English writers. Hardy died in 1928, when he was

The tiny hare knows the art of camouflage; his coat blends with the ground.

88 years old. He was buried in Westminster Abbey, which is a mark of great honor in England.

hare

The hare is an animal that belongs to the same family as the rabbit and looks very much like a large rabbit, except that it has longer hind legs and ears. It is found in all sections of the world except Madagascar and Australia. There are many different kinds of hare. Its color depends upon the climate in which it is found. Its usual color is tan or gray, but in northern regions it is white so that it cannot be seen against the snow. The hare can run very fast. It is also a good swimmer. A hare may have several litters of young a year, and they are born covered with hair and with their eyes open. The hare is sometimes killed for its skin, which is used as a trimming on coats; it is also killed for its meat, which tastes somewhat like chicken. The most common hare found in North America is the jackrabbit.

harem

The Moslems, or people who follow the Mohammedan religion, believe that the women of a family should live separately from the men. The apartment for the women in a Mohammedan family is called the harem. Harem means "the prohibited," or "private," and no man except the husband or a near relative of the women is allowed to enter it. A Moslem is allowed to have more than one wife, and in his harem would live his wife, or wives, his mother and unmarried sisters if they live with him, his unmarried daughters, and all his female servants. Mohammedan boys live in the harem with their mothers until they are about twelve years old; then they move to the men's apartment. Harems have been used in all the countries where Mohammedan people live, and in other countries of Asia. In the last hundred years there have been fewer harems because the customs governing the separation of the women from the men have become less strict.

Hargreaves, James

James Hargreaves was an Englishman who invented a machine to spin thread. Before this machine was invented, about two hundred years ago, all thread had been made by hand on spinning wheels such as you may have seen in pictures or in museums. These spinning wheels spun one thread at a time. The thread was then woven into cloth. At that time, in most households throughout the world the housewife made the clothes for the family, spinning the thread on spinning wheels and weaving the cloth on hand looms at home. Hargreaves' machine, which he called a *spinning jenny,* and the invention at about the same time of an automatic loom for weaving cloth, changed all this. English manufacturers became able to make cloth so cheaply that people could afford to buy it instead of making it themselves. This helped to make Great Britain the richest country on earth for more than a hundred years.

Hargreaves' neighbors destroyed the first jenny because they were afraid it would put many of the hand spinners out of work. They were wrong, because it finally turned out that the invention gave more people jobs. By the time Hargreaves died in 1778 there were thousands of jennies in England.

Harlem, a section of New York City, where many Negro people live: see the article on NEW YORK CITY.

Harlequin

Harlequin is a character you may have seen in children's plays or pantomimes or ballets. He is a kind of clown. His face is usually very white, and he often wears baggy trousers, a loose blouse with large buttons, and a two-pointed hat covered with bells and spangles. He sometimes seem sad because he cannot talk and has to express himself by hand movements and facial expressions. In the traditional, or very old, story he is always in love with Columbine, a lovely girl. He protects her until she is saved by the good fairy from another clown who tries to capture her. Harlequin is one of the oldest characters in stage history. In medieval times he was a demon, or evil spirit. Sometimes he was called the "Erlking." Later he became a kind of clown who was always lively and witty.

harmonica

The harmonica is a musical instrument. It is a mouth organ made of two short strips of metal and wood with small holes between them. When you blow through the harmonica, you produce different musical notes depending on which hole you blow through.

Another type of harmonica was very popular about 150 years ago. This instrument was made of several drinking glasses of different sizes and with different amounts of water in them. The player

The harmonica is one of the few musical instruments that fit into a boy's pocket and go with him on camping trips.

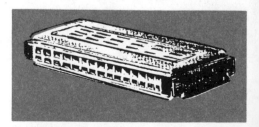

struck the glasses with his fingertips and each glass produced a different musical note. Benjamin Franklin made some improvements in this instrument, and two great composers, Mozart of Austria and Beethoven of Germany, wrote compositions for it.

harmony

Harmony is the study of how to make chords out of musical tones. A chord is a group of tones sounded at the same time. A melody, or tune, is said to be harmonized when other tones are sounded at the same time as the melody note, to give the whole a richer, fuller effect.

A melody is written in a certain key, or group of tones forming a scale. Each key has its own chords, which are built of notes a certain number of tones apart. The basic chord is called a *triad*, which means a group of three. Each tone in a chord is called a *voice*. In four-part harmony, the voices are called bass, tenor, alto, and soprano. The bass is the lowest, and the soprano is the highest. The soprano usually carries the melody, and the bass determines what the chord is. Since the chords are built in thirds, another tone is needed to make the fourth voice, and this is usually gotten by doubling, or repeating, one of the other tones.

Composers (writers of music) have been using harmony for only about 350 years, which makes it a recent development in the long history of music.

In ancient times music consisted only of melody. Then composers began to write two or more melodies to be played together. This is called *counterpoint,* and music written in this style is called *contrapuntal* or *polyphonic* ("many-voiced") music.

Since about the year 1750, most music has been *homophonic.* This means it is made up of one melody supported by chords, while polyphonic music is formed from two or more melodies going on at the same time. Homophonic music follows the rules and practices of harmony.

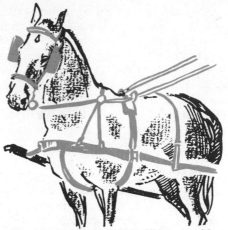

The harness crossing old Dobbin's shoulders below the neck enables him to pull his load without undue strain.

Today, composers are showing an increased interest in music based on the rules and practices of counterpoint.

harness

Harness is equipment that makes it possible for an animal to pull a load. The most common harness is that used for horses. Years ago in the United States all the work on farms and most of the transportation depended on horses, and harness-making was a very important business.

A horse's harness is made mostly of leather, but has some metal or wood on it. It is made of many different parts and all parts work together so that the driver can direct the horse and so that the animal can pull a heavy load without injuring itself. Most harness has a padded collar made of leather that is fitted around the neck of the horse. When the horse is not pulling a heavy load the collar may be exchanged for a padded breastband. Strips of leather or metal chains called *traces* are attached to the collar by pieces of wood or metal called *hames.* The traces are connected to the wagon itself, or in some cases to shafts, which are pieces of wood coming out from a crossbar on the wagon. This is called the *whiffletree* or *swingletree.*

The horse is directed by the reins that the driver holds in his hands. The reins are leather straps, and they are attached to the bit, a piece of metal running across the back part of the horse's mouth. The bit is held in place by a part of the harness called a bridle. When the driver pulls the reins the horse feels the movement in his mouth and turns in the direction in which he feels the pull.

Harold

Harold was the name of two kings of England, but the more famous was Harold II, though he was king for only a short time. Harold was born in 1022. He was the son of one of the greatest English nobles and, next to the king, was the most powerful man in England. When Edward the Confessor, King of England, died in 1066, he said that he wanted Harold to be the next king. At that time the leading nobles chose the king. They followed Edward's wish and made Harold king. But William, the Duke of Normandy, who lived across the English Channel in what is now a section of France, said that Edward had promised him the throne. In October of 1066 he invaded England. At the same time Norwegian armies were invading England in the north. Harold defeated the Norwegian armies and then went south to meet William at the small English town of Hastings. The Battle of Hastings lasted all day. The English fought bravely but they were defeated by the Normans. Harold was killed in the battle and William became king. He is now known as William I, or William the Conqueror. His victory is called the Norman Conquest, and after it the Normans ruled England.

harp

The harp is a large musical instrument with strings. It is sometimes five or six feet high. It is shaped like a triangle, with three sides, and can stand alone. The player sits beside the harp and plucks the strings with both his hands. Because the harp is so large and because it has more than forty strings, it has a wide range of tone. It sounds a little like a piano.

The harp is a very old musical instrument. Some kind of harp has been played at some time in almost every part of the world. The Bible says that a man named Jubal invented the harp. One kind of an-

The harp is the oldest stringed instrument. *Left:* The harpist's skill delighted the rulers of ancient Egypt. *Right:* In Africa, traveling harpists play and sing in the towns they visit. *Center:* A modern harp is an important part of a symphony orchestra.

NBC

cient harp was called a *psaltery.* David, in the Bible, sang while he played the psaltery. His songs are called *psalms,* and there is a book of them in the Bible. At first, harps had to be rather small because they were carried by players on long journeys. About five or six hundred years ago, strolling minstrels in Europe told long and exciting tales while they played their harps.

harpies

Harpies are creatures in Greek mythology, the stories the ancient Greeks and Romans told of their gods and goddesses. The harpies are goddesses of the storms, which means they control the storm winds. Also they play mean tricks on men. They appear in the *Iliad* and the *Odyssey,* the two most famous long poems in Greek literature.

A harpy is described as a very ugly creature. Sometimes it has a human face with animal ears, but usually it has the head of a bird and its wings and body are covered with feathers. It has human arms and legs but has claws instead of hands and has the feet of a large and fantastic bird. Harpies in literature represent danger or forces of evil that must be overcome by the hero in the story.

harpy

The harpy or *harpy eagle* is a large bird of prey. A bird of prey feeds itself by attacking and eating other birds or animals. The harpy is found chiefly in Central America. It is sometimes three feet long. It has a large bill and powerful talons, or claws. Its head and lower part are white, and its back is dark gray banded with black. It is different from other eagles because it has a double, rather than a single, crest on its head. The harpy hunts in the daytime, flying slowly until it sights its victim. It is named for the harpies, who were creatures in Greek mythology, the stories the ancient Greeks told about their gods and goddesses.

Harris, Joel Chandler

Joel Chandler Harris was an American writer. He was born in Georgia in 1848 and spent all his life in the South. He worked for the Atlanta *Constitution,* and it was in this newspaper that he first wrote about Uncle Remus. Uncle Remus was a kindly old Negro man who entertained the children by telling tales of Br'er (brother) Rabbit, Br'er Fox, and other animals. The tales became so popular that they were put into several books. Harris wrote other books, including a story of his own life called *On the Plantation,* but he is best known for the Uncle Remus stories. He died in 1908.

Harrisburg

Harrisburg is the capital of Pennsylvania. It is on the Susquehanna River, about a hundred miles west of Philadelphia, and it is surrounded by rich farms. Boats travel up the Susquehanna River to Harrisburg, and it is also a railroad center. The Enola railroad yards across the river are among the largest in the United States. About 80,000 people live in Harrisburg. Many of them work in iron and steel mills, and others make bricks, machinery, and clothing. Many books are printed in the city. Harrisburg is a handsome city, and the people are proud of their fine parks and beautiful public buildings. The state capitol is a magnificent domed building, with stately marble halls. There is an Education Building, with pictures on the walls that show the history of civilization, and a museum where there are many things recalling the history of the people of Pennsylvania.

Harrisburg was settled in 1712 by John Harris, and the city was named after him. His son built a ferry across the Susquehanna River, and for many years the town was called Harris' Ferry. In 1812, Harrisburg became the state capital.

HARRISBURG, PENNSYLVANIA. Population (1960 census) 79,697. Capital of Pennsylvania. County seat of Dauphin County. Settled in 1712.

Benjamin Harrison was the twenty-third President of the United States. He served from 1889 to 1893. He was defeated by Grover Cleveland when he ran for re-election to a second term.

Harrison was born in Ohio. His family for several generations had been prominent in the national affairs of the United States. His father was a member of Congress, his grandfather (William Henry Harrison) was President, and his great grandfather was a signer of the Declaration of Independence.

Harrison was a distinguished-looking man. He was tall and well-built, with a full beard and thick white hair.

HIS EARLY YEARS

Benjamin Harrison was born on August 20, 1833, at North Bend, Ohio. He grew up on the family farm and at first attended a local log-cabin school. Later, however, he was instructed by a private tutor, and he was a good student. He next attended Farmers College, and he finally graduated from Miami University. He had studied law and was admitted to the bar when he was only 20 years old. A few years later, he was considered one of the most capable young lawyers in the state of Ohio.

The Civil War interrupted his career as a lawyer. He volunteered for the Union Army and was commissioned a second lieutenant. His loyal service and bravery in battle won him several promotions, and he was eventually given the rank of brigadier general. After the war he returned to his law practice. Although he was not actively a politician himself, he was always very much interested in the welfare of his country and in the activity of the Republican Party.

HOW HE BECAME PRESIDENT

The people of Ohio elected Benjamin Harrison to the United States Senate in 1881, and during his six-year term as senator he won the respect of both parties. His term expired in March, 1888. The following November the Republican Party nominated him for president, to run against Grover Cleveland, who was then seeking re-election. Harrison won the election and served for just one term.

During his administration, the first meeting of the Pan-American Congress was held in Washington. This was the first time the people of North, South, and Central America had ever sent representatives to talk over problems they all shared and to make suggestions as to how they could help each other. It was also during Harrison's administration that the Sherman Silver Act was passed. This law compelled the government to buy huge amounts of silver each year. This was very costly, and upset the financial standing of the country. It had a great deal to do with Harrison's defeat by the Democrat, Grover Cleveland, in 1892.

After Harrison retired from the presidency, he went back to his law practice and wrote several books on government. He was so highly respected as a lawyer that the government of Venezuela called upon him for help when they needed a representative in a hearing concerning a border dispute.

He died at Indianapolis, Indiana, on March 13, 1901, at the age of 67, and was buried there.

BENJAMIN HARRISON'S TWO WIVES

Mrs. Caroline Lavinia Scott Harrison

was born in 1832 in Oxford, Ohio. She was the first head of the D.A.R.—the Daughters of the American Revolution. She married Benjamin Harrison when she was 21 years old. They had one son and one daughter. Mrs. Caroline Scott Harrison died in the White House in 1892.

Harrison's second wife was Mrs. Mary Scott Lord Dimmock, a widow. They were married in 1896 and had one daughter. Mrs. Mary Harrison died in 1948, at the age of 90.

WILLIAM HENRY HARRISON

William Henry Harrison was the ninth President of the United States. He served only one month in office, from March 4, 1841, to April 4, 1841. It was the shortest term ever served by any president. He caught cold at his inauguration, and he died a month later of pneumonia.

William Henry Harrison was nominated by the Whig Party to run against the Democrat, Martin Van Buren, who was seeking re-election. Although Harrison was elected, almost all the presidential term was served by the man who was his Vice President, John Tyler.

HIS EARLY YEARS

William Henry Harrison was born in Berkeley, Virginia, on February 9, 1773, before the Revolutionary War. His father, Benjamin Harrison, was one of the signers of the Declaration of Independence. His grandson, also named Benjamin Harrison, became the twenty-third President of the United States.

Young Harrison attended Hampden-Sidney College at Hampden-Sidney, Virginia, and later studied medicine at the College of Physicians and Surgeons in Philadelphia, Pennsylvania.

His career plans changed when he was 19 years old. He could see how badly the country needed good soldiers. There was trouble with the Indians, and troops were short. Harrison volunteered for the army and was commissioned a lieutenant. In 1792, he fought under General Anthony Wayne. He continued in the service with frequent promotions for his skill and bravery.

HOW HE BECAME PRESIDENT

In 1800, President John Adams appointed Harrison governor of the Indiana Territory. Afterwards he was also governor of the Louisiana Territory. In 1811, an Indian chief of the Shawnees, Tecumseh, succeeded in uniting all the Indians of the West against the white man. There was a battle at a place called Tippecanoe, about seven miles north of what is now Lafayette, Indiana. Because of Harrison's able command, he defeated the Indians with a force of six hundred men, and he won for himself the nickname of "Tippecanoe," which lasted for the rest of his life.

He made his home in Ohio, finally, and in 1816 the people of that state elected him to the House of Representatives. From 1825 to 1828 he served as United States senator from Ohio, and in 1836 he ran for President on the Whig ticket against Martin Van Buren. He was defeated. Four years later, in 1840, with John Tyler as his running mate, he again ran for President. The combination of his nickname and the name of John Tyler fell naturally into a rhyming campaign slogan—"Tippecanoe and Tyler too." The people of the country elected Harrison by a large majority, because by this time they were tired of the Van Buren administration. Harrison was 67 years old, the oldest President ever elected.

Harrison caught cold during his inauguration and developed pneumonia. He was a very sick man all through the one month during which he was actually president, and he did not have a chance to do anything at all in that office. He died on April 4, 1841. He was buried in North Bend, Ohio, where he had his home. John Tyler succeeded him.

MRS. WILLIAM HENRY HARRISON

Mrs. Anna Symmes Harrison was born in Morristown, New Jersey, in 1775. She was the daughter of Colonel John Cleves Symmes, chief justice of the supreme court of New Jersey and a veteran of the Revolutionary War. President and Mrs. Harrison had ten children, six sons and four daughters. Mrs. Anna Symmes Harrison died in 1864.

harrow, a machine used to break and smooth farm land: see the article on FARM MACHINERY.

Harte, Bret

Bret Harte was an American writer who wrote many stories about the western part of the United States in the days when it was first being settled. His full name was Francis Bret Harte. He was born in New York City, in 1836, but he moved to California when he was only 16, and he worked there as a printer and editor. He wrote most of his stories there. His most famous one, called "The Luck of Roaring Camp," was published in 1871. Harte later moved to England, where he died in 1902. His other well-known stories include "The Outcasts of Poker Flat" and "The Twins of Table Mountain."

hartebeest

The hartebeest is a South African antelope. It is a graceful animal and runs very swiftly; it can easily outdistance a greyhound, one of the fastest racing dogs. Its front legs are much heavier than its hind legs. Both the male and the female hartebeest have horns shaped somewhat like a lyre, which is a harp-shaped instrument. The hartebeest is red and has a long face with a naked nose. Formerly great herds of these animals roamed Africa from Cape Colony to Rhodesia, but now there are only a few animals left, and they are found only in remote districts.

Hartford

Hartford is the capital and largest city of the state of Connecticut. It is on the Connecticut River. More than 162,-000 people live there. Several of the biggest insurance companies in the world have their main offices in Hartford. There are important factories that make typewriters and firearms, and in East Hartford, a city of about 44,000 across the Connecticut River, are some of the world's most important aviation factories.

The capitol of Connecticut is a domed building on the side of a hill. In the Supreme Court building hangs the most

Conn. Development Comm.

The beautiful old State House in Hartford was built more than 150 years ago.

famous full-length picture of George Washington. This portrait was painted by Gilbert Stuart, a famous American artist. In Hartford is the place where the Charter Oak stood. This was an oak tree in which the early colonists hid an important document from the English governor, and you can read more about it in the article on CONNECTICUT. Trinity College for men was founded in 1823, and it has many fine old buildings. The home of Samuel Clemens (Mark Twain) is still used, as a library.

Hartford was an old Dutch trading post. In 1635 a group of colonists led by Thomas Hooker, a Puritan clergyman, settled there and called it Newtown. Two years later the name was changed to Hartford. In 1701, Hartford and the city of New Haven became the joint capital of Connecticut and remained so until 1875, when Hartford alone was made the capital. In 1814 the Hartford Convention took place in Hartford. Twenty-six delegates from New England met to discuss whether or not New England should continue fighting with the United States government in the War of 1812. Some of the delegates thought New England should secede (leave the Union) as the southern states did about fifty years later; but the war soon ended and New England did not secede. Also about this time Hartford was the center for a group of writers who were called the Connecticut Wits, or the Hartford Wits. They tried to create a literature that would be typically American, and also became interested in the political disputes of the time. Some of the Hartford Wits were Joel Barlow, John Trumbull, and Lemuel Hopkins, and they founded and wrote for a number of magazines.

HARTFORD, CONNECTICUT. Population (1960 census) 162,178. Capital of Connecticut. County seat of Hartford County. Settled in 1635.

Harun-al-Rashid

Harun-al-Rashid was the most famous caliph of Baghdad. He was born about 764 and died in 809. Caliph was the name given to the man who was the ruler of all the Mohammedan people. While Harun-al-Rashid was caliph, Baghdad, which is now the capital of Iraq, was the leading city of the Mohammedan empire. Harun-al-Rashid controlled all of southwest Asia as well as part of northern Africa. He lived in great splendor in Baghdad and was very generous to the poets and scholars of his time. Many of the stories told in the Arabian Nights are about Harun-al-Rashid, his wife Zobeide, and his vizier, or adviser, Graffir. Harun-al-Rashid is also spelled Haroun-al-Raschid.

Harvard

Harvard is the oldest university in the United States. The principal grounds and buildings are in Cambridge, Massachusetts. It was founded in 1636. In 1965 it had about 13,000 students, including those at Radcliffe College (see below), and more than 6,000 members of its faculty, or teachers, by far the highest ratio of faculty to students in the world. Besides its college for undergraduates, Harvard has schools in law, medicine, dentistry, business administration, theology, architecture, and others. The university is named for John Harvard, an

American clergyman who left his library of four hundred books to the University when he died in 1638.

The Harvard University Library has since become the world's largest college library, with more than 7,000,000 books. Harvard's property and endowment are more than 400 million dollars.

Until after World War II, Harvard was a college for men only, but Radcliffe College for women, also in Cambridge, had most of its courses taught by Harvard's professors. Since World War II, Harvard and Radcliffe have become almost the same as one coeducational university, and the men and women attend the same classes.

Five Presidents of the United States— John Adams, John Quincy Adams, Theodore Roosevelt, Franklin Delano Roosevelt, and John F. Kennedy—have been graduates of Harvard.

harvester, a machine that gathers grain and other crops: see the article on FARM MACHINERY.

Harvey, William

William Harvey was an English doctor who discovered that the blood circulates (moves around) the human body. He lived about 350 years ago. He was born in 1578 and studied in England and in Italy. At that time it was not known that the blood circulates. Harvey showed how the heart works and how the veins and arteries carry the blood to and from the heart. He died in 1657.

Hastings, Battle of

About nine hundred years ago, an English king called Edward the Confessor died without leaving an heir to succeed him on the throne. There were two noblemen, each of whom said Edward had promised the throne to him. One was Harold, an Englishman, and the other was William, Duke of Normandy, a region in the northern part of France.

William got together an army of about 10,000 men, made up of Normans and adventurers from all over Europe. They landed near Hastings on the southern coast of England. The Normans were cavalry troops who fought on horseback and with bows and arrows. The English under Harold were armed with spears, swords, and huge battle-axes. The English took up a position on a hill outside of Hastings, and William attacked with his cavalry. In between charges by the mounted Normans, they sent showers of arrows among the English troops, but the English stood firm most of the day. Then William used a trick to get some of the English down off the hill to a place where they would be easier to defeat. He had his horsemen pretend to run away. When the English left the hill to chase them, the horsemen turned and attacked. A small but strong group of English stayed on the hill around their king until evening, when Harold was killed by an arrow. One more attack by William killed most of the remaining English soldiers and put the rest to flight.

William became king of England as William I. In English history, William is known as William the Conqueror and his victory is called the Norman Conquest.

hat

A hat is a covering for the head. It may be made of felt, straw, silk, or fabric. A hat gives warmth, and it also protects the wearer from rain, snow, and the glare of the sun. Women often wear hats only to make themselves attractive or because they are going somewhere, for example to church, where it is customary to wear a hat. Men too may wear hats only so that they will be considered properly dressed. Hatmaking is a big business in the United States, where more than fifty million men's hats and even more women's hats are sold every year.

STYLES IN HATS

Men's hats have changed less, through

Men's hats are made in many styles, ranging from the formal top hat to the colorful hunting cap. But most men in the United States prefer an in-between style of hat that is informal enough for casual wear, yet conservative enough to be worn in any company.

Dobbs Hats

Millinery Fashion Bureau

Above: The simple, attractive cloche, which hugs the head and outlines the features, is one style of women's hat that remains fashionable year after year.

Right: Pretty as a picture in her pretty picture hat, the lovely lady of fashion succeeds in looking as if she had just stepped out of a bandbox.

Millinery Fashion Bureau

The hat styles shown here are: 1. A soft hat worn by Greek men on journeys. 2. A formal hat worn by Greek ladies to banquets. 3. Hat worn by women of Phrygia when St. Paul visited there. 4. A veil hat, popular among medieval ladies. 5. A sugarloaf hat, worn by 15th-century merchants. 6. A steeple hat, adorned with a bow. 7. An English merchant's hat in 1550. 8. A three-horned hat for formal wear. 9. A Spanish hat in 1570, resembling men's styles today. 10. The wildly decorated hat of a proud professional soldier. 11. A clergyman's hat.

the centuries, than any other article of their clothing, but gradually the soft felt hat has replaced most other kinds of men's hats. The snap-brim fedora is the most popular hat for a man. It is a felt hat and has a brim about 2½ inches wide, which most men wear turned down in front. The straw hat is popular with men who live in warm climates. Another popular hat is the homburg, which has a stiff brim that is turned up all the way around. Most men's hats are brown, gray, blue, or black. A man seldom spends more than $5 to $10 for a hat, but a very fine hat for a man may cost as much as $200.

Women spend a great deal more money on their hats than men do, and the styles of their hats change often. There are many types of hat popular with women, and a woman's choice of hat often depends upon the way she fixes her hair, the rest of her clothes, and the occasion for which she is wearing the hat.

Women's hats are generally more complicated than men's. They are also more colorful. They may differ in size from the tight-fitting Juliet hat and cloche to the wide-brimmed picture hat. Added decorations, such as veils, flowers, sequins, or ribbons, may be put on a woman's hat.

HAT MATERIALS

Most hats made in the United States are of felt. Also popular are hats made of straw, silk, and fabrics. In the ordinary felt hat, it is quite possible that the materials used were gathered from the far ends of the world. Most of the fur used for felt in the United States comes from the coney, rabbit, and hare. The fur is usually shipped from England, Scotland, Australia, Germany, France, and Austria.

1. A Pilgrim's hat from 1620. 2. The earliest of the tricorn style. 3. A Pilgrim woman's hat, simple but flirtatious. 4. A tricorn hat worn by ladies in 1750. 5. The men's version of the same style. 6. The bicorn hat worn by Napoleon. 7. The beaver top hat of 1795. 8. An informal "visor cap." 9. A poke bonnet, which kept the eyes from straying.

Making a handful of fine fur into a finished hat is a skill that requires craftsmanship.
1. Fur for one hat is weighed after being chemically treated to aid felting.
2. The fur is then shaped on a copper cone, which is dipped in water to tighten the fur.
3. It is next shrunk and hardened by being rolled under pressure while soaking wet.
4. Shrunk to one-third its original size, the domelike hat body is ready for shaping.
5. Metal fingers pull out the brim and the crown is given its familiar bell-like shape.
6. After blocking and ironing, the hat is oiled for luster. Last, the bands are sewn on.

Sometimes the American rabbit is used, but its fur is considered to be inferior. Higher-priced felt is made from the fur of the beaver, which makes the softest and strongest felt. The skins of more than eight million rabbits are used each year in the United States.

The silk used for silk hats and for the silk band on felt hats comes from China and Japan, as does the silk that is used for the linings of these hats. The silk is usually woven in American mills. More than ten thousand yards of satin are used in the United States each year for this purpose. Artificial silk is also used for linings and bands.

In the brim of a felt hat, to give it stiffness, is embedded a shellac solution, made from the lac bug of India. The leather in the hat band, which makes the hat fit and feel comfortable, is made from the skins of sheep.

HOW HATS ARE MADE

The way the fur is made into FELT is described in a separate article. For felt hats, the felt is made in a cone shape somewhat like that of an ice-cream cone but much larger. This is stretched over a *block,* a piece of wood cut in the shape of the "crown," or rounded top part, of the hat. On this block the felt is *pounced,* that is, it is rubbed or pounded until it is smooth. The brim is flattened out and ironed. Finally the cloth parts, the lining and band, are sewed on.

Women's felt hats are made in much the same way as men's hats, but women's cloth hats are a different kind of manufacturing, related to the garment industry. The cloth for many hats is cut at the same time and the hats are sewed by workers at sewing machines.

STRAW HATS

Straw hats are made from rice straw grown in Japan or China, from Tuscan straw grown in Italy, from bamboo grasses grown in the Philippines, and from the leaves of the screw pine tree. The Panama hat is a straw hat made from the Jipijapa palm tree that grows in South America, in Ecuador. The Panama hat is woven by hand, from moistened fibers of the palm tree.

Most straw hats are made in factories. The material is woven into braids before it is sent to the factory. There the braid is bleached and cleaned. It is moistened again before it is ready to be sewn. The hat is started by hand at the tip of the center of the crown. It is then fitted to a block of the desired size and a machine weaves or sews it to fit this block. Gelatin is used to stiffen straw hats. After the hats have been stiffened, they are blocked, or steam-pressed, into the correct shape. Finishing steps include further moistening, blocking, and ironing.

HISTORY OF HATS

People have worn all kinds of amazing and unusual hats. The savage of olden times wore palm leaves and animal skins to protect his head. Later, the Greeks wore skull caps and metal helmets with horses' manes and tails for decorations. The art of making fur into felt and then trimming and shaping it to make a hat was practiced more than three thousand years ago.

Hatmaking was one of the early industries in the colonies of the New World. It has always been practiced along the Atlantic Coast of the United States. Important hatmaking cities are Danbury and Norwalk, Connecticut, and Newark, New Jersey. New York City is the center for women's cloth hats.

Havana

Havana is the capital of Cuba and the largest city in the West Indies. *Habana* means "harbor" in Spanish and Havana, on the Gulf of Mexico, has one of the most beautiful harbors in the world. Ships bring machinery, cloth, and food to Havana, and carry sugar, tobacco, and fruit to other world ports.

More than a million people live in Havana. They make cigars that are considered the best in the world, and also perfume and rum. Outside the city are great plantations where sugar cane is grown.

The climate in Havana is very fine, and even during the winter the temperature is about 75 degrees, which is like a pleasant spring day in the United States. The summers are quite hot. Sometimes Havana is hit by severe hurricanes.

Before the Cuban Revolution of 1959, thousands of people went to Havana for vacations. It is an interesting and attractive city, with fine old Spanish buildings. Some parts of the city are modern, and there are many handsome hotels and beautiful parks. The capitol is an impressive building, with a splendid gold dome. It cost $20,000,000 and is the most beautiful in Latin America. There are some fine churches, and a magnificent opera house. When people come to Havana by ship, they pass Morro Castle, an old fortress that guards the entrance of the harbor. Morro Castle was built by the Spanish almost four hundred years ago to protect Havana from enemies.

The Spanish people founded Havana in 1519, and it was made the capital of Cuba in 1552. A United States battleship, the *Maine,* was blown up in Havana harbor in 1898; this was one of the incidents that started the Spanish-American War.

HAVANA, CUBA.   Population (1961 estimate) 1,158,203. Capital of Cuba.

ILLUSTRATED

WORLD

ENCYCLOPEDIA

LIBRARY
OF THE
LITERARY TREASURES

The novels, plays, poems, and other works of
the most celebrated and historic writers of
the English language in all lands and times

VOLUME
10

Ghosts — Hangman's House

Edited by ALBERT H. MOREHEAD
Designed by DONALD D. WOLF *and* MARGOT L. WOLF
With many new drawings by RAFAELLO BUSONI

ACKNOWLEDGEMENTS—Outlines in this volume were written by Elizabeth
MacLean, Dina Dellalé, Nancy Starrels, Hanz Holzer, Martin Keen, Robert
Condon, Christopher Lazare, Nicholas Bela, Susan Margulies, Phyllis Pollard,
Gerard Meyer, Mary Louise Birmingham, Sue G. Walcutt, Ernst J. Schlochauer,
James E. Tobin, Mildred Lee Marmur and the Editors.

Bobley Publishing a Division of
ILLUSTRATED WORLD ENCYCLOPEDIA, INC.

Ghosts

Play by Henrik Ibsen, 1828–1906.
Produced 1881. Several translations.
(RE, 4)

IN GHOSTS, IBSEN typically drama-
tized an aspect of the new scientific
knowledge that was rising to a peak
late in the 19th century. Here his peg
is the congenital aspects of syphilis
[a forbidden word in those times]
and the dire later consequences of the
disease, such as paresis. In the playwright's art Ibsen was never better,
especially in his skillful recounting of
past events in the dialogue without
slowing down the tempo of the current events.

Act I. ENGSTRAND, a crippled carpenter,
visits his daughter REGINE, who works for
the widowed Mrs. ALVING. Engstrand,
having saved money he earned working on
a new orphanage, intends to open a home
for seamen and wants her help him run the
tavern. Regine refuses because she intends
to work in the orphanage and because her
father is a drunkard. Pastor MANDERS,
then Mrs. Alving, come in as Engstrand
leaves. Mrs. Alving's son OSVALD has come
home to spend the winter. Manders wonders if the new orphanage, which has been
named in honor of Mrs. Alving's late husband, should be insured; some people
might consider insurance a lack of faith in
Divine Providence. Mrs. Alving says there
was a small fire at the orphanage the day
before, due to Engstrand's carelessness, and
Manders says that Engstrand drinks only to
relieve his pains. He asks Mrs. Alving to
let Regine live with her father, but Mrs.
Alving refuses. Osvald enters and Manders
berates him for being an artist and having
artist friends, who are immoral. Osvald
denies this and leaves. Manders reminds
Mrs Alving that she once left her dissolute husband and that he, Manders, persuaded her to go back, as her husband had
reformed. Mrs. Alving says that her hus-

band never reformed; he seduced one of
their serving girls, who then gave birth to
Regine. Mrs. Alving built the orphanage
only to counteract the talk about her husband's immorality. Osvald is heard making
advances to Regine in the adjoining room
and Mrs. Alving thinks she is hearing
ghosts—the ghosts of those who carried
on in the same room years before.

Act II. After dinner, Osvald leaves. Mrs.
Alving and Manders decide that Regine
cannot remain in the house, as she is the
illegitimate daughter of the late Alving.
Manders is furious that Engstrand married
the servant girl knowing she was pregnant,
and fraudulently pretended to be Regine's
real father. Mrs. Alving regrets not having
told Osvald about his father's true nature.
She speaks of the ghosts that keep haunting
her and wishes she had the courage to
banish them by letting the light in on
them. She berates Manders for not taking
her in when she left her husband—she
loved the pastor, but now she feels there is
no understanding between them. Engstrand comes in and asks Manders to conduct an evening service at the orphanage.
Manders accuses him of concealing the
truth about Regine's parentage. Engstrand
admits it but says he was not paid to marry
the pregnant girl, and Manders forgives
him. The two men leave and Osvald returns. He tells his mother he has had a
nervous breakdown and a doctor told him
his constitution was undermined due to the
sins of his father. He wants to take Regine
with him to Paris, where they can live joy-
fully. Before Mrs. Alving can say anything,
Manders returns and says he wants Regine
to help her father run his home for seamen. They hear shouts that the orphanage
is on fire and all rush out.

Act III. The orphanage has burned. Engstrand accuses Manders of having set fire
to it, but the pastor knows he will be under
public attack for having opposed insurance.
Mrs. Alving feels that the fire was all for
the best—the orphanage was a false memorial and would never have brought any
good to anyone. Engstrand offers to take

the blame for the fire and Manders promises to help him with funds for his home for seamen. Mrs. Alving tells Osvald about his father's dissolute life and that Regine is his half-sister. Regine also is told and then will not accept Mrs. Alving's offer of a home. She leaves to find Engstrand and Manders. Mrs. Alving tries to console Osvald and is almost happy that he is ill, for now she will be able to care for him. She talks to him of the future and how he

will be able to paint again when his depression and illness are cured. But Osvald tells her his illness is mental and that the doctor has told him it will gradually grow worse. He has saved enough morphine to kill himself. Mrs. Alving wants to run for a doctor, but Osvald makes her promise she will help him to die when it becomes necessary. She calms him. The sun rises and Osvald begs her to give him the sun, over and over again. He is insane.

The Adventures of
Gil Blas of Santillane

Novel by Alain René Le Sage, 1668–1747.

Published from 1715 to 1735. Translation from the French by Tobias Smollett published 1749; several other translations.

PART OF THE great reputation of *Gil Blas* stems from the fact that it has been called the first picaresque novel —that is, a novel about rogues or adventurers. It was not that, since the literary treatment of rogues goes all the way back to Cervantes and Rabelais and besides Le Sage's hero was disqualified by having a conscience; but undoubtedly *Gil Blas* was a great work worthy of its fame and the appreciation of it by English readers was helped along greatly by the fact that a major English novelist, Smollett, translated and sponsored it. The book is very long, more than 300,000 words, but it is amusing from start to finish. It is set in the early 1600s.

Chaps. 1–15. GIL BLAS, the son of a former soldier, is sent to school in the town of Oviedo by his uncle, GIL PEREZ, who then sends him to Salamanca to make his own way, giving him some money and a mule. During the journey, he sells the mule to buy a dinner for a fop who flatters him

at an inn. Gil Blas resumes his journey in the company of a newly married couple. The wife is plump and comely and the muleteer resolves to seduce her. To get rid of his other passengers he accuses them of having robbed him and threatens them. They flee to the woods. Gil starts back to rescue the woman but is intercepted by two horsemen, who take him to an underground cave. The cave is the sanctuary of a wealthy thieving order called The Brotherhood. The cook, LEONARDA, is made Gil Blas' superior with full power over him. At first he waits on table. He attempts to escape but is caught and beaten by a Negro servant and in time by the entire band. In the days that follow Gil Blas wins the confidence of his captors and asks to join the thieves on their raids. The captain, ROLANDO, gives consent and after six months in the cave Gil Blas is outfitted in a manner befitting a gentleman-thief. The bandits attack a coach, rob and kill four men, and take a girl captive. Gil Blas feigns illness to be excused from the next day's expedition. He gets the key from the cook and escapes, taking the girl with him. They ride to Astorga and put up at an inn, where the girl, Donna MENCIA, tells Gil Blas she was married; thought her husband was dead; became engaged to another man; and was reclaimed by her husband, who reappeared. The thieves killed her husband when they captured her. Donna Mencia's story is interrupted by officers who arrest Gil Blas.

The girl is not arrested. Gil Blas is freed when a passenger who was on the coach with him vouches for him. He proceeds to Burgos, where he finds Donna Mencia at a convent. She gives him 100 ducats to buy clothes and hints that her gratitude is far greater than a handful of ducats. Later he visits Donna Mencia and receives a present of 1,000 ducats from her. He leaves Burgos for Madrid.

Chaps. 16–21. At Valladolid, Gil Blas meets Donna CAMILLA, who says she is Donna Mencia's cousin. She and her brother, Don RAPHAEL, entertain Gil Blas and the girl persuades him to exchange rings. He believes the ring he gets to be very valuable and is smugly certain he has made a conquest. In the morning he finds the two dubious "cousins" gone and his portmanteau with them. Leaving the apartment, Gil Blas meets FABRICIUS, a friend from his native village, who gets him a job as footman in the house of SEDILLO, a boor and glutton. Gil Blas finds his work disagreeable but manages to conceal the fact and soon Sedillo dies and leaves Gil Blas his library, but it consists of worthless books. Gil Blas seeks out the doctor, SANGRADO, who treated Sedillo and becomes both his servant and his pupil. One day Gil Blas is called by an old lady to attend her niece, who turns out to be Donna Camilla. With the aid of Fabricius, Gil Blas gets back his ring but she declares her accomplice ran off with the money. She offers her personal jewelry and that of her aunt and Gil Blas and Fabricius take all of it and depart.

Chaps. 22–30. The aunt tells the story to the police and Gil Blas is once again in jail. Fabricius's master effects their release but the authorities confiscated Gil Blas' ring and the other jewelry. Gil Blas is now practicing medicine feverishly, but Dr. Sangrado's bloodletting and water cure seem only to result in swift death for all the patients. Gil Blas treats a handsome widow who is betrothed to a fiery Latin and when the widow dies Gil Blas is forced to flee the city to escape the Latin's wrath. He goes to Madrid and secures a position as valet to a mysterious man whose name and occupation are unknown. The authorities investigate the man and he wins their confidence by showing them a trunk filled

The maid entertains Gil Blas

with gold. On the street one day Gil Blas meets Captain Rolando, who invites him to rejoin the band of thieves. Gil Blas refuses, but his master saw him with Rolando and dismisses him. Gil Blas is next employed in the home of a playboy lord of Spain, whose household is ruled by a diabolical steward. The young lord lives a dissolute and Gil Blas leads the same life, but one scale down. They drink the same wine and while the young fop is entertained by the mistress Gil Blas is entertained by her maid. During this time the valets de chambre of the other lords are schooling him in superciliousness.

Chaps. 31–35. On the advice of his colleagues, Gil Blas steals some of his master's fine clothes and goes forth to seek an intrigue with a lady of quality. He meets one, sets an assignation, and tells her he is a cousin to the man he actually serves as valet. That night he accompanies his master to the home of an actress and the actress's maid, LAURA, is the "lady of quality" he met that afternoon. But they spend a pleasant evening together. Gil Blas now takes over duties as secretary to the lord. His work consists of forging letters from beautiful young ladies of Madrid. The lord reads these at dinner parties to amuse his companions, saying, of course, that they are genuine. But the lord is killed in a duel and Gil Blas is unemployed again.

Chaps. 36–40. Laura gets Gil Blas a position as steward in the home of her own mistress, the famous actress, where he will handle all household affairs, including the financial accounts. He succumbs to the general air of debauchery in the house, but soon he becomes satiated and disgusted. He quits and the steward of his deceased lord places him in the service of Don VIN-CENT, an old nobleman and widower, solely dedicated to raising his daughter, AURORA. One day the girl's duenna whispers to him of an assignation at midnight in the garden. Gil Blas meets Aurora, but contrary to his expectations Aurora confesses she is in love with a handsome cavalier she has never met. She wishes Gil Blas to quietly investigate the man, Don LEWIS. Gil Blas gets the required information, and though his report to Aurora is unfavorable she rewards him.

Chaps. 41–45. Don Vincent dies. Aurora inherits the estate and moves to a small castle in the country. She tells Gil Blas she cannot forget Don Lewis. She plans to go to Salamanca, where he is studying, disguise herself as a cavalier, meet Don Lewis, and extol the virtues and beauty of her "cousin" Aurora. She will engage two apartments and live in one as Aurora and in the other as the cavalier, "Don FELIX." Aurora and Gil Blas go to Salamanca. "Don Felix" intercepts a letter sent to Don Lewis by his latest mistress and shows it to Don Lewis, pretending it was written to herself. He reads it and believes the girl guilty. Aurora proposes they write abusive letters to the girl. They do so and she gives them to Gil Blas, who delivers only the note from Don Lewis. The affair is broken up and the undisguised Aurora is brought "onstage" the next day. The deception, with much dashing about, is accomplished and Don Lewis asks for Aurora's hand in marriage. Aurora reveals the deception to him but they are married and now Aurora places Gil Blas in the service of her husband's uncle, Don GONZALES DE PACHECO. The old man is decrepit in health and wasted of body but has a young mistress, EU-PHRASIA, who enlists Gil Blas' aid in a conspiracy to win her full favor in the old nobleman's will. Gil Blas pretends to accept but one day he discovers a young man concealed in Euphrasia's quarters and tells his master. Don Gonzales forgives Euphrasia, and dismisses Gil Blas as proof of his forgiveness, but does introduce Gil Blas to the home of the Marchioness DE CHAVES, where he is accepted for service.

Chaps. 46–55. The Marchioness entertains a daily gathering in her salon, the wits and intellectuals of Madrid. Gil Blas is attracted to a housemaid named PORTIA but the secretary to the Marchioness also favors the girl. A duel is fought and Gil Blas' life is spared on condition he leave Madrid immediately. At an inn Gil Blas hears of a fugitive the police are seeking and on the road he encounters Don AL-PHONSO, the fugitive. A thunderstorm is brewing and they find shelter in a hermit's grotto. In the morning the hermit is recognized as the rascally Don Raphael. He and his valet beg Gil Blas and Don Alphonso to join them as wanderers living by their wits, and all agree. They go to Valencia, disguise themselves as police and church authorities, and terrorize a converted Jew, whose strongbox they rob. Gil Blas and Don Alphonso suffer remorse and leave. They set out for Italy but on the road they stop at a castle, where Alphonso finds his true love, SERAPHINA. They are married and Gil Blas becomes steward of the household. He enters into a flirtation with a lady-in-waiting, but then he hears gossip of a young surgeon's nocturnal visits to her. Gil Blas challenges the surgeon to a duel but the doctor talks him out of it. He no longer cares for the lady and she, scorned, loathes him with a passion that causes him to leave.

Chaps. 56–65. The brother-in-law of Don Alphonso secures Gil Blas a position with the Archbishop of Grenada, copying manuscripts. The Archbishop suffers an attack of apoplexy and though he recovers he can no longer write coherently. He instructs Gil Blas to criticize but when Gil Blas does so he is castigated for his bad taste and dismissed. Gil Blas goes to the theater and the favorite actress turns out to be Laura. He determines to see her even though her "patron" is a wealthy Portu-

Gil Blas flees to Toledo

guese nobleman, the Marquis de MARI-ALVA. Laura deceives the marquis by addressing Gil Blas as her brother, and Gil Blas is invited by the marquis to become his personal secretary. His first assignment is to visit Laura and make apologies for the marquis, taking a gift. He spends the morning with the actress. That night Gil Blas learns his true identity is known and he flees to Toledo to seek sanctuary with the father-in-law of Don Alphonso. He cannot find him and goes to Madrid to seek favor at the court.

Chaps. 66–75. In Madrid Gil Blas encounters his old friend Fabricius, who is now a poet in the favor of a nobleman. Fabricius obtains a position for Gil Blas as secretary to Count GILIANO, a Sicilian. His duties are to spy on the servants and reduce household expenses. He does this and becomes the steward, hated by the rest of the staff. Gil Blas falls sick. The count returns to Sicily and the butler robs Gil Blas. His next job is with the Duke of Lerma as a rent collector. The Duke makes him a confidante and a messenger to the Duke's nephew, the Count DE LEMOS. His position is important, he even meets the King, but unfortunately he has not been paid nor has there been any mention of salary. He is poverty-stricken amidst splendor.

Chaps. 76–85. A colleague of Gil Blas warns him that he now knows too much to be dismissed and will most certainly go to jail by the Duke's order, but Gil Blas is summoned before the Duke and given a year's salary. In addition, he is permitted to take bribes from rich persons who desire favors from the Duke. He moves into a fine apartment, buys expensive clothes, and hires a valet. The valet, SCIPIO, schooled in intrigue, brings to Gil Blas a nobleman who killed a man in a duel and seeks a royal pardon. Gil Blas manages this and gets a cash reward. He shares his bribes with the Duke. He buys a house with a full staff and entertains nightly. He is summoned to the Count de Lemos and told to procure a young beauty for the Prince. Scipio finds one, named CATALINA, and the Prince is overjoyed with her charms, but Gil Blas suspects the girl and her duenna and learns that they own two houses, connected by a tunnel, and in the other house Catalina is the mistress of the Duke's chief secretary. He tells the Duke, but matters stand as they are. Scipio finds Gil Blas a bride with an enormous dowry. Gil Blas and SOLERO, his prospective father-in-law, agree to terms. Gil Blas remembers his old friend Don Alphonso and through the good offices of the Duke secures for him the governorship of Valencia.

Chaps. 86–95. The preparations for the wedding are well under way when suddenly Gil Blas is arrested, transported to the tower of Segovia, and thrown into a bare cell, with no charges against him. After two days the warden, whom Gil Blas befriended when he was in the service of the Archbishop, moves him to a room in the tower and feeds him fine foods and wine. Gil Blas has been imprisoned because the king has heard of his complicity in procuring a mistress for the Prince. The warden thinks the king's wrath will be dispelled in a couple of months. Scipio reports that soldiers and servants have ransacked his house, except for two bags of coins. Scipio insists on living at the prison. He says the Duke does not know of Gil Blas' fate and Gil Blas and Scipio decide to write to the Duke. Scipio delivers the letter but is rebuffed by the Duke. Gil Blas becomes very ill and when he recovers he is released from prison but is banished from Castile. He and Scipio buy mules and set out for Aragon. Solero has given his daughter in marriage to a rich merchant. Gil Blas visits Don Alphonso, now governor of Valencia, who rewards him with an estate at Luria in Valencia. Gil Blas goes to Oviedo to see his parents and arrives home in time to be at his father's bedside as he dies. He buries his father ostentatiously but is reviled by the townspeople, who think the money would have been better spent feeding the father while he lived. Gil Blas provides for his mother and leaves for his new estate.

Chaps. 96–105. Gil Blas and Scipio find their new home staffed with servants on the payroll of the governor but Gil Blas insists on hiring his own staff. In the city Gil Blas encounters the old bandit Don Raphael, dressed as a Carpathian monk. He tells Don Alphonso, but a few days later Raphael absconds with the monastery strongbox. Gil Blas meets and marries ANTONIA, the daughter of a neighboring farmer. The governor is host at the wedding and at his house. During the feast Scipio finds that one of Seraphina's maids, BEATRICE, is his wife, whom he deserted ten years before. They are reconciled and there is a double celebration.

Chaps. 106–115. Both Gil Blas and Scipio become fathers, but Gil Blas' wife and child die soon after. The King dies and the Prince succeeds to the throne. On the advice of Don Alphonso and Scipio, Gil Blas returns to Madrid and presents himself at Court. The new king recalls the service Gil Blas rendered him and orders the PRIME MINISTER to find suitable employment for Gil Blas. The Prime Minister sets Gil Blas up in great style and tells him to prepare propaganda to inform the people of Spain about the bad financial standing of the country and the fine efforts of the new king and Prime Minister to straighten matters out. In so doing, Gil Blas is forced to malign his former master, the Duke of Lerma, which he does without compunction. The propaganda is published and is very successful. Gil Blas roams the streets listening to the mood of the people, which he reports to his employer. Gil Blas' mother and uncle (Gil Perez) die. Gil Blas meets Fabricius, who now has a sponsor for his writings; his tragedy is presented and is practically hissed off the stage but the sponsor is so enraged at the audience that he doubles Fabricius's salary.

Chaps. 116–120. Scipio now having a family to provide for, Gil Blas supplies him with money for trade in the Indies on one of the Prime Minister's ships. Don Alphonso loses his governorship and is in trouble, because the Duke of Lerma is now a cardinal, but Gil Blas tells the Prime Minister how Alphonso got his post and the Prime Minister not only pardons Alphonso but makes him Viceroy of Aragon. The Prime Minister sends Gil Blas to Toledo incognito to watch a young actress named LUCRETIA. Gil Blas arrives on the eve of the *auto da fe* (burning of heretics), which he watches the following morning. He is horrified to see Don Raphael among the wretched awaiting execution. He goes to the theater and sees Lucretia; his old sweetheart Laura is her "aunt," actually her mother, and Gil Blas is not too sure but that he is the father.

Chaps. 121–125. Lucretia is called from Toledo and performs for the King. The King is smitten with Lucretia and Gil Blas is told to produce Lucretia as the King's mistress. Laura is willing; the girl has a virtue previously unassailable but after two or three meetings with the King she submits. Then she is so overcome with remorse that she enters a convent and soon dies of grief. Laura, to repent, enters the same convent. The King is peeved, the Prime Minister chagrined, and Gil Blas weighted with guilt. The Prime Minister has an illegitimate son in Genoa and sends Gil Blas to find the boy and educate him so that the Prime Minister can elevate him to a title and make him his heir. Gil Blas rents a house, staffs it, hires various tutors, and trains the boy well. Scipio returns from a most successful voyage and Gil Blas appoints him valet to the young man. All goes so well that the Prime Minister makes a very advantageous marriage for the boy. The Prime Minister presents Gil Blas with a king's patent raising him to noble rank. He is now Don Gil Blas.

Chaps. 126–130. Gil Blas again befriends Fabricius, who warns Gil Blas that the Prime Minister is losing favor and his days are numbered. The Prime Minister manages to avoid the conspiracy for some time, but then the Portuguese revolt and set up the Duke of Braganza as their king. The revolt is blamed on the Prime Minister, who has to resign. He takes up residence at Loeches and Gil Blas accompanies him. The Prime Minister is overcome with a strange melancholy and soon dies. Gil Blas is genuinely griefstricken.

Chaps. 131–133. Gil Blas is remembered handsomely in the will. He toys with the idea of entering a monastery but Scipio persuades him to return to his estate in Valencia. Scipio leaves the service of the Prime Minister's son and returns also. Scipio's daughter is being courted by a young man, Don JUAN, and Gil Blas meets Don Juan's sister, DOROTHEA, and falls insanely in love. He marries Dorothea and his life is serene and is blessed with two children.

God's Little Acre

Novel by Erskine Caldwell, 1903–
Published 1933 by Viking Press, New York. © 1933 by Erskine Caldwell. (NAL, S581; ML, 51)

IT IS NOT NECESSARILY the highest praise for a book to cite its sales records, but in the case of *God's Little Acre* the record is so outstanding that it must serve. In its paperbound Signet Books edition, *God's Little Acre* has been the most popular novel ever published and may have outsold its nearest competitor among all books by two to one. At last reports the total was 12,000,000 and going strong. The earthily sexy passages may have helped more than Mr. Caldwell would have wished, but he may take comfort in the general opinion that *God's Little Acre* is a great novel, sufficient to insure his literary immortality. His character Ty Ty is as fine a homely philosopher as any novelist would wish to create. God's little acre may be vile, but every other aspect pleases. The novel is quite short, about 65,000 words.

Chap. 1. TY TY WALDEN, two of his sons, BUCK and SHAW, one of his daughters, DARLING JILL, and Buck's wife, GRISELDA, live together in an old, ramshackle farmhouse in Georgia. They do little farming. For 15 years they have spent most of their time digging for gold and the land around the farmhouse is pockmarked with holes. In that part of Georgia a few nuggets have been found and many people, especially the Negroes, hopefully dig and dig. PLUTO, a fat man, who is running for sheriff because he has nothing else to do, tells Ty Ty about an albino "all-white" man down near the swamp who is supposed to be able to divine the location of gold.

Chap. 2. Ty Ty's other daughter, ROSAMOND, "loved off" to a mill town and mar-

Pluto comes upon Darling Jill taking a bath in the back yard

ried a mill man. His third son, JIM LESLEY, has moved off to Augusta and become a rich broker and refuses to speak to his family. Ty Ty has set aside one acre, which he calls "God's little acre"—just so God will know that Ty Ty has a little of Him in his heart. But whenever the family digs in this acre Ty Ty dedicates a different acre to God, for Ty Ty has promised to give any proceeds coming from God's little acre to God and he does not want to risk striking gold on God's plot.

Pluto asks Ty Ty if he can marry Darling Jill. Ty Ty says it would be all right with him but he doubts if the girl wants fat and lazy old Pluto.

Chaps. 3–4. When Pluto is ready to leave he finds his car has been swiped by the wild Darling Jill. He and Ty Ty plan to rope the albino and bring him back. Ty Ty suggests that Pluto drive over to Horse Creek Valley to get Rosamond and her husband, WILL THOMPSON, to help with the big gold-dig coming up. Ty Ty tells Pluto about the amazing beauty and modesty of his daughter-in-law, Griselda. Two Negro workers on the farm come up and say they are hungry and have nothing to eat. Ty Ty waves them off. He, Buck and Shaw leave in the old family car to capture the albino. Darling Jill returns and Pluto comes upon her taking a bath in the back yard. He stands staring at her ripe nudity, and she blows soap in his eyes.

Chap. 5. Darling Jill and Pluto go for Rosamond and Will. They find Rosamond in tears because Will is off drinking somewhere. He soon returns drunk and growls about how he intends, sometime, to have the lush Griselda. He talks about how the mill has been closed down for 18 months and people are practically starving but won't go back to work for $1.10 a day. He wants to break into the mill and turn the power on.

Chap. 6. The following morning Rosamond goes out to shop and Darling Jill seduces Will. Rosamond catches them. She beats Darling Jill and grabs a gun, which she shoots at Will's feet. She misses and then Will runs out of the house, naked. Rosamond and Darling Jill weep and console each other. Pluto holds Darling Jill naked, while Rosamond applies salve to her welts. Darling Jill wiggles and teases Pluto and runs off.

Chap. 7. Will manages a reconciliation with Rosamond. He still has a fierce impulse to turn the power on in the mill. He hates the union, which wants only useless and endless arbitration.

Chaps. 8–9. Ty Ty's place is full of excitement. The albino has been caught and everybody has been digging furiously at the spot where his divining indicated gold. The albino is young and handsome and flirts with Darling Jill. She drags him out into the yard and they make love. Ty Ty again lauds the beauty of Griselda, who blushes and hides her face.

Chaps. 10–13. The next morning the men are digging in the pit. Will taunts Buck and Shaw and a fight breaks out. The men go at each other with shovels. They are torn apart by Ty Ty, who knows that the real source of the conflict is Griselda. Ty Ty has not planted enough cotton to support the family the coming winter, so the whole family piles into the car and heads for Augusta to get money from Jim Lesley. In the city everyone but Ty Ty, Griselda and Darling Jill gets out of the car, being unwilling to face Jim Lesley. While the car is stopped prostitutes call down to Ty Ty from balconies. He wavers, but does not give in. They drive on to Jim Lesley's big white house on the hill, where they are rudely greeted. Jim Lesley's wife does not appear, as she is sick. Jim Lesley fixes a lecherous eye upon Griselda and Ty Ty immediately begins to praise Griselda's beauty. Ty Ty eventually gets the money he came for, and he and the girls get into the car. Jim Lesley leans in and puts his hands on Griselda, saying he will drag her from the car. Darling Jill starts the car. Jim Lesley's hands tear Griselda's dress as his arm is jerked from the car.

Chaps. 14–16. The following day everybody is back digging in the sweltering pit. Tension bristles between Buck and Will, and Will decides he wants to return home. Darling Jill persuades Pluto to take Will and Rosamond home in his car and she and Griselda go along for the ride. Buck is highly displeased. At Horse Creek Valley Will jumps out of the car and disappears for several hours. When he reappears he is agitated and says he and his friends have decided to break into the mill the following morning. Will feels like "God Almighty Himself." He tells Griselda he is going to tear all the clothes off her back. He does so, violently, passionately, in front of the others, and carries her off to another room. Rosamond remains silent and composed. Darling Jill is frantic with excitement;

Pluto is speechless. All of them remain awake that night. In the morning a friend drops in to tell Will that Pinkerton guards have arrived at the mill. Will leaves for the mill; the women soon follow him. They fear that Buck will find out what happened and will kill Will.

Chaps. 17–18. The Horse Creek Valley men break down a fence and smash their way into the mill. They take their posts at the looms and wait for the power to be turned on by Will Thompson, who is hailed as the leader. Suddenly the power goes on, then some shots are heard. Will Thomson has been shot dead and the backbone of the town's resistance is broken. The girls weep with agony. Pluto is frightened and Darling Jill comforts him with maternal love. They return home and when Ty Ty hears the news he moves God's little acre back under the house. Griselda tells Ty Ty that he has something in common with Will— they were both real men, as evidenced by their appreciation of her.

Chap. 19. A long, sleek car drives up and Jim Lesley steps out. He has come for Griselda. Ty Ty and Buck try to stop him from entering the house, but Jim Lesley is used to getting his own way. Buck finds him in the dining room with Griselda, with the other girls crouched behind a chair. Buck grabs a gun. Jim Lesley runs from the house, but Buck shoots him twice and he dies a few minutes later. Ty Ty is shattered. He looks about at his dug-up land and wishes he could smooth it all out with a sweep of his arm. He warns Buck that the sheriff will come. Buck kisses Griselda goodbye and walks away into the distance. Ty Ty wills that God's little acre follow Buck and always be under him. He then picks up his shovel and begins to dig. Griselda asks what happened to the gun that Buck used and without raising his eyes Ty Ty tells her Buck took it with him. She runs away and Ty Ty goes on digging.

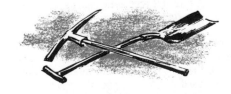

The Golden Ass of Lucius Apuleius

Novel by Lucius Apuleius, 2nd century A.D.

Published about 150. Various translations; translation from the Latin by Robert Graves published 1951 by Farrar, Straus, & Young, New York, © 1951 by Robert Graves. (PB, PL6)

THIS MAY BE the first extant novel, for it is a novel, though it is seldom so described. Within its structure as a novel *The Golden Ass* is a succession of tales, of which most were perhaps not original with the author and at least one certainly was not, the story of Cupid and Psyche. Some of the tales are bawdy and two or three might seem beyond the pale, but the book will disappoint anyone who has been led to expect pornography. It is the story of a man who was turned into an ass and of his adventures while in that form. Its title in Latin is literally "The Several Transformations of Lucius." It has had a tremendous effect on the novel through the ages and is good reading even today. Among other things it supports worship of the Egyptian gods Osiris and Isis, a pagan religion that appealed to a growing Roman minority at that time, and also Platonic philosophy; and it is refreshingly iconoclastic in its view of man as seen by his animal servants.

Chaps. 1–2. LUCIUS OF MADAURA is on his way to the town of Hypata in northern Greece. He meets a wholesale honey-buyer named ARISTOMENES who warns him not to go and tells him a story of a terrible occurrence in Hypata: Aristomenes and his friend SOCRATES went to an inn run by a witch, MEROE, who engaged in secret love rites and transformed into animals any men who refused to join in them. Socrates had offended her in this way, for that night two witches came to his bed and cut out his heart. Despite the warning, Lucius goes on to Hypata. He stays with a niggardly moneylender, MILO, and Milo's wife PAMPHILE, who dabbles in magic. Though warned by his cousin BYRRHAENA to be careful, Lucius enters into a romance with Pamphile's slave girl, FOTIS.

Chaps. 3–4. On the eve of the Festival of Laughter, at a banquet in Byrrhaena's house, Lucius hears the terrible Tale of THELYPHRON. Thelyphron lost his nose and ears while trying to prevent witches from devouring those organs on a corpse. Returning to Milo's house, Lucius kills three brigands who seem to threaten the house. He is haled into court on the day of the festival and is tried for their murder. After much laughter, Lucius learns that the brigands were really hanging wine-skins that Pamphile had enchanted to make them seem like men. Confounded by these strange deeds, Lucius persuades Fotis to sneak him into Pamphile's magic rites.

Chaps. 5–6. Lucius watches Pamphile change herself into an owl, the bird of wisdom. He begs Fotis to take Pamphile's drugs and change him too. Feeling that the noble Lucius has merely used her, Fotis changes him instead into an ass, the goddess Isis's most despised creature. Fotis promises to restore him the next day by bringing him roses to eat; but before she can do this, Milo's house is invaded by thieves. They feel fortunate to find an ass available, and Lucius is laden with heavy spoils and driven away to a wild cave presided over by an old hag. In order to comfort a beautiful girl named CHARITE, who is taken there as a hostage, the hag tells the famous Tale of CUPID and PSYCHE.

Chaps. 7–9. Venus sent her son Cupid to destroy a beautiful girl, Psyche ("soul" in Greek), who rivaled her beauty. Instead Cupid fell in love with Psyche and took her to a secret palace where he visited her by night. Psyche, who had expected to be exposed to a monster, listened to her jealous sisters and lighted a candle to see who her lover was. Cupid abandoned his distrusting wife and Psyche wandered the world, at last coming to Venus's house and begging help, for she was soon to give birth to a child. Venus set various impossible tasks for the girl. She made Psyche sort a pile of grain, but some ants assisted Psyche. Venus made Psyche fleece some golden sheep, and brambles came to her aid. Venus sent her to the Underworld for a pitcher of water from the River Styx, and Jove's eagle did the work. With the help of a speaking tower, Psyche also brought back some of the beauty of Proserpina, the queen of Hades, in a jar. At last Venus relented and permitted Psyche to join her husband; so Love and Rational Soul were inextricably wed. [The story of Cupid and Psyche is told more fully in another volume.]

Chaps. 10–11. Lucius, trying to escape with the hostage Charite, kills the old hag but is caught and beaten. Charite's lover comes to the cave, disguised as a bandit, and leads her and the ass to safety. In gratitude Charite's family sends Lucius to a stud farm, where he waits for the spring roses to bloom. While Lucius is there he hears that Charite's lover has been killed by his best friend, who also hoped to marry the girl. Charite pretends to encourage the murderer until she gets him to her room and in her power. Then she puts his eyes out and everyone flees the cursed estate.

Chaps. 12–16. Lucius continues a life of drudgery while misfortunes plague his various lecherous, conniving owners. A band of eunuch priests buys him but they are imprisoned for stealing. His next owner, a miller, is killed by his adulterous wife, who then disappears. Lucius is next stolen from a poor farmer by a Roman soldier, who sells him to a nobleman. The nobleman, THYASUS, learns that Lucius is a talented jackass who acts surprisingly mortal. He decides to exhibit Lucius at some degrading gladiatorial shows in the spring.

Chaps. 17–19. Lucius escapes, bathes seven times in the sea and offers a beautiful prayer to the Blessed Queen of Heaven. The goddess Isis descends and leads him to her mystery rites. There, a year after his first transformation, Lucius is changed back into a man. After regaining his goods, Lucius goes to Rome and accepts Osiris as the Lord of all Gods and Isis as the Queen of all feminine deities. Thus he achieves the highest spiritual state possible to a mortal after his long suffering as a hated animal living among bestial men.

Fotis mischievously changes Lucius into an ass

Goodbye, Mr. Chips

Novel by James Hilton, 1900–1954. Published 1934 by Little, Brown & Co.-Atlantic Monthly Press, Boston. © 1934 by James Hilton.

HILTON'S TRIBUTE to the familiar superannuated teacher was an unexpectedly successful tearjerker, producing not only a best-seller in the book stalls but also a successful play and motion picture. The book is very short, only about 25,000 words. It is very skillfully done and its record attests to the fact that it is one of the best things of its kind that have been written.

Chaps. 1–3. Mr. CHIPS—a nickname so time-honored that many think it is his real name—sits by the fire in Mrs. WICKETT'S boarding house one late November afternoon in 1933. His mind is clouded with memories. He thinks of the first day he came to teach at Brookfield. That was in 1870, when Chips was only 23. He had taught for a while at another school, but he had not been successful because he had not been able to discipline the students. Smiling, old Chips recalls the first punishment he meted out at Brookfield; it was to a boy named COLLEY who had slammed the lid of his desk. After that, Chips had had no trouble with discipline at all. Still smiling, Chips remembers that Colley's son had been at Brookfield too—and his grandson. Three generations of Colleys, and Chips had taught Latin to them all. When Chips was new at Brookfield he was full of ambition and had hopes of being headmaster, but he learned he was only run-of-the-mill, like Brookfield itself. As the years passed, he learned to love "his boys," to remember every one of them by name. To everyone Chips seemed like a typical bachelor but they were wrong, for Chips had once been married.

Chaps. 4–8. Chips had been at Brookfield 25 years before he met KATHERINE BRIDGES, who was 25. He had never liked women; they had always seemed so strange and demanding. But Katherine was different. He met her on a walking tour of the Lake District. They were married, even though Chips was old enough to be her father. Katherine conquered Brookfield as wholly as she had conquered Chips. Everyone loved her and obeyed her. She was good for Chips and helped broaden his views and opinions. She taught him compassion. She taught Brookfield, too. Once Kathy convinced Chips that the school should play a soccer match with the boys from the London slum mission that Brookfield supported. The idea was revolutionary but the game was a huge success. When Kathy died in childbirth, only three years after they were married, Chips was desolate. She and the infant died on April 1, 1898—April Fool's Day. Chips did not even notice the little pranks the boys played that day.

Chaps. 9–13. Life at Brookfield had been good, but there had been some bad moments. Once a new headmaster had tried to make Chips resign. That was in 1908. The headmaster had called Chips old-fashioned because he refused to teach Latin by the "new" methods. But all the school rallied around Chips and he did not leave. The hardest years of all were the World War I years. Every day there was a new report of old Brookfieldians killed in action. Chips had retired when he was 65 but was called back to Brookfield for the "duration." The board of trustees asked him to act as headmaster and he agreed, his heart swelling with pride. Years later people still talked about Chips' courage during the German bombings and how one day he conducted his Latin class as though nothing were happening, while there were tremendous explosions all about.

Chaps. 14–18. Then the war was over and Chips moved back to Mrs. Wickett's. He was still a part of Brookfield—he prepared the school directory, attended Old Boys' dinners in London, and met visiting dignitaries. His reputation for "funny" sayings grew. He used to send boys into peals of laughter when he said he thought a Wurlitzer was a German sausage, or when he made some obscure Latin puns. Chips always tried to learn the names of new boys as they arrived, but this was becoming more and more difficult. Nevertheless, Chips still invited the boys to tea. Brookfield had been home for 63 years.

Reflecting about his past, this chilly November afternoon in 1933, Chips hears a rap at the door. Mrs. Wickett is out. He goes to the door and finds a little boy standing there, a new boy just arrived that week. The boy asks for "Mr. Chips," saying he was told that Chips had been looking for him. Chips smiles. It is an old schoolboy joke being played on the youngster. Chips says, "Yes, come in." He says he has wanted to have the boy to tea. They chat and at 5 o'clock promptly, Chips dismisses the boy in a gentle fashion. He dies quietly that night in his sleep. The boy will always remember that it was he who said goodbye to Mr. Chips.

The Good Companions

Novel by J. B. Priestley, 1894–
Published 1929.

THIS ONE NOVEL was sufficient to establish John Boynton Priestley as an important novelist, but he wrote several later novels that were as well received. In *The Good Companions* his characters won the sympathy of readers and critics and the adventures of those characters made the book continuously interesting.

Book I. Chaps. 1–3. JESS OAKROYD is a Yorkshireman 45 years of age, neither ugly nor handsome, with a nagging wife and a repulsive son. When he loses his job he decides to leave his unpleasant home and travel about England in search of adventure. On that same day, ELIZABETH TRANT, who has inherited several hundred pounds from her father and is considered an old maid, decides to leave her home. She is surfeited with reading. She buys her nephew's car and starts out on her journey. INIGO JOLLIFANT, a tall, thin youth of 26, an instructor at a school for boys, who is unhappy and has an urge to write fantastic tales, at his birthday party gets drunk and speaks his mind to the tyrannical wife of the headmaster. He is dismissed and leaves the school on that same day.

Chaps. 4–6. Jess Oakroyd dashes out of his house with no idea where he is going.

A passing lorry gives him a lift. When the driver and his helper stop at an inn for the night, Jess discovers the lorry is carrying stolen cloth. The next morning his companions are gone and with them all his money. Jess starts walking and comes upon a peddler in another lorry. The peddler's assistant does not show up for three days so Jess stays and helps the peddler. When it is time for him to leave, Jess comes upon Miss Trant's car, which has stalled. She appeals to Jess to fix it. It begins to rain and they take shelter under a tree. Miss Trant is drawn to the twinkling little man and they exchange stories. Miss Trant stopped at an inn for the night and next morning her car was driven off by mistake by ERIC TIPSTEAD and EFFIE, a barmaid with whom he was leaving his wife. Mrs. Tipstead and Miss Trant took Tipstead's car and caught the runaway couple. Tipstead chose to return with his wife, leaving Effie in tears with Miss Trant. A telegram arrived with the news that Miss ELSIE LONGSTAFF, sister of the sniffling Effie, was stranded with her theatrical troupe and needed money and her theatrical kit. Miss Trant was on her way with these things when her car stalled. The rain becomes a storm and Miss Trant and Jess go to a little tearoom, where they meet Inigo Jollifant and his banjo-playing friend, MORTON MITCHAM. So Miss Trant, Jess and Jollifant are brought together.

Book II. Chaps. 1–4. Elsie is younger and prettier than her sister Effie. She tells Miss Trant about the misfortunes of the "Dinky

Doos," her theatrical troupe; the manager has left them stranded with four weeks' back pay due them. Impulsively Miss Trant decides to take over the company. She changes the name of the troupe to "The Good Companions" and invites both Jess and Jollifant to join them. The talent in the group consists of SUSIE DEAN, the young and pretty soubrette; JERRY JERNINGHAM, the handsome song-and-dance man; and Elsie, who dances and sings with music-hall gusto. Miss Trant is their manager, Jollifant the pianist, and Jess the man of odd jobs. The first appearance of The Good Companions is not very successful but their second engagement is and makes the entire cast happy. Just after this success Miss Trant is surprised by a visit from her sister, HILDA, who tries to get her to leave the troupe, but Miss Trant refuses. Jess Oakroyd is having the time of his life. Susie Dean is his favorite because she reminds him of his daughter LILY, who is married and living in Canada. Jess is disturbed when he receives a letter from his son, saying that a policeman has been looking for him, because Jess cannot think what he might have done. He remembers that the night he left home he helped a drunken man home. Then Jess meets an old neighbor in a pub and is relieved to learn that there are no charges against him.

Chaps. 5–7. The Good Companions travel by train from one town to another. One day Susie Dean misses the train and Jollifant jumps off to be with her while she waits for the next train. Jollifant realizes that he is in love with her and he tells her so, but she is not yet interested in marriage. The morale of the troupe becomes low. Quarrels become frequent and even Miss Trant finds it difficult to hold on to her fraying temper. After a performance with only three people in the audience she calls a meeting and suggests closing the show, but Jess persuades them to take the bad luck with the good and they agree to go on.

Book III. Chaps. 1–3. The Good Companions are a hit in most of the towns they play, but Miss Trant is tired of show business. She has recouped most of her money and she is persuaded to make a last fling by hiring a large theater to give each of the players a chance to shine before visiting London producers. Jollifant, who has been composing gay songs for Susie, is tired of waiting for her to become a star. He goes to London, where a famous music publisher accepts his songs; but Jollifant refuses to sign a contract unless the publisher comes with him to hear Susie sing the songs. The publisher accompanies Jollifant but the evening's performance is a fiasco because the owner of the local movie houses has hired a gang to set fire to the hall. A riot ensues and Miss Trant is hurt. The publisher leaves after refusing to have anything further to do with Susie.

Chaps. 4–6. Elsie leaves the troupe to marry. Miss Trant is in the hospital under the care of Dr. HUGH McFARLANE. It is not too long before they find themselves in love. Jerry Jerningham marries the rich Lady PARTLIT. She is about 30 years older than he and it is obvious that he has married her for her money and the three theaters she owns in London's West End. Jerry is true to his friends and they join the cast of his new revue. Susie is ecstatic, as she is to be the female star and Jollifant is to compose the music. Jess discovers the guilt of the movie operator who started the riot in the theater and the police free Miss Trant of any financial responsibility.

Jess Oakroyd receives a telegram from his son informing him that Mrs. Oakroyd is seriously ill. Shortly after Jess returns home, she dies. The morning of the funeral, he receives a letter from Miss Trant telling him of her marriage to Dr. McFarlane and asking him to come to them if he has no other plans. But Jess is going to Canada to visit his daughter Lily and, if he likes it there, to stay. Susie, who keeps postponing her marriage to Jollifant, sends Jess all the press clippings about the Good Companions. Jollifant sends him the recordings of his new songs. Jess proceeds to his new life, treasuring his theatrical experience.

The Good Earth

Novel by Pearl Buck, 1892–
Published 1931 by The John Day Co.,
   New York. © 1931 by Pearl S. Buck.
   (ML, 15; PB, C111)

NO ONE DISPUTES the place of *The Good Earth* as a classic of this century and it is considered to have contributed more to its author's winning the Nobel prize for literature (1938) than any other single title has done for any other Nobel-prize winner. A novel may have any of several main themes and *The Good Earth* superlatively answers to at least three. It is a timeless portrayal of timeless and universal human beings. It is a historical novel, giving the modern reader of English a better insight than any other book has given into the condition of the Chinese people in the early 1900s when the habits of a millenium persisted but were on the brink of being totally and suddenly overthrown. And it is a social and political sermon, though it never becomes unpalatable as a sermon might to one who is reading for relaxation only. The character O-lan is so great that an actress in motion pictures fell into an Academy Award just by being given the rôle.

Chaps. 1–4. WANG LUNG, a typical poor Chinese farmer who barely subsists on a small plot of land, is to be married. His aged father has arranged for him to be given a slave girl from the great House of HWANG in the nearest city. His father admonished him to take a girl who is strong but not good-looking (so that she would not have appealed to the young lords). Wang Lung washes himself all over, though there is a shortage of water, and dons clean and unpatched clothes. He spends most of his total hoard of six silver dollars for the wedding feast that night and the last dollar to tip the surly gatekeeper at the House

of Hwang. He is overawed by the OLD MISTRESS, who calls in the big, ugly slave girl O-LAN and pronounces them man and wife between puffs on her opium pipe. The Old Mistress gives her slaves away when they are marriageable because she wants to win favor in heaven. O-lan follows her husband home, and on the way he pauses to light incense at the shrine to the two little gods he hates and fears. At once O-lan takes over all heavy duties in the house, serving Wang Lung and his father as a totally submissive slave, and also she works beside Wang Lung in the field all day. She leaves the field just long enough to enter the hut and have her first child, a son, unassisted; then she goes back to hoeing and plowing.

Chaps. 5–6. The great House of Hwang is running out of money. The OLD LORD and Old Mistress indulge themselves with new slave girls and opium, the Young Lords live extravagant lives in Chinese and foreign cities, and the daughters need big dowries. O-lan whispers this to Wang Lung and he buys a small piece of Hwang land with money from a good harvest. O-lan bears a second son. Wang Lung comes to be recognized as a prosperous citizen.

Chaps. 7–10. The next year O-lan gives birth to a daughter. Crows fly across the field. These are evil omens but Wang Lung defiantly sells his wheat—which is sparse, for there is a drought—and buys more land. Famine falls upon the land and there is little to eat in Wang Lung's house. O-lan is with child again. Her milk dries up and her baby daughter cries constantly from hunger. The little money that Wang Lung has hidden is of no use, for there is no food to buy. Wang Lung's UNCLE, his father's brother, comes to beg. The uncle and his family are idle and shiftless, and Wang Lung turns him away. The uncle spreads rumors that Wang Lung is a rich man with hoarded food, and at night the villagers come to take food by force. When they find nothing but a few dried beans and a handful of corn, they seize the furniture. O-lan stops them, and they listen to her because they are not evil men except when they are starving. CHING, Wang Lung's nearest neighbor, a small, silent man, is ashamed. He takes the beans he found and leaves, speechless. Wang Lung resolves to sell some land and take his family to the great city of the south, where there is food to buy. Grasping speculators come, seeking to buy land cheap. O-lan skillfully persuades Wang Lung not to sell land and sells their furniture instead. It seems almost impossible for them to make the long journey with the old father and the emaciated children, but Ching brings them a handful of red beans and this puts heart into them. O-lan's child is born and she kills it; anyway, it was only a girl. As soon as she can walk they set out for the south.

Chaps. 11–14. Crowds of people ride the unfamiliar and feared "firewagons" to the great city and live there, like Wang Lung and his family, just outside the city's outer wall, in huts made of mats. Such people live in the greatest poverty in spite of the city's markets full of food and air of wealth. Wang Lung rents a riksha and draws passengers through the streets and O-lan and the children beg. There is never enough money, but with what there is one can buy food. Wang Lung hears young men on

Lotos in the teahouse

street corners shouting that if the rich would share there would be no poor people. Wang Lung does not quite understand. He thinks only of his lands. O-lan, who knows his longing, offers to sell their daughter, who is feeble-minded but pretty, into slavery so that they can return home. Wang Lung is tempted, but he loves his daughter and he will not sell her to be beaten or ravished in a great house. One night crowds break into the inner city where the great lords live. Wang Lung, borne along helplessly, finds himself in the inner court. A fat, soft lord, terrified, offers him money to spare him. Wang Lung takes all his money and takes his family north to his land.

Chaps. 15–17. One night Wang Lung finds a small, hard package between O-lan's breasts. In it are jewels. With her knowledge of great houses, she knew where to look for hiding places while the inner city was being looted. Wang Lung takes the jewels from her to buy more land, but she pleads for two little pearls and he lets her keep them, "just to feel at times." Wang Lung takes the jewels to the Great House. He finds there is no one there except the shabby Old Lord and a female servant, CUCKOO, who is in full control of the Old Lord and the few possessions he has left. She is happy to sell Wang Lung land in return for jewels. Wang Lung hires Ching as steward over the field hands now working for him. O-lan does not work in the fields any more, since she is the wife of a rich man. She bears twins, a boy and a girl, and both are healthy, but Wang Lung is still fondest of his "poor fool," his idiot oldest daughter. Wang Lung's only shame is that he cannot read, and businessmen laugh at him and cheat him. For this reason he sends his two older sons to school and neither of them works on the land.

Chaps. 18–24. Wang Lung becomes aware that O-lan is not comely, her feet were not bound, and she is too plain a wife for such an important man. At a teahouse in the town he finds Cuckoo in charge. She has let the ruined Great House. Cuckoo offers him his choice of the prostitutes and he chooses LOTUS, a beautiful, spoiled woman. He can think of nothing but Lotus. To make her happy he makes O-lan give back the two pearls. He makes Lotus his second wife and installs her in his house,

Pear Blossom likes old men because they are so kind

later bringing Cuckoo to be her attendant. On the day that Lotus comes, O-lan goes out and hoes the fields as she used to do. She will not go near the second wife. In spite of his prosperity Wang Lung is plagued with trouble. His uncle, who with his whole family has been living at Wang Lung's expense, reveals that he is leader of a troop of robbers, so that it is too dangerous for Wang Lung to put him out. Swarms of locusts descend on the fields and devour the crops. Wang Lung discovers that his eldest son, tired of waiting for his betrothed to grow old enough to marry, spends most of his time with Lotus. Wang Lung beats both of them and sends the boy south to study.

Chaps. 25–26. O-lan is in great pain with "a fire in her her vitals." The doctor says that she cannot live. Wang Lung sits besides her bed, neglecting Lotus and his land. O-lan will not die until she has seen her eldest son wed, so the boy is recalled from the south and is married to his betrothed. O-lan is content, and dies. Wang Lung's father, distraught, also dies in his sleep.

Chaps. 27–30. Although the worst famine Wang Lung can remember is on the land, Wang Lung's eldest son persuades him to buy the inner courts of the Great House of Hwang. The house is deserted now except for the poor who live in the outer courts. Wang Lung's first grandson is born, and his second son is betrothed. His eldest son insists that he buy the outer courts of the Great House. Wang Lung is now lord of the house he once feared to enter.

Chaps. 31–34. The wars have come close to the village. Wang Lung's uncle's son, a soldier, brings hordes of his friends to the house and there they stay, eating and drinking. In an attempt to placate the uncle's son, Wang Lung offers him a slave, PEAR BLOSSOM; but she is a delicate child who hates young men and Wang Lung is sorry for her and gives his uncle's son another slave instead. At last the soldiers leave, but there is no peace in the house. The wives of the sons quarrel and their children bicker. The youngest son wants to be a soldier and Wang Lung offers a slave if the boy will stay at home, but when the boy chooses Pear Blossom Wang Lung is suddenly angry and refuses. He is nearly 70 years old, but one night he calls Pear Blossom to him. She says she likes old men, because they are kind. He appeases Lotus with gifts. The youngest son, finding that his father has taken Pear Blossom, runs away. Pear Blossom serves Wang Lung well and is happy with him even when his lust is spent.

Now Wang Lung cannot think long on any subject. His grandsons grow and learn and they tell him there has been a revolution. One day, with Pear Blossom and his "poor fool" and a few servants, Wang Lung moves back to the earthen house on his own land. He hears his two older sons, who are now great and wealthy men in the town, discussing how they will divide his land after his death. Wang Lung cries out that they must not do this, that it is the end of a family when they begin to sell their land. His sons reassure him, swearing that they will never sell the land, but over his head they look at each other and smile.

The Good Soldier Schweik

Novel by Jaroslav Hasek, 1883–1923. Published 1929. Published in the U.S. 1930 by Doubleday & Co., New York, in a translation from the Czech by Paul Selver. © 1930 by Doubleday & Co.

THE DISARMING ARMED MAN, the eternal enigma to Army brass, has been a proper theme of every war. American readers met him during World War I in *Dere Mable* and during World War II in *See Here, Private Hargrove*, and *No Time for Sergeants*. But the most uproarious of them all, the true classic, is *The Good Soldier Schweik*. Hasek wrote nothing else that has contributed greatly to his reputation, perhaps because he died when he was 40. His short stories, published before and after *Schweik*, have been widely praised.

Book I. Chap. 1. JOSEF SCHWEIK, a stocky, round-faced citizen of Prague, earns a livelihood by the sale of mongrel dogs for which he forges pedigrees. Mrs. MULLER, the cleaning woman, tells him that Ferdinand has been shot and Schweik says he knows a Ferdinand the chemist and a Ferdinand the manure collector. Which one does she mean? She says it was the Archduke Ferdinand, the fat one, and Schweik says it's easier to shoot a fat one. He goes to his favorite café and gets into a discussion of the assassination with BRETSCHNEIDER, a plainsclothes policeman, who is not exactly sure he knows what Schweik has been talking about but arrests Schweik for high treason on general principles.

Chaps. 2–6. Schweik is taken to be cross-examined and greets his inquisitors affably. He is told to take the idiotic expression off his face, but he replies that he can't help it—he was discharged from the army as being officially weak-minded. He blandly admits to being guilty of a long list of preposterous charges. Schweik informs his cellmate that the cross-examination was fun—not like olden times when they made you walk on red-hot iron and drink molten lead. Schweik is again taken before the police commissioner and willingly signs a confession. The following morning Schweik is taken to court and asked if he signed the confession under pressure. He answers that everything was done in proper fashion. The judge decides Schweik must have a mental examination. He is sent to three serious medical authorities who question him and receive offhand and intriguing answers. They declare him an imbecile and he is taken to the lunatic asylum. Two other doctors test his reflexes and pronounce him a malingerer. The doctors order his discharge but Schweik says they can't do it until after lunch. He causes quite a scene and is arrested for disorderly behavior and taken to the commissariat of police. On a corner a crowd is reading the emperor's proclamation of war. Schweik shouts: "Long live Franz Josef! We'll win this war." This starts a riot. The baffled police cannot figure out charges against him and he is told to get out. At liberty again, he runs into Bretschneider, who has been told at head-quarters to pretend he wants to buy a dog from Schweik and in this way observe Schweik's actions. Schweik proceeds to sell the detective a series of hideous freaks as full-blooded pedigreed animals and pockets a tidy sum for each of them.

Chaps. 7–9. The Austrian army is doing very badly and Schweik is drafted. He is in bed with rheumatism, but nothing daunted he puts on a military cap and has Mrs. Muller push him in a wheelchair to the medical board, where he brandishes a pair of crutches and shouts, "To Belgrade, to Belgrade!" He avows he will serve the emperor till he is hacked to pieces. The doctor calls him a malingerer and he is sent to military prison with men who have all kinds of malingering diseases—consumption, cancer, diabetes, kidney infections, and so on. Schweik receives the usual treatment, including swathing in cold wet sheets, large doses of aspirin and quinine, stomach-pumping twice a day, and a massive colonic irrigation. He takes it all cheerfully but complains that it really isn't helping his rheumatism. Schweik and almost all the other malingerers are declared fit for duty, including three in the last stages of consumption. A man with one leg and another with genuine cavities in his teeth are released. Schweik is taken to chapel to hear the chaplain, OTTO KATZ, preach a sermon. Schweik bursts into tears and the chaplain takes him aside and accuses him of shamming. Schweik readily admits it, but says he felt the sermon needed a re-formed sinner. Katz takes a liking to Schweik and has him made his orderly.

Chaps. 10–11. Otto Katz, born a Jew, is overly fond of drinking and has the sacramental wine well laced with grog. Schweik often has to escort the babbling Katz home from a drinking party and put him to bed. The chaplain, out of funds, sends Schweik to borrow money from several officers and tells him to "pitch any yarn you please." Schweik returns with much more cash than Katz had expected and when Katz asks him how he managed it, Schweik says he merely told the officers that the chaplain was involved in a paternity case. The chaplain is so distressed that he drinks five bottles of brandy. Several days later Schweik assists the chaplain in

a field mass, though he is unfamiliar with the routine. The chaplain is in a good mood, as he is using a large silver trophy cup, filled to the brim, as a substitute chalice.

Chaps. 12–13. Katz loses Schweik in a card game to Lt. LUKASH, an officer with a reputation for being hard on his batmen and soft on the ladies. Schweik ingratiates himself with his new master by procuring a bona fide Pomeranian for him, but the dog was stolen from an estimable booby of a colonel, who punishes Lukash by ordering him to the front. Lukash retaliates by taking Schweik with him, but Schweik merely says, "It'll be a good thing if you and me was to fall together fighting for the emperor."

Book II. 1–5. On the train, Schweik innocently asks a trainman how the alarm brake works and somehow the brake is pulled and the train is stopped. Schweik is ordered to report to the stationmaster at the next town. The train pulls away without him and Lukash heaves a sigh of relief. Schweik talks his way out of his troubles, but immediately is involved in new ones, since Lukash has his papers and his ticket. Schweik is ordered to buy a ticket and when he says he has no money the lieutenant tells him he can walk there for all he cares. Schweik starts his journey on foot, in the wrong direction. The next morning he is taken to the police station, where the sergeant is sure Schweik is a Russian spy. Schweik, not knowing he is under suspicion, readily agrees with every leading statement the sergeant makes. The sergeant sends Schweik, in the custody of a policeman, to headquarters in another town. The journey is cold and the two men, handcuffed together, stop for occasional drinks. They arrive in a happy state. The captain believes Schweik's story and puts him on a train. Schweik affably reports to Lukash, who turns pale and puts him in the guardhouse. The regiment is transferred to another town and Schweik is in the prisoners' car. A chaplain, deep in his cups, has mistakenly boarded the car and Schweik takes good care of him and puts him to bed. The next day the train stops at a town and the chaplain gives Schweik money to buy food and wine. Schweik gives it to Lukash and gets back in Lukash's good graces. Lukash goes to the theater in town, sees an attractive woman, and writes a note to her, which he instructs Schweik to deliver at 10 o'clock the next morning. Schweik gets to drinking with an old buddy and finally delivers the letter at noon, when the woman's husband is home for lunch. A free-for-all follows and Schweik and his buddy are arrested. Schweik maintains he wrote the letter himself, and when asked to copy it for a handwriting comparison he claims that overnight he has forgotten how to write. But the colonel refuses to give official sanction to a civilian complaint and Schweik and his buddy are set free. The colonel appoints Schweik company orderly under Lt. Lukash, and Schweik takes a series of messages over the phone, and in his zeal he fouls up everything and makes Lukash late for a staff meeting. He receives one message in what may be code, decides the caller must have been an idiot, and throws it away.

Book III. Chaps. 1–4. The regiment receives new orders and entrains for the Russian front. En route, the captain gives the officers a new code based on page 161 of a novel. The other officers are completely bewildered because they have volume I of the novel and the captain has volume II. Schweik is the culprit—he has issued a copy of volume I to each officer because, as he subsequently explains, anyone reading a novel would naturally start with the first volume. At a small town, Lukash sends Schweik out to buy a bottle of brandy. A young lieutenant who has been trying to get something on Schweik finds the bottle on him, but Schweik tells him it is filled with a yellowish water from a nearby pump. The lieutenant cleverly orders Schweik to drink it all and Schweik coolly complies. Five minutes later Schweik reports to Lt. Lukash, tells him what has happened, and begs to report that he will soon be drunk as a lord. The train finally reaches its destination and Lukash sends Schweik and a couple of others ahead to arrange billets in the next town. The mayor of the town attempts to talk them into going on to the next town, but Schweik threatens to hang the mayor and when the company marches into town, there are plenty of beds available. Once again Lukash sends Schweik ahead to find quarters. Schweik's reaches a pond where an escaped Russian prisoner is bathing. Schweik wonders how he would look in a Rusian uniform and tries it on. An Austrian patrol comes by and he is arrested as a Russian fugitive and put in a labor gang.

Schweik reports to the lieutenant that he will soon be drunk as a lord

The Story of Gösta Berling

Novel by Selma Lagerlof, 1858–1940. Published 1894. Translation from the Swedish by Pauline Bancroft Flach published 1898 by Little, Brown & Co., Boston.

THE FIRST NOVEL by Selma Lagerlof is still rated high among her works. It is a skillful blending of Swedish folk superstitions with modern (19th century) life in Miss Lagerlof's native Värmland district of Sweden. Miss Lagerlof never actually reveals whether the superstitions are to be taken as an agency of the events of the novel or merely as coincidence. The characters are complex and most of them are developed fully. The novel is of moderate length, about 140,000 words.

Introduction. Young GÖSTA BERLING is the minister of a poor parish in the Western Värmland. Everybody in that cold, gloomy region drinks, but Gösta has overstepped the bounds and complaints are made to the bishop. The bishop comes to investigate and Gösta, on his first Sunday in church for many weeks, delivers an eloquent and impassioned sermon. The bishop is pleased and exonerates him. Captain CHRISTIAN, a drinking companion of Gösta, rudely warns the bishop to leave his friend alone. Gösta fears the bishop may think him responsible for the loutish Christian's threat and he flees from his home. He wanders through the snow-covered forests and over the icy roads and reaches the village of Bro in a disheveled, miserable condition. He steals some grain and sells it to buy brandy, then in drunken remorse he staggers out of town and throws himself in a snowbank to die. He is saved by a large, coarse woman who takes him to her estate at Ekeby. She tells him her name is MARGARETA and that she once loved a poor young man but was forced to marry the supposedly wealthy Major SAMZELIUS. Her husband turned out to have very little money, but her former lover returned a rich man. She had an affair with him and when he died he left his seven estates to her and the major. She is now mistress of Ekeby, owner of iron mines, and the most powerful person in the region. But she cannot forget the curse her own mother put upon her for living in sin. Gösta Berling becomes a guest at Ekeby. He falls in love with EBBA DOHNA, the sister of a count, but she dies (perhaps having killed herself rather than marry a dismissed priest). Gösta feels he is doomed to suffer.

Part I. Chaps. 1–3. Seven years later Gösta is still living in the bachelor wing of Ekeby, with eleven other pensioners who are kept in comfort through the generosity of Margareta. Capt. Christian is one of the pensioners. They occupy their time in drinking, card-playing, and retelling stories of their past glories. On Christmas Eve they are carousing when SINTRAM, master of the local iron works, enters dressed as the devil. The men believe he actually is the Evil One. He tells them he has a contract with Margareta that allows her to continue as mistress of the seven estates in exchange for the soul of one of the pensioners every year. They are horrified and forget her many kindnesses to them. Gösta refuses to believe until Sintram tells him that Margareta told Ebba Dohna Gösta was a dismissed priest and Ebba killed herself. The "devil" agrees to cancel his contract with Margareta if the pensioners make a pact with him. They can have the seven estates in order to save their souls if they act like gentlemen for a year. If any one of them does something sensible, useful or effeminate during that time they will all lose their souls and the estates will go to someone else. The pensioners sign the contract in blood. The next day, at the great Christmas feast, Capt. Christian drunkenly denounces Margareta as an adulteress. Major Samzelius orders her from the estate, claiming he never knew he owed the seven estates to his wife's infidelities. Gösta does not defend Margareta because he blames her for the

death of Ebba. Margareta feels that a judgment has been visited on her but she warns
the other guests of dire things. She leaves
and the major moves to his own little farm,
placing the pensioners in charge of the
seven estates in the hope that they will ruin
the property.

Chaps. 4–7. Gösta goes to a ball at a
neighboring estate and meets ANNA
STJÄRNHÖK, a beautiful young woman
who is engaged to be married. She falls in
love with Gösta and his passion is aroused.
He takes her for a sleigh ride and they are
attacked by wolves and just manage to get
back safely. Gösta believes the wolves are
instruments of judgment upon him and he
renounces Anna. At a ball at Ekeby the
beautiful and sought-after MARIANNE SIN-
CLAIR acts in a tableau with Gösta. They
are attracted to each other and kiss, which
seems to be part of the scene. During the
ball Gösta plays cards with Marianne's
father and wins his money, watch, and fur
coat. Sintram, who is standing by, suggests that the old man stake his daughter
against all that Gösta has won. Sinclair does
and Gösta wins. While Gösta goes to dance
with Marianne, Sintram tells Sinclair that
the kiss was not part of the tableau. The
old man leaves in a rage. Marianne walks
home in the snow but when she arrives her
father has locked her out. She pleads in vain
and finally leaves the door and throws herself in a snowdrift. Gösta finds her half-
frozen and takes her back to Ekeby. Later
that night Margareta comes to Ekeby and
commands the servants to oust the pensioners. Marianne overhears her and once again
goes out into the frozen night, this time to
summon Major Samzelius. The major takes
his pack of muzzled bears to Ekeby with
Marianne and frightens Margareta away.
Margareta says she will go to seek release
from her mother's curse.

Chaps. 8–9. Marianne is ill with small-
pox at Ekeby. She loses her beauty but
Gösta is faithful. Marianne's father, who is
about to auction off all his belongings because he does not want Marianne to inherit
them, relents when he hears of her illness,
rushes to Ekeby, and takes her home. Now
Gösta is angered because she went without
leaving a message for him. He tells her he
does not love her any more. She protests
that she still loves him.

Chap. 10. Margareta has been arrested
for trying to retake Ekeby and is a prisoner
in the bailiff's house. The bailiff gives a
party and the pensioners are among the
guests. Count HENRIK DOHNA (Ebba's
brother), an ugly, stupid man, is there with
his young and beautiful wife ELIZABETH.
Elizabeth asks Gösta to help Margareta but
he refuses; then when Gösta asks her to
dance, she refuses. Gösta broods, and as the
party is breaking up he grabs Elizabeth and
drives madly off with her in his sleigh with
the others in hot pursuit. During the excitement two of the pensioners free Margareta.
In the sleigh, Gösta forces his kisses on the
struggling Elizabeth and then in sudden
remorse takes her home. The stupid count
berates his wife for refusing to dance with
Gösta and orders her to kiss Gösta's hand.
The proud Elizabeth obediently approaches
Gösta but he is embarrassed and tells her
she must not debase herself. To prevent her,
Gösta puts his hands in the fire, but a friend
pulls him away from the hearth.

Chaps. 11–12. Sintram tells Anna
Stjärnhök that when she let Gösta go she
sent his soul to the devil. Anna is frightened
and is sure Sintram is the devil himself. She
hears that Gösta and Elizabeth are in love
and see each other often. Anna tells Elizabeth the story of Ebba Dohna. She does not
tell Elizabeth that Gösta was the man, but
Elizabeth hears a poem by Gösta that tells
the same story she has just heard from
Anna. She sends him away.

Part II. Chaps. 1–7. Gösta decides as
penance to marry a poor, humble girl. He
chooses a half-crazy peddler of brooms.
Elizabeth goes on foot to beg Gösta not
to marry this BROOM-GIRL. She is trapped
on the breaking ice near Ekeby and the
dam begins to give way. Gösta and others
struggle to save the dam and prevent the
raging waters from inundating the town.
Gösta rescues Elizabeth and the two are
joyous in their reunion. Countess MARTA,
the mother of Henrik, tells her son that
Elizabeth is unfaithful. Henrik makes Elizabeth wholly subject to his mother's commands. Marta humbles Elizabeth, making
her do household chores and wait on guests,
and tortures her. After a month Elizabeth
runs away. She meets the pensioners on a
river barge, loaded with iron from Ekeby
on the way to market, and they hide her.

The pensioners lose their iron in a storm and one more disaster has befallen Ekeby. Henrik gets an annulment of his marriage to Elizabeth. A witch curses Countess Marta for not giving her food. She invokes a plague of magpies that almost drive the countess mad.

Chaps. 8–13. The pensioners hold a concert to distract the melancholy Gösta and they succeed in making him cheerful again. The pensioners will not let Henrik attend church, considering him unworthy to sit in the house of God. The count and his mother move to a faraway place. Capt. LENNART, who was falsely accused of theft by Sintram and sent to jail, comes back to town. The pensioners get him drunk, paint a horrible face on him, and take him home. His wife refuses to admit him and the captain, thinking it is God's will, devotes himself to helping the poor peasants. He wanders through the countryside giving aid and comfort and countering the evil wrought by Sintram.

Chaps. 14–18. Marianne Sinclair seeks to get away from her father, whom she fears and detests, by becoming engaged to her penniless cousin, Baron ADRIAN. Her father suffers a stroke and becomes more human, and Marianne is further pleased to learn that Adrian really loves her. Drought comes to the land and the people

The estate burns to the ground

blame the hardhearted and miserly pastor of the parish. Gösta, remembering his own shame as a priest, counsels the pastor to change his ways and help the people. The next Sunday the pastor prays for rain and as a torrent comes down, he dies of happiness. Gösta is summoned by Elizabeth, who has been living with a peasant family. She has given birth to a son, and though Henrik is the father, he refuses to remarry Elizabeth. She wants the child to have a father and Gösta agrees to marry her, though he fears he will only bring ruin to Elizabeth. Their marriage makes Elizabeth the mistress of Ekeby. The child dies. Major Samzelius is severely bitten by one of his bears and dies just before Christmas.

Chaps. 19–22. The broom-girl disappears and the peasants think the pensioners have harmed her and storm Ekeby. The pensioners distract them by holding a great feast. Then the peasants mistake Elizabeth for the broom-girl and are about to carry her off, but the body of the broom-girl is found, dead from a fall in the forest. One of the pensioners becomes temporarily insane and believes Elizabeth is a witch. To get rid of her he sets fire to Ekeby. He recovers his senses, but the estate is burned to the ground. Lennart is killed by a brawler, and now the pensioners regret their prank that kept him from his wife and join in the mourning. Sintram tells Gösta he is going to destroy everyone. Gösta bargains with him and agrees to take his own life if Sintram will spare the others. He disappears but Elizabeth sends searchers into the forest and he is found and brought back. Elizabeth tells him that the pensioners have started to rebuild Ekeby, that he is needed as the leader, and that he must give up his bargain with Sintram.

Chap. 23. Margareta comes back to Ekeby, ill; but she has seen her aged mother and has been forgiven. The pensioners' year is up and they have won in their pact with Sintram—they have worked and they have acted sensibly. Since they have done this not for themselves but for others, Sintram —the force of evil—has lost. News comes that Sintram is dead. Margareta offers Ekeby to Gösta and Elizabeth, but they prefer to live simply and help others. Margareta dies. Gösta sums up how much has been learned during the year of joy and sorrow.

The Grapes of Wrath

Novel by John Steinbeck, 1900– Published 1939 by Viking Press, New York. (ML, 148)

THIS IS ONE of the best examples of the propaganda novel in American literature, ranking with *Uncle Tom's Cabin* as an example of the art though not as a historical phenomenon. Steinbeck had tried straight propaganda once before (*In Dubious Battle*, 1936) and had not done it well. In *The Grapes of Wrath* he made virtually no mistakes. His characters are real, reasonable, and sympathetic, and he even permits an interlude of gaiety to break into their misery. The abuses he attacks—shameful treatment of itinerant agricultural workers in California—really existed. Ma Joad is widely considered the best character Steinbeck has created. The book is moderately long, approaching 200,000 words. The title is from the first stanza of "The Battle Hymn of the Republic."

Chaps. 1–6. Drought, duststorms and exhaustion of the soil have ruined the land in Oklahoma and parts of neighboring states. Sharecroppers can no longer raise enough to feed themselves and pay rent. Banks are foreclosing mortgages and the big land companies are evicting the farmers, and farming the land with "cats," giant tractors. The dispossessed farmers are migrating westward to California. TOM JOAD, just paroled from a prison term for killing a man in a fight, hears this from a truckdriver who gives him a ride. Walking the last stretch toward the Joad farm, Tom meets JIM CASY, a former preacher, and they share a bottle of whiskey. Casy has given up his calling, and now lives a derelict existence, because he can no longer see the difference between virtue and sin. Casy decides to accompany Tom. They find the Joad farm deserted. A neighbor, MULEY GRAVES, comes by and tells Tom that the Joads have been evicted and have moved to Tom's UNCLE JOHN'S farm. Muley himself has been evicted but obstinately refuses to move. He hides near his old farm and lives on what he is able to catch for food; he has two scrawny cottontail rabbits, which he shares with Tom and Casy.

Chaps. 7–10. The next morning Tom and Casy walk the 8 miles to Uncle John's farm and find the family preparing to leave permanently in an old Hudson Super-Six sedan that they have converted to a truck. Throughout Oklahoma, predatory buyers are buying up farm equipment and furniture at distress prices, and heartless, dishonest used-car dealers are selling jalopies, at $50 to $100 each, that will hardly run; but Tom's 16-year-old brother AL is already a remarkably good mechanic and has bought a car in good condition for $75. The rest of the family are Tom's parents, PA and MA JOAD; his older brother NOAH; his sister ROSE OF SHARON, who is several months pregnant, and her husband CONNIE RIVERS; Tom's sister RUTHIE, 12, and brother WINFIELD, 10; GRAMPA, GRANMA, and Uncle John. They have $154 in all. Now, with Tom and Casy, there are twelve to go. They sell everything salable, but for almost nothing. They slaughter and pack as much meat as possible. They load the truck—overload it to the limit. Tom must break parole by crossing the state line, but this does not deter him. They pile into and onto the truck and go, with Muley waving goodbye.

Chaps. 11–13. The Joads join the long caravan of cars headed westward on Route 66. The journey is hot and uncomfortable, but there is little complaining. Stops are made along the roadside at night for cookfires and sleep. At one stop they meet a farm couple from Kansas, IVY WILSON and his wife SAIRY. At this stop Grampa has a stroke. Casy forces himself to pray for Grampa but the old man dies. The Joads decide to bury Grampa secretly; they have not enough money to live the extra days they would have to spend if they reported the death. Then the Joads join forces with the Wilsons, who have only $30 but whose 1925 Dodge will relieve some of the load on the truck. They travel on together.

Chaps. 14–17. In the Texas Panhandle the Wilson car breaks down. It seems most sensible to send part of the party on ahead, but Ma Joad refuses absolutely to let the family be split. At last everyone yields to the indomitable woman's will and Al and Tom go off in the truck to buy used parts. The family settles in a roadside camp where a bitter man, returning from California, informs them that the only jobs in California will not keep them alive because the market is flooded with emigrants like themselves and employers are paying starvation wages. The Joads refuse to be disheartened and when the Wilson car is ready they drive on into the mountains of New Mexico.

Chaps. 18–20. They cross the Painted Desert and finally reach California, but they still have the long desert to cross. They camp for a night, and while Ma is preparing dinner a state trooper tells her they can only spend the night because "Okies" are not wanted around those parts. Another returning emigrant tells the men that they will be exploited and treated like animals wherever they go in California. Grimly they head for the truck-farming section of the state. Noah abandons the party to stay by a river and fish. Sairy Wilson becomes too ill to continue and Ivy makes the Joads go on without them. Granma is all tuckered out and barely conscious. She dies the night before the Joads enter the lush San Joaquin Valley, but Ma keeps it a secret because any delay would prevent their making it. At Bakersfield they turn Granma's body over to the local coroner and pay what they can afford for her burial. They go to a camp outside of town, a collection of tents and shacks called, like all such camps, Hooverville. They are told how California farm-owners keep the Okies starving—especially the Okies' children, so that the parents will work all day for one inadequate meal. Any attempt at organization by the Okies is met with beatings and jail for those deemed to be the leaders. The Joads learn this lesson personally when a brutal deputy sheriff

Loading the truck

The deputy tries to arrest a man and is knocked to the ground

comes to Hooverville with a contractor looking to hire cheap hands to pick his crops. The deputy threatens to burn down the camp so the people will have no shelter and must accept the low wage. There is an argument. The deputy tries to arrest a man and is knocked to the ground. He pulls his gun and shoots wildly, wounding a woman in the hand. Casy kicks the deputy into unconsciousness. He warns Tom to run, and he stays behind. Four armed men arrive and Casy takes the blame for all that happened. They take him away to jail. Rose of Sharon's husband, Connie, deserts. Uncle John, fed up with all their troubles, spends some of their last money on whiskey, to get release from all the misery and hardship. The next day the Joads head southward to possible work.

Chaps. 21–26. The Joads are now part of the desperate horde who outbid one another for any work available, down to 15 cents an hour or less. They reach a government camp at Weedpatch and for the first time since they left Oklahoma they are given understanding and decent treatment. There are shower rooms, flush toilets, and other conveniences. The campers have a chance to voice their grievances and settle their problems through committee action. There is even a brief evening of fun, with dancing and music. Tom gets a job at 25 cents an hour digging ditches and laying pipes. The other Joad men find it impossible to obtain any work. Tom is laid off and the family, hungry and with no income at all, has to leave the government camp and look for work. They are directed to a ranch that is hiring peach pickers. When they reach the place they are escorted through the gate by state police, through lines of men and women shouting at them and brandishing their fists. Everybody except Rose of Sharon picks peaches for a nickel a pail and at the end of the day they have all picked enough to earn about $1.50. Ma buys food from the company store, is appalled by the prices, but buys what she can to feed the family. After dinner Tom goes for a walk but is stopped by a guard, who tells him a bunch of damned reds are picketing the ranch. Tom crawls under the fence and walks down the road. He meets Casy and some others who tell him they are striking because they had been promised 5 cents a pail, but were given 2½ cents—not enough to feed a family. The little group is suddenly attacked by the police or company men and Casy is clubbed to death. Tom goes berserk, grabs a club, and beats a man to the ground. He knows he has killed the man and runs, reaching the Joad shanty safely. The next morning the wages goes down to 2½ cents, yet hundreds of workers come to apply for it, nearly all with hungry children. That night the family hides Tom in the loaded truck and they leave to go back to Weedpatch. They reach a string of boxcars on a railroad embankment and see a sign saying "cotton pickers wanted." They take the jobs and live in a boxcar, and Tom goes into the woods to hide.

Chaps. 27–29. The boxcars make the best home the traveling Joads have had except for the government camp. Ma takes food to Tom every day. Ruthie, in a childish argument, tells some other children about Tom's being in hiding, and Tom has to leave. He plans to do what Casy was do-ing—lead the workers in a fight for a decent life. Al is now Pa's right hand but he is in love with a girl, AGGIE WAINWRIGHT, in another boxcar and wants to marry her and work in a city as a mechanic. Rose of Sharon goes out to pick cotton with the family; she gets a chill as rain begins to fall, and her labor pains begin. The rain comes down in torrents and swishing waters surround the boxcar. Ma and some neighbor women tend Rose of Sharon while the men frantically build levees, but the levees do not hold. Rose of Sharon's baby is born dead. The waters are over the floor of the boxcar and the family is forced to leave. The truck is under water and they walk until they reach a barn. Here they find a boy trying to comfort his father, who is dying of starvation. He is too weak to eat and must have milk. Ma looks at Rose of Sharon and she looks back with an understanding light in her eyes. The others go out. Rose of Sharon lies down beside the emaciated man and gives him the milk that was meant for her stillborn child.

Graustark

Novel by George Barr McCutcheon, 1866–1928.
Published 1901.

THE ROMANTIC NOVEL about the tiny Balkan or eastern European principality was all the rage around the turn of the century and Graustark deserves a place at the top of the list, along with *The Prisoner of Zenda.* In its time *Graustark* was McCutcheon's principal work, but now he is better remembered for *Brewster's Millions.*

Chaps. 1–2. GRENFALL LORRY, urbane, wealthy, not quite 30, and bored, is on a train out of Denver bound for the East. He becomes infatuated with a dark-haired, blue-eyed girl traveling with an elderly couple, as well as a maid and manservant. Lorry fails at a couple of elaborate stratagems calculated to effect an introduction to the girl. In West Virginia, the train stops at a small mining town. The girl strolls a short distance into town and Lorry follows her. The train pulls out unexpectedly without them. Lorry telegraphs ahead for the train to stop at a station four miles ahead. Then he hires a stagecoach, and after a wild and perilous chase along rough mountain roads they catch the train. Lorry still has not learned the girl's name but he does learn that she is from Graustark, a small European country whose capital is Edelweiss.

Chaps. 3–4. The girl's chaperones, who are her Aunt YVONNE and Uncle CASPAR, are grateful to Lorry and invite him to dinner, where he learns that the girl is Miss GUGGENSLOCKER. He is disappointed, because he is sure she must be the daughter of a butcher, a brewer, or a cobbler, but he is no less fascinated by her. In Washington he takes the girl and her aunt for a drive around the city, and he again is their guest at dinner. He has a moment alone with the girl, who invites him to come visit her in Graustark.

Chaps. 5–6. Lorry tries to do some work in his uncle's law office, but is unable to concentrate. He curses himself for a love-sick fool and takes the night train to New York. At the steamship offices he cannot find anyone named Guggenslocker on the passenger list, but on the pier he sees the girl at the ship's rail. He daringly throws her a kiss and when she throws a kiss back he is wafted to heaven. After pining all summer, he goes to Europe. In Paris he meets his Harvard classmate, HARRY ANGUISH, an art student. Anguish enthusiastically joins him in his search for Miss Guggenslocker. They arrive in Graustark and put up at the best hotel and make inquiries about the Guggenslockers. No one has heard of the name.

Chap. 7. Lorry and Anguish go to see Baron DANGLOSS, the chief of police, to inquire about the Guggenslockers. Dangloss is at first helpful, but as their story unfolds he becomes hostile and suggests that their search will be futile. On the way back to their hotel, the two men see Miss Guggenslocker and another young lady riding in a luxurious carriage. The eyes of Lorry and the girl meet. When the men return to their hotel, a groom hands Lorry an invitation from Miss Guggenslocker to accompany her messenger on the following afternoon, for a visit to her home.

Chaps. 8–10. After dinner, Lorry and Anguish take a stroll in the darkened town of Edelweiss. They lie down on the grass under a hedge to rest, and they overhear three men plotting to kidnap Princess YETIVE of Graustark. Lorry and Anguish decide to foil the plot themselves. They hide near the palace. The conspirators chloroform, bind and gag the guard, and substitute one of their own men. Lorry and Anguish knock out the false guard and go on to the castle. In the darkened halls, they become confused. Lorry enters the princess's antechamber, where her lady-in-waiting, Countess DAGMAR, sleeps. She wakes and calls for the guard, DANNOX, and she is incredulous when Lorry tells her that Dannox is in a plot to kidnap the princess, but he manages to convince her. She goes to warn the princess and Lorry sees in the

light of the doorway that the princess is Miss Guggenslocker. Dannox runs in and hits Lorry on the head. As he is losing consciousness, he sees Anguish run in shooting. When he regains consciousness, he and Anguish are heroes, and that night eight plotters are caught and shot. But Lorry is angry because with these plotters dead there is no way of finding out who was behind the conspiracy.

Chap. 11. The princess visits Lorry in his sickroom. She tells him that he and Anguish will be royal guests in the castle. Lorry and the princess talk and he tells her he loves her. She admits that as a woman she loves him, but that as a princess she cannot and they must remain simply friends. He insists that he will find some solution.

Chaps. 12–13. From Count HALFONT, the elderly man of the train trip, and from Countess Dagmar, Lorry learns about local conditions. Graustark, 15 years before, lost a war to its neighbor Axphain. The peace treaty required Grustark to pay 20,000,000 gavvos plus interest. The payment is due in a few weeks. Graustark cannot raise more than half the money, and failure to pay means ceding to Axphain a ruinous amount of territory. Crown Prince LORENZ of Axphain is enamored of Princess Yetive, and so is GABRIEL, the Prince of Dawsbergen, Graustark's neighbor to the south. Gabriel, in return for her hand, will lend Graustark the needed money. Later that night, Yetive tells Lorry that she abhors both her royal suitors but that she is soon to be betrothed to Prince Lorenz. Lorry believes that the instigator of the kidnap plot was Prince Gabriel of Dawsbergen.

Chaps. 14–15. Lorry and Anguish return to the hotel. Several days later, Anguish bursts into their room to tell Lorry he is sure Gabriel was the leader of the kidnap attempt; he has just heard Gabriel speak, downstairs in the foyer, and it was the voice of the chief plotter. He and Lorry tell Baron Dangloss and they all go to the castle, but they cannot see the princess. Countess Dagmar tells them that Yetive has accepted Prince Lorenz, to save her country. They leave the castle in dejection.

Chaps. 16–17. Lorry and Anguish go to a café. Prince Lorenz and some of his officers are there, and Lorenz is toasting the princess and boasting of the kisses he

On the way to the dungeon

with him and discovers his companion is the princess in a soldier's uniform. The princess tells Lorry he is to stay at a monastery high in the mountains until he can escape. She confesses her love for him, but refuses to leave Graustark with him.

Chaps. 20–21. Anguish, upon hearing of Lorry's escape, rushes to the castle and tells the princess and Countess Dagmar that since Lorry has disappeared from Graustark he, Anguish, has no excuse to remain. The two women acquaint him with Lorry's whereabouts and the princess says she will decree that Anguish is to remain in Graustark as a hostage. Prince BOLAROZ, the late Prince Lorenz's father, rages into Edelweiss and says that if the murderer of his son is found and executed by the time the Graustarkian debt to Axphain is due, he will give Graustark a ten-year extension of time. Lorry chafes over his confinement and goes back to the castle with Quinnox.

Chaps. 22–24. On the day before Graustark must pay its debt, Gabriel offers the needed money in return for Yetive's hand. Both Count Halfont and the Princess angrily refuse the offer. That night Quinnox allows Lorry to go to see Yetive in her boudoir. Lorry is determined to give himself up for trial, in order to save Graustark, but Yetive persuades him to return to the monastery. As he is leaving, Gabriel appears at the door. In a jealous rage he accuses Yetive of having a lover. Quinnox appears, says he has been present all the time, and that Lorry is his prisoner. Gabriel says that if Lorry is in the tower dungeon the next day, he will believe the story.

Chaps. 25–26. The people of Edelweiss are in despair on the morning of the day the debt is due. With all the nobles in the throne room, Princess Yetive asks Prince Bolaroz for an extension of time. He refuses. Captain Quinnox and Lorry burst into the room; Lorry is determined to sacrifice himself. Yetive publicly declares her love for him. Anguish cries out that he knows the real murderer of Lorenz—that an accomplice has confessed the crime to him. Prince Gabriel turns savagely on one of his retinue, thereby giving away his guilt. Bolaroz is satisfied, gives Graustark a ten-year extension, and suggests a treaty of friendship. Lorry has a few minutes alone with Yetive, but leaves downcast because

will have from her. Angered, Lorry knocks him under a table and challenges him to a duel. Prince Gabriel looks on with satisfaction. The seconds of Prince Lorenz arrive at the hotel and a duel is arranged for early the next morning. But the next morning Baron Dangloss has Lorry and Anguish taken to the tower of the royal dungeon. Prince Lorenz was found stabbed to death in his bed and a trail of blood led to Lorry's door. Captain QUINNOX, of the princess's bodyguard, arrives at the tower with an order, signed by the princess, for Lorry's arrest. Baron Dangloss reluctantly carries out the formal arrest—reluctantly because all Graustark is glad the hated betrothed of their beloved princess was killed.

Chaps. 18–19. Captain Quinnox brings Lorry a note from Yetive, saying that the way has been prepared for his escape. Lorry refuses to go without seeing the princess again. Late that night a guard brings another note from Yetive which seems to tell him she will see him again. He changes clothes with the guard and leaves the dungeon. A carriage is waiting outside to spirit him away through the stormy night. Lorry questions the young soldier who is riding she will not promise to marry him. Anguish says that his accusation of Gabriel was pure bluff based on a shrewd guess.

Chaps. 27–28. Count Halfont tells Lorry he regrets that Lorry is not a prince but, since he is not, it is impossible for him to marry Yetive. The following day Princess Yetive assembles the nobles and tells them of her determination to marry Lorry. She asks them to revise the laws so that Lorry can become Prince Consort and their first male child, the Prince Regent. Thus Lorry could never become ruler of Graustark. The nobles finally consent.

Three months later, Lorry and Yetive and Anguish and Dagmar, two honeymooning couples, leave Graustark for a trip to America.

Great Expectations

Novel by Charles Dickens, 1812–1870. Published 1860–61. (PB, PL50)

GREAT EXPECTATIONS is one of Dickens' best novels, though for many years it was not very high in the popularity ranking of his works. Most of the characters are typical Dickens (which is by no means bad) and have their counterparts in some or all of his other novels, but Miss Havisham is an original creation. Left at the altar in her youth, she sat the rest of her life in her wedding dress, waiting for the bridegroom to arrive. Miss Havisham's ward Estella might have been equally effective, and the book would have been many times better, if Dickens had let her finally go the way of Miss Havisham. Dickens must have had this in mind, and almost to the end he left the way open for it. But then, as always, he bowed to the public taste and gave his book a happy ending.

Chaps. 1–6. PHILIP PIRRIP, called PIP, is in the churchyard near the marshes when he is accosted by an escaped convict in fetters, who makes him promise to bring food and a file. Pip, an orphan about 10 years old, lives with his sister and her husband, JOE GARGERY, the town blacksmith. When Pip takes the food and the file to the marshes he comes upon another escaped convict, whom he manages to avoid. He tells his acquaintance of the day before, who seems to be infuriated. That day (Christmas), while Joe's family including Pip's Uncle PUMBLECHOOK are at dinner, a sergeant appears and asks Joe to fix a pair of handcuffs. Pip and his uncle follow the sergeant, who is seeking a pair of escaped convicts. The convicts are caught and Pip's man is careful to say that he stole the food and file from the blacksmith, so that Pip cannot be blamed.

Chaps. 7–9. About a year later, Pip has started his schooling at an institution run by Mr. WOPSLE'S great-aunt, where he is given considerable assistance by BIDDY, her granddaughter. Joe never had any schooling and is anxious for Pip to have it. Mrs. JOE (Pip's sister) is very excited when Miss HAVISHAM, an eccentric and mysteriously isolated lady in town, invites Pip to come to her house to play. Uncle Pumblechook takes Pip to Satis House, where Miss Havisham lives. Pip is admitted by a beautiful but insolent girl of about his own age, named ESTELLA, who takes him to a room where Miss Havisham sits, dressed as for a party, with candles about her. She tells him to play cards with Estella. When he is let out he is told to return in six days.

Chaps. 10–17. Pip has a curious adventure at a tavern called the *Three Brave Bargemen,* to which he takes a message to Joe. He sees Joe and Wopsle in a conversation with a stranger who stirs his rum with a file. The stranger gives Pip "a shilling"— wrapped in two £1 notes—with a cryptic message that Pip interprets as meaning they come from the convict he helped. Pip pays his second visit to Miss Havisham's. It is her birthday, and several relatives are visiting. Pip gets into a fight with a pale young gentleman, whom he soundly trounces. He is rewarded by a kiss from Estella. The visits to Miss Havisham go on for some time. She is always dressed in an elaborate white gown. At length it is time for Joe to put Pip on as his apprentice, and Miss Havisham pays Pip's fee. His visits to Satis House end, but his contact with Miss Havisham and Estella has made him conscious of his own lack of refinement and education. DODGE ORLICK, an assistant at the forge, makes uncomplimentary remarks about Mrs. Joe, for which Joe knocks him down. Pip calls on Miss Havisham and learns that Estella has gone to the continent to complete her education. Returning home, he meets Orlick. At the house his sister is lying on the floor, unconscious. Someone has struck her a savage blow. The officers who come from London cannot find the culprit and Mrs. Joe cannot speak. To help around the house, Joe calls on Biddy, who proves very quick in learning to interpret Mrs. Joe's wishes. Mrs. Joe seems to have most friendly feelings for Orlick, who soon becomes almost part of the family—to Biddy's distress, for Orlick has a strong affection for her and she does not reciprocate.

Chaps. 18–33. Pip visits Miss Havisham on his birthday each year, and each year she gives him a guinea. After four years of Pip's apprenticeship, a lawyer, Mr. JAGGERS, whom Pip has seen at Miss Havisham's house, tells Pip and Joe that a certain friend, who does not wish to be identified, has expressed the intention of leaving Pip a considerable fortune. In other words, Pip has "great expectations." Therefore Pip must leave his present life for London, to learn to live like a gentleman. Joe willingly relinquishes his rights in Pip, but Pip fails to recognize the great-hearted qualities of his brother-in-law and suddenly sees only the uncultured, rough-mannered laborer. Pip suspects that Miss Havisham is his benefactor, though he has no hint of any such thing from the lawyer. In London, Pip is turned over to Jaggers' clerk, young Mr. WEMMICK. Pip is to share lodgings at Barnard's Inn with young Mr. HERBERT POCKET, whose father, MATTHEW POCKET, is to be Pip's tutor. Mr. Pocket, Jr., turns out to be the pale young gentleman with

Pip meets young Mr. Pocket

whom Pip once fought. That does not prevent their getting on very well together now. Herbert teaches Pip polite behavior and also tells him Miss Havisham's story— the story of a faithless fiancé who failed to appear for the wedding, after which Miss Havisham became the recluse that Pip knows, always dressed for a wedding. The Pocket residence being quite an impossible place in which to live, because of Mrs. Pocket's dictatorial nature, Pip continues to make his quarters with Herbert Pocket. Pip becomes well acquainted with Wemmick and visits his home in Walworth, where Wemmick lives with his old, deaf father, whom he addresses as "Aged Parent." Pip dines with Mr. Jaggers and meets two of his fellow students, BENTLEY DRUMMLE and STARTOP. Joe Gargery brings news that Estella is back from the continent. Pip at once makes up his mind to go back and see her. Estella is now a grown woman, and a very beautiful one. Orlick is working for Miss Havisham as a porter. Pip returns to London madly in love with Estella. He confides this fact to Herbert, who reciprocates by confessing that he is in love with CLARA—but her father is a most difficult and unpleasant man. Pip has the honor of escorting Estella to Richmond, where she is to be introduced to society.

Chaps. 34–38. Pip and Herbert always spend more than their allowances and are constantly in debt. Pip's sister, Mrs. Joe, dies and Pip returns for the funeral. Shortly afterward, both he and Herbert come of age. Jaggers increases Pip's allowance most substantially and Pip is able to transfer a goodly sum to Herbert as a loan, without letting Herbert know the part he played. Wemmick, who arranges the matter, is falling in love with Miss SKIFFIN. Drummle is paying court to Estella and she seems to welcome his suit, which is painful to Pip, who still adores Estella.

Chaps. 39–46. Pip is 23 years old now, and the possessor of a considerable income, which he has always believed to come from Miss Havisham. He is alone at home one evening when a strange man calls on him. The man is crude, roughly dressed and workworn. Pip learns, with a shock, that this man is his benefactor, not Miss Havisham. It is the convict whom Pip befriended so long ago, and he has returned to see the gentleman he has made of Pip, though he does it at the risk of his life, for the penalty of discovery is death. The man moves in as Pip's Uncle PROVIS. Herbert is sworn to secrecy, and the two young men agree that they must get Uncle Provis—or ABEL MAGWITCH, which is his real name—out of England as soon as possible. They hear his story and learn that he was victimized by one COMPEYSON, a gentlemanly swindler—the other convict Pip saw on the marsh. (Compeyson is also the faithless lover who jilted Miss Havisham.) Pip goes to see Miss Havisham and Estella once more, and learns that Estella is to marry Drummle. On his return to London he receives a note warning him not to go in his lodgings. They are being watched by someone. Magwitch has been secretly moved to a house on the shore of the river. Pip is to obtain a boat and row each day on the river, so that it will be a familiar sight and excite no suspicion when he rows Magwitch to a steamer later for his escape.

Chaps. 47–51. Pip learns that it is Compeyson who is watching him. Pip dines at Jaggers' house, and certain things about Jaggers' housekeeper convince Pip that she is Estella's mother. This is confirmed when Wemmick relates the woman's story. Estella marries. A fire at Satis House nearly results in Miss Havisham's death, but she is saved by Pip, whose hands are badly burned. On his return to London, Pip hears from Herbert a story that shows clearly that Magwitch is Estella's father.

Chaps. 52–59. The attempt to place Magwitch on the Hamburg steamer is a failure, due to Compeyson's espionage. Magwitch is captured, but before he is overpowered he deals Compeyson his death blow. Magwitch is held for trial, but he dies in prison before the trial takes place. Before he dies, he has the comfort of knowing that Pip has developed a real affection for him, and it also pleases him that Pip loves Estella deeply. After the death of his benefactor Pip suffers a long illness. When he returns to his old haunts, Miss Havisham has died and Joe is married to Biddy. Eleven years later he sees Estella. She is now a widow, but it is clear that she will now marry Pip.

The Great Galeoto

Play by José Echegaray, 1832–1916. Produced 1881.

THE TITLE of the first English translation was *The World and His Wife*. Echegaray was a Spanish Nobel Prize winner (1904). This has been his most popular play in the United States. The title is explained in the outline.

Prologue. Don JULIAN finds his young ward ERNEST trying to write a play but lacking a good idea. Don Julian advises a hunting trip, or at least a new plot. After Don Julian leaves inspiration comes to Ernest. He will write a play based on a story from Dante, the story of the violent and passionate love of Francesco and Paolo, and his play will be called "The Great Galeoto."

Act I. Julian tells TEODORA, his beautiful young wife, that he is worried about Ernest's future. Ernest feels that he lives on alms in Julian's house. Julian suggests that Ernest become his secretary and receive a salary. Ernest accepts. Don SEVERO, Julian's brother, and MERCEDES, Severo's wife, are certain that an affair is going on between Ernest and Teodora. "All Madrid" is gossiping about it. Severo tells Julian, who retorts that the story is a filthy lie but privately begins to entertain suspicions.

Act II. Having heard the rumors, Ernest moves out of Julian's house into a poorly furnished garret. Don Julian, filled with remorse, begs him to return. Julian is accompanied by Severo, who confesses that he foolishly gave credit to shabby innuendoes. Ernest challenges Viscount NEBREDA to a duel, for publicly voicing the slander, and Julian, too, wishes to challenge Nebreda. Severo's son asks Ernest who Galeoto was, and Ernest replies that he was a panderer who acted for Launcelot and Guinevere and who was used as a symbol of pandering in the romance of Francesco and Paolo. Ernest declares that all too often society as a whole is a Galeoto, forcing a man and woman together against their wills. Teodora comes to Ernest to prevent his duel with Nebreda. They hear a noise on the stairs and Teodora hides in Ernest's bedroom. Severo's son bursts in and reports that Julian has been severely wounded by Nebreda. A few seconds later Julian appears, supported by Don Severo. Despite Ernest's protests, Severo takes Julian into Ernest's bedroom. Teodora is discovered and Don Julian collapses.

Act III. Julian lies at home in grave condition. Ernest has fought and killed Nebreda. He comes to Julian's house to offer an explanation of what took place. Mercedes orders him turned away, but Ernest tells Mercedes that Teodora was in his rooms only to prevent a duel that would smudge Julian's honor. Mercedes dismisses this as a flimsy excuse. She goes to Teodora and tries to force her to confess love for Ernest. Teodora maintains that all her love is for Julian. Still unconvinced, Mercedes tries again to turn Ernest away but he persists and sees Teodora, who tells him they must never meet again. Ernest goes on his knees before her and Severo comes across them at this very instant. Severo seizes Teodora and drags her across the room, but Ernest intervenes and forces Severo to kneel before Teodora. Julian staggers into the room, half-delirious, and challenges Ernest to a duel. Severo and Mercedes carry Julian to his room. A cry of anguish is heard and Teodora hurries to Julian's room but Mercedes orders her out of the house. Julian has died without heirs, so the house belongs to Severo. Ernest protests again that Teodora is innocent. Severo screams that Ernest is a liar, then makes a menacing gesture toward Teodora. Ernest steps forward to protect her. He shouts that at last society has driven Teodora into his arms, against both their wills. Society, armed with stupidity and prejudice and gossip, has acted the panderer, the Galeoto, toward him and an innocent woman.

The Great Gatsby

Novel by F. Scott Fitzgerald, 1896–1940.

Published & © 1925 by Charles Scribner's Sons, New York.

EXCEPT FOR Hemingway and perhaps Faulkner, F. Scott Fitzgerald has probably influenced a greater number of young, talented novelists than any other modern writer. *The Great Gatsby* was the Fitzgerald novel that won them in the first place. The majority of readers will call it his best work. It is the book of the "lost generation" for which Fitzgerald was spokesman, and no one saw more keenly than he, or expressed so well, not only the things his generation did but why they did them. For a picture of the early postwar, early Prohibition era, *Gatsby* is the book.

Chap. 1. NICK CARRAWAY, 1915 Yale graduate, a member of a wealthy family, has come to New York in 1922 to learn the bond business. He rents a small house in the fashionable town of West Egg on Long Island. Next to his house is the sumptuous estate of the mysterious JAY GATSBY, who gives a big, open-house party every night. Nick is invited to dinner by his cousin DAISY BUCHANAN and her husband, TOM, both very rich, who live in the even more fashionable town of East Egg, which is visible across the bay. Also at dinner is Miss JORDON BAKER, an outstanding woman golfer. In Daisy, Tom, and Jordon Nick sees forced gaiety but actual boredom and discontent. Tom and Daisy have an argument, and Jordon tells Nick it is because Tom has a mistress. Upon returning from the Buchanans', Nick sees Gatsby for the first time, standing in front of his mansion and apparently disturbed.

Chap. 2. Tom introduces Nick to MYRTLE WILSON, his mistress, who lives in a little town halfway between West Egg and New York. She is the wife of the local garage mechanic, GEORGE WILSON. Tom maintains an apartment in New York to which she goes on the pretext that she is visiting her sister. At the apartment Nick also meets Myrtle's sister, Catherine. She tells Nick she has been to one of Gatsby's parties and that she is afraid of Gatsby. Catherine also says that Myrtle and Tom hate their respective mates but that Tom cannot get a divorce because Daisy is a Catholic. Nick knows this is not true.

Chap. 3. Throughout the summer Gatsby is host at parties attended by large crowds of people, most of whom do not even know Gatsby. There is plentiful food and liquor, a full orchestra, and lavish entertainment. On the evening that Nick attends his first party at Gatsby's, he believes he is one of the few guests to be formally invited. Jordan Baker is there. No one knows anything about Gatsby's background and there are many extravagant rumors about him—he is a murderer, a gangster, a former German spy. Gatsby tells Nick he was stationed in France during the war and seems to remember Nick from overseas. Gatsby tries to be friendly with Nick but Nick is not very sociable that summer. However, during the summer Nick sees Jordan a great deal.

Chap. 4. One July morning Gatsby calls on Nick at Nick's house. Gatsby is always restless and never has much to say. Nick privately has some doubts when Gatsby says he is from a wealthy Midwest family and was educated at Oxford. He shows Nick a picture taken at Oxford and a medal he won during World War I. Gatsby says he has traveled about to forget a sad thing that happened to him. Nick goes to lunch in New York with Gatsby, who introduces him to a gambler named WOLFSHEIM, who seems to be well acquainted with Gatsby. At tea, Jordan reveals that Daisy, as a popular girl in Louisville, was deeply in love with an army lieutenant stationed nearby. The lieutenant was sent overseas and Daisy married Tom, and Jordan believes that despite Daisy's love for the lieutenant Daisy was actually in love with Tom until he started seeing other women. It was not till six weeks ago that Daisy learned that the young army lieutenant had turned up as the fabulous Jay Gatsby across the Sound. Gatsby has told Jordan he bought his mansion just to be near Daisy. Across the bay between West Egg and East Egg he can see a green light that marks the Buchanans' place. Gatsby asks Nick to invite him and Daisy to tea so that he can meet her again.

Chap. 5. Daisy accepts Nick's invitation to tea. Gatsby, nervous and embarrassed, also comes. Nick leaves them alone together and when he reënters the room Gatsby seems like a new man. He takes Nick and Daisy on a tour of his elaborate mansion.

Chap. 6. Jay Gatsby's real name is James Gatz, and he is the son of poor, shiftless and unsuccessful farm people from North Dakota. He was haunted by fantastic conceits and dreams of glory. As a young man Gatsby worked for DAN CODY, a millionaire prospector who was growing old and slightly senile. Cody died and left Gatsby $25,000, but Gatsby never got the money. Gatsby became a gentleman legally when he was commissioned an officer in the U.S. Army. Gatsby is determined to repeat the past, not just erase it and start over. He wants Daisy to tell Tom she never loved him, and then marry Gatsby. Daisy and Tom attend one of Gatsby's parties, but Daisy does not enjoy the artificiality and Tom takes an instant dislike to Gatsby.

Chap. 7. Suddenly, and without explanation, Gatsby stops giving parties and fires all his servants, except a crew he has hired through the gambler Wolfsheim. Gatsby tells Nick he has taken these steps to prevent the servants from gossiping, as Daisy comes to visit him often. Nick and Gatsby are invited to lunch at Daisy's house, at which time Tom faces the realization that Daisy and Gatsby love each other. Daisy, Tom, Gatsby, Nick and Jordan decide to drive to New York. Gatsby and Daisy take Tom's coupé, and Tom drives Gatsby's large, expensive, yellow car. On the way to town, Tom stops for gas at the garage owned by George Wilson. George does not suspect that Tom is his wife's lover but he is aware that she is unfaithful to him. He tells Tom he is going to move out West with his wife. There is tension when the group arrives in New York. Tom confronts Gatsby with the knowledge of his relationship with Daisy, whereupon Gatsby tells Tom that Daisy never loved him. Daisy says that at one time she did love Tom, but now she is planning to leave him. Tom has had Gatsby investigated and reveals that Gatsby

Tom stops for gas at the garage owned by George Wilson

is associated with the bootlegging business. Gatsby and Daisy drive back to Long Island in his yellow car, the others following in Tom's coupé. On the way back to East Egg, Gatsby's car, driven by Daisy, is involved in an accident. Myrtle Wilson, thinking the yellow car is still being driven by Tom, runs out on the highway and the speeding car hits and kills her. Daisy does not stop.

Chap. 8. Nick advises Gatsby to leave town for a while, as the police are sure to trace the car to him. Gatsby refuses, still hoping that Daisy will leave her husband for him. Wilson, sure that the driver of the yellow car was Myrtle's lover, traces the car to Gatsby, goes to Gatsby's house, and shoots Gatsby in his swimming pool. Wilson then shoots himself. Both die.

Chap. 9. Nick attempts to find some of Gatsby's friends to attend his funeral, but there seems to be none. Daisy has gone away with Tom. Gatsby's father, HENRY G. GATZ, a tired old man, comes for the funeral. He speaks of Gatsby's youth and how he dreamed of a great future. There is no one at Gatsby's funeral but his father, Nick, and one other man who had been to a few of Gatsby's parties. After Gatsby's death, Nick feels that the East is haunted for him and decides to return to the Midwest. He and Jordan almost reached the point of marriage, but inexplicably they drifted apart. Before he leaves, he meets Tom once more. Tom confesses that he told Wilson it was Gatsby who drove the yellow car. Tom feels no guilt or remorse. Nick muses on the spoiled darlings of life, Tom and Daisy, who never suffer the consequences of their irresponsible acts, and on the dreamers such as Gatsby, who vainly pursue the future while time carries them inexorably back into the past.

The Green Bay Tree

Novel by Louis Bromfield, 1896–1956. Published 1927 by F. A. Stokes, New York. (NAL, S1025; PB, 56)

CRITICAL OPINION of Louis Bromfield has been mixed, some critics considering him a major American novelist and some dismissing him as merely a popular one. This is not strange, since his novels ranged from quite poor to very good. The novel that was most successful, *The Rains Came* (1937), was very far from his best. *The Green Bay Tree*, his first novel, has best stood the test of time. Its interesting characters are women and when Bromfield based a play on it, in 1927, he called the play *The House of Women*. The theme of *The Green Bay Tree*, as of all of Bromfield's early novels, is the unrest and defiance of a new generation to the conservatism and tradition of an old family. The title occurs in the Bible, Psalm 37:35: "I have seen the wicked in great power and spreading himself like a green bay tree."

Chaps. 1–6. Mrs. JULIA SHANE, an old woman of wealth, position, and character, lives in a mansion in a provincial midwestern town. The mansion has lost its value and style since it has been surrounded by railroad yards, steel mills, and immigrant workers' homes, but Mrs. Shane refuses to move, because of sentiment. Mrs. Shane's younger daughter, IRENE, is shy and religious and seems unable to cope with the business of life. Mrs. Shane's older daughter, LILY, a warm, attractive girl of 24, is in love with the governor of the state, who is 20 years her senior. She is pregnant with his child but she refuses to marry him. Irene, delicate and neurotic, is haunted by an image of the governor opening the door of Lily's room.

Chaps. 7–13. Mrs. Shane wants to send Lily abroad before her condition can become known and cause a scandal. WILLIAM HARRISON (WILLIE), a businessman, asks Lily's hand in marriage, but she dislikes his cringing manner and decides to go to France. William's mother suspects the reason for the trip but there is little talk in the town. In Paris Lily lives well, and she

decides to stay there. She sends a telegram
to her mother, announcing the birth of her
son, JEAN. Irene tells her mother that she
wants to join the Catholic Church. Mrs.
Shane, coming from a long line of Scottish
Presbyterians, is appalled at the idea. She
makes Irene promise not to be converted
as long as she (Mrs. Shane) lives.

Chaps. 14–30. Four years later Lily
comes home unexpectedly for a visit. Lily
tells her mother that she has been baptized
by the opportunistic but kind Mme. GIGON
and has a respected position in French society. Lily gives parties in the old Shane
mansion and for a while the gaiety of
former days almost subdues the sound of
the surrounding mills. William Harrison,
now a mill owner, takes Lily and Irene on a
tour of the mill and again asks Lily to marry
him. She refuses, because he is neither
exciting nor strong. Irene is teaching English to the millworkers and has an obses-
sive interest in their problems. She has
made one friend among them, a handsome
Russian, STEPHAN KRYLENKO. Lily meets
her cousin, ELLEN TOLLIVER, who wants
to study the piano in New York, and to
get away from the drab life of her home.
She idolizes Lily, because Lily has lived in
Paris. Lily, catching some of Ellen's en-
thusiasm for France, longs to return and
when she hears that her small son has
measles she is only too glad to leave. Ellen
Tolliver marries a New York salesman and
escapes from the mill town.

Chaps. 31–48. Irene continues her work
among the mill hands. Krylenko becomes a
leader of the immigrant workmen. He reads
Rousseau and Marx and becomes a revolutionary. Irene feels close to him and in
her shy way even loves him. She has become righteous and smug and confesses to
her mother that she hates Lily. Irene con-
tends that of the two sisters only the
younger is loved by God. Irene also tells
her mother that she will never marry and
that she wants Krylenko to remain pure
and free of any woman. She wants him to
be a saint. Krylenko organizes a strike at
the mill and Irene is proud of his work. Mrs.
Shane asks Lily to come back from France
because she has only a few more months to
live. Lily writes that she will return as soon
as she has placed her son in a school in
England. Lily comes home and finds her

mother very weak. The town is up in arms
and the strikers riot in the streets. Lily
brings comfort to her mother and tells her
charming stories about her grandson, Jean.
Several days later Julia Shane dies in her
sleep.

Chaps. 49–54. Irene gives the workers
permission to meet on the grounds of her
house. Lily listens to Krylenko speak to the
crowd in several languages. She is moved by
the passion of his words and when he is
hurt by the police in a fight, Lily takes him
into the house, binds his wounds, and
promises to hide him from the police.
The police come to the house, do not find
the hidden Krylenko, and leave when Lily
avows that she has not seen the strike
leader. Afterwards Lily and Krylenko
embrace. Irene breaks in on them and cries
out in fury that Lily has ruined her saint
and is damned forever. The next morning
Lily leaves Krylenko a note saying that
Irene has gone away and that she also is
leaving. She wants him to remain in the
house and tells him that she loves him. He
stays in the great house, sending words of
encouragement to the strikers, but the strike
fails. Then he disappears.

Chaps. 55–67. Ellen Tolliver's husband
dies and Ellen goes to Paris, where she becomes a successful, glamorous concert
pianist, taking the name of LILLI BARR.
Rumors of war stir Paris. Lily Shane takes
a lover, Baron CESAIRE, a military man,
who is kind and dignified. Irene has entered
a convent at Lisieux. The shock of seeing
Lily with Krylenko has shattered her faith
in humanity and now she devotes herself
entirely to God. Lily follows Krylenko's
career as a strike leader and hopes for his
ultimate success. She is frightened at the
thought of becoming old and of losing her
son, who is growing up and is attending a
military academy.

Chaps. 68–70. Willie Harrison comes to
Paris. His arrival awakens memories of
Krylenko and Lily is sad. He tells her that
he has quit the mill and come to Europe to
lead his own life. The mill now belongs
to a company that evicted the strikers from
the company houses and blacklisted them,
so that they find it impossible to find work
anywhere else. Harrison's mother is dead
and an epoch has come to an end in the
midwestern town. Lily learns that her old

home was burned and decides to sell the property to the town and forget that she ever lived there. After Willie's visit Lily writes to Irene, who has taken the name of Sister MONICA. This letter, like hundreds of others Lily has written to her sister, remains unanswered.

Chaps. 71–77. The Archduke of Austria is assassinated and war comes to Europe. The baron joins his regiment and Jean leaves his academy to fight for France. Lily moves to her house at Germigny on the Marne with Mme. Gigon. She is warned, by a friend in the War Ministry, to leave France, but she decides to stay. The Germans approach Germigny. Mme. Gigon suffers a fall and lies unconscious. Lily runs to the little church in the country town and brings the priest back to hear the confession of her friend and companion. Lily tells the priest the story of her own life and of the love she has for Krylenko. The baron briefly visits Lily and tells her a battle near Germigny is imminent. When he has left to rejoin his regiment, Lily weeps.

Chaps. 78–84. The battle goes badly for the French and the Germans take possession of the town. A German officer calls on Lily. He tells her he does not hate and does not want to kill but all men are caught in the war as flies in a spider's web. After he has gone, Lily looks through binoculars and sees that the Germans intend to blow up a bridge that the French must use in their retreat. She takes her revolver, hides in the brush, and kills the three Germans at the bridge. She is brought back to her house by some French soldiers and falls ill. When she recovers she is decorated by the French Government for her heroism. Cesaire is listed as missing in action and Jean is in the hospital, recovering from the amputation of his right leg. Lily moves back to Paris and becomes friendly with a French diplomat, RENÉ DE CYON. She uses some of her wealth to aid returning soldiers. She is becoming more and more like her mother in character.

Chap. 85. At a convention for American politicians in Paris, Lily meets her ex-lover, the governor, and finds him vulgar and the life he stands for repulsive. She is glad that she renounced the governor and that she is now married to René de Cyon. He appreciates her qualities and she makes a perfect wife for a man of politics. In 1920, a card from the convent at Lisieux informs Lily that Sister Monica has died, and in the newspapers Lily reads that Stephan Krylenko has died in Moscow.

The German officer tells Lily that he is a fly in a spider's web

Green Grow the Lilacs

Play by Lynn Riggs, 1899–1954.
Produced in New York, 1931. Published
1931 by Samuel French, New York.

ON THIS PLAY was based the Rodgers
and Hart operetta *Oklahoma!*, ensur-
ing the lasting fame of the play. *Oklahoma!* was the most successful musical
show that had been known up to its
time (it was produced in 1943).
Green Grow the Lilacs itself leaned
heavily on its music—folk ballads of
the West, chiefly those sung by the
character Curly. But *Green Grow the
Lilacs* is also a charming piece of writing and characterization. The title is
from a line in a ballad sung by Curly.

Scene I. Outside the Williams farmhouse
in Indian Territory (later Oklahoma) on a
June morning in 1900, a tall young cowboy,
CURLY MCCLAIN, is singing and Aunt
ELLER asks him to come in. She says that if
she wasn't an older woman and he wasn't
so young and smart alecky, she'd marry
him. Curly says he wouldn't marry her or
any of her kinfolk, including Miss LAUREY
WILLIAMS; but he gives himself away by
asking where Laurey is. Aunt Eller taunts
him with the fact that Laurey pays no attention to him. He boasts about his prowess
as a bulldozer and she makes disparaging
remarks about his being bowlegged. Curly
says he wants to take Laurey to a party that
Old Man PECK is giving across Dog Creek.
Laurey overhears and comes in, saying she
heard someone singing like a bullfrog. She
asks Curly if he has a buggy with red wheels
and a spanking team and Curly says he has
a surrey with a fringe on the top, but then
says he hasn't. Laurey flounces out of the
room, but reappears and says she is going
to the party with JEETER, the hired hand.
Curly asks Aunt Eller to go to the party
with him and tells her he really has hired
the surrey. Then he goes out to look for
Jeeter.

Scene 2. Laurey is in her bedroom preparing for the party. She acts very short
with Aunt Eller, who surmises that she is
in love. Laurey tells of once having seen
a house burn to the ground and how sad it
made her. She says she sometimes fears
Jeeter may set their house on fire and she
confesses that she is frightened by the hired
hand. A wagon drives up with ALI HAKIM,
a peddler, and ADO ANNIE CARNES. Aunt
Eller buys an eggbeater and Laurey and Ado
buy trinkets, garters, and face whitening.
They hear shots from the smokehouse,
where Curly has gone to find Jeeter, and
they all rush out.

Scene 3. When Curly goes to the smokehouse to find Jeeter, the hired hand is
looking at postcards. They exchange taunts.
Jeeter shows Curly his pictures and a pair
of Colt .45 revolvers. They start playing
cards. Jeeter starts musing about violent
crimes, which he follows in detail, most
of them having to do with men murdering
young girls and trying to dispose of their
bodies. When Curly admits that he comes
to see Laurey, Jeeter becomes angry and
forbids him to step foot on the place. Curly
compares him to a scared rattlesnake and
Jeeter snatches up a gun and pulls the
trigger, splintering the wall. Curly points to
a knot in a plank, picks up the other gun,
and blows the knot out. Aunt Eller and
Laurey arrive. Laurey is impressed by
Curly's marksmanship. Ali Hakim comes in
and Jeeter buys a wicked-looking knife.
Curly counters by buying a pair of brass
knuckles.

Scene 4. The party is in full swing at
Old Man Peck's place. Jeeter asks Laurey
why she doesn't like to be alone with him.
He tells her how he tries to get her alone
at the ranch and he suddenly seizes her in
his arms. At first she is hysterical but suddenly her fears vanish and she tells him he
is nothing but a mangy dog and someone
might shoot him. Laurey finds Curly and
tells him she is afraid. He holds her and
kisses her and asks her to marry him.

Scene 5. Curly and Laurey have been
married and are sneaking through a hay-
field hoping to escape the shivaree, the

post-wedding hazing ritual. The shivaree begins and all the neighboring men, who have been hiding in the fields, make suggestive remarks, manhandle Curly, and try to surround Laurey. In the midst of the uproar a haystack begins to burn and Jeeter appears, drunk, carrying a flaming torch, and threatening to burn the bride and groom to cracklings. He pulls out his knife and rushes at Curly. But he trips, and after groaning and whimpering he lies very still. The men persuade Curly to come with them and give himself up to the law.

Scene 6. Ado Annie and Aunt Eller, sewing in the living room, are worried because Laurey has not eaten or slept since Curly was taken away. They hear the dog barking outside and Curly appears. Laurey is thankful that they have let him off but he confesses that he broke out of the prison. Aunt Eller is wild, because she knows he will be followed. Curly tells Laurey not to worry, as he has heard that the hearing will be purely perfunctory. The posse arrives, but Aunt Eller gives the men a piece of her mind and they agree to leave Curly and Laurey alone until the next morning, when Curly will be freed at the hearing.

The Green Hat

Novel by Michael Arlen (Dikran Kouyoumdjian, 1895–1958).
Published 1924. Play produced 1924 in New York.

AS A NOVEL The *Green Hat* was no work of art, perhaps because its Armenian author was not at home writing in English, but its story is a most dramatic one and the play based on the novel was a great success. It was one of Katharine Cornell's early triumphs. The basic theme is that the heroine Iris March, who affects flamboyant green hats as an act of bravado, married her brother's hero. The hero turned out to be unworthy while Iris herself was actually pure; but rather than disillusion her brother, Iris let her own reputation be smudged. Her brother became an alcoholic anyway, from shame that his sister had (as he thought) so betrayed his hero. While the play was running in 1924–25, most cities did not permit the word syphilis to be uttered on the stage and "a vile disease" was substituted.

Chap. 1. 1. The author lives in a flat in Shepherd's Green, London. Above him lives a misanthropic drunkard, GERALD MARCH. The author's bell rings and on the street he sees a green hat, the kind worn *pour le sport*, and a large yellow Hispano-Suiza. **2.** The girl in the green hat asks if Mr. March is in. He escorts her to Gerald's apartment. She is Gerald's twin sister, IRIS STORM, and has not seen her brother for ten years. They find him drunk. Iris explains that Gerald's youthful hero died and he never got over it. **3.** Iris has heard of the author from a mutual friend, HILARY TOWNSHEND. She has a drink of water in his flat and they talk. She calls herself "a house of men . . . of their desires and defeats and deaths" and tells him there is a curse on the Marches. He admires a ring on her finger. It was given her by her dead husband and she shows him how it falls off her finger; it is beautiful but loose. A policeman rings to inquire about the Hispano-Suiza. When the author returns to his flat he finds Iris asleep in his bed. **4.** In the morning Iris talks about the beast that comes to her in a dream. She says she is sorry they cannot be friends but she gives him a telephone number.

Chap. 2. 1. Gerald is described through the eyes of Hilary Townshend and GUY DE TRAVERT, both great friends of Barty March, father of Iris and Gerald. Gerald wrote a novel, then cut away from his friends, partly because his sister had become déclassé. Hilary describes Gerald as having been a "dark, diabolical schoolboy"; and Guy, who was his colonel in the Grena-

diers during the war, calls him a "young,
hellfire idiot." **2.** Proceeding with the
description of Gerald: The author remembers his never having an overcoat and being
a solitary drunkard. Gerald's novel *The
Savage Device* was a story of adventure in
which the hero plucks a wife from a San
Francisco dive, the hero being obviously
patterned on BOY FENWICK, Iris's husband
and Gerald's hero, and the woman being
inspired by Iris herself. Iris at 18 was in
love with NAPIER HARPENDEN, but his
father, Maj.-Gen. Sir MAURICE HARPEN-
DEN, opposed any marriage. **3.** When
Gerald is told of Iris's call he does not believe it, then he calls his sister a beast. The
author moves to new lodgings and loses
track of Gerald for two weeks. He calls Iris
but finds she is on the continent. From there
she sends him box of stationery.

Chap. 3. 1. The author meets Gerald at
a newsstand. He offers Gerald money.
Gerald counters by insisting that he himself accept a fiver, and sends his love to
Iris. **2.** Hilary Townshend and Guy de
Travert are described, as symbols of England. Guy has a wife who insists that he is
cruel, and she threatens to take a lover but
never does. **3.** The author talks to Hilary
about Iris. Hilary says the Marches are
cursed. The author discovers that Iris is
very rich, having been left a fortune by her
second husband, the steel magnate HECTOR
STORM. Her first husband, Boy Fenwick,
committed suicide on their wedding night.
4. This happened in Deauville. The report
was that Boy killed himself "for purity,"
after discovering that his wife was unchaste.
Iris condoned the report, though it ruined
her reputation. Hilary admits that Fenwick
was not quite sane but says he acted in the
depths of sudden despair and destroyed the
girl by exalting himself. Hilary says that
Iris was loved extravagantly by both her
husbands.

Chap. 4. 1. The author goes with Hilary
to a night club in Carlton House Terrace,
where the aristocracy foregathers. There
they see VENICE POLLEN, who is to marry
Napier Harpenden. HUGO CYPRESS, dancing by with his wife, SHIRLEY, asks if they
have seen the evening paper, about a friend
of theirs. Hilary leaves the table and returns
to say that Gerald is in an awful mess. Iris
comes in with a colonel, then Guy comes in,

Gerald is a suicide

most unsmiling. **2.** The author finds himself with Iris in the Hispano-Suiza. She
insists on seeing Gerald before she goes
abroad the next day. The author has learned
Gerald has been fined for indecently an-
noying a woman in Hyde Park and is ap-
pealing the charge. They go to Shepherd's
market and the author climbs to Gerald's
flat. He comes back and tells Iris that her
brother is drunk again, but actually he has
blown his brains out.

Chap. 5. 1. Some months later the writer
is in Paris. An acquaintance, CHERRY
MARVEL, tells him that Iris is seriously ill
at a nursing home; she has had an operation.
The author has previously had a long letter
from Iris, blaming him for some sort of
predicament in which Iris then found herself. Iris has admitted to Guy that she had
a son by Storm before her second husband
died but that the baby died. **2.** The author
goes to the nursing home, but a nun tells
him that Mrs. Storm is rather wild. The
nun will not let him in.

Chap. 6. By tipping the lay sister (as she
turns out to be) the author gets into the
hospital. He has a talk with CONRAD
MASTERS, a celebrated doctor, who explains

that Iris is very ill with septic poisoning and has lost her desire to live. He finds that septic poisoning comes after one has had a baby or an abortion and that it is not necessarily fatal. Napier stops by the hospital to inquire about Iris, not realizing the gravity of her illness. When Masters hears that Napier has been Iris's lover, he suggests a visit from Napier may inspire her to live, but Napier decides that he has to leave Paris with his wife, Venice.

Chap. 7. Napier is again urged to stay over and try to pull Iris through her crisis, but he refuses to upset his plans. Masters then decides that the author himself must make a second visit to Iris to persuade her to fight for her life.

Chaps. 8–10. The author sees Iris. She is very frightened and confesses that no one wants her, including God. She tells him that he has probably saved her life and seems satisfied when she learns that Napier does not suspect that he was the cause of her near brush with death. She assures the author that she will never again return to England. But later Hilary, Guy and the author see Napier and Iris together in a cab in London. Guy suggests that since it is very hot they should get up a swimming party. The author drives to Maidenhead with Iris and she buys a green hat on the way. When they go swimming Iris saves Venice from drowning, although it is obvious to everyone that Napier and Iris are contemplating an elopement.

Chap. 11. The principal characters meet at Sir Maurice Harpenden's, where they review the tangled threads of the romance between Napier and Iris. Iris accuses the old man of having wickedly broken up her girlhood romance with his son. For the first time it is revealed that Fenwick killed himself because he had syphilis while Iris, when she married him, was a virgin. Napier wants Iris to go away with him but Venice reveals that she is bearing Napier's child. Iris drives off in the Hispano-Suiza and intentionally kills herself in an accident.

Green Mansions

Novel by W. H. Hudson, 1841–1922. Published 1904; in U.S. published by Alfred A. Knopf, New York. (ML, 89)

As a novel of nature, the supernatural, and romance, *Green Mansions* is an outstanding work of this century. William Henry Hudson was American by parentage, Argentine by birth, British by adopted nationality. He was a naturalist as well as a novelist and his novels are dependable as well as beautiful in their descriptions of natural life.

Prologue. The narrator of the prologue is the only person who knows the story of Mr. ABEL's sojourn in the desert. The only visible symbol of this sojourn was a flower-decorated urn filled with ashes in Abel's house. Abel was a Venezuelan who had come into a fortune. People liked him well enough, and speculated about him, but none knew much about him. The narrator shared with Abel a great love of poetry, and the two became good friends, so that Abel consented to tell the narrator about his unusual experience.

Chap. 1. As a young man of 23, Abel is involved in a plot to overthrow the Venezuelan government. The plot fails and Abel is forced to flee. He decides to explore the wilderness region south of the Orinoco River, which is inhabited by tribes of primitive peoples. At Manapuri Abel falls ill of a fever, which keeps him incapacitated for six months. He meets a kindly trader, Don FANTA, who arranges for a group of friendly Indians to take Abel with them to a place where the climate is better. Abel is facile at learning the Indian dialects and as a result manages to get along with the natives. He is befriended by RUNI, the chief of an Indian tribe, and settles down to live among Runi's people.

Chaps. 2–3. Abel explores the lovely forest near the village, though the Indians warn that it is a dangerous place. Abel thinks their fears are merely superstition. In the wood he hears an exquisite melody that seems to resemble a human voice, but he fails to see the creature, be it human or not, that has made the sounds. One day he bribes one of the Indians, KUA-KO, to accompany him to the wood. Kua-Ko says that the Indians never kill any of the animals in the wood, for fear the daughter of DIDI would cause them to be killed. Abel infers that the Indians invented this superstition of a daughter of the water-spirit to explain the strange melodic voice. Kua-Ko runs from the wood in fear, leaving Abel behind. Abel hears the melodic voice again and becomes certain that it is a human voice.

Chaps. 4–5. Kua-Ko teaches Abel how to use the zabatana, a weapon for killing game. After several days, Abel revisits the wood. This time he does not hear the melodic voice but he has a strange adventure while watching a spider tracking its prey. The spider's maneuvers are so amusing that Abel feels like laughing, whereupon he hears a clear trill of merry laughter nearby. The next day he pushes farther into the wood and suddenly comes upon a girl, an exquisite, delicate creature, who is playing with a bird. She does not seem afraid, but she disappears. Abel goes back into the wood repeatedly and hears the voice in different places, but can see nothing. Kua-Ko offers Abel his sister in marriage if Abel will slay the mysterious girl with a poisoned arrow. The girl, says Kua-Ko, is the daughter of an evil being and prevents the Indian from hunting in the wood. Abel rejects the idea angrily.

Chap. 6. Abel is about to hit a poisonous coral snake with a rock when the girl boldly steps out of the forest. Immediately the snake seems to lose its anger and curls up about her foot. The girl is lovely, with a bright, luminous skin coloring and an ethereal appearance. When Abel moves to put his arm about her slender body to detain her, the snake bites him. Abel fears that he will die from the deadly bite, and implores the girl to help him. She appears grief-stricken but apparently has no knowledge of medical care. Abel tries to leave the wood but is lost. A storm has arisen and

Abel, groping his way, goes over the edge of a precipice and loses consciousness.

Chaps. 7–8. Abel awakens in a hut occupied by an old man, NUFLO, and the girl, whose name is RIMA. Rima has saved Abel by having him brought to the hut. However, in the hut she seems to have lost the brighter aspect he saw in the wood. Nuflo reveals that they eat no meat, because Rima will not permit the killing of animals. When Abel has recovered somewhat, he goes walking in the wood. Rima seems to be once again the tantalizing, elusive creature he had first known. Rima speaks of her mother, who is dead, and tells Abel that they once lived in the village of Voa, but will tell him no more.

Chap. 9. As the days pass, Rima becomes silent and shy, and is only occasionally around. Nuflo goes off every day to a secret hiding place where he eats meat alone, so as not to offend Rima. He tells Abel that Rima's mother died young and that he took the child away to a better climate. Nuflo will not hunt in the wood, declaring that in that wood is one law, the law of Rima. Abel discovers that he loves Rima.

Chaps. 10–11. Abel returns to the Indian village for a short visit, but he returns to Rima the next day. A storm comes on and Abel gets lost again, but Rima leads him back to Nuflo's hut. Rima wishes Abel to tell her about the whole world, because she feels there must be people in the world who would understand her mysterious speech and thoughts and feelings. She asks Abel to go with her to seek her mother's people. Abel tells her it is impossible to cross the mountains of Riolama, and in a flash Rima knows that Riolama is her real name and also the name of the place her people are from.

Chaps. 12–13. Rima is angered that Nuflo never told her about Riolama and demands that he now take her there. She prays to her mother for revenge on Nuflo. Her prayer reveals that she loves Abel, though she does understand this emotion. Nuflo fears the curse and agrees to make the trip. While preparations are being made, Abel returns to spend a few days with Runi, who is now suspicious of him. Runi steals Abel's pistol and tries to keep him prisoner in the village, but Abel sneaks back to the forest of Rima.

Chaps. 14–15. Nuflo tells Abel Rima's story. About 17 years before, as a fugitive from the law, he went to Riolama and took shelter in a cave. Here he met a strange, wonderful-looking woman whose foot had been injured and who was about to give birth to a child. Nuflo took her to Voa, a village, where the child Rima was born. Mother and child would go into the wood and commune with each other in their wonderful language. Rima also learned Spanish from the villagers. The mother grew weak and on her deathbed implored that Rima, who was also frail, be taken to a cooler mountainous region. Nuflo agreed to do so and built the hut where Abel had found them.

Chaps. 16–17. After an 18-day journey they arrive at Riolama, but Abel dissuades Rima from climbing the mountain to see her mother's country, telling her she might wander for years and that probably her people no longer exist. The brightness seems to go out of Rima and they fear she is dying, but gradually she seems to regain life. Abel holds her in his arms and kisses her. A radiance overspreads her face, and Abel explains that the emotion she has felt for him is love. Rima then insists on returning to her wood alone, because she has many things to do and can get there faster alone. Abel is against it, but Rima has her

way. She will await his homecoming in rapturous expectation.

Chaps. 18–19. After another long, hard journey, Nuflo and Abel arrive in the wood of Rima. The hut is burned down and there is no sign of her. Abel comes upon some Indians of Runi's tribe in the wood, a place where they never would enter previously. He returns to the village and learns that the Indians found out Rima was gone and began hunting in the wood. Then one day Rima returned. The girl, frightened, climbed a tree, and to destroy her the Indians burned her in the tree. Abel is stunned and filled with rage. He leaves the Indians, killing Kua-Ko in his flight.

Chaps. 20–22. Abel seeks help from the tribe of Manango, a deadly enemy of Runi, and eventually this tribe kills Runi's tribe. Abel returns to the wood of Rima, where he lives in solitude in a small shelter he builds there. His health deteriorates, and he fears he is going mad. He still holds the hope that the Indians lied about Rima's death, but he finds the burnt tree and gathers up the ashes of Rima. Food becomes difficult to find, and he grows weaker. Finally he decides that Rima herself would prefer it if he left the wood. After a bad journey, Abel makes it to the coast. With him is the urn of sacred ashes that he has destined to mix with his own.

Abel comes upon some Indians of the Runi tribe

The Green Pastures

Play by Marc Connelly, 1890–
Produced Feb. 26, 1930, in New York.
Published and © 1930 by Rinehart
& Co., New York. (ML, G21)

THOUGH THE OUTLINE may make it appear a burlesque, this modern classic is a reverent retelling of the Book of Genesis. With its background music by a Negro choir, it is tremendously effective and touchingly beautiful. The play is based on stories (published in 1928 as *Ol' Man Adam an' His Chillum*) by Roark Bradford, who was an artist superior even to Joel Chandler Harris in this field of dialect stories.

Act I. 1. In a class of Sunday School children in a Negro church in Louisiana, the preacher, Mr. DESHEE, tells the children to listen to the story of Creation as he pictures it to them. The lights go down. 2. The angels, all Negroes, are holding a fish fry in a typical picnic setting. The Angel GABRIEL enters and announces "de Lawd God Jehovah." The LORD enters, wearing a black Prince Albert coat, and exchanges greetings with the adoring angels. He tries some custard and says it needs more firmament. The Lord decrees the earth as a place to drain off the firmament and also decrees man. He decides to go down to inspect earth and leaves Gabriel in charge of heaven. 3. The Lord sees that Adam is lonely so he creates Eve and tells the two to enjoy themselves in the garden, but not to eat the forbidden fruit. As the stage darkens, Mr. Deshee is heard asking a child what happened to Adam and Eve, and the girl replies that they ate the fruit and were driven out of the garden and that they had CAIN and ABEL. 4. Cain is shown standing over the body of Abel. The Lord tells Cain that he'd better "git." 5. Cain finds a young, enticing girl in the Parish of Nod and he decides to board with her folks. The Lord considers this bad business. 6. In his private office in heaven, the Lord is going over affairs with Gabriel, who picks up his trumpet. The Lord warns him not to blow until the time comes. Gabriel reminds the Lord that he has not been down to earth in 400 years. The Lord decides to pay the earth a visit. 7. The Lord, dressed as a preacher, walks down a country road on a Sunday morning. He finds the flashily dressed people violating the Sabbath, and men who seem to be kneeling in prayer turn out to be crapshooters. The Lord is about to wipe all people off the face of the earth when he meets NOAH, who mistakes the Lord for a fellow preacher and invites him to a chicken dinner at home. 8. The Lord tells Noah of the coming rain. He tells Noah how to build an ark and instructs him to take his family and two of every kind of animal aboard. Noah asks to be allowed to take two kegs of liquor, but the Lord, causing a clap of thunder, insists on one keg. 9. Noah and his sons, HAM, SETH and JAPETH, are building the ark while the people jeer and carry on scandalously. Thunder is heard and the rain comes down as the people scatter. The animals are led aboard the ark as the stage darkens, and a choir sings "De ol' Ark's a-moverin'." 10. Noah is a little drunk; his wife scolds him and Noah sends a dove out with an olive branch. The Lord visits Noah and tells him to start making the earth bloom again. Gabriel doesn't think much of the possibilities, but the Lord hopes it will work out all right.

Act II. 1. The Lord is in his office with ABRAHAM, ISAAC, and JACOB, discussing a new plan to cure men of their continuing wickedness. He asks them to help him choose a leader and they suggest MOSES. The Lord agrees. 2. The Lord appears to Moses and to overcome his skepticism causes a bush to burst into flame. He then calls in AARON to help Moses. He gives Moses a rod and teaches him some tricks to confound the wicked PHARAOH. 3. Moses and Aaron appear before the Pharaoh in his palace and Moses turns the rod into a serpent, brings a plague of flies, and asks the Pharaoh to let his people go. The

Pharaoh agrees but then changes his mind. Moses calls for the death of every firstborn Egyptian child and when the Pharaoh sees his dead son he allows the Hebrews to leave Egypt. 4. The Hebrews are on the march with JOSHUA leading the army and Aaron leader of the priests. The Lord gives Moses the Ten Commandments and when Moses breaks the Tablets the Lord is displeased and says Moses cannot go on to the promised land, but he takes the old man to Heaven with him. The choir sings, "Joshua fit de battle of Jericho," and in the darkness Mr. Deshee is heard saying things didn't work out once again and the people of Israel were taken to Babylon in bondage. 5. The King of Babylon enters a night club with several flashy girls, and the fat, corrupt High Priest of the Jews joins him. A prophet enters and reproaches them for their sinful conduct. He is shot by the king's guard. The high priest attempts to placate the Lord with an offering of silver, but the Lord appears and in a voice of doom says he has had enough of sinning. 6. Abraham, Isaac and Jacob visit the Lord in his office and plead with him, as they have been doing every day for hundreds of years, to go back to their people. He refuses, but he sees the shadow of the prophet HOSEA and hears the voice of HEZDREL, a soldier guarding the temple in Jerusalem from the attacking Romans. The Lord decides to pay a visit to earth. 7. The Lord, dressed as a country preacher, hears Hezdrel say they all must fight to the death for their God. The Lord asks Hezdrel why he has such faith, as God has abandoned man, and Hezdrel answers that God is no longer the Jehovah of wrath and vengeance but the God of Hosea, the God of mercy. The Lord asks if it isn't the same God, and Hezdrel says he doesn't know but that they have found Him through suffering. The Lord thanks Hezdrel for teaching him so much. 8. The Lord sits in heaven with the angels gathered around his chair. He tells Gabriel that mercy comes through suffering. Even God must suffer. A voice from below is heard forecasting the Crucifixion. The angels sing "Hallelujah, King Jesus!"

The Lord sits in Heaven with angels gathered around His chair

Grimm's Fairy Tales

Tales by Jakob Grimm, 1785–1863, and Wilhelm Grimm, 1786–1859. Published 1815.

THE BROTHERS GRIMM were great scholars in linguistics and lexicography. Their researches into language caused them to encounter many of the legends of medieval Europe and they collected them in what became the best-known book of fairy tales. As a result, any volume collecting the most famous fairy tales, such as Cinderella, Sleeping Beauty, Little Red Riding Hood, Snow White, and similar ones, is more than likely to be called "Grimm's Fairy Tales." Actually, it has long since been observed that the German versions of these stories are too cruel for children brought up by the accepted standards of today: The enemies of the "good" characters are far too likely to be put to death in some horrible way, or at the very least subjected to torture. Therefore the revised versions actually published for children are more likely to be based on the French versions of Charles Perrault (1628–1703) and even some of those have required considerable expurgation or revision to make them suitable for today's humanistic tastes.

HANSEL AND GRETEL

HANSEL and GRETEL are children of a poor woodchopper. There is not enough food for the family and their callous stepmother persuades their father to take them into the woods and abandon them. The first time the father does this, Hansel leaves a trail by dropping shiny pebbles all along the way, so the children find their way back home. The father tries again and this time Hansel tries to leave a trail by dropping crumbs from a slice of bread he has in his pocket, but birds eat the crumbs and the children are hopelessly lost, tired and hungry and frightened. A little bird guides them to a clearing in which there is a tiny cottage all made of gingerbread, cake, and candies. They eat their fill, but an old woman, a witch, who owns the cottage, catches them and makes them her prisoners. She plans to fatten up Hansel and eat him, and she makes Gretel her servant and treats her cruelly. The witch does not see very well, and each day she tells Hansel to put forth his arm so that she may feel it and see if he is fattening. He holds out a dry bone and makes her think he is too thin to eat. One day she decides to eat him anyway, and heats up the oven. She tells Gretel to put her head inside the oven and find out if it is hot enough. Gretel, warned by the bird, pretends she does not know how. The angry witch puts her own head inside, to show how it is done, and Gretel pushes her in and slams the door. That is the end of the wicked witch. Gretel releases Hansel, and a great crowd of birds—the ones that ate the crumbs—repay the children by taking gems and pearls from the top of the cottage, where the witch had hidden them, and dropping them into aprons that the children hold. Now Hansel and Gretel are rich. The birds show them the way home, where their father is happy to see them.

THE SLEEPING BEAUTY

After many years of childlessness, a king and queen finally have a beautiful baby daughter. In honor of her birth the king gives a party to which he invites twelve out of the thirteen fairies in the kingdom. One by one, the fairies give presents to the little princess. Just as the twelfth fairy's turn comes, the uninvited fairy arrives, furious at the king for slighting her. She decrees that when the little princess is 15, she will prick her finger with a spindle and die. The twelfth fairy now steps forward to present her gift. She cannot undo the evil but she can soften it. The little princess will not die, but she and all in the palace will fall asleep for 100 years.

Hoping to avoid the misfortune altogether, the king has every spindle in the kingdom destroyed. But on her 15th birthday, the princess wanders into a strange room in the palace and finds an old woman spinning. She begs the woman to let her try, and as soon as she touches the spindle she pricks her finger and she and everyone in the palace fall asleep. A hedge of thorns grows up around the palace. Many princes try to break through it but no one succeeds

The sleeping beauty is rescued

until, 100 years later, a handsome, daring young prince manages to get through. He makes his way past all the sleeping people in the palace to the tower where the princess lies. He kisses her and she wakes. Instantly the spell is broken. Everyone in the palace wakes and everything is just as it was 100 years ago. The prince and princess are married and live happily ever after.

RAPUNZEL

A man and woman who have long wanted a child live next door to a beautiful garden that belongs to a witch. One day the wife is overcome with desire for a radish from that garden and persuades her husband to get one for her. The witch catches him. She permits him to take the radishes but makes him promise to give her his first-born child. A little daughter is born to the couple soon after. The witch claims her, names her RAPUNZEL, and takes her away. When Rapunzel is 12 years old she has long golden hair. The witch shuts her up in a tower without doors or stairs. When the witch wishes to enter the tower, she stands beneath its only window and calls: "Rapunzel, Rapunzel, let down your hair." Then Rapunzel lowers her beautiful gold braids and the witch climbs up. One day a prince happens by and sees the witch do this. When the witch has gone, he calls out to Rapunzel.

She lowers her hair and he climbs up. They fall in love and decide to escape as soon as the prince has brought Rapunzel sufficient silk to make a ladder. But the witch learns of their plan. She cuts off Rapunzel's hair and carries the girl to a desert. Then she fastens Rapunzel's braids to the window latch and waits till the prince comes and climbs up. When he is told he will never see Rapunzel again, he leaps from the window and is blinded by a thorn bush into which he falls. For years he wanders through the land and at last he chances to come upon Rapunzel. She falls into his arms and weeps. Her tears moisten his eyes and cure his blindness. He takes her to his kingdom, where they live happily ever after.

THE FISHERMAN AND HIS WIFE

A fisherman lives with his wife in a ditch by the sea. One day the fisherman hooks a huge flounder. The flounder begs the fisherman to let him go, as he is not a real fish but an enchanted prince. The fisherman lets him swim away. That night he tells his wife the story and she orders him to return the following day and ask a favor of the enchanted fish. He must ask for a fine cottage in which to live. The fisherman goes back to the sea and tells the fish of his wife's demand. He is told to return home—the wish has already been granted. The wife is not content. She wants a fine stone mansion. This wish too is granted, but still she is not content. She wants her husband to be king, then emperor, and then Pope. Each new demand is granted, and each time the fisher-

The fisherman and the fish

man begs her to be happy with what she has, but she can never be satisfied. One morning, as she sees the sun rise without herself bidding it to do so, she decides she must be lord of the sun and moon. She tells her husband of this new wish, and trembling with fear he goes down to the sea, which is now rolling and roaring in anger. He tells the fish that his wife wishes to be lord of the sun and moon. "Go home to your ditch again," says the fish. And there they live to this very day.

RUMPELSTILTSKIN

A poor miller, wishing to impress the king, tells him he has a daughter who can spin straw into gold. The king, a greedy man, orders the girl brought to him and puts her in a room filled with straw. He tells her that if she has not spun it all into gold by the following morning she must die. As the girl sits alone, wondering how to save her life—for she knows nothing of how to spin straw into gold—a little man comes in. He asks what she will give if he spins all the straw into gold. She gives him her necklace and he spins the straw into gold in a twinkling. The next day the king puts the girl into a still larger straw-filled room, with the same command. Again the little man appears and this time the girl gives him her ring. On the third day she has nothing left to give the little man and he makes her promise to give him her first-born child. Then he spins the straw into gold. Soon after this, the girl marries the king and they have a baby. The little man appears to take the child, but the young queen pleads with him and he tells her if she can guess his name in three days she may keep her baby. For two days the girl guesses all the names she knows but none of them are right. On the morning of the third day her messenger tells her that while wandering in the woods he saw a little man dancing on one leg, shouting: "Today I stew, tomorrow bake, the next day I the queen's child take; how fortunate nobody knows my name is RUMPELSTILTSKIN." When the little man returns the queen calls him Rumpelstiltskin; he screams and stamps his foot so hard that it sticks in the ground. He cannot get it out and pulls so hard that it comes off. He goes hopping away, never to be heard from again.

The girl and Rumpelstiltskin

CINDERELLA

[Note: The Cinderella of The Brothers Grimm differs from the French and English Cinderella stories. It does not include the Fairy Godmother or the pumpkin and rats and mice that become carriage, horses, and footmen. Also, in the Grimm version, the Grand Ball lasts three days. Cinderella's stepmother and sisters are finally punished with cruel deaths, not recited in most published versions today and not included in this outline.]

A rich man loses his wife and is alone with his daughter. He marries a widow with two ugly daughters. These three hate the little girl because she is so beautiful, sweet, and kind. They clothe her in rags and make her do menial work; she has no bed and at night she huddles in the warm ashes on the hearth, so she is called CINDERELLA. The father goes to the fair and asks what the women wish him to bring back as presents. His two stepdaughters demand beautiful jewels and clothing, but Cinderella asks only for a green hazel twig. He brings it, and Cinderella plants it in the garden, where soon it becomes a tree. A dove makes its home in the tree and is Cinderella's friend.

A great ball, lasting three days, is to be held at the royal palace so that the prince may choose his bride. The ugly sisters make elaborate preparations. Cinderella begs to be allowed to go. Her stepmother agrees that Cinderella may go if she can sort out all the good peas that the stepmother drops in the ashes, and put them in a bowl within two hours. This is impossible, but Cinderella's friend the dove brings its friends and they do the job. Then the stepmother says that in one hour Cinderella must clean two pans full of peas. Once again the birds come and do the job. Still the stepmother will not let Cinderella go to the ball, for Cinderella has no dress to wear. The ugly stepsisters and their mother go off and Cinderella is left alone. She runs out to her hazel tree and begs it to shake down some fine party clothes on her. Her rags disappear and she is clad in lovely shining garments, with dainty gold slippers [in English versions, glass slippers; properly, fur slippers]. She goes to the ball and the prince is entranced with her. She has been warned by the hazel tree that she must be home by midnight, or else her finery will disappear. She slips away in time the first night, and the second. The prince tries to follow her, and once he thinks he sees her enter the yard of the house where she lives, but when he looks he sees only a shabby, ragged kitchen maid. On the third evening the prince has pitch placed on the grand staircase. When Cinderella slips out, one of her slippers is caught in the pitch. The prince determines to find the foot that fits the slipper. He goes to Cinderella's house and both of the ugly sisters are determined to make the shoe fit. The foot of one is too long, and she cuts off a bit of her big toe. The other's foot is too wide, and she snips off a bit of the side of her foot. In each case the little dove whistles warnings to the prince to "see the blood on that shoe," and the prince finds he has been tricked. Cinderella finally comes out and puts on the slipper. It fits perfectly, and as she is standing there her rags disappear and she is once more dressed in her ballroom finery. The prince places her on his horse and they ride away to live happily ever after.

CINDERELLA (ENGLISH VERSION)

The wife of a rich man dies, leaving him with one daughter. He marries again, a widow with two ugly daughters. Jealous of their stepsister's beauty, they send her to live in the kitchen, where she must do the dirtiest work, wear rags, and tend the cinders. Because of this, they call her CINDERELLA. Several years later the king announces a ball, to last for three nights, at which his

The ugly sisters dress

son will choose a bride. The two ugly sisters spend weeks preparing themselves. The big night comes and they set out for the ball. Cinderella is left weeping by the grate. Magically an old woman appears before her and tells her she shall go to the ball. The old woman converts some mice and a pumpkin into a beautiful horse and carriage. Then she turns Cinderella's rags into the most beautiful gown in the world, and Cinderella has fur slippers [in traditional but incorrect English versions, glass slippers]. The old woman warns Cinderella that each midnight all her splendor will vanish and her dress will turn to rags. At the ball the prince is entranced with Cinderella and dances with no one else all evening. At midnight, remembering the old woman's warning, Cinderella hurries home. She does the same the next night. But on the third night she remains a few moments too long and as she runs away, at the first stroke of twelve, she drops one of her slippers. The prince finds the slipper and orders his heralds to search the kingdom for the maiden whose foot it fits. When the herald arrives at Cinderella's house, the two ugly sisters try desperately to squeeze their big feet into the slipper, but without success. Then Cinderella emerges from the kitchen and begs to try. The sisters laugh, but Cinderella puts the slipper on and it fits perfectly. Her rags turn into the beautiful ball dress again. The prince marries her amid much pomp and rejoicing.

SNOW WHITE AND ROSE RED

A poor widow lives in a hut by the side of the forest with her two daughters, who are called Snow White and Rose Red. One wintry night a big black bear knocks at the door and begs to come in and warm himself. The widow lets him in and the girls play merrily with him. Every night after that, all winter long, the bear comes back to play with the children. When spring comes he tells them he must go to guard his treasures from the evil dwarfs who remain below ground all winter. Not long after the bear leaves, Snow White and Rose Red come upon a dwarf who is caught in the cleft of a log by the end of his beard. To release him, the girls are forced to cut off a piece of his beard. Instead of being grateful, he scolds them for ruining his beautiful beard. He picks up a sack of gold and runs off. A few days later they meet the dwarf again. This time he has caught his beard in a fishline. Once again they free him by snipping his beard, and once again he scolds them. Then he picks up a bag of pearls and runs away. A third time the girls free him, when a great eagle picks him up by the beard and is about to carry him off. Soon after this incident, the girls come upon a clearing in which they see the dwarf, surrounded by jewels and gold. The bear comes out of the forest and starts after the dwarf. The dwarf begs him to eat the girls instead,

The bear kills the dwarf

but the bear kills the dwarf with a single blow. The bear's rough coat falls off, revealing the shining golden clothes of a handsome prince. He explains that he was bewitched by the evil dwarf, who stole all his fortune. The dwarf's death has released him. He marries Snow White and his brother marries Rose Red and they all live happily ever after.

THE ADVENTURES OF TOM THUMB

Tom Thumb, the smallest boy in the world, is the son of a very poor woodcutter. When there is a famine in the land, the woodcutter is forced to take Tom and his six brothers out to the wood and abandon them. The first time he does this, Tom leaves a trail of pebbles and he and his brothers find their way back. The second time, Tom leaves a trail of breadcrumbs, but these are eaten by the birds and the little boys are lost. In the distance they see the lights of a cottage and they go to it. A woman opens the door and tells them this is the house of an ogre, who will surely eat them, but the boys would rather stay than be torn by the wolves in the forest. When the ogre comes home he smells the boys and wants to kill them for tomorrow's lunch, but his wife persuades him to wait till morning. That night Tom and his brothers sleep in a room with the ogre's seven daughters, each of whom has a crown on her head. When the daughters fall asleep Tom takes their crowns and puts them on his brothers' heads and his own head. In the middle of the night the ogre comes into kill them, but when he feels the crowns on their heads he thinks they are his daughters and he ends up killing his daughters. Tom and his brothers escape as soon as the ogre leaves. The next morning the ogre puts on his 7-league boots and sets out after Tom and his brothers. He stops to rest and falls asleep. Tom, who is nearby, creeps up and steals the 7-league boots. Then he takes ten steps to the king's palace. There he is employed to carry messages to the king's army, which is a long way off but which Tom can reach in a short time because of the boots. He makes enough money to support his entire family for the rest of their lives. When the ogre wakes up he does not notice that his boots are missing. He comes to a bog that he could have crossed in one stride with the boots. He steps into it and sinks to the bottom, and that is the end of him.

LITTLE SNOW WHITE

A queen gives birth to a little girl as white as snow, with cheeks as red as blood and hair as black as ebony. She names her Snow White. Soon after, the queen dies and the king marries another wife, who is beautiful, proud, and haughty. She has a magic mirror and every day she asks her mirror, "Mirror, mirror, on the wall, who is the fairest in the land?"—and the mirror tells her she is. But Snow White grows prettier and one day the mirror says Snow White is the fairest in the land. Outraged, the queen orders a huntsman to take Snow White into the woods and kill her. The huntsman takes pity on the little girl and lets her run away [a modified variety of charity, for he consoles himself with the thought that the wild beasts will kill her]. He kills a pig and shows the queen its heart as Snow White's. Snow White runs till she comes to a cottage that belongs to seven dwarfs. They agree to let her live with them and take care of the cottage. But the queen learns of this from her magic mirror and sets out to kill Snow White. Disguised as a peddler, she goes to the cottage while the dwarfs are away and shows Snow White a bodice, lacing the stays so tight that Snow White falls, breathless. Believing her dead, the queen goes home; but when the dwarfs return they unlace Snow White, who recovers. Again the queen, in disguise, calls on Snow White. This time she shows a poison comb, and when Snow White puts it in her hair she falls as though dead. But when the dwarfs return they take the comb out of her hair and she recovers. The next time the queen comes with a poisoned apple. Snow White takes one bite and falls dead. The dwarfs cannot revive her this time. They put her in a glass casket where they can see her all the time. The queen is delighted, for now the mirror tells her she is the fairest in the land. After many years, a handsome prince happens by and sees Snow White lying in the casket. Overcome by her beauty, he begs the dwarfs to let him take her. Seeing how much the prince loves her, they agree. When the prince moves Snow White, the piece of apple falls out of her throat and she comes to life. The prince takes her to his kingdom, where they are married. When the queen learns that Snow White is alive, she is so enraged that she rushes out of the castle and is never heard from again.

Growth of the Soil

Novel by Knut Hamsun, 1859–1952. Published 1917. Published 1921 by Alfred A. Knopf, New York.

KNUT HAMSUN WAS AWARDED the Nobel Prize in literature immediately after the publication of his *Growth of the Soil;* and, as has been noted before, the Nobel Prize is most likely to be awarded to an author immediately after the publication of a successful work. In this novel Hamsun took as his theme the time-honored one of a man's love of land and his reward from it. Pearl Buck's *The Good Earth* is similar in theme. Hamsun lost the respect he had enjoyed in Norway (and some other countries) when he proved to be a collaborationist with the Germans in their invasion of Norway in 1940.

Book I. Chaps. 1–2. ISAK, a sturdy rock of a Norwegian, with an iron beard, walks north. He is carrying a sack containing some food, and a few tools. At night he lies down on the heather, puts his head on his arm, and sleeps. Finally he halts at a range of pasture and woodland with a rich green hillside and a stream. He sets to work to build a hut of turf and stones. He strips birch trees of bark and carries a great load of the bark all the miles back to the village, where he exchanges it for food, more tools, and a cooking-pot. Isak later acquires three goats. He is seeking also a woman to help him, but he and his goats live through the winter alone.

In the late spring of that year a sturdy, brown-eyed, full-built, coarse young woman with large, strong hands appears at the hut, says vaguely she is on her way to see her kin, and remains with Isak. Her name is INGER. Isak is very happy with her. True, she speaks peculiarly because of a harelip; but Isak is no beauty himself. He now works twice as hard and begins to build a larger house. Inger makes a trip into the village and is gone so long that Isak believes she has deserted him, but she returns, leading a cow. Isak is delighted but fears she has stolen the cow.

Chaps. 3–4. Isak continues to work very hard, and his good fortune increases. The cow has a calf, and Isak buys a bull. On returning from a trip to the village he finds he has a son. The boy is named ELESEUS. A kinswoman of Inger, OLINE, comes to visit, and Isak is relieved to learn that the cow really is Inger's. Isak and Inger work as hard as ever and their goods increase; they survive a drought and a deluge. Inger has another son, named SIVERT for a wealthy uncle. One day a wandering Lapp, OS ANDERS, stops by to beg food. From his pack he takes a dead hare and this terribly frightens the pregnant Inger.

Chaps. 5–7. The local official or *Lensmand,* named GEISSLER, comes to survey Isak's farm, for it is on government land. Isak is told that for a small fee he can buy it. Geissler names the farm Sellanraa. He sees Eleseus playing with some heavy stones and takes a few along, thinking they may be ore samples. Inger gives birth to a girl with a harelip, and she strangles the infant and buries it. Oline, visiting again, snoops about and finds the grave. Inger accuses Oline of having sent the hare with Os Anders, to mark the unborn child, and she beats Oline with a heavy wooden spoon. Oline, obviously guilty, accuses Inger of murder and says she will inform the authorities. She does, and Inger is tried for her crime. The magistrate is sympathetic and Inger's sentence is only 8 years. Oline comes to Sellanraa to take care of the children.

Chaps. 8–9. Isak is very lonely without Inger and has endless troubles with nasty, clever, thieving Oline; but Oline is good to the children. Another family, that of BREDE OLSEN, takes up a homestead in the wilderness, between Sellanraa and the village. A telegraph line is strung over the land. Isak refuses the job of caretaker and it goes to Brede, who is an indifferent farmer.

Chaps. 10–11. Geissler, who has quit his post as Lensmand, obtains a pardon for Inger. Inger was pregnant when she left

for prison and has given birth to another daughter, LEOPOLDINE, who is perfectly formed. Geissler buys from Isak the copper ore on his land for 200 daler and a share in the earnings. Isak goes to the boat to meet Inger and Leopoldine. Inger has had her harelip surgically repaired. She has learned city ways and is less simple and warm. She brings with her a sewing machine.

Chaps. 12–14. Isak works as hard as ever. He sets up a sawmill and puts up more buildings. Inger spends most of her time at her sewing machine, astounding the girls from the village with her skill and doing much work for them free. She asks Isak for a servant girl and a gold wedding ring and she takes care not to have any more children.

Chaps. 15–16. Geissler, grayer, somewhat shabby, comes to visit. He shows Isak how to build irrigation sluices to save his parched crops. Then he wanders off on his way to Sweden. More settlers take up land between Sellanraa and the village. One, AXEL STROM, names his place Maaneland because it looks beautiful in the moonlight. Brede Olsen's oldest daughter, BARBRO, goes to Maaneland to do the woman's work. Inger becomes pregnant again and Isak gets the village smith's girl, JANSINA, as a servant for her. Inger gives birth to a girl and Isak names her REBECCA. The second son, Sivert, is now a young man and like his father is a hard worker and lover of the soil.

Chaps. 17–18. Eleseus comes home from school, quite dandified but a good sort. Oline reports that Uncle Sivert is on his deathbed and young Sivert goes to him and finds him feeble but up and about. Geissler brings a party of wealthy men, his wife's relatives, who buy Isak's mining property for 1,000 daler. Geissler, surveying Sellanraa, calls Isak a margrave, a landed squire. Uncle Sivert dies and it is found that he was not rich but actually penniless. Eleseus becomes enamored of Barbro, but she turns him down, preferring Axel. He pines for a while.

Chap. 19. Brede Olsen has let his farm, Breidablik, go to pot and now is forced to sell it. Isak wants to buy it for Eleseus but Inger wants Eleseus to have a professional career in the city.

Book II. Chap. 1. At the auction, Axel Strom buys Breidablik for his brother. Brede is about to lose his job as inspector of the telegraph lines because of neglect. Eleseus goes back to town to seek employment.

Chap. 2. One day Axel finds Barbro lying near a stream, dazed. She has just given birth to his child, which she has buried nearby. She recovers, but she quarrels constantly with Axel. She empty-headedly boasts that this was her second child; the first she threw into the harbor at Bergen. She returns Axel's engagement ring.

Chap. 3. Early in the winter, Barbro leaves Axel. One day when Axel is felling a tree it falls on him, pinning him to the ground. Brede Olsen comes along but he is angry because Axel is to have his telegraph inspection job and he simply walks away. It begins to snow. In one last effort, Axel shouts for help. Oline, wandering past, comes to his aid. Now aged and poverty-stricken, Oline installs herself in Axel's house as his servant. A new settler, ARONSEN, builds a general store, called Storborg.

Chaps. 4–7. The copper mine goes into production and Aronsen flourishes on the wages of the free-spending miners. Then, suddenly, the mine is shut down, the ore vein having played out. Geissler owns the tract of land to the south of the mine and the mine officials offer to buy it, but Geissler asks a price so high that the deal falls through. Barbro is arrested and tried in Bergen for the murder of her infant. At the trial, Axel is absolved of complicity; Barbro takes all the blame. She is given a suspended sentence and is remanded to the care of the wife of the Lensmand, HEYERDAHL.

Chaps. 8–9. Isak buys Aronsen's store, Storborg, for Eleseus. Geissler finally sells his mining land, but the mining engineers say they must work the lode from the far end, many miles away. Eleseus runs his store inefficiently and is in town on buying trips most of the time. ANDRESEN, who was Aronsen's chief clerk, keeps the store going.

Chaps. 10–12. Barbro comes back to Axel. The Lensmand's wife caught her sneaking out at two in the morning and dismissed her. Barbro seems chastened and wiser. She has marriage banns put up for herself and Axel. Oline puts off going away, on one excuse or another, until one night she dies quietly in her sleep. Eleseus admits failure at the store and leaves for America. He is never heard of again. The store goes to Andresen, who is to marry Leopoldine. Middle-aged, still sturdy, Isak and Inger are wealthy, respected, reasonably contented, for theirs is the strength of the soil.

Oline comes to the aid of Axel, pinned under a tree

Gulliver's Travels

Satire by Jonathan Swift, 1667–1745. Published 1727. (ML, 100 & T32; Viking, P37; RE, 10; PB, PL51)

JONATHAN SWIFT would probably be quite amazed to learn that today *Gulliver's Travels* is treated almost exclusively as a book for children. Swift wrote the book as a satire on social and political life of his times. The book appeals to children, when it is somewhat bowdlerized, because it places its hero Lemuel Gulliver in fantastic or fairy-tale situations. *Gulliver's Travels* consists of four parts, in which Gulliver travels to imaginary lands where reside respectively tiny creatures, giants, cloud-dwelling optimists, and noble horses. In each case Gulliver can contrast their society with the Europe of his day. The noblest society was that of the horses. They made Gulliver ashamed to be a man. Some of Swift's comparisons were echoed a century and a half later by Mark Twain.

Part 1 (A Voyage to Lilliput). **Chap. 1.** I, LEMUEL GULLIVER, was born in Nottinghamshire, England, and after three years at Cambridge and apprenticeship to a prominent London surgeon I signed aboard a ship to serve as its doctor. I made several trips to far-off corners of the world, then settled down to marry MARY BURTON. But I was not successful as a doctor and on May 4, 1699, I again signed aboard a ship, the *Antelope,* bound for the East Indies. In November a storm sank the ship. I escaped in a lifeboat but high waves forced me to abandon it and my friends. I swam to a previously undiscovered island called Lilliput, where I collapsed with fatigue on the beach. When I awoke, I found my whole body fastened to the ground with threads. Hundreds of tiny creatures, not six inches high, surrounded me on all sides. When I tried to rise, they shot arrows at me that caused my face and hands to smart. Afraid that they might blind me, I decided to submit to their will. A royal entourage approached and the Lilliputians erected a stage so that the EMPEROR could behold my huge frame. The emperor had me fed some of their cattle, which were about the size of a lark's wing. I devoured enormous quantities. Then I was taken to the capital city of Mildendo and housed outside the city gates in a temple whose front portal was 4 feet high. I was chained to the door and guarded by hundreds of soldiers.

Chaps. 2–3. The emperor and his court climbed a tower of the temple to observe The Man Mountain, as they called me. The emperor was a few inches taller than his subjects. He wore European-Asiatic clothes. We communicated by signs. The emperor ordered two ministers to search me and remove harmful objects. They took my watch, razor, and pistols, but promised to return them later. I had won over the emperor and he refused to have me shot with poisoned arrows, as some of his counselors advised. I became more beloved when I donated my handkerchief to serve as a field for horseback skirmishes and stood with my legs apart so the soldiers could parade through them. After frequent petitions I was at last loosened from my chains, but I was not permitted to leave the kingdom. I was promised enough food and drink every day to satisfy 1,728 Lilliputians. Without any provocation, I found a mortal enemy in the Lilliputian admiral, SKYRESH BOLGOLAM.

Chaps. 4–5. I was finally allowed to see the capital, with a special escort so that I would not crush anyone. Shortly afterward I became involved in politics. The emperor's loyal subjects belonged to the Low-Heeled faction and were opposed by courtiers who wore high heels. Foreign affairs were troubling the emperor. Lilliput was endangered by its traditional enemies from the nearby island of Blefuscu. The two islands had fought for centuries over the proper way to break an egg. Now the Blefuscudians were invading Lilliput. I swam to Blefuscu, terrified the enemy into leaving their ships, and drew the fleet with me back to Lilliput. The emperor conferred numerous honors upon me. I refused to crush the Blefuscudians completely, but they sued for peace and thanked me for my generosity. I again proved serviceable by saving the palace from destruction by fire. I had drunk plenty of wine and I urinated on the burning buildings.

Chaps. 6–8. I was suspected of carrying on a love affair with the Treasurer's wife. This cost me the emperor's favor, though I established my honor in the affair. My enemy, the admiral Skyresh, had succeeded in poisoning the emperor's mind, and though the emperor refused to kill me he agreed to blind me. I fled to Blefuscu, where I was welcomed with great warmth; but the Emperor of Blefuscu received word from Lilliput that I must be blinded. Fortunately I found a small boat and escaped. I was taken aboard an English ship and returned home in 1702.

Part II (A Voyage to Brobdingnag). Chaps. 1–4. On my next voyage to the East, in 1703, I left the main ship to gather water from the unexplored land of Brobdingnag. I wandered away from my fellow sailors and was picked up by a huge creature, taller than a church steeple. He carried me to his farmhouse, where his enormous wife and children toyed with me. I realized that they did not want to harm me. I was put to bed in a handkerchief. Two rats attacked me and I killed them with my needlelike sword. I was protected by the farmer's daughter, GLUMDALCLITCH (or "little nurse"). She taught me her language but could not persuade her father to keep me at home. He put me in a cage and exhibited me to other Brobdingnagians. I was bought by the KING and QUEEN, who allowed Glumdalclitch to take care of me in a doll house in the Palace. Once I was attacked by bees, but I killed three of the huge creatures and kept them as proof of my experience. The queen's dwarf, who measured about 30 feet high, took a dislike to me. I traveled with Glumdalclitch throughout the kingdom and saw the Brobdingnag temple, which was 3,000 feet high.

Chaps. 5–7. I continued to have adventures, such as getting caught in a hailstorm in which the pellets were the size of tennis balls. The king liked to talk with me about the states of Europe and I delivered five lectures. I was unable to persuade him that Europeans are not "the most pernicious race of little odious vermin that Nature ever suffered to crawl upon the surface of the earth." I tried to persuade the king to manufacture cannon and gunpowder, but he was horrified at the notion. I concluded that the Brobdingnagians were not interested in progress.

Chap. 8. The king, after two years, took me on a journey to the southern part of his kingdom, near the sea. I traveled in a special wooden crate, cradled in Glumdalclitch's lap. One afternoon the girl handed me over to a page so that I could walk on the beach. After enjoying a brisk walk, I asked the page to put me back into my crate. He did so, then went off to find some birds' eggs. The tide swept my crate out to sea, where I was rescued by an English merchant ship. I arrived home in 1706. I found that my wife and children looked undernourished in comparison with the giants.

Part III (A Voyage to Laputa, Balnibarbi, Luggnagg, Glubbdubdrib, and Japan). Chaps. 1–4. In 1707 the ship on which I was making my third great voyage was seized by pirates and I was cast adrift in a lifeboat. I landed on an island and saw some men fishing on the shore. I was surprised to see the mountainous part of the island rise up into the air above my head. When I called to the people, they lifted me up by pulleys into the strange land of Laputa. The sky-dwellers, or Laputans, were the royal and intellectual classes of the island of Balnibarbi but had cut themselves off from the common people below and the Balnibarbarians had finally claimed their independence. The Laputans spent so much time in contemplation that their eyes turned either inward or toward the heavens. Their heads inclined either left or right. Nobody except the women paid any attention to me. The king did nothing but study geometry and music. They had a very orderly realm, but the houses were too symmetrical and the food too unappealing. The poor women wanted very much to return to the earth. At my request, I was lowered to the earthly land of Balnibarbi. There the neglect of the inhabitants appalled me. The only order in this country was maintained at the Academy in the capital city of Lagado.

Gulliver is attacked by huge bees and kills three of them

The academicians had been trained above in Laputa.

Chaps. 5–6. I spent some time in the Academy debating with numerous professors. I was astounded by the things that these learned doctors were trying to do, such as to abolish all words. Their methods of teaching were also strange. They forced students to swallow wafers inscribed with ink so that the writing could penetrate their stomachs and brains. I listened attentively to their discussions of ways for uncovering government conspiracies.

Chaps. 7–11. I made a side journey to Glubbdubdrib, or the Land of Sorcerers. The governor of that island received me with great cordiality and summoned ghosts out of the past to entertain me. I saw many famous people, such as Julius Caesar, Pompey, and Alexander the Great. The Greek philosopher Aristotle told me that he was wrong in many of his deductions about natural philosophy and that thinkers such as Newton in our own time were making the same mistakes because logic can never yield absolute truth. I then proceeded to the island of Luggnagg. There I was received by the king with great hospitality, but I had to perform the usual ceremony of licking the dust beneath his throne. The most interesting people on this island were

the Struldbrugs or Immortals, who are born with a red spot on the forehead and who live forever. Their lives were extremely miserable, for after the age of 30 they became morose. Although they were immortal, Struldbrugs were subject to old age and sickness. Therefore after the age of 90 they were exiled from the rest of society. The Luggnaggians offered to give me some Struldbrugs to take back to England but I refused. They might have taught Englishmen to welcome death, but they might also have monopolized our nation's highest positions. Next I visited Japan, where I was welcomed by the emperor, but I stayed for only a short time, then boarded a Dutch vessel for Amsterdam and returned to England in 1710.

Part IV (A Voyage to the Country of the Houyhnhnms). **Chaps. 1–4.** On my last great adventure I was made prisoner by mutinous sailors who put me out to sea in a boat. I arrived at an island where I saw some strange creatures known as Yahoos. These creatures resembled human beings except that they had pointed claws, hairy bodies, and mean faces. They tried to attack me, but I drove them away. Then I was found by a beautiful horse, who communicated with me by striking his hoof on the ground. I learned that the horses, called

Houyhnhnms (pronounced *whinnums*), were masters of the filthy Yahoos. The horse invited me to his house, which resembled a simple stable, and there I dined on oats and milk. My host, whom I called MASTER, and his family taught me the horse language, which resembles Dutch. The Master was shocked to learn that in England the Yahoos control the horses, but on learning this he was not at all surprised that Englishmen are famous for their wars and corruption.

Chaps. 5–8. Although I tried very hard to explain how wars arose, my Master could see no logical reason for their taking place. He also asked why education did not bring about perfect justice such as existed in his own land. He did grant that England must produce some noble creatures, because I showed such wit and understanding. In the end, my Master showed his typical horsesense by suggesting that a lack of reason was responsible for all English ills. With-

out reason there can be no virtue. He noted that most Yahoos in his land were governed by emotions and fancies that led to lewdness and laziness.

Chaps. 9–12. I heard a great debate among the horses as to whether they should exterminate the Yahoos entirely. Although the issue was decided negatively, I began to sympathize with the Houyhnhnms. I disliked the thought of going back to England, where people were so much like the Yahoos. My happiness was broken one day when the Houyhnhnms decided at their great debate that I was too Yahoolike to continue living there. My Master and his family provided me with a canoe and I left them with many tears and fond farewells. After a sea voyage and some further adventures, I arrived back in England in 1715. From that day to this, I have been unable to share the company of my family. I spend all of my time in the stable conversing with my horses.

Hamlet

Play by William Shakespeare, 1564–1616.
Produced about 1602.

FOR MORE THAN 300 years *Hamlet* has been accorded every evidence that it is the greatest work of both literature and drama in the English language. It is the most read, the best known, the most quoted, and the most often performed; its title rôle is the one every actor most wishes to play. Amid such general acclaim a self-respecting critic can hardly call *Hamlet* Shakespeare's greatest work for fear he be considered a sheep following the lead of others. Nearly anyone else is willing to admit it. ❡ There was probably a Danish or Juttish king named Hamlet (earlier

spelled Amleth); legend sets his time around the year 700. Shakespeare does not follow the traditional stories very closely, and he gives most of his characters Latin names. The prince Amleth (junior) was a youth at school in the west (France or Belgium) when his father was killed by his uncle. He returned, feigned madness, and worked out an elaborate plan for revenge, which succeeded; but young Amleth himself did not die when he killed his uncle. He lived and became king of the land. The original versions imply an incestuous feeling between Hamlet and his mother, and most scholars have interpreted parts of Shakespeare's play to be an acceptance of this part of the story.

Act I. 1. On the ramparts of Elsinore Castle in Denmark HORATIO, friend of Prince HAMLET, joins MARCELLUS, an offi-

cer of the guard, to see a GHOST that appears nightly. The ghost resembles young Hamlet's father, King Hamlet, recently dead. **2.** Hamlet, recalled from school, pays his respects to the new king, his father's brother CLAUDIUS, who immediately married Hamlet's mother, Queen GERTRUDE. Claudius sends envoys to ask the king of Norway to stop the invasion of Denmark by his nephew Prince FORTINBRAS. LAERTES, son of the king's chief minister, POLONIUS, asks and is given leave to return to France. Left alone, Hamlet delivers his *first soliloquy*—"O! that this too too solid flesh would melt"—in which he regrets that suicide is forbidden by God and decries his mother's remarriage—"Frailty, thy name is woman!" Horatio and Marcellus tell Hamlet of the ghost. **3.** Laertes, leaving for France, warns his sister OPHELIA not to count on Hamlet's marrying her, because a prince does not have free choice. Polonius gives Laertes a series of famous "precepts," ending with "This above all: to thine own self be true." **4–5.** Hamlet, on the ramparts, meets his father's ghost and is told that Claudius murdered his father by dropping poison in his ear while he slept in the garden and that Gertrude was a party to the plot.

Act II. 1. Polonius sends his servant REYNALDO to France to observe the behavior of Laertes. Ophelia tells Polonius of Hamlet's strange behavior lately and Polonius concludes that Hamlet is mad with love of Ophelia. **2.** Claudius asks ROSENCRANTZ and GUILDENSTERN, courtiers and former companions of Hamlet, to attend Hamlet and keep him from doing mischief. The envoys return with a promise from Norway that Fortinbras will not attack. Polonius tells Claudius his theory of the reason for Hamlet's madness. Then Polonius talks to Hamlet, whose speech is cryptic and seems mad. It is the same when Hamlet talks to Rosencrantz and Guildenstern. Polonius brings in a company of strolling actors, who give a sample performance for Hamlet. Hamlet asks them to play, for the king and court, the *Murder of Gonzago,* with certain changes he will make. When they leave, Hamlet delivers his *second soliloquy,* beginning "O! what a rogue and peasant slave am I" and ending "The play's the thing/Wherein I'll catch the conscience of the king."

Act III. 1. The king and queen are worried about Hamlet's mental condition and

Hamlet and the Ghost

the king is afflicted by conscience. Hamlet delivers his *third soliloquy*, "To be, or not to be; that is the question." He concludes that suicide would be a blessing if one could be sure of nothingness, but the fear of the unknown hereafter deters would-be suicides. Ophelia. interrupts him and he rejects her, telling her to go to a nunnery. The king and Polonius, who were hidden, hear and are sure Hamlet is mad. **2.** The actors put on the play and, coached by Hamlet, duplicate the murder of Hamlet's father as Hamlet heard it from the ghost. The king is stricken by conscience, stops the performance, and leaves. Hamlet is now sure the ghost's story was true. Rosencrantz and Guildenstern, then Polonius, approach Hamlet but he talks mad to them. He ends the scene with his *fourth soliloquy*: " 'Tis now the very witching time of night/When churchyards yawn, and hell itself breathes out." **3.** The king is overcome and kneels alone to confess his guilt and pray. Hamlet sees him and delivers his *fifth soliloquy*, "Now might I do it pat, now he is praying"—but he will not kill Claudius because then Claudius, killed while praying, would go to heaven. **4.** Hamlet is summoned to his mother's room. Polonius is hiding behind the curtain. Hamlet accuses his mother of murder; then, detecting someone behind the curtain, stabs and kills Polonius, thinking it is Claudius. The ghost appears to Hamlet, but to Gertrude he is invisible.

Act IV. 1–3. Hamlet is being sent to England, attended by Rosencrantz and Guildenstern, ostensibly with messages to the English king. **4.** On their way, Hamlet, Rosencrantz and Guildenstern encounter Fortinbras at the head of an army. Left alone, Hamlet delivers his *sixth soliloquy*, beginning "How all occasions do inform against me" and ending "From this time forth,/My thoughts be bloody, or be nothing worth." **5.** At Elsinore, Ophelia goes mad from grief over Hamlet's madness and renunciation of her. Laertes returns in anger to kill Claudius, to avenge his father's death, but Claudius convinces him that it was Hamlet's doing. **6.** Horatio receives a letter from Hamlet that he is in Denmark. Horatio speeds to join him. **7.** Claudius receives a message from Hamlet, saying that he is returning to court, and Claudius promises to help Laertes revenge himself on Hamlet. Gertrude tells Laertes that Ophelia has drowned herself.

Act V. 1. Hamlet and Horatio walk through a graveyard. Hamlet muses upon the skull of YORICK, the king's jester, whom he knew and loved as a boy, and on the common fate of all things mortal. The funeral procession of Ophelia enters and Hamlet declares that his grief at her death is greater than anyone else's could be. He challenges Laertes but they are not permitted to fight. **2.** Hamlet, back in the castle, tells Horatio how the treacherous king sent him to England bearing letters instructing the English king to put him to death; but Hamlet opened and changed the letters and sent Rosencrantz and Guildenstern on to their deaths. Hamlet is invited to give a fencing exhibition with Laertes. Claudius has poisoned Laertes' rapier, so when Hamlet is hit he is doomed, but in a scuffle the men change rapiers and Laertes is hit and poisoned. Claudius offers Hamlet a poisoned cup to drink, and Hamlet refuses it but Gertrude takes it and drinks before Claudius can stop her. Hamlet, aware what is going on, uses his last strength to stab and kill Claudius. All four die. As Hamlet is dying, Horatio proposes to kill himself too, but Hamlet urges him to stay alive so that the world may know the true story. Fortinbras enters with his army and assumes control of Denmark.

Hangman's House

Novel by Brian Donn Byrne, 1889–1928.

Published & © 1926 by Appleton-Century-Crofts, New York.

THIS EXCELLENT NOVEL by an excellent novelist is a story of adventure and intrigue in Ireland during the period (after World War I) when the Irish were struggling with England for independence. There is some contemporary Irish politics in it but not so much that the reader need understand it to enjoy the story. During the period covered by the novel, numerous Irish revolutionaries were gathered in New York as refugees and Donn Byrne, American-born, was personally familiar with them and their plotting.

Chap. 1. DERMOT MCDERMOT of Dermotstown, not yet 25, stops to talk to the ancient lodgekeeper of his place in the Wicklow Hills in County Dublin and hears that his cousin JOHN D'ARCY is back from abroad and staying at "Jimmy the Hangman's," his name for Lord GLENMALURE, Lord Chief Justice of Ireland. The mission of the "twister," as D'Arcy is known unfavorably. by the local folk, is to marry the lord's daughter, CONNAUGHT. Dermot visits with his mother, a Quaker lady, who came from Philadelphia to Ireland with her husband, now dead, and also lost her elder son, DESMOND, in the Boer War. Dermot tells his mother that he is going to ask Lord Glenmalure for his daughter's hand in marriage. She has misgivings.

Chap. 2. Connaught is a pretty girl who was educated in a convent and at 18 in-

Dermot visits the dying Lord Glenmalure and learns he was a rebel

herited a large fortune from her grandfather. She is interested in horseracing, in riding, and in the new sport of greyhound racing. Her father discovers that he is incurably ill and wishes Connaught to marry. The only young man she cares for is Dermot. Glenmalure says that Dermot's being the best gentleman rider in the county is not enough reason. He writes to ask John D'Arcy, son of an old schoolmate of his, to come to Glenmalure. D'Arcy, a member of the Irish rebel party, is a suave, burly man with a great reddish-brown beard (which Glenmalure forces him to shave off). Connaught becomes enamored of D'Arcy. Glenmalure interrogates D'Arcy about his connection with the rebels who are exiled in Paris, and specifically with PATRICK HOGAN and his sister MAEVE, with whom D'Arcy's name has been linked, but receives evasive answers.

Chap. 3. Dermot asks for Connaught's hand. Her father reminds him that Connaught wants a big career for her husband—adulation, position, luxury, and glamour. Dermot says he would not sell Dermotstown and get into politics, and Glenmalure tells him Connaught will marry D'Arcy.

Chap. 4. In New York a group of Irish rebels select Patrick Hogan to go back to lead the cause. He is the son of old DINNY HOGAN, the irreconcilable, known to the rebels as The Citizen.

Chap. 5. Connaught is badly neglected as Lord Glenmalure plans a political career for

John D'Arcy. Politicians gather at the hall. Occasionally she plays tennis with her fiancé. She finds out that the servants do not think highly of D'Arcy. She also hears that Dermot is in love with her, though he has stayed away out of propriety. Her father tells her he has not long to live and she must marry D'Arcy within a week.

Chap. 6. Connaught seeks out Dermot and tells him she does not love D'Arcy. Dermot bravely answers that John is a fine man and everything will be all right. They hear a boy singing the old rebel song, "Shan Van Voght" (The Poor Old Woman, meaning Ireland). The boy says that he learned the song from a man in the mountains, a man called the Citizen. When John D'Arcy hears of the incident he turns pale and asks for a description of the Citizen. His knees sag and he staggers off for a drink.

Chap. 7. Dermot suffers when Connaught marries John but decides that she has made a wise choice. The couple leave on their honeymoon. Dermot visits Lord Glenmalure, who is dying, and learns from him that he was a rebel in his youth. The old man dies and Dermot sends a telegram to Waterford to intercept Connaught and John.

Chap. 8. Dermot finds Connaught a hard, white-faced woman since her marriage. Riding after the hounds, they see a stranger on a wild horse that tries to throw him until he croons to it a refrain from "Shan Van Voght." D'Arcy is turned down by the politicians, now that Glenmalure has died. The stranger on the wild horse asks D'Arcy if he was in Paris in '95 and D'Arcy replies that he was never in Paris in his life. Connaught asks why he lied and John answers that he doesn't want to be bothered with foreigners. Connaught finds out that John has informed on the stranger, who is being hunted by the constabulary.

Chap. 9. D'Arcy's estate becomes a meeting place for shady characters, gamblers, heavy drinkers, and crooked horse trainers and bookies. Connaught turns over her horses to a man named ROBINSON to train. After a greyhound race, Dermot meets a monk on the road, singing "Shan Van Voght." Dermot recognizes him as the man on the wild horse at the Tara Hunt but promises not to give him away.

Chaps. 10–11. The winter passes. Dermot learns that there is suspicion about a forthcoming horse race, the Dundrum Handicap, because John D'Arcy has laid heavy bets against Connaught's entry, the Bard. Connaught tells Dermot she is having trouble finding a jockey. On the day of the race the horse is still riderless and Dermot volunteers to ride it but John forbids Connaught to accept. There is a near scene but Dermot rides anyway and wins the race. He and Connaught find John sobbing and learn that Dermot, by winning, has cost John £10,000, which he needed desperately. Connaught tells him she has money. Dermot turns away in disgust. A blind man with a quaint old overcoat compliments Dermot on his race. Dermot recognizes the Citizen.

Chaps. 12–14. John kills the horse, Bard. Dermot threatens to kill John but his Quaker mother restrains him and Connaught tells him her husband is only a poor crazy man. She leaves for England and John is reduced to entertaining bookmaker's touts, barmaids, and potboys. He tells Dermot he has only kissed Connaught once, on their wedding day, and he wants money to

go to Florida or California. Dermot asks why he is afraid of the Citizen, and D'Arcy, in his cups, tells of having a long affair with Hogan's sister Maeve, whom he finally left, after they had had a child, to come to Ireland and marry Connaught. Dermot offers to lend him money if he will make a happy home for Connaught, and offers to intercede with the Citizen, but to his horror he learns that John is married to Maeve. He attacks him but is restrained. He tells D'Arcy to get out.

Chaps. 15–19. Connaught returns from England and Dermot tells her that John is gone for good. Dermot finds the Citizen and pleads with him for Connaught's sake to be quiet about D'Arcy. The Citizen agrees but says D'Arcy is marked for death. Connaught tells Dermot she was a wife in name only and she confesses her love for Dermot. Dermot seeks out the Citizen again, for D'Arcy's marriage to Maeve obviously made his marriage to Connaught illegal, but the Citizen says Maeve died before D'Arcy married Connaught. John returns to Glenmalure, having heard of Maeve's death. He accuses Dermot and Connaught of adultery but is convinced that everything has been circumspect. Connaught returns to England.

Chaps. 20–22. Dermot is left alone in Dermotstown. John is at Glenmalure, deserted by his servants. He has taken in tinkers, the Irish gypsies, to tend his house. Dermot hears from Connaught that she is coming to Ireland for a few days to attend the races. D'Arcy's tinkers tell him that a man is spying on the house and he suspects it is the Citizen. He finds the Citizen on the grounds and they enter the house together. D'Arcy has sprinkled the inside with kerosene. He shoots the Citizen and sets the house afire, but Dermot drags the Citizen out of the burning building. John, caught inside, jumps to his death. Dermot tends the Citizen's wound and helps him escape, then is united with his beloved Connaught.